Sexuality:
A Nursing Perspective

Sexuality:
A Nursing Perspective

Fern H. Mims
M. S. N., Ed. D., and F. A. A. N.
Professor of Nursing
School of Nursing
University of Wisconsin–Madison

Melinda Swenson
R.N., M.S.N.
Clinic Coordinator
Planned Parenthood of
South Central Indiana

McGraw-Hill Book Company
New York   St. Louis   San Francisco   Auckland   Bogotá   Düsseldorf
Johannesburg   London   Madrid   Mexico   Montreal   New Delhi   Panama
Paris   São Paulo   Singapore   Sydney   Tokyo   Toronto

NOTICE

Medicine is an ever-changing science. As new research and clinical experience broaden our knowledge, changes in treatment and drug therapy are required. The editors and the publisher of this work have made every effort to ensure that the drug dosage schedules herein are accurate and in accord with the standards accepted at the time of publication. Readers are advised, however, to check the product information sheet included in the package of each drug they plan to administer to be certain that changes have not been made in the recommended dose or in the contraindications for administration. This recommendation is of particular importance in regard to new or infrequently used drugs.

SEXUALITY: A NURSING PERSPECTIVE

2 3 4 5 6 7 8 9 0   FGFG   8 3 2 1 0

Library of Congress Cataloging in Publication Data

Mims, Fern.
    Sexuality : a nursing perspective.

    Includes index.
      1. Sexual disorders--Nursing. 2. Sex (Psychology)
--Nursing. 3. Sick--Sexual behavior. I. Swenson,
Melinda, joint author. II. Title.
RC556.M55   616.6   79-14951
ISBN 0-07-042388-1

This book was set in Times Roman by University Graphics, Inc. The editors were Laura A. Dysart and Irene Curran; the cover was designed by Mark Wieboldt; the production supervisor was Jeanne Selzam.
Fairfield Graphics was printer and binder.

To our husbands,
Al Mims
and
Daniel Willard

Contents

PART **3** REPRODUCTIVE DECISION MAKING

PART **4** SEXUALITY AND HEALTH DISRUPTIONS

PART **5** ADVANCED INTERVENTION AND RESEARCH

Preface

Another textbook on human sexuality? In recent years there have been numerous new books in the field. Some are edited collections of readings, some take a sociological, biological, or medical model approach. Very few are specific to health care providers. Fewer still are focused on nursing. Hence another textbook on human sexuality.

As teachers of baccalaureate and master's level students we see a need for a text which not only presents research and theory but also helps with the transfer of this knowledge to nursing practice. We have prepared this book using direct and specific nursing goals and interventions.

The principal tool for the transfer of theory to practice is the Mims-Swenson Sexual Health Model. This conceptual framework relates content in human sexuality to the nursing process and is used throughout the book as a teaching-learning model and as an assessment device for clients and for nurses themselves. Since its development in 1976 the Sexual Health Model has been applied successfully by nursing students, teachers, and nurses in practice. It allows for several levels of intervention based both on the needs of the client and the abilities of the nurse. Consequently, interventions for the less-knowledgeable or less-comfortable nurse are suggested at a level different from that of the experienced practitioner. As a student becomes more aware and more at ease with the subject of human sexuality, the complexity of suggested nursing intervention increases.

We believe some of the chapters present new and exciting materials for nurses. Convenient brief sexual history forms are presented which enable the nurse to expand the routine health history to include sexuality. Until now sexual history forms have been complicated, time-consuming, and frankly, inquisitive. These newly devised questions (a set for the adult and a separate set for the child) ask for only necessary information, are nonthreatening and nonjudgmental, and are readily adaptable for most client situations. A special chapter on the examination of male and female genitalia and reproductive organs is included, which provides clear direction for relating physical assessment skills to the field of sexual health promotion.

A unique chapter on psychosexual responses to health disruption provides special help for nursing interventions in the promotion of sexual health. There is also a thorough and updated chapter on pharmacologic modification of sexuality. Contemporary issues in life-style choices, written by two women who are Harvard law students, is a highlight of the book.

Clinical examples are presented in the new problem-oriented nursing assessment form. This method of recording information and progress notes also is a means to communicate the nursing process. Many schools and agencies have already adopted problem-oriented records, and others are predicted to follow. Therefore, the problem-oriented format in this book is attractive as well as current.

The approach throughout is the promotion of sexual health in primary or secondary health care nursing. In primary care the focus is on prevention and health maintenance of individuals, families, and groups through anticipatory guidance. In secondary health conditions the focus is on the care of individuals with an acute, chronic or terminal illness affecting sexual health. This area is concerned with processes and mechanisms which reduce complications of illness, minimize the impact of hospitalization and treatment on the sexuality of clients and family, and to facilitate sexual adaptation to illness and disability.

Writing a book is more difficult than we had imagined. Topics which may seem essential to some nurses have been left out, usually because they are already presented in great depth in more specialized books. The area on health disruption covers specific health conditions, but not all that affect sexuality. We suspect that most nurses will find it challenging to transfer and modify nursing approaches presented in this book for clients with other health disruptions affecting sexuality.

The Sexual Health Model can also be adapted as a foundation for curriculum design, providing for basic, intermediate, and advanced level instruction. The last two chapters of the book offer information and suggestions for education programs, research, and sexual therapy.

Our goal has been to present basic nursing material clearly and concisely, with practical considerations and real-life examples included as often as possible.

We expect our readers to be nursing students, teachers of nurses, and professional nurses in primary (ambulatory) and secondary (inpatient) care settings. We expect that we are not always right, and that both our philosophies and our knowledge will change over time. For now, a nursing textbook on sexual health is needed, and that is what we have done our best to provide.

Fern H. Mims
Melinda Swenson

Sexuality:
A Nursing Perspective

Part One

Introduction

Chapter 1

Sexual Health: A Model for Nursing Education and Nursing Practice

All people are sexual, regardless of age, health, or situation. Some are engaged in sexual relationships, some are not. Some believe the sexual component in their lives to be very important, while others find sexuality relatively unimportant. Nurses are sexual and are influenced in their practice of nursing by their sexual feelings, behaviors, beliefs, attitudes, and knowledge. Clients and patients are sexual and their total health is influenced by their sexual feelings, behaviors, beliefs, attitudes, and knowledge. How the client and nurse respond to sexuality is influenced by what has been learned. The content of learning is in turn influenced by the norms and values of society.

Most nurses believe they have a responsibility of promoting sexual health in their practice and are asking: How is sexuality integrated into the practice of nursing? When should sexuality of the client be assessed? Who should gather information about sexual concerns of patients? What can be done to promote sexual health among nurses and those to whom they provide care?

The Mims-Swenson Sexual Health Model was developed to provide a framework for self-assessment, for client assessment, for intervention, and for planning nursing education. The model is based on the P-LI-SS-IT model of Annon.[1] The Annon version is used for the behavioral treatment of sexual problems and is not appropriate for use by most nurses. The Mims-Swenson model is specifically designed for use by nurses. It provides a means of self-assessment for nurses, provides nurses with direction for interaction with clients, and provides an organizational base for curricula in human sexuality.

To be effective in providing sexual health care, nurses must

    1   Develop a sound and comprehensive body of knowledge about sexuality;

    2   Confront feelings, values, and attitudes of sexuality in themselves and in those differing in sexual orientation and practices;

    3   Develop assessment, intervention, integration, and communication skills in all aspects of sexual health.[2]

Since some nurses share the largely biased and negative attitudes toward sexuality which have been seen throughout history, then meeting these requirements entails considerable time and effort. Many nurses believe their own patterns of sexual behavior and their own code of morals to be "right" and those which differ to be "wrong." This egocentricity and ethnocentricity will not promote sexual health.

In the past 10 years, scientific knowledge about human sexuality has expanded immensely; at the same time social attitudes have changed and continue to create controversy. Although an increasing number of schools of nursing are offering courses in sex education and other schools are attempting to integrate sexuality into related curriculum offerings, there are still many professional nurses who have not had proper educational experiences to prepare them to include sexuality as a legitimate consumer concern. It is the purpose of this book to enable nurses to promote sexual health care of their clients through the use of the Sexual Health Model (Fig. 1-1).

The life experience level (Fig. 1-2) includes both destructive and intuitively helpful behaviors that are products of living experiences in a society that continuously gives double and confusing messages regarding sexuality. Because there have been many taboos, myths, and stereotypic responses toward normally occurring erotic behaviors, many individuals internalize negative attitudes and behaviors about sexuality at a very early age.

In classrooms, clinical practice, workshops, and inservice programs it becomes apparent that many students and practicing health professionals have misconceptions, misinformation, and stereotypic values regarding sexuality. Some of the testing statements that are used in measuring knowledge in sexuality are

    1   Impotence in men over 70 is nearly universal.

    2   Certain conditions of mental and emotional instability are demonstrably caused by masturbation.

    3   Homosexuals have a body build with distinguishing features.

    4   A woman's chance of conceiving is greatly enhanced if she has had an orgasm.

    5   Exhibitionists are latent homosexuals.

    6   Vaginal-penile intercourse is the most satisfactory method of sex relations.

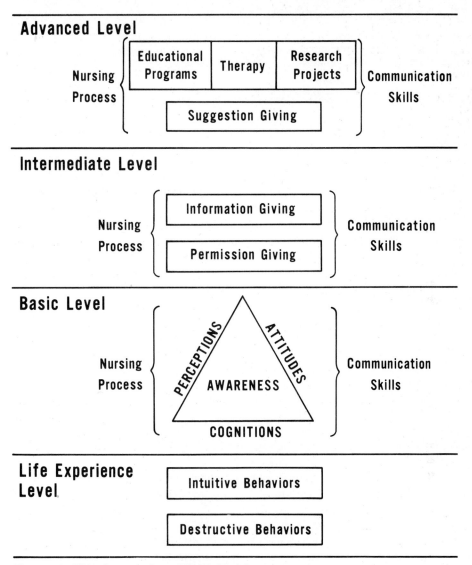

Figure 1-1 Mims-Swenson Sexual Health Model.

7 Sex offenders are oversexed.

8 Pornography stimulates people to commit criminal sex acts.

9 The average registered nurse is equipped to be helpful to clients with most sexual concerns.

10 Complex sexual problems can be cured very easily.

All the above statements are false. Yet many registered nurses and students in nursing believe them to be true. These are only a few of the many fallacies,

Intuitive Behaviors

Destructive Behaviors

Figure 1-2   Life experience level.

myths, and stereotypic biases that prevent nurses from providing effective health care. An understanding of sexual functioning requires knowledge of sexual anatomy, physiology, and psychosexual development and the effects of depression, chronic stress, learned patterns, and social influences on sexuality. Sexuality is influenced by the complicated interplay of physiological, psychological, and social forces. Many nurses have intuitively developed a variety of positive feelings, behaviors, and attitudes that provide a reasonable working base for sexual choices, values, and rational behaviors. The problems encountered at the life experience level involve separation of destructive behaviors from those that would facilitate sexual health. After identifying destructive attitudes and behaviors, the discarding and replacing processes require study, planning, and practice.

Awareness is created by the interactions of perceptions, attitudes, and cognitions. Awareness is fluid and constantly changing due to changes in sexual mores. For example, the equal rights movement has deeply influenced attitudes, perceptions, and cognitions regarding sexuality. Awareness can be unsettling, since it may create concerns and raise questions about fundamental matters that were taken for granted a generation ago. According to Pomeroy: "People are more willing now to test, to inquire, to experiment, and to communicate about sex. Still, being human, it is easier for us to accept new shibboleths, new myths, new stereotypes, than to think for ourselves."[3]

Sexuality is an area to which many people attach strong emotions, dogmatic religious ideas, strict legal sanctions, and a wide variety of rigid opinions. On the other hand, others may have amorphous values that are useless as a base of support. Neither extreme seems to assist the nurse in providing therapeutic intervention. A better approach incorporates a balanced viewpoint, which recognizes one's own value system, while simultaneously being accepting and supportive—or at least nonjudgmental—of the values of others.

Practitioners who operate exclusively from the life experience level may provide haphazard sexual health care. Therefore, the acquisition of the basic level awareness (Fig. 1-3) is absolutely necessary for all nurses in order to be helpful regarding sexual concerns. To be effective practitioners of nursing in the field of human sexuality, nurses have to recognize basic facts about themselves and their clients. The nurse must acknowledge how emotions and sexual values will affect therapeutic intervention. The values, concerns, and personal experiences of the nurse must be separated from those of the client. To accomplish this separation, the nurse must clarify his or her own values before attempting to assist the client in value clarification. Awareness is a level reached through

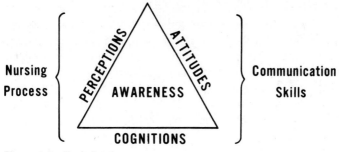

Figure 1-3 Basic level.

honest group participation, unbiased reading, the objective evaluation of a variety of experiences, feedback from others, and introspection and self-assessment.

Awareness is not static and researchers and practitioners are constantly revising and broadening the area of sexuality. Many public issues such as abortion, pornography, incest, rape, and homosexuality continue to require rigorous study and action. There continue to be many aspects of sexuality that are not measurable in the right and wrong columns of behavior for all people at all times. Awareness and acceptance of changing values, issues, and behaviors provides a working base for the other levels of intervention. Awareness is raising one's consciousness, and is the first step in being able to learn, to practice, and to teach nursing.

The intermediate level (Fig. 1-4) includes communication skills of giving "permission" and giving information. Nursing process, communication, counseling, and teaching skills are used in permission and information giving. Permission sanctions sexual thoughts, fantasies, and behaviors that occur alone or between informed, consenting adults. Many sexual concerns are alleviated simply by giving the client permission to engage or not engage in specific sexual behaviors. Permission often begins with history taking when the practitioner conveys to the client that sexuality is an important component of health. Taking a sexual history gives permission to talk about sex. Permission may begin when the nurse acknowledges verbal and nonverbal messages of sexual concern. For example, the client facing impending surgery may need permission and encouragement to relate feelings and fears of rejection and loss of a highly valued body part. Clients may have doubts and fears concerning the ability and wisdom of resuming sexual intercourse following an illness. If coital activity is not dis-

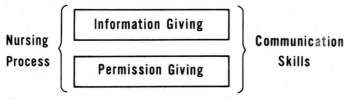

Figure 1-4 Intermediate level.

cussed, people with short- and long-term illnesses may have many doubts, concerns, and fears that may lead to false assumptions that they should not engage in sexual activities. A handicapped client and/or partner may need permission to acknowledge sexual needs even though they cannot master coitus. Some clients need permission to acknowledge an increased or decreased libido during developmental and situational crises. Some clients need permission to enjoy oral-genital sex and masturbatory or homosexual activities in which they are participating. Others need permission to feel comfortable about life-style choices such as celibacy, heterosexuality, homosexuality, and autosexuality.

Nurses must assess the client before giving permission or information. Not all clients need permission or information and might feel "pushed" in one direction or another by a nurse who is too eager. The nurse must not give permission for behaviors that are beyond what the client wants or is able to handle. Nurses can give themselves permission not to intervene with some clients, permission not to know everything, and permission to refer problems that they cannot handle. Permission giving would be detrimental without the ability to provide accurate information. Many clients do not have basic information concerning anatomy, physiology, and the sexual response cycle. Skills in counseling and patient teaching will be helpful in supplying needed information in promoting sexual health. Clients have the right to know that certain disease processes, medications, operations, and other treatments may be responsible for changes in sexuality. Without information, temporary dysfunctions may develop into long-term dysfunctional patterns that are difficult to change. Information is also helpful in anticipatory guidance for clients and their partners. Frustration, anger, fear, guilt, distrust, and suspicion between partners are often alleviated or held to a minimum when accurate information is given to both partners about developing or existing physical and mental health conditions.

Information giving is also important for specific segments of the total population. For example, adolescents and young adults need information regarding reproductive biology, fertility control, sexually transmitted diseases, pregnancy, abortion, and conjugal practices. Sex education in elementary and high schools has not been a universal practice and a vast number of families have not provided adequate sex education. The nurse will continue to have opportunities and responsibilities in helping to provide accurate information to people of all ages in both primary and secondary health settings.

The advanced level (Fig. 1-5) includes suggestion giving, therapy, educational programs, and research projects. Suggestion giving requires specialized knowledge of specific conditions of sexuality. Various techniques, different positions, specific exercises, and methods of communication to achieve sexual gratification may be given to the client in the form of specific suggestions.

Sensate focus is an example of a specific suggestion which prescribes a comprehensive communication process to achieve sexual responsiveness. The sensate process begins by focusing on tenderness, affection, understanding, and warmth of pleasurable touching. The purpose of sensate focus is to enable the receiving and the giving partner to discover what experiences are most pleasur-

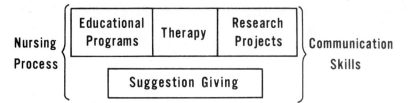

Figure 1-5 Advanced level.

ble for each of them. Suggestions are given for each partner to experience the sensuous dimensions of hard, soft, smooth, rough, warm, and cold. Some couples move through each prescribed exercise with creativity while others need detailed instruction and positive reinforcement with each suggestion. Both partners are encouraged to use "I" statements and to learn as much as possible about themselves and their partners. Some couples require specific exercises and tasks to help them identify obstacles that impede sexual responsiveness. Others benefit from movies and other audiovisual materials.[4]

Sexual therapy may offer an interpretation of the psychodynamics and transactional factors of sexual conflict. Methods in which nurses have participated to provide sexual therapy include solo practice, cotherapy, sex counseling clinics, group counseling, marital counseling, and family counseling. A few examples of the types of problems that clients present to nurse therapists are incest, unwanted pregnancy, rape, impotence, dyspareunia, orgasmic dysfunction, premature ejaculation, homosexual panic, altered body image following an illness or handicap, effects of aging or disease on sexual health, and specific psychological stresses. In the treatment of sexual problems, the therapist utilizes knowledge and skills of crisis intervention, sensate focus exercises, assertiveness training, psychotherapy, deconditioning techniques, desensitizing techniques, group process, role playing, communication games, gestalt techniques, and behavior modification. However, it is not expected that nurses will be competent in all areas or in the use of all techniques. Advanced education and clinical experiences help nurses clarify their interests and formulate specific treatment approaches. Understanding the approaches of sex therapy will help other nurses make appropriate referrals.

Nurses with advanced education and experiences in human sexuality have many opportunities to plan and conduct educational programs for professionals, groups of adolescents, families, and patients. Sexuality programs should focus on building awareness, increasing knowledge, and acknowledgment of feelings, biases, prejudices, and attitudes of self and others. This emotional content challenges the nurse educator to use a creative format to meet the divergent needs of each group.

Moving from the basic level upward through the intermediate and advanced levels usually is accomplished by further education. A basic course in human sexuality would enable most nurses to function at the intermediate level. Additional clinical experience will enhance the ability to provide specific suggestions to clients with more complex concerns. Post-baccalaureate education experience may enable some practitioners to design educational programs, engage in sex therapy, or conduct sex research. Workshops, inservice education, and special programs will be discussed in Chap. 20. All nurses can use the model to determine their level of interaction with clients, and some nurses may have to confine themselves to the basic level if they are uncomfortable with giving information or permission.

The needs and opportunities in research of the many components and aspects of sexuality are abundant. Practitioners and educators need answers to specific questions and they should be able to combine efforts in research and evaluation of sexual health programs and of clinical practice. The final chapter in this book presents sex therapy and sex research in greater depth.

APPLYING THE NURSING PROCESS IN SEXUAL HEALTH

Nurses with different educational preparation and nursing skills find various opportunities and methods to apply the nursing process in the promotion of sexual health. Nurses have opportunities in assisting clients in developing, maintaining, or coping with sexual responses in health and in illness. The assessment process initiates or incorporates some or all of the following:

1   Collecting information regarding clients' sexual attitudes, behaviors, feelings, and beliefs. The sexual history is the tool for gathering this information
2   Incorporating information from the medical diagnosis and other pertinent illness data
3   Incorporating information from physical examination and laboratory findings
4   Determining mental and emotional status and functioning
5   Securing family, social, and cultural data

An interpretation of the data is necessary to establish a nursing assessment.

Following the assessment, both short- and long-term goals need to be established. The goals are highly dependent on the assessment data and the skill of the nurse. Some general goals that may be adopted for a wide variety of nurse-client interactions and activities that promote sexual health care include:

1   Assisting the client in acquiring accurate knowledge in order to eliminate sexual myths, stereotypes, and misconceptions
2   Assisting the client in determining and "owning" feelings about his or her own and others' sexuality (e.g. guilt, fear, anger, ignorance, denial)
3   Helping the client understand the complexity of the multiple strands of motivation that affect responses
4   Exploring with the client possible alternative sexual options and expressions to meet needs identified by the client
5   Exploring methods of mastering performance to provide sexual gratification for self and partner

6 Determining the client's perceptions and expectations of sexual functions and dysfunctions

7 Establishing the knowledge, attitudes, and specific behaviors that facilitate accomplishment of past, present, and future developmental tasks

The plan and rationale in the nursing process follows the assessment and goals and is dependent on the skill of the nurse. The plan will most likely include some or all of the Sexual Health Model methods of implementation which include eliminating destructive behaviors on building on intuitive health behaviors, increasing awareness, permission giving, information giving, suggestion giving, teaching, and sexual therapy.

In the nursing process the evaluation supplies the information that indicates the effectiveness of the nursing plan. Client responses to each goal must be evaluated and readjusted if data suggest a change in goals. Data to measure the achievement of a goal can be obtained from the client, partner, family, nurse, physician, laboratory findings, and multidisciplinary resources.

COMMUNICATION

For many reasons, sex is difficult to discuss seriously. People may find it easier to make jokes about sex than to discuss their real concerns. Nurses are no exception, and may frequently feel that they should not talk about sex with clients. Some nurses feel it is "too personal," "too embarrassing," or "nosey." These comments reflect the nurse's own discomfort.

The section on education, at the end of this book, outlines ways for nurses and others to increase their level of comfort with sexuality through a desensitization-resensitization process. Awareness can then be enhanced by increasing one's knowledge level. When a nurse is able to balance cognitive awareness with an awareness of personal values and attitudes, nursing intervention in the area of sexuality will become easier.

In talking with clients about sexual concerns, the following guidelines may be helpful:

1 Approach the situation with an attitude of acceptance and honesty about your own level of expertise.

2 Provide a quiet, private place to talk.

3 Provide a relaxed and unhurried atmosphere. It may take a long time for clients to say what they want to say. Listen without impulsively rushing in to supply an answer.

4 Use direct eye contact as much as possible.

5 Do not write during the interview. Notes should be written later. (A possible exception is when you are writing the problem list. The client should participate in formulating the list.)

6 Sit as close to the client as is comfortable for both of you. Do not sit behind a desk or across the room.

7 Ask open-ended questions rather than questions requiring merely a yes or no response.

8 If the client does not bring up sexual concerns, use a *review* statement ("As you probably already know," . . .) or a *universality* statement ("Most people who have had this surgery wonder about when they can safely resume sexual relations. . . .").

9 If the client has no questions or concerns, it is usually not appropriate to press for a lengthy discussion. The client may be more willing to discuss sexuality at a later time or actually may have no concerns.

10 Communication clues can come from content of discussion, perception, and thoughts. It is helpful to think about the central themes coming from the client and the thoughts and perceptions about these themes.

11 Nonverbal clues include appearance and behaviors during an interview. Assess if the client is demonstrating evidence of disequilibrium by anxiety, inability to concentrate, unrealistic perceptions, and disorganization in work and/ or social situations.[5]

12 Communication about sexuality requires observation of not only what the client does and says but what is repeatedly avoided. These observations require time and skill in order to make an accurate assessment.

13 Exploration of covert messages with direct feedback can be useful for some clients. Gestures and actions can reinforce what is being said and make it more meaningful. However, gestures can communicate a different meaning from the words that are spoken. Therefore, the nurse needs to clarify the meaning of gestures, tone of voice, and other behaviors that do not seem to correspond with the oral communication. This can be done by a statement such as, "You say you are comfortable with homosexuality but I seem to be getting messages to the contrary. What does that mean?" or "You say you feel okay about homosexuality but it seems to me that you are really upset about it. Help me get this straight in my head." The nurse will need to be comfortable with most topics of sexuality and at the intermediate level before the last four suggestions are used.

PROBLEM-ORIENTED NURSING ASSESSMENT

In this book, the Sexual Health Model is put into practice using the problem-oriented method[6] as a means of recording the nursing process and nursing care plan.

The *problem list* is the base of the record. As sexual concerns and problems are identified by the client and the nurse, they are numbered, dated, and listed. Clients legally have access to their medical records and should be aware of any problem identified. Problems which commonly arise might include the following:

Inadequate sexual information
Desires contraception
Depression associated with marriage problems
Gender identity concerns

Gonorrhea contact
Adolescent pregnancy
Allergic to penicillin

As a problem is resolved, it is moved to the inactive status. If more information changes a problem, it becomes inactive, and the new problem is assigned a new number. A number is never used twice.[7]

Subjective Data

This comes directly from the client, and may be presented as a quotation. For example, "I'm worried about an infection I have" or "I wish I knew what to tell my daughter about menstruation" or "Maybe I shouldn't have sex since I've had this heart attack."

Objective Data

This comes from nursing observation, laboratory results, medical diagnoses, and other documented sources. It includes anything seen, touched, smelled, or heard by the nurse. The findings of the physical examination might be summarized as objective data.

Assessment

The nurse takes all the available information and says, "So what does this all mean?" The nursing diagnosis, or assessment, is the best possible guess as to what is going on with the client.

Plan

The nursing care plan has four major components:

1 Gather further information
2 Establish long- and short-term goals
3 Nursing interventions planned for the future
4 Education for the patient

SUMMARY

Nurses need help in determining what they are and are not prepared to do in the promotion of sexual health. The Sexual Health Intervention Model is helpful in defining and communicating various levels of expertise based on knowledge, attitudes, and transmittal skills in nursing practice. The model may also be used as a tool for self-evaluation, in the planning of learning experiences, and in educational programs. Implementation experiences indicate that nurses and students are able to relate and apply the nursing process to intervention activities included in one of the four levels of the Sexual Health Model.

REFERENCES

1   Jack Annon, "The P-LI-SS-IT Model," *J. Sex Educ. Ther.* **2**:1–15 (1976).
2   Fern H. Mims, "Sexuality in the Nursing Curriculum," *Nurs. Educ.* **2**(2):20–23 (1977).
3   Wardell B. Pomeroy, "Interview: Sexual Myths of the 1970's," *Med. Aspects Hum. Sexual.* **11**(1):63–74 (1977).
4   William H. Masters and Virginia Johnson, *Human Sexual Inadequacy,* Little, Brown, Boston, 1970, pp. 67–91.
5   Donna Aquilera and J. Messick, *Crisis Intervention,* 3d ed., Mosby, St. Louis, 1978.
6   Lawrence Weed, "Medical Records That Guide and Teach," *N. Engl. J. Med.* **278** (1968).
7   P. D. Larkin and B. A. Backer, *Problem-Oriented Nursing Assessment,* McGraw-Hill, New York, 1977.

Chapter 2

Historical Background

This chapter supplies a brief overview of sex and sexuality in modern America to provide background material for understanding taboos, stereotypes, responses, misconceptions, and myths that influence sexual behaviors of today. Sexuality has always been a human concern but sexual beliefs and attitudes change over time. Sexuality in modern America is complex and intertwined with religious and social values of the people who immigrated in the seventeenth and eighteenth centuries. This chapter highlights only a few of the historical events in a simplistic manner. The aim of presenting this material is to emphasize the complexity of the subject and to create interest for further study of background material in order to better understand present approaches of sex education and sexual health care.

In early America, during the seventeenth century and the beginning of the eighteenth, social and economic life centered on the family, with religion being the governing force. Sexuality, within marriage, was considered an important binding force with the need and expectation of procreation. Families, politics, and religions were all male-dominated, and clear expectations, consistency, and role models were provided for both male and female offspring. Children were expected to obey and help their parents with family responsibilities. Sexual offenses that created the greatest concern were those that had the potential of threatening the family structure, such as incest, illegitimate births, and adultery. During this period rape and fornication were viewed with a degree of tolerance; however, sexuality with animals caused great concern.[1]

ROMANTICISM AND REFORMATION

During the first half of the nineteenth century, with the industrial, scientific, and sexual revolutions, there was a protest movement of equal rights for women, marital reform, eugenics, birth control, and free love. Americans were beginning to have conflicts over what the nation had been and what they had hoped it would be. For a few years there was a hope of transforming labor into pleasure and there was the beginning of experimentation with communal living. Some 200 communities were established with different patterns of matrimony and sexuality, which indicated social pluralism rather than abandonment of sexual mores. One of the best-known nineteenth-century American social experiments was the Oneida Community at Oneida, New York. The community was founded by John Humphrey Noyes with objectives centered around improving the quality of sexual and social relations between men and women, concerns of birth control, and improving the quality of offspring. The Oneida system set up a central committee that gave consent to a male and female member to live together as man and wife. This type of relationship could be easily dissolved with no commitments or concerns. The marriage contracts of this community were arranged, complex, controlled for procreation, and not easily dissolved. The offspring of the chosen marriages were expected to be biologically superior.[2]

During this period not many individuals participated in communal living, but there were many changes that took place in all parts of the society. The double standard for male and female sexual behaviors was beginning to diminish. Many books on marriage and sexual physiology were published. Although the books contained misinformation, stereotypic beliefs, and fantasy materials, they were very popular with the general population. Authors tried to provide some scientific information and connote that sex was pleasurable. This period was short-lived since the sexual and economic freedom of women caused great concern in regards to the social stability of the traditional family structure. By 1820, women's freedom had been supplanted by the Victorian sexual ethics of "purity."[3]

VICTORIANISM

The Victorian era was repressive in all aspects of sexuality. Later marriages, until the male had achieved success, were encouraged. Virility was established by the ability to delay sexual gratification. Art and Shakespearean plays were either banned or censored because they were thought to be obscene. The woman's sexuality was denied; she was expected to have no sexual interest, only a desire to be pure. The "nice" woman had sexual relations as a sense of duty or for reproduction, but never from desire. Sexuality could be described only by scientific definitions and words that hinted of sex disappeared or were supplanted by euphemisms. Some examples of common euphemisms are that legs became limbs, breasts were bosoms, women's underclothing became "unmentionables," chicken breast became white meat, and women were not seduced but "betrayed."[4]

Masturbation or having frequent coitus was considered wasteful and lacking in self-control. Preserving semen was advocated for health purposes. Masturbation was considered sinful, self-abusive, and was believed to cause various emotional and physical illnesses. In some cases it was believed that death was caused by masturbatory activities. Other physicians claimed that masturbation caused baldness, impotence, insanity, mental decay, and acne. Devices to prevent masturbation included a four-pointed penile ring and a toothed penile ring that made contact with the penis when it was erect. Another complex device was used in the prevention of nocturnal emissions, by causing a bell to ring when there was an erection. Early medical literature indicates that physicians advocated such practices as the castration of sexually active children, clitoridectomy, cauterization of the genitals and prostate, applying leeches to the base of the penis to begin bleeding, hot poultices to the genitals, hot mustard hip baths, and wearing protective devices such as a chastity belt to make sexual arousal difficult and painful.[5,6]

During the Victorian period it was expected that men be rigid and have control over all sexual impulses and activity. For women the lack of sexuality was a valued feminine quality; consequently, if a woman experienced sexual feelings and desires she also experienced guilt and shame. With the "purity" concept of women prevailing, prostitution began to increase. Many clients of prostitutes were married men who were unable to fulfill sexual needs at home. The black woman slave and the prostitute helped to meet the sexual needs of this society. These two groups of women helped to keep the wife "pure" and permitted the man to degrade and control women.

According to Staples:

> The sexual availability of slave women allowed white men to put white women on a pedestal, to be seen as the goddesses of virtue. In a way this became a self-fulfilling prophecy. White women were held aloof from the world of lust and passion and in many cases became more inhibited emotionally, sexually, and intellectually because of the oppressive presence of slavery. Consequently, while the white woman's experiences and status inhibited sexual expression, the black woman's encouraged it.[7]

The end of slavery did not change these sexual practices. Many Southern white men did not have sexual relations with white women until they married. They also assumed that the black man had a strong desire for the white woman, who was guarded from meeting with him as an equal. As Jessie Bernard writes, "The white world's insistence on keeping Negro men walled up in the concentration camp (of the ghetto) was motivated in large part by the fear of their sexuality."[8] Finally, after emancipation, the black woman's marriage was legally recognized and black men began to demand that black women be treated with respect and courtesy and not be raped and seduced by white men.[9]

According to Haller and Haller, during the Victorian period many physicians and writers of marriage manuals made a great effort to control sexual excesses. Sylvester Graham believed that

> An ounce of semen equaled nearly forty ounces of blood. Graham concluded that sexual excesses lowered the life force of the male by exposing his system to disease and premature death. Demanding that men radically change their diet to include such foods as unbolted wheat, rye meal, hominy, and graham flour, he also hoped that healthy and robust husbands would limit their sexual indulgences to twelve times each year. More frequent intercourse would impair the male's constitutional powers, shorten life, and increase liability to disease and suffering. Graham's dietary rules and his views on intercourse eventually became common currency among physicians who saw in male abstinence a means for not only replenishing nervous energy, but also for radically changing the prevailing views of sexuality in the nineteenth century.[10]

From this period it was learned that sexuality of the male or female could not be eliminated, not even controlled, and there was a need to make sexuality more positive and a part of the normal human experience.

THE TWENTIETH CENTURY

By 1900 America had become a society of abundance with an economic emphasis on consumption. The values of the people shifted from savings, thrift, and self-control to spending, enjoyment, and spontaneity. These same values applied to the sexual sphere. There was no societal value on controlling coitus and saving semen. Instead, the male model became an individual who enjoyed himself. The average woman was left with more inhibitions. Advertising began to apply sex as a selling device. Beautiful young women were employed to drape cars, pose for magazine covers, and be a man's playmate. During this period it became evident that sex and sexuality were enjoyable and could no longer be controlled and remain invisible. Most critical opponents of this movement gave up hope of censorship of art and literature and began to concentrate on pornography.

After World War I new influences included jazz, the flappers, the "red-hot-mamas," and sex queens. Women, with the rising hemlines, were no longer expected to be sexless. The Nineteenth Amendment to the Constitution gave women the right to vote, which increased their opportunities and freedom. However, men were still defining sexuality for both men and women.

Physicians began to challenge the idea that sexual activities, including masturbation, were harmful to health. Sigmund Freud introduced the libido theory and claimed that sexuality is a major force in human development from birth to death. Medical advances, the emphasis on employing some type of contraceptive method, and effective treatment of venereal diseases served as an impetus to enjoy sex.

Soon after World War II, Alfred Kinsey and colleagues conducted a non-clinical investigation of sexual behavior within American society. The sexual activity of 5300 males and 5940 females was sociologically investigated. *Sexual*

Behavior in the Human Male was published in 1948 and *Sexual Behavior in the Human Female* appeared in 1953.[11,12] These studies expanded the knowledge of what average people say they do sexually; however, it was acknowledged that these data were dependent on the honesty of the subjects. These two reports showed a discrepancy between male and female sexual practices. Early in the 1950s Christine Jorgensen underwent a surgical operation for sex reassignment that received national publicity. In 1953 Hugh Hefner published the first issue of *Playboy,* which made sex and nude photographs acceptable for the newstand magazine consumer. In 1956 oral contraception, the "pill," was introduced as an effective conception control.[13] The pill gave the woman more freedom but also gave her more responsibility in the enjoyment of sex for herself and her partner.

All the above changes in the 1950s helped create liberation and awareness in the 1960s. As the young became more outspoken in politics and sex, they became more of a threat to the older generation and to traditions. The older generation felt a rejection of many of their values such as sex and race inequality, patriotism, and virginity. The number of young people and their energies were too much to combat; consequently, the young people made their impact on changing sexual values in society.

William Masters and Virginia Johnson, under the auspices of the Reproductive Biology Research Foundation in St. Louis, Missouri, spent several years in clinical research in an intensive interrogation (medical, social, and psychosexual) of both laboratory study subjects and clinical research populations. *Human Sexual Response* (1966) and *Human Sexual Inadequacy* (1970) are reports of research that explored the physiology of the human sexual response and the treatment approaches to sexual problems.[14,15] This work provided important data on the following: (1) physiological and psychological response phenomena during sexual activities; (2) alterations of these phenomena in the aging population; and (3) therapeutic modifications of varieties of sexual dysfunction based on psychophysiological information of sexual response patterns.[16]

In the 1960s and 1970s the experiments in living were of a greater variety and more numerous than those of the nineteenth century. These experiments and options included communes, group marriages, swingers, multiple love relationships, open marriage, and premarital trials in living together. Extramarital sexual relationships with the consent of the partner were accepted by some married couples.

In 1973 the American Psychiatric Association ruled that it no longer considers homosexuality to be a "mental disorder" and urged that all discrimination against homosexuals cease. In 1974 the Washington State Court of Appeals upheld a lower court decision that denial of a marriage license to two gays is neither unconstitutional nor discriminatory. The Court's opinion was based on the argument that marriage is primarily for the procreation and education of children.[17] The courts have generally found a gay household, whether male or female, unsuitable for raising children. However, in 1974, a judge in Tacoma, Washington, granted a lesbian permanent custody of her three children without preventing her from living with her lover.[18] In 1978 basic human rights of homosexuals were still being pursued by those against oppression and persecution for sexual preferences. Some of those opposed joined the Anita Bryant campaign and claimed that homosexuality is a religious issue rather than a constitutional rights issue.

In 1973 a Supreme Court decision permitted early termination of pregnancy. However, the abortion issues were not settled with that decision. Those in the Right to Life Movement fought abortion and the antiabortion laws of many states remained on the statute books, despite the ruling of unconstitutionality.[19] Using federal and state funds for those who could not afford an abortion became a controversial issue in 1977–1978. According to Faye Wattleton, President of the Planned Parenthood Federation of America (1978), the organization would have three principal public policy targets: "To restore to the poor access to safe, legal abortion so cruelly destroyed in two-thirds of the states by recent federal and state actions limiting payments for abortion under Medicaid; to place reproductive biology research and contraceptive development at the highest level on the nation's research agenda; to formulate and pursue a national strategy for reducing the incidence of teenage pregnancy." Wattleton claimed that "one out of seven pregnant girls used contraception and eight out of ten teenage pregnancies were unintended. Much needs to be done in health services and educational programs if the tragic prospect of many hundreds of thousands of children bearing children each year is to be ended."[20]

During this decade a great emphasis and momentum for change in equal rights came from the black and women's movements. Much of the women's movement was aimed at female consciousness raising and legalizing equal opportunities and responsibilities in all aspects of living. The new feminism brought forth an increased awareness of the true meaning of "equality of women" and of the prejudices to which women had been subjected for many years. As women struggled to free themselves from overt and covert discrimination, male-female role stereotypes were being questioned, and definitions of male and female sexuality needed to be reexamined and reevaluated.[21] In 1976, Kelly suggested that there were three distinct types of men emerging:

> **1** *The New Masculinist,* who enjoys sharing in the atmosphere of equality, finding it liberating, refreshing and manageable. He sees women as sexual equals and is free to share his spectrum of emotions with others.
> **2** *The Male Traditionalist,* who feels more comfortable in the dominant role of guide, protector and provider for women. He tends to believe that men should be the sexual aggressors, that they should appear strong and controlled as well as controlling, and the double standard is legitimate.
> **3** *The Mediator Male,* who attempts to straddle both worlds. His attitude toward sexuality tends to follow a somewhat opportunistic path of convenience and manageability.[22]

Some women and some men wanted to preserve the traditional sex roles of femininity and masculinity and created as many blocks and turmoil to prevent changes as the law would allow. Human rights were also beginning to extend to the sexual birthright of individuals with physical and mental disabilities, the young, and the aging population.

In the 1960s and 1970s a fair amount of energy was spent on defining pornography and determining the social, behavioral, and medical implications of erotic materials. The United States Commission on Obscenity and Pornography began its work in 1968 and made its report in 1970.

> The majority of the members of the Commission concluded that explicit sexual materials could not be considered to play a significant role in the causation of delinquent or criminal behavior among youth or adults. Rather, they concluded that much of the "problem" regarding materials which depict explicit sexual activity stems from the inability or reluctance of people in our society to be open and direct in dealing with sexual matters.[23]

The report was not accepted by President Nixon and the Senate rejected the findings and recommendations. In the late 1970s the "adult book stores" flourished in most large cities, and those opposed to sexually explicit materials were out to "protect" the children from the "underground" exposure to erotica. In 1977 the United States Supreme Court had five obscenity cases and 22 states had active obscenity bills before their legislative sessions. From these exercises society learned that there were no simple answers regarding censorship to control morals and values of human sexuality. It appeared that the battles to control obscenity were never-ending.

In spite of increased educational programs for the public and an increase in contraceptive methods, the number of unwanted pregnancies increased in the 1970s. In the late 1970s there were 30,000 pregnancies in preadolescents (ages 11 to 15) annually. In the adolescent group (ages 15 to 19) there were 1 million pregnancies yearly (almost 20,000 per week) or 1 in every 10 females in this age group. The age of unwed mothers became younger than in previous decades. In California there were 32 reported births to 12-year-old mothers during 1974. In 1978, Calderone reports that requests for contraceptive advice from girls as young as 9 years old were posing a problem in San Francisco.[24] In the older group of potential parents, contraceptive practices brought forth more responsibility from men as well as from women, and more couples elected not to have children.

According to Burgess and Holmstrom, Uniform Crime Reports from the Federal Bureau of Investigation indicated a 121 percent increase in reported cases of rape between 1960 and 1970. In 1970 over 39,000 cases were reported in the United States.[25] By 1977, child and wife abuse required funds for special attention and study.

After Masters and Johnson claimed that half of all marriages were troubled by significant, if not serious, sexual problems, there was a dramatic increase in professionals who called themselves sex therapists. There was some effort by the American Association of Sex Educators and Counselors to develop criteria sufficient for the certification of sex therapists, educators, and counselors. Concurrent with the interest in sex therapy and counseling was the development of sexuality as a legitimate field of academic pursuit with its own research and literature. The number of programs increased each year, with the length of programs varying from 9 months to 4 academic years.

The Hite Report, the results of a 5-year study of 3019 women on their sexuality, was published in 1976.[26] Shere Hite explains that limiting the definition of sex only to sexual intercourse is an absurdly confining concept. She suggests that sex be called instead physical relations, which would have a much broader implication, and could include all the kinds of physical communicating that human beings can do with each other, from touching to cuddling, friendly kissing, passionate kissing, and intercourse of all kinds.[27] Like the Kinsey studies, the methodology, the biases, the subjects, and the researcher of the Hite report will receive criticism.

In reviewing the history, some writers speak of the 1960s and 1970s as a sexual revolution. Other authors describe this period as one of sexual enlightenment and sexual revelation. In any case, the social changes have made an impact on all segments of the population. Perhaps the range of acceptable sexual behaviors and options is still emerging or expanding and will further influence American society in the future. Whether these trends will be slowed, reversed, or sidetracked for a while is difficult to predict due to the complexity of the subject.

SEXUAL HEALTH CARE EDUCATION

In September 1972 the World Health Organization (WHO) of the United States began an investigation of the competence of health professionals to deal with human problems in the field of human sexuality. The investigation was sought because the competencies of health professionals in sexuality were seriously questioned. The public was finding physicians, nurses, and paramedical personnel ill prepared to provide the help they needed with sexual difficulties. The investigation reported that "little in the way of relevant teaching in the field of human sexuality is to be found in the curricula of most medical and nursing schools throughout the world."[28]

In 1972, these concerns were reinforced by a study of the emotional responses of 113 graduating medical students at the University of Southern California as to what they considered the impact of their education on their existing sexual attitudes and knowledge. The research demonstrated that the subjects felt grossly inadequate, both intellectually and emotionally, to deal with the sexual problems commonly encountered by physicians in clinical practice. Over half of the subjects felt that their medical education had failed to significantly increase their understanding of human sexuality. Forty-eight percent felt unable to work adequately with homosexual conflicts or anxiety and 50 percent felt unable to deal adequately with sexually provocative patients. The most striking finding concerned the belief that their own sexual conflicts and anxieties paralyzed their sense of clinical adequacy.[29] In the review of the literature for this same study, Woods reported that only 10 years ago one investigation made the shocking discovery that nearly half of a large group of medical students and one in five faculty members subscribed to the long-discredited belief that masturbation frequently causes mental illness.[30]

A survey of American medical schools in 1963 showed that only one school had any required systematic instruction on the subject of marriage and human sexuality. Another school offered a course as an elective.[31] After reviewing the history of sexuality, it is evident that women before the 1960s were controlled or greatly influenced by men. Consequently, nursing, a profession composed primarily of women, was inclined to follow the male medical profession and not include sexuality in the curriculum. The editorial staff of *Nursing Outlook* devoted the greatest portion of the November 1970 issue to human sexuality. According to the editor, sexuality—an important dimension of life—is still clothed in Victorian garb and hidden in the closets of our minds. It is perhaps the least comfortable aspect of humanity that nurses deal with and the least understood.[32] A study of human sexuality course evaluation by Mims et al. was reported in *Nursing Research* in 1973. The results indicated a tremendous need for this subject matter.[33] According to a survey conducted by Goodwin in 1975, professional nurses believed that a variety of experiences other than their formal nursing education was helpful in preparing them to discuss sexual concerns with patients.[34] Lief and Payne report that both nursing students and graduate nurses are less knowledgeable and more conservative concerning sexuality than college graduates.[35] Several studies in the 1970s have shown that both medical and nursing students lack knowledge and sophistication regarding sexual feelings, attitudes, values, and beliefs.[36–38]

It is evident that sexuality has become an important aspect of total health care and that there will be more pressure for professionals to be adequately prepared. For example:

> California mandates sexuality study for professionals. Beginning in 1978, any person in California "applying for a license, registration, or the first renewal of such license . . . as a licensed marriage, family and child counselor, a licensed clinical social worker or as a licensed psychologist shall, in addition to any other requirements, show by evidence satisfactory to the agency regulating such business or profession, that he or she has completed training in human sexuality as a condition of licensure . . . and the curriculum for an applicant for a physician's and surgeon's certificate (must) provide for adequate instruction in human sexuality."[39]

It is hoped that other states will not need to mandate that professionals prepare for sexual health care, but rather that the health professions will take on this responsibility. It is also important that sexual health care be undertaken with some constraints and continual evaluation to prevent new misconceptions, taboos, and stereotypes supplanting the old ones. Pomeroy had demonstrated this fear as follows:

Old versus New Sex Myths
1 Old myth: Deep, prolonged therapy is necessary to cure sex problems.
   New myth: Sex problems can now be cured by simple tricks.
2 Old myth: Women are basically disinterested in sex.
   New myth: Women have become so sexually aggressive that men can't keep up with them.
3 Old myth: Masturbation is immature and harmful.
   New myth: Masturbation is a more fulfilling sexual experience than intercourse.

4   Old myth: Female orgasm is perverse or a rarity.
    New myth: Female orgasm is a glorious experience that changes a woman's life.
5   Old myth: Love is essential to satisfying sex.
    New myth: Love is irrelevant to sex. Technique and a sense of fun are everything.
6   Old myth: Homosexuality is "sick" and all homosexuals lead wretched lives.
    New myth: Homosexuality is equally as rewarding as heterosexuality.
7   Old myth: Unusual sexual fantasies signify mental disturbance.
    New myth: All sexual fantasies are healthy.
8   Old myth: Vaginal orgasms are superior to clitoral orgasms.
    New myth: Women experience no difference between vaginally induced and clitorally induced orgasms.
9   Old myth: A large penis is needed to satisfy a woman.
    New myth: Penis size is totally irrelevant to female pleasure.
10 Old myth: Simultaneous orgasms are the best sexual experience.
    New myth: Sequential orgasms are best.
11 Old myth: Well-adjusted young people are chaste.
    New myth: All contemporary adolescents are promiscuous.
12 Old myth: The lower classes have a much more varied and active sexual life.
    New myth: Extraordinary sexual activity is the domain of the upper classes.
13 Old myth: Any woman who is raped probably wanted it.
    New myth: Many women fantasize rape, and therefore must enjoy it.[40]

SUMMARY

The history of sexuality in America supplies background material for understanding the beginnings of taboos, stereotypic responses, misconceptions, and myths that may have outlived their usefulness. The 1960s, known as a period of social reform or social change, created a great deal of controversy and change in sexual activities. Some people believe this period to be a sexual revolution; others claim that it was the beginning of a period of sexual enlightenment or sexual revelation. Enlightenment or revelation seems to be more appropriate to describe the changes in sexual health care. Before the 1960s medical and nursing curricula did not include sexuality as a course of study. The social changes ushered in the right and responsibility of health professionals to study sexual behavior. In the following decade the literature in education, psychology, medicine, social work, allied health, and nursing was bulging with articles and books on many aspects of sexuality.

Finally, there is an understanding and acceptance of the fact that sexuality has a tremendous impact on individuals, family, and the nation's health status. It is verbally accepted by most professionals and those organizations that are responsible for any type of health care. Methods of providing health care are dependent on the needs of the client and skills of those delivering care. Both needs and skills should be accurately assessed before sexual health care is attempted.

Concurrent with the acceptance of sexuality as a legitimate health concern has been the recognition and development of sexuality content in the disciplines of health, behavioral, and social sciences. Gradually each discipline is recognizing and establishing basic requirements for different types of activities. The evaluation of sexuality as an academic field is at the stage when there is a great deal of confusion. Many difficult questions need to be answered.

LEARNING ACTIVITIES

1 Each student selects a period in American history and determines the relationship of sexuality and major societal issues. Compare and contrast the different issues and periods in small groups (6 to 10) of students.

2 Compare and contrast the sexuality of men with that of women during each period of American history.

3 Discuss and compare the sexual myths and fallacies of the past and those proposed as the new sexual myths of the 1970s (Pomeroy).

4 Each student should make a list of what he or she feels are the most severe problems in health care arising from biased attitudes of the past. Discuss with other members of the class.

SUGGESTED READING

Calderone, Mary S.: "Eroticism and a Norm," in *Human Sexuality,* 2d ed., Eleanor Morrison and Vera Bonosage (eds.), Mayfield, Palo Alto, Calif., 1977, pp. 39–48.

Elder, M. S.: "Nurse Counseling on Sexuality. An Unmet Challenge," *Nurs. Outlook* **18**:38–40 (1970).

Haller, John, and Robert Haller: *The Physician and Sexuality in Victorian America,* University of Illinois Press, Chicago, 1974.

McCary, James L.: "Sexual Myths and Fallacies," in *Modern Views of Human Sexual Behavior,* James McCary and Donna Copeland (eds.), Science Research, Chicago, 1976, pp. 286–312.

Pomeroy, Wardell: "Sexual Myths of the 1970's," *Med. Aspects Hum. Sexual.* **11**(1):62–74 (1977).

REFERENCES

1 Sam Wilson, Bryan Strong, Leah Clark, and Thomas Johns, *Human Sexuality: A Text with Readings,* West, St. Paul, Minn., 1977, p. 5.

2 Norman Sussman, "Sex and Sexuality in History," in Benjamin Sadock, Harold Kaplan, and Alfred Freedman (eds.), *The Sexual Experience,* Williams & Wilkins, Baltimore, 1976, p. 54.

3 Wilson, op. cit., p. 7.

4 Sussman, op. cit., p. 57.

5 Ibid., pp. 59–62.

6 Wilson, op. cit., p. 8.

7   Robert Staples, "The Sexuality of Black Women," in Leonard Gross (ed.), *Sexual Behavior,* Spectrum, Flushing, N.Y., 1974, p. 24.

8   Jessie Bernard, *Marriage and Family among Negroes,* Prentice-Hall, Englewood Cliffs, N.J., 1966, p. 75.

9   Staples, op. cit., p. 25.

10   John Haller and Robert Haller, *The Physician and Sexuality in Victorian America,* University of Illinois Press, Chicago, 1974, p. 97.

11   Alfred C. Kinsey, et al., *Sexual Behavior in the Human Male,* Saunders, Philadelphia, 1948.

12   Ibid.

13   Sussman, op. cit., pp. 66–67.

14   William Masters and Virginia Johnson, *Human Sexual Response,* Little, Brown, Boston, 1966.

15   William Masters and Virginia Johnson, *Human Sexual Inadequacy,* Little, Brown, Boston, 1966.

16   Fritz A. Freyhan, "Scientific Models for Sexual Behavior from the Clinician's Point of View," in Joseph Zubin and John Money (eds.), *Contemporary Sexual Behavior: Critical Issues in the 1970's,* Johns Hopkins, Baltimore, 1973, pp. 269–270.

17   Tom Hurly, "Gay Couples and Straight Law," in Eleanor Morrison and Vera Borosage (eds.), *Human Sexuality,* 2d ed., Mayfield, Palo Alto, Calif., 1977, pp. 331–332.

18   Ibid.

19   Evalyn Gendel, "Sexuality, Health and Social Policy: A SIECUS Statement," *SIECUS Rep.* **1**(6) (1973).

20   Judy Lemsrud, "Abortion Rights—Advocate Ready for Battle," *Wis. State J.,* sec. 3, February 6, 1978.

21   Eleanor Morrison and Vera Bonosage, "Male and Female Roles in Transition," *Human Sexuality,* 2d ed., Mayfield, Palo Alto, Calif., 1977, p. 107.

22   Gary F. Kelly, "College Males and the New Masculinism," *SIECUS Rep.* **5**(1):1 (1976).

23   W. Cody Wilson, "Facts versus Fears: Why Should We Worry about Pornography?" in Morrison and Bonosage (eds.), *Human Sexuality,* Mayfield, Palo Alto, Calif., 1977, p. 354.

24   Mary S. Calderone and Terry Herb, "Thoughts on Preadolescent Pregnancies," *SIECUS Rep.* **6**(3):11–12 (1978).

25   Ann Burgess and Lynda Holmstrom, "Rape Trauma Syndrome," in James McCary and Donna Copeland (eds.), *Modern Views of Human Sexual Behavior,* Science Research, Chicago, 1976, p. 270.

26   Shere Hite, *The Hite Report: A Nationwide Study of Female Sexuality,* Macmillan, New York, 1976.

27   Leah Schaefer and Wardell Pomeroy, "The Hite Report: Two Professionals' Views," *SIECUS Rep.* **5**(2):15 (1976).

28   *SIECUS Report,* "World Health Organization Asks: Are Health Professionals Competent to Deal with Human Sexuality?" **1**(6):4 (1973).

29   Sherwyn Woods, "Sex and the Uptight Doctor," *Med. Opin.* **I**(1):14 (1972).

30   Ibid.

31   Robert H. Coombs, "Sex Education in American Colleges," in Clark Vincent (ed.), *Human Sexuality in Medical Education and Practice,* Charles C Thomas, Springfield, Ill., 1968, chap. 5, p. 63.

32 Jeanne D. Fonseca, "Sexuality—A Quality of Being Human," *Nurs. Outlook* **15**(11) (1970) (editorial).

33 Fern H. Mims, Rosalee Yeaworth, and Stephen Hornstein, "Effectiveness of an Interdisciplinary Course in Human Sexuality," *Nurs. Res.* **23**(3):248–253 (1974).

34 Trena Goodwin, "Sexual Concerns and Questions Which Patients Present to Registered Nurses in Selected Areas of Nursing Practice," unpublished thesis, University of Cincinnati, 1975, pp. 58–68.

35 Harold Lief and Tyana Payne, "Sexuality Knowledge and Attitudes, *Am. J. Nurs.* **75**(11):2026–2029 (1975).

36 Mims et al., op. cit., pp. 248–253.

37 Fern H. Mims, Lewis Brown, and Robert Lubow, "Human Sexuality Course Evaluation," *Nurs. Res.* **25**(3):187–192 (1976).

38 Joshua Golden and Edward Leston, "Medical Sex Education: The World of Illusion and the Practice Realities," *J. Med. Educ.* **47**:761–771 (1972).

39 *SIECUS Report,* " 'Do You Know That,' California Mandates Sexuality Study for Professionals," **5**(5):5 (1977).

40 Wardell B. Pomeroy, "The New Sexual Myths of the 1970's," *SIECUS Rep.* **5**(6):1 (1977).

Chapter 3

Sexual Responses and Dysfunctions

Sexual responses elicit activity and reactions from the muscular, vascular, endocrine, and neurological systems, and ultimately affect the overall functioning of the body. However, in this chapter only the major physiological changes and responses of the sexual organs will be reviewed. For a thorough study of the physiological sexual responses, other sources are recommended in the suggested readings at the end of the chapter. The techniques of sexual stimulation, coital positions, and the most common male and female sexual dysfunctions will also be introduced in this chapter. It is mainly an informational chapter with few specific suggestions for nurses. Later chapters cover nursing interventions.

MALE SEXUAL ANATOMY AND PHYSIOLOGY

The male external genitalia include the penis, scrotum, two gonads (testes), epididymis, and parts of the vas deferens. The internal genitalia consist of the vas deferens, seminal vesicles, ejaculatory ducts, prostate, and Cowper's glands (Fig. 3-1).

The main parts of the *penis* are known as the shaft, glans, and bulb. A cross section of the shaft shows two corpora cavernosa lying side by side, one corpus spongiosum, urethra, arteries, veins, nerves, and skin (Fig. 3-2).

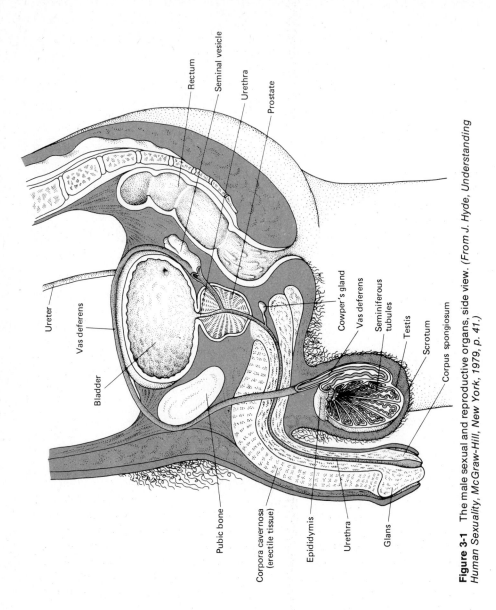

Figure 3-1 The male sexual and reproductive organs, side view. *(From J. Hyde, Understanding Human Sexuality, McGraw-Hill, New York, 1979, p. 41.)*

Ureter

Vas deferens

Bladder

Rectum

Seminal vesicle

Urethra

Prostate

Cowper's gland

Vas deferens

Seminiferous tubules

Testis

Scrotum

Corpus spongiosum

Glans

Urethra

Epididymis

Corpora cavernosa (erectile tissue)

Pubic bone

The corpora cavernosa and corpus spongiosum, sometimes called spongy bodies, are composed of erectile tissue, which fills with blood to bring about an erection. It is believed that the blood is prevented from draining out through the veins by special valves, which are closed by a reflex action. Nerves of the parasympathetic division of the autonomic nervous system control the diameter and the valves of the penile blood vessels. According to Kaplan:

> An additional lower erectile reflex center has been discovered in the higher cord. The sacral center seems to mediate erection in response to direct tactile stimulation of the genitals, while the higher center produces erection primarily caused by psychic stimulation. Cerebral centers which influence the erectile reflex have been located in the midbrain and in various loci of the limbic cortex.[1]

The glans is composed of the anterior end of the corpus spongiosum and corpora cavernosa. The surface is filled with nerve endings, especially at the corona. At the tip of the glans is a meatus, the external opening of the urethra. The bulbocavernosus and the ischiocavernosus muscle cover the backward extensions of the spongy tissue which helps to propel ejaculate through the urethra.

The *testes* are oval glands measuring about 1 in wide, 1½ in long, and ¾ in thick. The seminiferous tubules, within the testes, produce the sperm cells. Besides producing sperm, the testes are involved in the production of testoster-

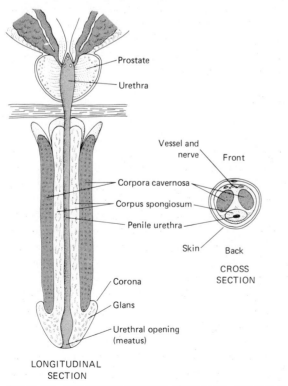

Prostate

Urethra

Vessel and nerve   Front

Corpora cavernosa

Corpus spongiosum

Penile urethra

Skin   Back

CROSS SECTION

Corona

Glans

Urethral opening (meatus)

LONGITUDINAL SECTION

Figure 3-2   The internal structure of the penis. *(From Hyde, op. cit., p. 42.)*

one. The testes lie in the saclike *scrotum,* which is composed of two compartments, each containing a testis and epididymis. The *epididymis* is a tubule which is part of the channel through which sperm pass to the outside. It holds sperm until they are needed.

The *vas deferens,* or ductus deferens, is the continuation of the tail of the epididymis. It connects to the seminal vesicle and empties into the *ejaculatory duct* in the *prostate gland.* It carries sperm from the epididymis to the ejaculatory duct. The ejaculatory duct is usually closed, and the ejaculatory process is under the control of the sympathetic subsystem of the autonomic nervous system. It is believed that through the hypogastric plexus the sympathetic nervous system innervates the muscles of the epididymis, vas deferens, seminal vesicles, and the prostate, which causes ejaculation of the fluid into the urethra. The prostate surrounds the ejaculatory ducts, which partially house the semen until ejaculation. The *semen* is composed of spermatozoa, seminal fluid, and secretions from the epididymis, seminal vesicles, prostate gland, and Cowper's glands.[2-4]

FEMALE SEXUAL ANATOMY AND PHYSIOLOGY

The female external genitalia include the mons pubis, (or mons veneris), labia minora, labia majora, clitoris, and vaginal orifice (Fig. 3-3). The internal genitalia consist of the gonads (two ovaries), fallopian tubes, uterus, and vagina (Fig. 3-4).

The external genitalia are collectively called the *vulva* and consist of the mons pubis, labia majora, labia minora, and the vestibule. The *mons pubis,* a mound directly in front of the pubic bone, is a highly sensitive area. Receptors in the mons respond to touch, pressure, and weight to produce sexual excitement. Some women prefer manipulation of the mons area rather than the clitoris. The *labia majora,* "large lips," are covered with hair on the outside while sweat glands are prevalent on the inside. These lips serve as a protection of the vagina, labia minora, and urinary opening. During sexual excitement, the labia majora separate and flatten to expose the labia minora, clitoris, and vaginal opening. The *labia minora* are folds of pigmented skin possessing many blood vessels, sweat and oil glands, and sensory receptors. Levels of sexual excitement are detected by the color changes from pink to bright red of the labia minora. The minor lips provide protection for the clitoris and the two Bartholin's glands (a homologous structure to the Cowper's gland). Their exact function remains questionable. However, in the young woman, they produce one or two drops of clear mucuslike fluid that helps in lubricating the opening of the vagina. There is some atrophy of these glands with aging.

The *clitoris,* a small cylindrical, erectile structure composed of fused corpora cavernosa, is usually not more than 1 in in length. Like the penis, the clitoris is composed of the shaft and glans, and is generously supplied with sensory nerve endings.[5-7]

The internal organs of the female consist of two ovaries, uterus, two fallopian tubes, and vagina (see Fig. 3-5).

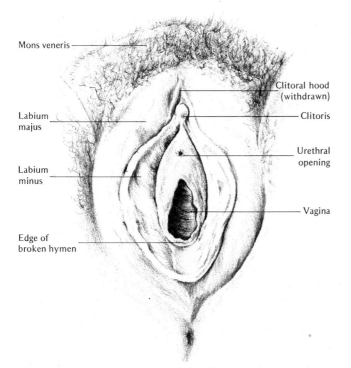

Mons veneris

Clitoral hood
(withdrawn)

Labium
majus

Clitoris

Urethral
opening

Labium
minus

Vagina

Edge of
broken hymen

Figure 3-3 Female external genitalia. *(From B. Goldstein, Introduction to Human Sexuality, McGraw-Hill, New York, 1975, p. 34.)*

The *ovaries* are almond-shaped organs about 1 in in length that are supported by a fold of peritoneum called the *suspensory ligament*. Each ovary has many follicles that contain immature ova. At puberty with growth and production of estrogen and progesterone, the immature ova begin to ripen and one is released each month. After the ovum is discharged, the lining of the follicle is filled with corpus luteum. The ovum is propelled by the many cilia on the wall of the *fallopian tubes* toward the uterus.

The *uterus,* a hollow pear-shaped organ about 3 in long, is located in the pelvic cavity between the bladder and rectum and hangs slightly below and between the fallopian tubes. The internal mucus, or endometrium, goes through changes with a shedding each month. Walls of the uterus contain longitudinal and circular muscle fibers that interlace, creating a forceful contraction during orgasm and during the birth process. The muscles of the pelvic floor help with bladder and bowel control, and the pubococcygeus muscle is an important muscle of sexual function (Fig. 3-6).

The *vagina* is usually in a collapsed state, but is capable of considerable dilation. Lining of the vagina expands in both length and width, which accommodates the penis during sexual intercourse. The hypogastric plexus of the sympathetic nervous system serves the uterus, fallopian tubes, and part of the vagina. These nerves stimulate the genitalia to contract during periods of the sexual response cycle.

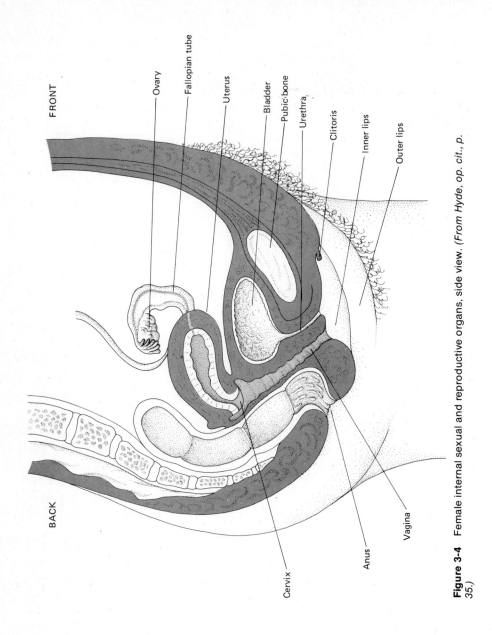

FRONT

Ovary

Fallopian tube

Uterus

Bladder

Pubic bone

Urethra

Clitoris

Inner lips

Outer lips

BACK

Cervix

Anus

Vagina

Figure 3-4 Female internal sexual and reproductive organs, side view. *(From Hyde, op. cit., p. 35.)*

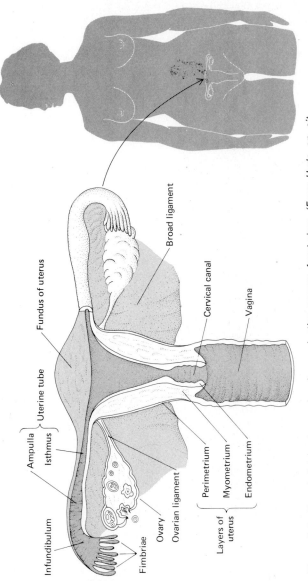

Figure 3-5 Female internal sexual and reproductive organs, front view. (*From Hyde, op. cit., p. 36.*)

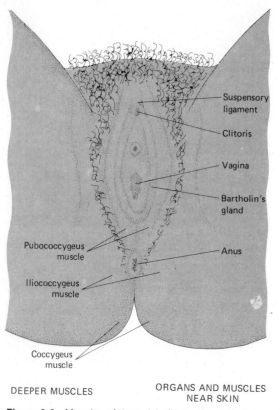

Suspensory
ligament

Clitoris

Vagina

Bartholin's
gland

Pubococcygeus
muscle

Anus

Iliococcygeus
muscle

Coccygeus
muscle

DEEPER MUSCLES   ORGANS AND MUSCLES
                              NEAR SKIN

Figure 3-6   Muscles of the pelvic floor. *(From Hyde, op. cit., p. 37.)*

SEXUAL RESPONSE CYCLE

Masters and Johnson divide the physiological responses to sexual stimuli into four successive phases: (1) excitement, (2) plateau, (3) orgasm, and (4) resolution[8] (Figs. 3-7 and 3-8). The excitement stage develops from any source of bodily or psychic stimulation that produces erotic feelings sufficient for penile erection and vaginal lubrication. In both male and female, there is vasocongestion, an accumulation of blood, particularly in the genitals, which leads to tumescence of the penis or clitoris. Sexual tension is also noted by a generalized bodily reaction of vasocongestion and myotonia, a muscular tension throughout the body. The excitement phase for the male also includes a flattening, thickening, and elevation of the scrotum, with the testes beginning to elevate. In some females, and to a lesser extent in males, there is a skin response called the *sex flush:* the breasts begin to enlarge, and the nipples become erect. The uterus enlarges and moves upward, the vaginal barrel expands and lengthens, and the labia minora change in color, varying from bright red to deep wine. In both male and female, breathing becomes heavier, with both the heart rate and the blood pressure increasing.

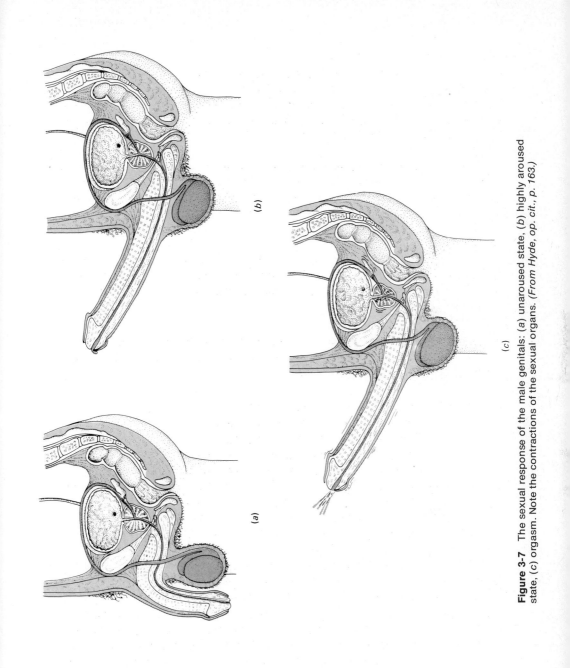

Figure 3-7 The sexual response of the male genitals: (a) unaroused state, (b) highly aroused state, (c) orgasm. Note the contractions of the sexual organs. (*From Hyde, op. cit., p. 163.*)

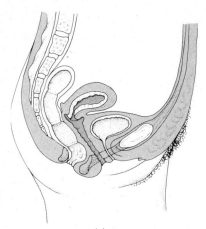

(a)

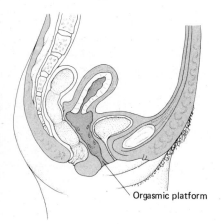

Orgasmic platform

(b)

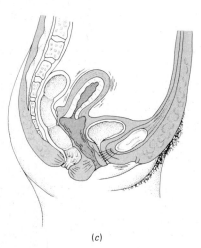

(c)

Figure 3-8 Sexual response of the female genitals: (a) unaroused state, (b) highly aroused state (plateau), (c) orgasm. Note the contractions of the muscles surrounding the vagina. *(From Hyde, op. cit., p. 165.)*

In the plateau phase, sexual tension becomes more intensified, and if stimuli and drive are maintained, orgasm will occur. In this phase, local genital vasocongestive responses are pronounced. The penis is distended to its capacity and testes may enlarge by 50 percent. Often there are a few drops of clear mucoid fluid on the glans of the penis, probably coming from the Cowper's glands. In the female, vasocongestion continues to bring about color changes of the labia minora. In the young woman, the Bartholin's glands secrete a few drops of mucoid secretion, but it is insufficient to lubricate the vagina. The uterus continues to move from the pelvic floor and the clitoris retracts in a flat position behind the symphysis pubis. There is a building of the orgasmic platform, a swelling due to blood congestion of the outer third of the vagina. Sympathetic control becomes evident in both sexes, with acceleration of heart rate, increase in blood pressure, increase in breathing rate, and myotonia.

The orgasmic phase might be considered the more pleasurable of the sexual sensations. Orgasm is a physiological response of the entire body, usually lasting only a few seconds. In the male, there are involuntary contractions of the penile muscles, seminal vesicles, prostate, urethra, and rectal sphincter. Heartbeat, breathing rate, blood pressure, and respirations increase. The ejaculatory spurt of semen changes with age. In the young man, the semen spurts from 12 to 20 in and often diminishes to only seepage in the older man. In the female, there is a great variation in the physiological response and subjective awareness of orgasm. Usually, there are 3 to 15 contractions of the labia minora, lower third of vagina, uterus, rectum, and external urethral sphincter. Orgasm may differ physiologically in pattern and intensity from time to time in the same woman. Some females have the capacity of multiple orgasms with each one of them being highly pleasurable. The potential for multiple orgasmic response remains throughout the woman's life.

The resolution, the last of the phases, is approximately 10 to 15 minutes long if there is an orgasm. The time is lengthy if there is no orgasm and can last several hours in either male or female. Usually, for the male, the vasocongestion partially disappears in 5 to 10 seconds with full detumescence occurring in 5 to 30 minutes. The flush disappears and a light film of perspiration can be detected on the soles of feet and palms of hands. Immediately following an orgasm, most males have a physiological refractory period which involves a temporary lack of response to sexual stimuli. The refractory period is variable in duration, ranging from a few minutes in the young man to a week or longer for some older men. In the female, the congestion disappears with the color and size of the labia majora, clitoris, uterus, and breasts returning to normal in 10 to 15 minutes after orgasm. Usually, there is no physiological refractory period for the female.[9-11]

TECHNIQUES OF SEXUAL STIMULATION

Manual Stimulation

Auto and reciprocal genital manipulation are often used as foreplay or may be used to obtain orgasm. Self-manipulation or self-pleasuring centers around an erogenous zone and is sometimes called *masturbation*. The erogenous zone may be any part of the skin containing numerous receptors that when stroked causes sexual arousal. The most frequent form of hand-genital stimulation of the male is a firm gripping and stroking manipulation of the penis by hand. Women frequently stimulate the clitoral shaft and labia minora. Since these structures are quite sensitive, they are pressed and rhythmically stimulated by the fingers with a gentle stroke. Some women manipulate the breast and mons area as a whole. In both male and female, hand manipulation is the most common method of manual stimulation. However, other objects such as pillows, towels, bedclothes, or vibrators are used to produce orgasm.

Oral-Genital Stimulation

There are three types of oral-genital stimulation practiced by a sizable number of adults: cunnilingus, fellatio, and cunnilingus-fellatio combination ("69"). Cunnilingus comes from Latin meaning "to lick the vulva"; fellatio is derived from the Latin *fellare*, meaning "to suck"; and soixante-neuf, French for 69, refers to oral-genital contact between two individuals.[12] In cunnilingus, there is a kissing, sucking, licking, and tongue exploration of the minor vaginal lips, the clitoral shaft, and the opening of the vagina. Women vary as to what feels good, and what is sexually stimulating may vary from day to day with each woman. According to the Hite Report, 42 percent of the study population of 3019 women orgasmed regularly during oral stimulation.[13] In fellatio, the oral-genital activity has many variations. Sucking, licking, and movements of the tongue in a circular fashion around the glans, the shaft of the penis, and sometimes the testicles are used in the excitement stage. Movement of a thrusting up and down motion is used in the plateau and orgasmic phases. The combined methods of fellatio and cunnilingus, referred to as 69, allows both persons to be stimulated at the same time.

Anal-Genital Stimulation

Some people find the anus to be sensitive and prefer having anal stimulation over all other types of sexual practices. The anus is not as elastic as the vagina, thus requiring gentleness, gradual entry, and extra lubrication.

Genital-Genital Coitus Stimulation

Coitus is generally thought to mean a coming together of the male and female sexual organs of penis and vagina.

Coitus may be described as having a wide variety of purposes. The usefulness of sexual intercourse in reproduction is not a controversial subject. Describing coitus as a method of expressing a reciprocal love relationship is also a common practice. According to some women respondents in the Hite Report, "I love it; to me nothing else is really sex."[14]

Coital Positions

It is believed that the coital positions that are most commonly used in a particular culture are highly correlated with the social status of the sexes in the society.

Where the woman's sexual satisfaction is deemed as important as a man's, the woman-on-top position seems to be predominant. In cultures where the primary coital position is face to face, man on top, the female's social status is most often less privileged than the male's. An increased variety of coital methods may be an indication that the social status of sex roles is changing.[15]

Individuals and couples vary as to the preferred position of coitus. The most common positions, with infinite variations of each, are sitting face to face; lying face to face (Fig. 3-9), man above; face to face, woman above; face to face, both partners standing; rear entry; and side coital position. The man above is probably the most widely used position in our society. Some of the most common positions are shown in Figs. 3-10 to 3-16.

SEXUAL PROBLEMS OR DYSFUNCTIONS

As noted in Chap. 2, society is in a period of transition with the final stabilizing point not being clear at this time. During this change or maturational period, individuals will probably continue to experience difficulties in sexual functioning. Many of these problems are classified as sexual dysfunctions. These conditions still lack specificity and the research data necessary to describe specific subtypes and related factors. In this chapter, the sexual problems, dysfunctions, or complaints will be considered the major diagnosis. In subsequent chapters, the same sexual dysfunctions will appear as potential secondary conditions of physiological and psychological abnormalities.

Change in Libido (Decreased and Increased)

In a broad sense, libido may be defined as the sexual motivation, urge, or desire for sexual activity. Libido fluctuates within each person and varies from person to person. Libido is influenced by the interplay of physiological, psychological, and social functioning. Physiologically, the neural control of sexual functioning is organized in such a manner that sexual responses are intricately and reciprocally influenced by all levels of the brain. The genital organs and the cerebral sex centers send impulses to and receive impulses from virtually all the neural centers and circuits. This includes the peripheral nerves, sensory nerves, sympathetic, and parasympathetic systems. There is also evidence that both male and female libido and sexual responsiveness require that the brain and the genitals receive an adequate blood supply with specific hormones. Physiologically, a temporary inhibition of the central nervous system or lowered androgen levels may cause a temporary decrease in libido. Some of the causes or contributing factors of a decreased libido are (1) drugs that depress the central nervous system; (2) drugs that cause a psychomotor depression; (3) large doses of antiandrogens; (4) conditions that damage the androgen supply, such as adrenalectomy or castration; (5) impaired hepatic function; (6) chronic painful syndromes, such as cancer, arthritis, and cardiac disease; (7) dyspareunia; (8) depression; and (9) aging process. The causes and contributions to a decreased libido are numerous, complex, interrelated, and the exact relationships are not always understood.[16]

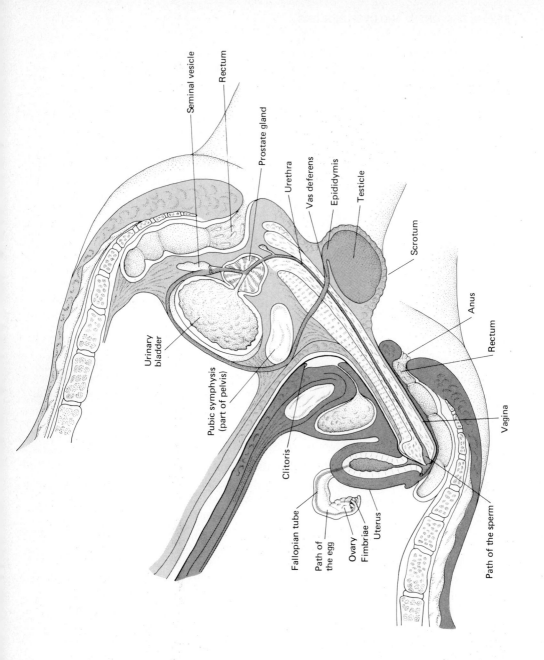

Figure 3-9 Penis and vagina in face-to-face coitus. *(From Hyde, op. cit., p. 91.)*

Figure 3-10 Face-to-face coital position, man above, woman below. *(From B. Goldstein, Introduction to Human Sexuality, McGraw-Hill, New York, 1975, p. 148.)*

Figure 3-11 Face-to-face coital position, woman's legs fully elevated. *(From Goldstein, loc. cit.)*

Figure 3-12 Woman above, man below, in face-to-face coitus. *(From Goldstein, op. cit., p. 149.)*

Figure 3-13 Side by side, face-to-face. This position and the woman-on-top position (Fig. 3-12) allow maximum stimulation of the woman. *(From Goldstein, loc. cit.)*

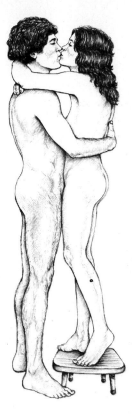

Figure 3-14 Face to face, standing, allows maximum freedom of movement for both male and female. *(From Goldstein, op. cit., p. 150.)*

Figure 3-15 A variation of face-to-face coitus. *(From Goldstein, loc. cit.)*

Figure 3-16 One of several rear-entry coital positions. *(From Goldstein, loc. cit.)*

In a society that places so much emphasis on sexuality, it might be expected that an increased libido would always be a welcome change. However, a drastic change in libido can cause a major problem unless there is a conscious awareness of the process and an acceptance of increased sensitivity to sexual stimuli. In puberty and adolescence, there is an increase in libido for both male and female. Neurological and hormonal factors are enmeshed and responsible for dramatic body and psychological changes in sexual urges. The increase in sexual drive produces an increase in pleasure as well as creating problems for the young recipient. A few adolescents become sexually active, with coitus, as early as 11 or 12 years of age. However, it is likely that some of these young people become active because of peer pressure rather than from an increase in libido. Other adolescents learn to sublimate with athletics, hobbies, and music in order to control libido.[17] The nurse may be instrumental in helping families explore the rights and responsibilities of sexual urges of their teenagers.

Not many physical or mental illnesses increase libido. Damages to the brain such as temporal and frontal tumors and accidents can increase or decrease libido. In the cyclic manic-depressive states, there is often an increase in libido in the manic phase.

The use of drugs, the aphrodisiacs, to enhance libido has a long but unsuccessful history. In most drugs labeled aphrodisiacs, the positive effect in enhancing erotic behavior comes from the placebo effect. The amphetamines and cocaine are reported to enhance libido for some people but for short periods of time, and the addicting potential is more likely to diminish rather than increase libido. Hallucinogens, LSD (lysergic acid diethylamide), mescaline, and marijuana have been reported by some users to increase libido, while others report inhibited sexual responses.[18]

Impotence

Impotence is the inability to achieve an erection of the penis necessary for coital connection. Impotence may be primary or secondary. In primary impotence, the man has never achieved an erection sufficient for coitus with a partner, although he may have had erections while masturbating or spontaneous erections. In secondary impotence, the man functioned in coitus for some time prior to the development of the erectile dysfunction. Both types of impotence can be due to physiological or psychological factors or a combination of both. The vascular reflex mechanism fails to pump sufficient blood into the cavernous sinuses of the penis to make it hard and firm. The exact relationship of psychic factors and learned sexual behaviors on erectile difficulties is not completely understood.

Physiological Factors   The physiologically related causes or contributing factors are associated with the hormonal, vascular, and neural mechanisms. Endocrine disturbances that may cause impotence are hypothyroidism, Addison's disease, hypogonadism, Klinefelter's syndrome, acromegaly, and diabetes mellitus. Diabetes will be discussed in Chap. 16.

Neurological disorders that destroy the function of the sacral cord or of the lower thoracolumbar sympathetic fibers may affect erection. Damage to genitals, the perineal nerves, and the hypogastric plexus may result in impotence. Some of the surgeries that cause extensive damage to the genital nerve supply include radical perineal prostatectomy, abdominal-perineal bowel resections, and other extensive abdominal explorations. These conditions usually do not affect libido, only erectile abilities. In renal diseases, the peripheral neuritis associated with uremia may be the underlying cause of impotence. Conditions that affect testicular functioning such as tumors, mumps, and traumas may also cause impotence. The vascular diseases, which include thrombosis of veins and arteries of the penis, sickle cell disorders, and leukemia may impair erection. Any condition that causes local irritability during sexual activity such as urethritis or prostatitis can be responsible for impotence.[19,20]

There are a large number of drugs that decrease sexual responses. Sedatives depress the central nervous system and chronic use may cause neurological damage. Other drugs act on the genitals by blocking the nerves controlling the smooth muscle and blood vessels of the genitals. Some of these drugs are used in the treatment of hypertension, peripheral vascular disorders, and ophthalmologic disorders.[21]

The antipsychotic drugs, phenothiazines, may produce impotence. The antidepressants, tricyclics, and monoamine oxidase inhibitors may produce potency problems. Some of the drugs used in an attempt to enhance sexuality, such as the amphetamines, may initially alter sensations but used over a longer period of time, there is a gradual loss of ability to achieve an erection. The habitual heroin user has difficulty with erection but evidently no long-term damage is done and the inhibitory effects of heroin are reversible.[22] Drugs and their specific effects on sexuality are discussed in greater depth in Chap. 13.

Psychologically Related Causes and Contributions   The relation of psychological factors and impotence is complex. Some men have problems with erection when associated with coitus, while others can obtain an erection during foreplay but lose the erection in different phases of sexual activity. It is not uncommon for a man to have an erection with several different sexual partners but be impotent with a specific partner.

Primary impotence is often associated with psychological factors. Family and societal taboos, restrictions, controls, and individual performance anxiety may be interrelated and the basis of a pattern of erectile failures. If erection of the penis is associated with pain, fear, or guilt, the man is likely to inhibit the response. The inhibitions and controls can be responsible for a conditioned response. The impotence may be associated with a complex interaction of punishment and reinforcement derived from significant others. Psychological causes of primary impotence are often associated with traumatic early sexual experiences.

Secondary impotence is most often associated with feelings of inadequacy, guilt, rejection, or anger concerned with immediate situational factors. Some of these troublesome factors are general unhappiness, boredom associated with a particular female partner, economic or work tensions, body image anxiety, marital discord, infidelity in partner, performance anxiety following an unsuccessful attempt, and aging anxiety. Body image following surgery such as ostomies and prostatectomies is usually altered substantially and can prove to be detrimental to potency. Any condition that is responsible for a reactive depression can have negative effects on potency.

Ejaculatory Disturbances

Ejaculation is the emission of seminal fluid from the penis. Disorders of ejaculation are premature ejaculation, retarded ejaculation, retrograde ejaculation, and nonejaculation.

Premature Ejaculation   There has been much controversy and disagreement on the definition of premature ejaculation. Some clinicians claim there is no such clinical syndrome. Masters and Johnson consider premature ejaculation as a condition in which

> . . . a male cannot control his ejaculatory process for a sufficient length of time during intravaginal containment to satisfy his partner at least fifty percent of their coital connections. If the female partner is persistently non-orgasmic for reasons other than rapidity of the male's ejaculatory process, there is no validity to the definition.[23]

When there was less concern of the woman's needs and she was not expected to respond sexually, premature ejaculation was defined as the inability to maintain erection to achieve vaginal insertion. Perhaps the significant factor of the present concern of most men is that sexual gratification is relatively low when there is rapid ejaculation. Men desire to delay ejaculation to increase sexual fulfillment for self and partner. The greatest part of the problems associated with ejaculation is very often a learned or conditioned response used to relieve anxiety or guilt about sexual performance. In our society, the beginning coital experiences of a young man are often focused on orgasm and not on the interpersonal aspects of a sexual relationship. Initially the woman may not be interested and may encourage the premature ejaculations. Later, these conditioned responses become sexual patterns with the interaction becoming plagued with anger and anxiety about performance. Premature ejaculation responds by treating the couple with desensitization of sexual guilt, removal of performance anxiety, and the lowering of penile excitability.[24]

A few physiological conditions that may be responsible for ejaculatory disturbances are neurological disorders that interfere with peripheral nerves or spinal cord reflex centers. Irritability and damage to the genitals are sometimes thought to be responsible for premature ejaculation.

Retarded or Inhibited Ejaculation   Retarded or inhibited ejaculation may be primary, when it has always been present, or secondary, when it develops after previous normal ejaculation. In primary retarded ejaculation, the causes are usually psychological and are similar to those of premature ejaculation. A few of the psychological factors related to this condition are fear of impregnating the partner, fear of loss of control, a high value on controlling, and general hostile feelings toward the partner. Secondary ejaculatory incompetence is more often a symptom of interpersonal problems within a relationship.

Ejaculatory incompetence may result from some neurological disorders where there is an interference of sympathetic innervation to the genitals. The antiadrenergic drugs used in the treatment of hypertension can block the autonomic sympathetic response and impair ejaculation. The phenothiazines, such as Thorazine and Mellaril, have some inhibiting effects on ejaculation for some men.[25]

Retrograde Ejaculation   Retrograde ejaculation is the discharge of semen into the bladder rather than through the urethra (see Fig. 3-17).

> Two sphincters are involved in ejaculation: an internal one, which closes off the entrance to the bladder during a normal ejaculation, and an external one, which opens during a normal ejaculation, allowing the semen to flow out through the penis. In retrograde ejaculation, the action of these two sphincters is reversed; the external one closes, and thus the ejaculate cannot flow out through the penis, and the internal one opens, permitting the ejaculate to go into the bladder.[26]

Sensation of ejaculation is reported to be similar to normal ejaculation. The causes can be associated with surgery of the lower urinary tract, transurethral surgery of the prostate, deep pelvic dissection, retroperitoneal lymph node dissection, and trauma to the pelvis with injury to the bladder neck or sacral

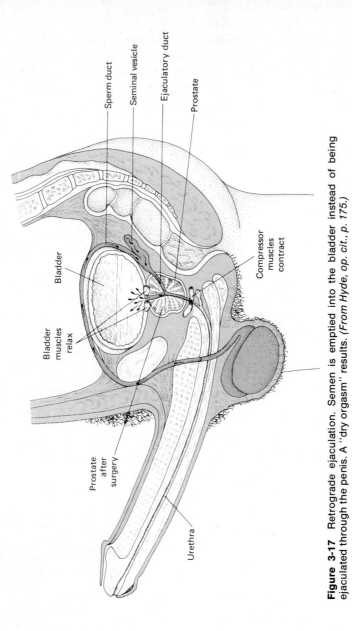

Sperm duct

Seminal vesicle

Ejaculatory duct

Prostate

Bladder

Compressor muscles contract

Bladder muscles relax

Prostate after surgery

Urethra

Figure 3-17 Retrograde ejaculation. Semen is emptied into the bladder instead of being ejaculated through the penis. A "dry orgasm" results. *(From Hyde, op. cit., p. 175.)*

nerves. It can be caused by chemical ganglionic blockers used in the treatment of hypertension. For some men it has been one of the first signs of diabetes mellitus which is associated with neuropathy. Finally, a spinal cord injury may interfere with the sympathetic nerve supply and cause retrograde ejaculation.

Any abnormal function of the sexual organs can create anxiety about sexual performance and self-esteem. Lack of seminal fluid may be traumatic and threaten the masculinity of the man. The woman may take responsibility for the lack of ejaculate and wonder what she is doing wrong. One of the presenting complaints may be infertility. If the couple agrees, the sperm may be recovered from the urine and used in artificial insemination to produce pregnancy.[27]

Dyspareunia

Some clinicians and authors apply the term dyspareunia only to women. Others use the term to denote the occurrence of pain experienced by either the male or female during the sexual act. There seems to be no adequate rationale to limit the term to only females. There are many organic causes for pain in both the male and female. Some of the physiological causes for dyspareunia are outlined in Table 3-1.

As noted in Table 3-1 there are many causes for coital discomfort in both male and female. There are also many complex psychological factors related to dyspareunia, especially in the female. For the male, psychological problems are more likely associated with impotence and ejaculatory difficulties than with dyspareunia. In the woman, fear is probably the main etiologic factor. Some of the fears revolve around concern of unwanted pregnancy, of social exposure, of pain with penetration, of losing control of one's psychological or physiological body functions, of fantasied conflicts based on various beliefs and myths, and of unresolved maturational conflicts. Fear seems to be the common denominator of the fantasied event, whether it is experienced as pain, shame, or guilt. Since the psychological factors relating to dyspareunia are usually complex, the organic causes of coital discomfort should be explored before there is any attempt at diagnosing the psychological causes.

A basic nursing approach entails (1) a careful and detailed sexual history including when, where, and how the pain began; (2) a thorough physical and pelvic examination, taking notice of any manipulations that cause acute sharp pain, intermittent twinges of pain, general discomfort, or aching sensations. Some discomfort may be noted on entrance to vagina due to lack of lubrication, painful scars at the vaginal opening, or locally inflamed or irritated areas. The discomfort in the midvaginal area is more commonly associated with urethritis and cystitis. Some of the most common causes of pelvic discomfort are associated with varicosities, endometriosis, pelvic inflammatory disease, and prolapsed ovary. Most nurses will need to refer to or have a consultation with a competent gynecologist, urologist, or psychotherapist in order to administer effective nursing care for diagnosis and treatment of coital discomfort.[33]

Table 3-1 Causes of Dyspareunia

Physiological causes of dyspareunia in women	Physiological causes of dyspareunia in men

I. Vaginitis
  a. Vaginal infections
    1. Trichomonas
    2. Monilia
    3. Bacterial
    4. Venereal warts
    5. *Escherichia coli*
  b. Sensitivity reactions to
    1. Chemical contraceptives
    2. Douche preparations
    3. Rubber condoms
    4. Hygiene sprays or deodorants
    5. Semen
    6. Bubble bath
  c. Atrophy
    1. Senile
    2. Radiation
  d. Inadequate lubrication
  e. Disuse
  f. Radiation vaginitis
II. Episiotomy scar or too tight repair
III. Vaginismus (spasm of muscles around vagina)
IV. Pelvic pathology
  a. Infections (gonorrhea)
  b. Neoplasms
  c. Congestion
  d. Inadequate repair of cystocele or rectocele
  e. Foreshortened after total hysterectomy
V. Endometriosis
VI. Intact hymen or traumatized hymenal remnant
VII. Cervicitis and cervical lacerations
VIII. Ovarian prolapse
IX. Retroversion of the uterus
X. Clitoral pain
  a. Inflammation: trichomonas
  b. Adhesions
  c. Allergic reactions
  d. Ulcers
    1. Genital herpes
    2. Chancroid
    3. Granuloma venereum
    4. Basal cell carcinoma
    5. Necrotizing fasciulitis in diabetes
	I. Inflammation and infections of external genitalia
	  a. Balanitis—inflammation of glans penis
	  b. Posthitis—inflammation of the prepuce, usually in uncircumcised males
	  c. Balanoposthitis—condition often associated with phimosis or smegma
	  d. Anterior urethritis—associated with urethral stricture, urethral diverticulum, or periurethral abscess
	  e. Epididymitis—often associated with a prostatitis and bacteria descending via the vas deferens
	  f. Orchitis—inflammation of testes, may be due to venereal diseases
	  g. Meatus urinarious—inflammation of the external urethral meatus
	  h. Cellulitis or abscess of the scrotal wall or penis
	  i. Anal lesions—fissures and fistulas, hemorrhoids, and proctitis
	II. Curvature of the penis
	  a. Hypospadias with ventral chordee (penile curvature with urethra opening on the underside of the penis)
	  b. Epispadias with dorsal chordee (penile curvature with urethra opening on the upper side of the penis)
	  c. Dorsal chordee
	  d. Ventral chordee
	  e. Traumatic injury (trauma to the penis, usually in the erect state)
	  f. Phimosis
	III. Lesions or tumors
	  a. Testicular tumors
	  b. Carcinoma of the penis
	  c. Venereal warts
	  d. Herpes progenitalis
	IV. Priapism (persistent erection of the penis)
	  a. Secondary to trauma
	  b. Secondary to sickle cell anemia and spinal cord injury

Table 3-1 Causes of Dyspareunia (continued)

Physiological causes of dyspareunia in women	Physiological causes of dyspareunia in men
e. Masses	V. Internal genitalia
1. Vulvar varicosities during pregnancy	a. Prostatitis (may be due to prolonged abstinence from sexual relations)
2. Venereal warts	b. Seminal vesiculitis
3. Abscesses	c. Prostatic calculi
4. Tumors	VI. Miscellaneous health conditions
a. Benign	a. Arthritis
b. Malignant	b. Fractures
XI. Urethritis	c. Metastatic malignancies
a. Infection	VII. Conditions of female genitalia
b. Estrogen deprivation	a. Inadequate lubrication
c. Urethral diverticulum	b. Poor repair of vaginal hysterectomy
XII. Inelastic tissues	c. Lymphogranuloma venereum
a. Estrogen deprivation	d. Allergens
XIII. Anal and bowel lesions	1. Contraceptive creams
a. Colitis	2. Rubber condoms or diaphragms
b. Thrombosed hemorrhoids	3. Douch preparations
c. Diverticula (rectosigmoid)	4. Hygiene sprays and deodorants
d. Proctitis (usually caused by anal intercourse)	5. Externally applied lubricants
e. Anal fissures and fistulas	6. Inability to tolerate normal vaginal secretions
f. Rectosigmoid tumors	

Source: References 28 to 33.

Orgasmic Dysfunction

Orgasmic dysfunction is a woman's inability to achieve orgasm through physical stimulation. In primary orgasmic dysfunction, the woman has never had an orgasm. In secondary dysfunction, there has been at least one instance of orgasm.

Since Kinsey's study in 1953, there have been a large number of studies concerning sexual practices and types of sexual satisfaction. In most studies of sexual practices, orgasmic difficulties appear to be the most prevalent sexual complaint of women. Whether the female orgasm is clitoral or vaginal has been a subject of great controversy. At this time, most people believe that physiologically female orgasms are alike. According to Kaplan:

> It is now believed by many authorities that all female orgasms are physiologically identical. They are triggered by stimulation of the clitoris and expressed by vaginal contractions. Accordingly, regardless of how friction is applied to the clitoris, i.e., by the tongue, by the woman's finger or by her partner's, by a vibrator, or by coitus, female orgasm is probably almost always evoked by clitoral stimulation. However, it is always expressed by circumvaginal muscle discharge.[34]

Most clinicians believe that psychosocial factors are largely responsible for primary orgasmic dysfunction. The psychological influences are numerous, inter-related, and complex. The orgasmic reflex may be conditioned, controlled, and greatly influenced by interpersonal relations. Some negative influences stem from double messages, double standards, and expected sexual repressive activities experienced in the normal growing-up process. The taboos and stereotypes promote ignorance, fear, and guilt about sexual activity. Other early traumatic sexual experiences such as punishment for masturbatory activities or sex play, witnessing violent conflict between parents, sexual abuse as children, rape, and an unpleasant first coital experience may be responsible for ambivalence, fear, or an overcontrol of self. Orgasm may be unconsciously associated with vulnerability and the fear of losing control over sexual feelings that stem from hostility or lack of trust. Other situational factors such as the fear of pregnancy, fear of venereal diseases, and a nonprivate environment influence orgasmic responses. None of these factors are mutually exclusive and are extremely difficult to unmask.

According to Shere Hite:

> The right to orgasm has become a political question for women. Although there is nothing wrong with not having orgasms, and nothing wrong with empathizing with and sharing another person's pleasure, there is something wrong when this becomes a pattern where the man is always having an orgasm and the woman isn't. If we make it easy and pleasurable for men to have an orgasm and don't have one ourselves, aren't we just "servicing" men? If we know how to have orgasms, but are unable to make this a part of a sexual relationship with another person, then we are not in control of choosing whether or not we have an orgasm. We are powerless.[35]

Vaginismus

Vaginismus (Fig. 3-18) is due to an involuntary spasm of the muscle surrounding the vagina, specifically of the vaginal levator ani muscles. These spasms usually occur whenever there is an attempt to introduce an object into the vagina. Women suffering from vaginismus can be sexually responsive and experience orgasm through clitoral stimulation or sexual play. Problems tend to multiply with each unsuccessful penile entry. Vaginismus may lead to a phobic avoidance pattern of coitus hysteria or to a secondary impotence in the male partner. In primary vaginismus, the male who is chosen as the sexual partner will often be nonaggressive and appear to be a super considerate gentleman.

Any of the pathological causes of dyspareunia of the pelvic area can also be responsible for a vaginismus conditioned response. The pathology can be surgically removed but the vaginismus response is not automatically relieved. The negative contingency associated with coitus cannot be surgically removed. In secondary vaginismus, the woman was able to have intercourse for a period of time but due to dyspareunia, sexual trauma, sexual aversion, etc., the muscles begin to involuntarily protect the opening of the vagina. Interestingly, in the less severe form of vaginismus, it may be possible to put a finger in the vagina, to insert a tampon, or to use a speculum, and only the penis is prevented from entering the vagina.[36]

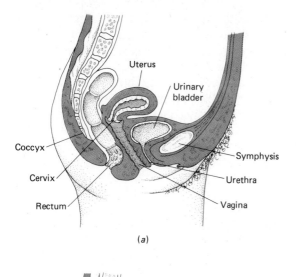

Uterus

Urinary
bladder

Coccyx

Symphysis

Cervix

Urethra

Rectum

Vagina

(a)

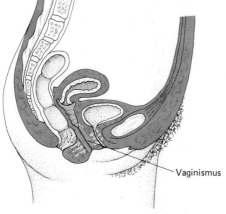

Vaginismus

(b)

Figure 3-18 Vaginismus. (a) Normal vagina and other pelvic organs, side view. (b) Involuntary constriction of the outer third of the vagina. *(From Hyde, op. cit., p. 417.)*

SUMMARY

Much of the material in this chapter is based on the work of Masters and Johnson published in 1966 and 1970. The sexual response cycle is described in four ascending stages. One or more of the seven most common coital positions that are shown (Figs. 3-10 to 3-16) are enjoyed by many couples. Other people experiment to develop variations of these positions that make coitus more enjoyable for them. Many clinicians believe that the overwhelming majority of sexual dysfunctions evolve from psychological or attitudinal determinants. Structural, hormonal, and neurological deficiencies are known to be responsible for a few sexual problems. Etiology of sexual dysfunction may be a combination of physiological and psychological factors, but this relationship is often not understood. There is at this time a lack of controlled research to determine the exact relationship between client variables and specific dysfunctions. In the future, studies of different investigators need to be compared in order to increase our knowledge of the many facets of sexual responses and dysfunctions.

This chapter can serve as either a review of or an introduction to sexual anatomy and physiology, sexual response cycle, techniques of stimulation, coital positions, and sexual dysfunctions. The content of these first three introductory chapters will be expanded and have repetitive application in the remaining sections of this book.

LEARNING ACTIVITIES

1 Define fellatio, foreplay, cunnilingus, and impotence.
2 Compare and contrast the four phases of sexual responses in the male and female.
3 What are the lay terms for coitus, autosexuality, orgasm, libido, anal intercourse, and the most common coital position in this country?
4 Name the homologous structures of the male and female internal and external genitalia.

SUGGESTED READING

Masters, H. William, and Virginia Johnson: *Human Sexual Inadequacy,* Little, Brown, Boston, 1970.
Sadock, Benjamin, Harold Kaplan, and Alfred Freedman: *The Sexual Experience,* Williams & Wilkins, Baltimore, 1976, chap. 3, pp. 79–127.
Kaplan, Helen Singer: *The New Sex Therapy,* Brunner/Mazel, New York, 1974.

REFERENCES

1 Helen Singer Kaplan, *The New Sex Therapy,* Brunner/Mazel, New York, 1974, p. 17.
2 Bernard Goldstein, *Introduction to Human Sexuality,* McGraw-Hill, New York, 1976, pp. 5–31.
3 Virginia Sadock, "Sexual Anatomy and Physiology," in Benjamin Sadock, Harold Kaplan, and Alfred Freedman (eds.), *The Sexual Experience,* Williams & Wilkins, Baltimore, 1976, pp. 79–97.
4 James Leslie McCary, *McCary's Human Sexuality,* 3d ed., Van Nostrand, New York, 1978, pp. 47–62.
5 Goldstein, op. cit., pp. 32–59.
6 McCary, op. cit., pp. 63–73.
7 Sadock, op. cit., pp. 95–103.
8 William Masters and Virginia Johnson, *Human Sexual Response,* Little, Brown, Boston, 1966, p. 4.
9 Ibid., pp. 286–293.
10 Kaplan, op. cit., pp. 7–12.
11 Goldstein, op. cit., pp. 156–160.
12 Ibid., p. 134.

13 Shere Hite, *The Hite Report,* Macmillan, New York, 1976, p. 232.
14 Ibid., p. 289.
15 Goldstein, op. cit., p. 151.
16 Kaplan, op. cit., pp. 80–85.
17 Gordon Jensen, "Adolescent Sexuality," in *The Sexual Experience,* Williams & Wilkins, Baltimore, 1976, pp. 142–155.
18 Kaplan, op. cit., pp. 98–99.
19 Ibid., pp. 80–85.
20 Judd Marmor, "Impotence and Ejaculatory Disturbance," in *The Sexual Experience,* Williams & Wilkins, Baltimore, 1976, pp. 403–406.
21 Alfred Freedman, "Drugs and Sexual Behavior," in *The Sexual Experience,* Williams & Wilkins, Baltimore, 1976, pp. 403–406.
22 Kaplan, op. cit., pp. 98–101.
23 Masters and Johnson, op. cit., p. 92.
24 Marmor, op. cit., pp. 409–410.
25 Kaplan, op. cit., pp. 316–335.
26 J. S. Hyde, *Understanding Human Sexuality,* McGraw-Hill, New York, 1979, p. 175.
27 John Donnelly, "Retrograde Ejaculation," *Med. Aspects Hum. Sexual.* **9**:51–52 (1975).
28 Paul Fink, "Dyspareunia: Current Concepts," *Med. Aspects Hum. Sexual.* **6**:28 (1972).
29 James Semmens and F. N. Semmens, "Dyspareunia," *Med. Aspects Hum. Sexual.* **8**:85–86 (1974).
30 John Wear, "Cause of Dyspareunia in Men," *Med. Aspects Hum. Sexual.* **10**:140–153 (1976).
31 Sumner Marshall, "Painful Urogenital Conditions Which Impede Coitus," *Med. Aspects Hum. Sexual.* **10**:111–112 (1976).
32 Mary Jane Gray, "Clitoral Pain," *Med. Aspects Hum. Sexual.* **10**:105–106 (1976).
33 A. R. Abarbanel, "Diagnosis and Treatment of Coital Discomfort," in Joseph LoPiccolo and Leslie LoPiccolo (eds.), *Handbook of Sex Therapy,* Plenum, New York, 1978, pp. 241–259.
34 Kaplan, op. cit., p. 29.
35 Hite, op. cit., p. 63.
36 Alan Wabrek and Carolyn Wabrek, "Vaginismus," *J. Sex Educ. Ther.* **2**:21–24 (1976).

BIBLIOGRAPHY

Beach, Frank: *Human Sexuality in Four Perspectives,* Johns Hopkins, Baltimore, 1976.
Boston Women's Health Book Collective: *Our Bodies, Ourselves,* Simon and Schuster, New York, 1976.
Browning, Mary, and Edith Lewis (compiled): *Human Sexuality: Nursing Implications,* American Journal of Nursing Co., New York, 1973.
Byrne, Donn, and Lois Byrne (eds.): *Explaining Human Sexuality,* Thomas Y. Crowell, New York, 1977.
Delora, Joann S., and Carol Warren: *Understanding Sexual Interaction,* Houghton Mifflin, Boston, 1977.

Gagnon, John H.: *Human Sexualities,* Scott, Foresman, Glenview, Ill., 1977.

Goldstein, Bernard: *Introduction to Human Sexuality,* McGraw-Hill, New York, 1976.

Green, Richard (ed.): *Human Sexuality: A Health Practitioner's Text,* Williams & Wilkins, Baltimore, 1975.

Hettlinger, Richard: *Human Sexuality: A Psychosocial Perspective,* Wadsworth, Belmont, Calif., 1975.

Hite, Shere: *The Hite Report,* Macmillan, New York, 1976.

Hyde, Janet S.: *Understanding Human Sexuality,* McGraw-Hill, New York, 1979.

Kaplan, Helen S.: *The New Sex Therapy,* Brunner/Mazel, New York, 1974.

Katchadourian, Herant, and Donald Lunde: *Fundamentals of Human Sexuality,* 2d ed., Holt, New York, 1975.

LoPiccolo, Joseph, and Leslie LoPiccolo: *Handbook of Sex Therapy,* Plenum, New York, 1978.

Masters, William, and Virginia Johnson: *Human Sexual Response,* Little, Brown, Boston, 1966.

Masters, William, and Virginia Johnson: *Human Sexual Inadequacy,* Little, Brown, Boston, 1970.

McCary, James Leslie: *Human Sexuality,* 3d ed., Van Nostrand, New York, 1978.

McCary, James L., and Donna Copeland (eds.): *Modern Views of Human Sexual Behavior,* Science Research, Chicago, 1976.

Mims, Fern H. (ed.): "Symposium on Human Sexuality," *Nurs. Clin. North Am.* **10**:517–607 (1975).

Sadock, Benjamin, Harold Kaplan, and Alfred Freedman: *The Sexual Experience,* Williams & Wilkins, Baltimore, 1976.

Taylor, Donald (ed.): *Human Sexual Development,* Davis, Philadelphia, 1970.

Wiseman, Jacqueline P. (ed.): *The Social Psychology of Sex,* Harper & Row, New York, 1976.

Woods, Nancy F.: *Human Sexuality in Health and Illness,* Mosby, St. Louis, 1979.

Part Two

Typical and Atypical Psychosexual Development

Chapter 4

Psychosexual Development

The purpose of this chapter is to present, in tabular form, a summary of sexual growth and development. The table includes expectations of normal psychosexual and physical-sexual development and possible disturbances or disruptions of normal. Following Table 4-1, the various sections discuss in greater detail the period of development with emphasis on the nursing interventions required. The reader is cautioned to avoid arbitrary assignment of a label based on age in years alone. Each client must be assessed in terms of psychological and emotional development as well as chronological age.

EMBRYONIC PERIOD (GENETIC SEX AT CHROMOSOMAL LEVEL)

At conception, a zygote must have at least one X chromosome to survive. Errors at conception may be caused by factors such as exposure to radiation, medication, or environmental pollutants. Due to spontaneous abortion, the number of defective fetuses conceived is greater than the number of defective babies born.[1] Frequently there is no apparent explanation for unusual chromosomal configurations. These errors may be evident by amniocentesis or at birth, but they may also go unnoticed until the child is at the age of puberty or beyond. For example,

Table 4-1   Summary of Stages of Sexual Development

Sexual growth expectations	Sexual growth disturbances
Embryonic period	

Fertilization determines chromosomal sex
  Female   XX
  Male   XY
	Chromosomal error causing Turner's syndrome (XO), Klinefelter's syndrome (XXY), and other anomalies

Fetal hormonal period	
In XY, testes form at 6–7 weeks of gestation and produce androgen In XX, ovaries form at 12 weeks of gestation and produce no androgen	Androgen insensitivity syndrome (testicular feminizing syndrome) causes XY genotype to develop female external genitalia Adrenogenital syndrome causes XX genotype to develop male external genitalia Ambiguous genitalia caused by hormone excesses or enzyme deficiencies
Birth	
Gender assignment	Error in assignment due to ambiguous genitalia
Infancy (birth to 18 months)	
Oral sensitivity Need for tactile stimulation Stimulation of external genitalia by self or others; pleasure from touching	Oral deprivation caused by weaning too early Touch deprivation causes miasma, possible mental retardation, and possible death
Orgasmic potential in females Erectile potential in males Reinforcement of gender identity	Blurred identity causes later core identity confusion
Sense of "goodness" or "badness" of body Gradual capacity to distinguish "self" from "other"	Disturbance of basic trust-mistrust
Toddler period (age 1–3)	
Gender identification leads to development of core gender identity Anal phase—learns control of bowel and bladder	Anxiety about acceptable behaviors for boys and girls Strict toilet training leads to shame and doubt or compulsive behavior or castration anxiety
Genital fondling and masturbation to produce pleasure; exploration of body parts Learns sex role differences and identifies differences between male and female role models	Restriction of genital play leads to poor self-image
Develops vocabulary relating to genital anatomy, elimination, reproduction Sensual-erotic activities such as rocking, swinging, hugging people and toys	Lack of proper vocabulary may cause communication problems in later years Difficulty in expressing affection

Table 4-1 Summary of Stages of Sexual Development (continued)

Sexual growth expectations	Sexual growth disturbances
Preschool (age 4–6)	
Oedipal attachments to opposite-sex parent	Excessive attachment; seductive behavior of parent toward child
Identification with same-sex parent	Lack of identification leads to later gender identity confusion
Learns about sex roles	Anxiety caused if parents are intolerant of behavior which does not conform to common stereotypes of sex role behavior
Sex play. Exploration of own body and genitals and those of playmates	Overreaction of parents leads to guilt, feeling that sex is evil
Masturbation	Failure to explain cultural expectations leads to inappropriate behavior in public
School age (6–10)	
Same-sex friends	
Curiosity about sex (no "latent period")	Lack of information reinforces fears and may lead to development of negative, rigid views about sexuality
Sharing of sexual fears and fantasies	Misinformation gained from peers may be confusing or frightening
Interest in physical and emotional aspects of sexual development: menstruation, nocturnal emissions, secondary sex characteristics, pregnancy, abortion	
Increasing self-consciousness and self-awareness	
Use of "dirty words" for shock value	Overreaction of parents may cause increased usage
Preadolescence and puberty (10–13)	
Concerns about body image (acne, genital size, sexual development)	Lack of positive experiences leads to poor self-image
Menarche	Fears relating to onset of puberty before receiving any information or from receiving no information
Seminal emissions	
Learning self-control	Limits too rigid or overprotective parents may prevent the development of self-confidence. No limits may delay the development of an internal sexual value system
Testing behavior limits	
Homosexual experiences as part of same-sex friendships	Overreaction of parents may lead to fear, guilt
Early adolescence (age 13–15)	
Testing of self as primary source of behavior control	Conflicts with parents and society over testing of limits and controls
Beginning opposite-sex friendships	Failure of parents to take feelings seriously leads to lack of trust and loss of communication
Learning heterosexuality	
Dating, "puppy love," and crushes	

Table 4-1   Summary of Stages of Sexual Development (continued)

Sexual growth expectations	Sexual growth disturbances
Early adolescence (age 13–15) (continued)	
Awkwardness in first sexual encounters	Anxiety over inadequacy or lack of partner or lack of orgasm
Half of teenage population will not have intercourse	Anxiety over whether virginity is "normal"
Masturbation and mutual masturbation (petting)	Compulsive, mechanical masturbation which is used as an escape from everyday problems
Sexual thoughts and fantasies	
Late adolescence (age 16–19)	
Learning intimacy in a heterosexual relationship	Inability to trust another or to successfully participate in close relationships
Takes responsibility for sexual activity	Unplanned pregnancy and precipitous marriage
	Sexually transmitted diseases
Exploration of sex role behaviors and sexual life-styles	Transsexualism: error or confusion in core gender identity. May begin in childhood. Transvestism: cross-dressing for sexual gratification. Fetishism: compulsive sexual attraction for an object as a substitute for a person
Half of teens will not have sexual intercourse until in their 20s	
Young adult (20–35)	
Learning to give and receive pleasure	Inability to communicate with partner about sexual needs
Knowledge of sexual response cycle enhances sexual relationship	Sexual dysfunction: premature ejaculation, inorgasmic, dyspareunia
Long-term commitment to sexual relationship (heterosexual or homosexual; possible bisexual)	Promiscuity or irresponsible behavior which involves coercion or nonconsent
	Homosexual panic caused by feeling "trapped" into this sexual preference
Experimentation and curiosity about sexual positions and variety of sexual expressions	Stereotypic sexual behavior
	Fear of experimentation
	Boredom
Elaboration of sexual techniques	
Responsible reproductive health	Spread of sexually transmitted diseases
	Failure to have yearly Pap smear
Decisions about childbearing	Unwanted pregnancy. Multiple abortions
	Child abuse/neglect
Development of sexual value system while learning tolerance for values of others	Sexual amorality. Rigid, inflexible beliefs about sex
Middle adult (30–55)	
Understand and accept body image changes relating to menopause and male climacteric	Anxiety, relationship problems caused by changes in sexual performance or sexual interest
Mastery of consequences of lower hormone production (vaginal atrophy,	Panic about losing sexual prowess
	Depression/denial

Table 4-1   Summary of Stages of Sexual Development (continued)

Sexual growth expectations	Sexual growth disturbances
Middle adult (30–55) (continued)	
slower erections) which may affect sexual intercourse	
Focus on quality rather than quantity of sexual encounters	Sexual dysfunction: secondary impotence, secondary inorgasmia
Relinquish control of children's sexual behaviors and sexual preferences	Attempts to control sexual behaviors of adult offspring
Menopause	Crisis of dealing with loss of reproductive ability
Late adulthood (over age 55)	
Development of new ways to achieve sexual satisfaction or sexual intimacy after loss or illness of partner	Withdrawal, bitterness, guilt, or sexual dysfunction
Understanding and accepting own sexual needs and needs of others	Coercion or lack of self-control leading to voyeurism, exhibitionism, molesting
Accepts slowed sexual response cycle without necessarily stopping sexual relationship	Conformity to cultural stereotypes regarding sexuality and aging

a child with Turner's syndrome appears to be a normal female with female external genitalia. Not until mental retardation (a frequent consequence of Turner's syndrome) or primary amenorrhea is investigated is it discovered that the child has no ovaries. The child and her parents (and the child is usually a girl, and has been raised as a female) will need compassionate and sensitive care from the whole genetics team usually involved in such cases. The nurse is especially well prepared to provide this care at the basic level of nursing intervention. The parents will need help with grieving and perhaps with anger. They will need a sympathetic listener who also can remind them that their daughter is still a healthy girl despite her inability to bear children. Intermediate-level intervention for the child and the parents will include explanation of the fact that she will not menstruate like her friends or be able to become pregnant. They can be assured that estrogen therapy will help her to develop secondary sex characteristics such as pubic and axillary hair and larger breasts. Discussions of marriage and adoption may be postponed until the child is older: as a young adolescent her greatest worries probably center around her appearance and her need not to seem different from her friends.

FETAL PERIOD AND BIRTH

During the first 8 to 12 weeks of gestation, sexual differentiation of the external genitalia occurs. Gonadal sex is determined by hormonal influences on the basic chromosomal sex. If androgens are present, an XY zygote will develop male genitalia if the cells are sensitive to androgen. If androgen insensitivity exists, the

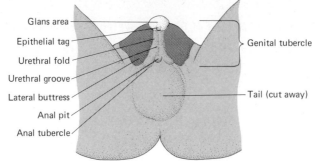

UNDIFFERENTIATED

Glans area
Epithelial tag
Urethral fold
Urethral groove
Lateral buttress
Anal pit
Anal tubercle

Genital tubercle

Tail (cut away)

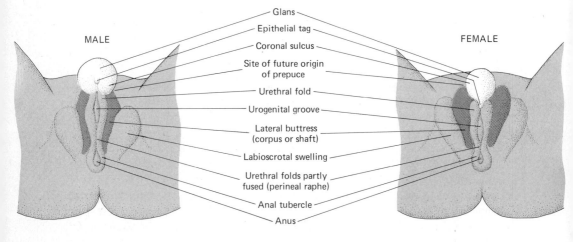

MALE

FEMALE

Glans
Epithelial tag
Coronal sulcus
Site of future origin
of prepuce
Urethral fold
Urogenital groove
Lateral buttress
(corpus or shaft)
Labioscrotal swelling
Urethral folds partly
fused (perineal raphe)
Anal tubercle
Anus

FULLY DEVELOPED

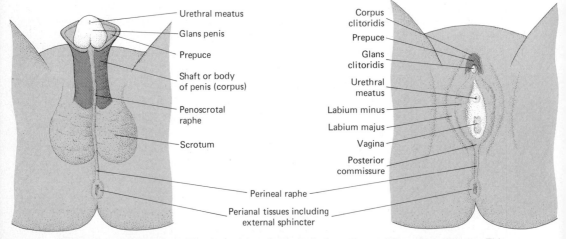

Urethral meatus
Glans penis
Prepuce
Shaft or body
of penis (corpus)
Penoscrotal
raphe
Scrotum

Corpus
clitoridis
Prepuce
Glans
clitoridis
Urethral
meatus
Labium minus
Labium majus
Vagina
Posterior
commissure

Perineal raphe
Perianal tissues including
external sphincter

Figure 4-1 Development of male and female genitalia from the undifferentiated stages. This occurs during prenatal development. Note homologous organs in the female and the male. *(From J. Hyde, Understanding Human Sexuality, McGraw-Hill, New York, 1979, p. 54.)*

XY genotype will develop female genitalia. (The development of the male and female genitals from the undifferentiated stages is shown in Fig. 4-1.) Another hormonal error, adrenogenital syndrome, causes the XX genotype to develop male external genitalia.

Although such abnormalities are relatively rare, nurses in hospital nurseries, public health nurses, and nurses in other settings may find themselves in a counseling situation with the parents of such a child.

When any baby is born, parents usually ask two things (not necessarily in this order): "Is it healthy and intact?" and "Is it a boy or a girl?" In the case of ambiguous external genitalia, neither question can be satisfactorily answered. The baby has been born "sexually unfinished."[2] The new parents can be devastated by seemingly minor details: what to name the child, what to put on the birth certificate and birth announcements, what color clothes to put on the baby. Of course, these problems are of major importance and should be approached with seriousness and pragmatism. A nurse could help parents find a "unisex" name appropriate for either a boy or girl (Kim, Tracy, Kerry, Chris). Announcements can be postponed until a gender assignment has been made. The term "sexually unfinished" may be one way parents can explain the problem to anxious friends and relatives.

Early and accurate gender assignment is crucial. From the first few moments after birth parents, knowingly or unconsciously, relate differently to male and female babies. Males are handled more roughly and are referred to as "tougher" or "stronger." Baby girls are handled more gently, are held more, and are referred to as "delicate," "pretty," or "sensitive." However, an error in gender assignment probably can be safely corrected up until the age of 18 to 24 months.

INFANCY

Infants need to be touched. Studies done after World War II proved that lack of stimulation caused infants to be retarded in growth and development and could even cause death. The baby's mouth is particularly sensitive and the sucking needs partly reflect satiation of hunger and partly simply the need for oral gratification. Babies' senses take in what feels good.[3] Weaning a child too quickly from breast or bottle may be related to emotional problems ranging from prolonged thumb sucking to more severe behavioral problems.

Close contact (holding, cuddling, playing) by a consistent mother or mother substitute is essential to normal psychosexual development. The baby must have an identity and a "personhood" in order to develop gender identity, sex role identity, and sexual relationships.

In all the growth phases, the nurse at the basic level must be genuinely interested, able to be trusted, and must provide accurate and nonjudgmental information. Availability and concern do not just "happen"—nurses must be sure to make themselves available in an unhurried, quiet environment so that questions and concerns can be discussed freely.

The public health nurse, pediatric nurse, postpartum nurse, and nurses in other settings can effectively help parents to understand and to encourage the psychosexual development of their young children. This development in infancy is the basis for future sexuality. Parents need to hear from a knowledgeable and trustworthy person that it is healthy for a baby to use its mouth to explore its environment or that the baby will not be harmed if they allow genital self-pleasuring. Young infants are sensitive to touch and tone of voice, and parents can be reminded of this phenomenon so that they avoid making even playful disparaging remarks such as these: "Look at Jimmy's poor, nasty little penis." "Susie is a messy little stinker." Children learn through verbal and nonverbal messages how the parents view their bodies, and soon adopt the same attitudes.

Although gender identity reinforcement is necessary, parents sometimes are confused about how to accomplish this goal without teaching sex role stereotypes. Nurses should model behavior for parents by relating directly to the baby. Praise the baby's health, draw attention to the child's developmental task accomplishments, and show pleasure in the child's pleasure in himself or herself.

TODDLER

As the child learns to walk and to talk, independence from parents is greatly increased. The child learns from peers, relatives, siblings, television, and other sources in addition to the parents. Sex role behavior, sex role differences, and sex role expectations become clearer to the child. Not only does the child see behaviors and body parts, but also begins to talk about these. "The child's concept of body image and awareness of sex identity are essential precursors and components of his or her adult sexuality."[4] Parents, assisted by health care professionals, can provide a vocabulary for their children that emphasizes matter-of-fact attitudes, acceptance of sex differences, and a positive feeling about genitals, reproduction, and elimination. Since toilet training occurs during this period, and since Freud and others have called it the anal phase, parents need to be prepared with the proper vocabulary before the child is old enough to talk. Anticipatory guidance provided by the nurse can make this time more comfortable for both parents and children. Robmault[5] cites the major tasks of this period to be "joyful interaction with people" and "body control."

Nurses also can emphasize the normalness and healthiness of masturbation in the young child. For many parents, this concept is difficult. They may agree, intellectually, that masturbation is not harmful, but their "gut reaction" still is to say "no-no" when Johnny fondles his penis.

Exploration of attitudes and feelings also entails giving information and suggestions about ways of coping. Acknowledgment of conflicting feelings is a way of giving permission to parents to ventilate their confusion.

PRESCHOOL

Most young children play "doctor" or some other game that involves exploration of body parts. This kind of activity reflects healthy curiosity and interest.

Parents sometimes find, however, that even though they understand that this behavior is normal, they still react with shock or anger. Guilt feelings, perhaps left over from their own childhood experiences, affect the way parents deal with "doctor games." Nurses can aid parents by assisting them to anticipate sexual curiosity in their children. Cognitive rehearsal is a useful strategy in providing anticipatory guidance. The nurse and parent can role-play possible responses in an attempt to find one that the parent feels is comfortable and is not destructive or guilt-producing. Parents should be encouraged to seek out opportunities for their young children to see and to discuss the body parts of both girls and boys. Feelings about being a boy or being a girl, attitudes toward family members, and the ability to love and to trust are developed during these early years.

Parents also must be ready with answers to questions about where babies come from, breast feeding, and the differences between the bodies of grown men and women and young boys and girls. Identification with same-sex parent also leads to comparisons in penis size, breast size, and body hair distribution. Parents need not wait until asked (some children never ask) but should offer information frequently to the child. Volunteering information establishes the parent as "askable." Of course, the level of understanding of the individual child must always be considered. Regardless of age, the child can learn to use accurate, acceptable terms; parents may need encouragement to use "penis," "vagina," "urine," and similar words because many adults are not comfortable with this vocabulary themselves. Insistence on baby-talk references to body parts and functions may hinder the child's communication later. Nurses help parents to help their children.

Despite incest taboos which exist in most cultures, some parents behave in seductive, sexually inviting ways with their children. Children find seductive behavior confusing, and later life-style confusion or sexual variants sometimes are seen as related to a seductive parent. Sleeping in the same bed, genital fondling, or coercion to participate in overt sexual activity all are forms of seductive behavior. Some parents are unaware that they are seductive, and respond to nonthreatening discussion by changing their ways of relating to the child. Other parents need more extensive counseling in order to deal with their needs and feelings.

SCHOOL AGE

Freud's idea of the latency period was never a claim that sexuality in the school-age child was nonexistent. Rather, sexuality at this age is more relaxed or subdued, at least in Western culture. Perhaps the child simply learns that in "polite, adult company" sexuality is not an acceptable topic for conversation. However, during these years most children discover and explore a great number of genital activities alone, with same-sex peers, and with opposite-sex peers. Sex does not disappear, but the changes are smoother and more tranquil.

Sexual roles are practiced and skills for carrying out sex roles are learned. Same-sex friendships predominate. Impulse control and appropriate public behavior are developed. The child acquires knowledge of genital anatomy, sometimes by comparison with the bodies of friends. Masturbation, usually alone, is not only normal, but is healthy.

Children of this age who do not learn which sexual behaviors are socially acceptable probably need help in therapy or counseling situations. Obsessive behavior, defiance, or total sexual repression is indicative of problems. Although all children experiment with both heterosexual and homosexual roles, exclusive interest in the sex roles of the opposite sex may indicate future homosexual preferences.

Nurses assist parents to understand the sexual curiosity and sexual activity of school-age children by providing accurate information before and during this developmental phase. The child also requires help from the school nurse, public health nurse, pediatric nurse, and family nurse in the form of sympathetic listening, access to books and other resources, and answers to specific questions. The sexual history can be used as a way to let the child know that sex can be discussed with the nurse in a comfortable, confidential atmosphere.

ADOLESCENCE

The onslaught of hormones during this period causes the previously tranquil child to become irritable, unpredictable, and difficult to live with. Children as well as parents need help to cope with seemingly altered personality characteristics. Patterns of behavior change quickly and radically, leaving child and parents bewildered and often angry.

Parents need help in understanding the utter seriousness of their children's concerns about appearance, relationships, and sexual development. The inequity in growth between girls and boys adds to the confusion. In addition, parents and children must begin to "let go" of each other as independence increases. Nurses must encourage communication between parents and children, even if the child seems to relate more easily to the nurse than to the parent. The preadolescent might not even talk at all, but attempts to communicate on the part of the parent will not go unappreciated.

Ideally, the nurse has had time over the years to develop a trust relationship with children and their parents, so that by the time of adolescence, the nurse is a valuable friend and counselor. Due to the mobility of our culture and to our frequently episodic approach to health care, the nurse, the adolescent, and the parent may meet for only a brief encounter. Nevertheless, these situations can be critically important to the development of the adolescent and to the peace of mind of the parents.

At the basic level, the nurse must prove to be a trustworthy resource. Confidentiality and honesty are important to teenagers and should be carefully assured. The nurse, in order to be "askable" must be available, must have made time to sit down and talk, and must give complete and serious attention to the adolescent's concerns. A sense of humor is a helpful attribute when working with teens, although it must not be contrived or forced. Whether in a primary or secondary setting, nurses can let adolescents know that questions about sexuality are appropriate and welcome. The sexual history is one way to indicate willingness to discuss sexuality. Strict confidentiality is an absolute prerequisite to the sexual history of an adolescent. The history is a private part of the medical record and should not be available to parents.

In addition, nurses are a resource to parents, either alone or in discussions with their teenaged children. Parents can be encouraged to ask questions privately or in joint conferences.

Sex education in school and at home must include basic biological facts which explain hormonally induced body changes (menstruation, nocturnal seminal emissions, secondary sex characteristics), facts relating to reproductive potential (intercourse, contraception), and attitudes toward sexuality (value systems, marriage, sexual variation).

The best source for this information is from the parents themselves. Nurses assist by giving books, pictures, and other materials to parents, who, in turn, educate their children. However, since many parents are reluctant to be the teachers of their children (because they are embarrassed, or lack communicative skills, or feel such information is harmful), public schools and churches frequently provide sex education programs. The nurse consultant is a valuable resource for these programs, both in their development and in their presentation. The nurse's openness and trustworthiness will make him or her an important contributor to parents and to children. Since a child's developing sexuality is associated with increasing independence from the family, it may be difficult for parents to reconcile themselves to providing sex education.

Information and permission can be given in response to requests or can be provided in anticipation of concerns. Particularly important is preparation for puberty. Preadolescents who are prepared for the onset of menstruation or nocturnal emissions are not frightened by these important body changes. The universality statement provides a good way to begin giving information. Since adolescents are particularly likely to receive misinformation from peers, the nurse must not only provide accurate facts but also help to dispel myths and fallacies. Sexuality, especially as it relates to contraception, venereal disease, and abortion, is vitally important for the adolescent.

The teenager needs information about expectations of normal growth and development and about the "normalness" of masturbation, fantasy, and sex role confusion.

Information for adolescents and parents is available in many excellent books and films. For some people, reading or watching a film may be a less-threatening way to learn. Presentations in youth groups, parent organizations, churches, and schools provide a basic information source and can establish the nurse as a reliable and approachable resource for teens and parents as well. Information must always be accurate and absolutely nonjudgmental. The nurse must carefully examine his or her own values and biases, and attempt to keep moralistic messages out of the presentation. Adolescents can be encouraged, of course, to examine and possibly revise or reaffirm their values and moral beliefs in regards to sexuality. The important thing is that adolescents learn to respect the value systems of others while simultaneously adhering to their own—a difficult and complex task for anyone.

Specific suggestions are based on the particular questions which arise as the adolescent develops and grows. Early questions relating to menstruation, size of body parts, nocturnal emissions, and boy-girl relationships can be the springboard for suggestions. The range can be from simple (how to use a tampon) to complicated (how to tell my mother I'm pregnant). Later questions which need suggestions in response might be how to have sex without getting a disease or how to feel better after breaking up with a girlfriend.

There is a certain "normal craziness" in adolescents. Very few are seriously disturbed or require intensive therapy. However, suicide remains a high cause of death in this age group and the "communication gap" still divides families at times when they most need each other's support. Therefore, the nurse must be alert to the manifestations of important problems: anorexia nervosa, compulsive behavior, using sex in a violent way, unintended pregnancy, and core gender identity confusion. Referral for therapy is necessary if the nurse is not specifically trained to provide such intensive counseling. Whenever possible, parents and teenagers should participate together in therapy sessions, so that they can learn how to help and support each other.

ADULTHOOD

The passage from adolescence to adulthood is subtle and inconsistent. The changes are not measurable nor are they necessarily related to age.

The body changes which beset the adolescent are more or less complete. The adult is expected to be responsible for his or her own body and own health. Knowledge of body functions and basic health and safety is important simply for the sake of survival.

However, knowledge of basic human sexuality and genital health is neither easily obtained nor easily taught. Adults are expected to be the primary sex educators of their children even though the adults have themselves received very little correct sex information. Educators and others have said that sex education in the schools must begin "early." A good adjunct to sex education for children is sex education for their parents and for other adults.

Simply knowing the physiological sexual response cycle can make the experience of arousal and intercourse more satisfying for a couple. If they understand the need to give and receive pleasure, they strengthen the human relationship as well. Many sexual dysfunctions such as uncomplicated premature ejaculation, dyspareunia, and female orgasmic disturbances are resolved by acknowledgment of the problem, permission and information, and simple suggestions.

Since many adults were raised in a society where discussions of sexual topics were allowed only in locker rooms or doctor's offices, permission even to talk about sex is a major change for these men and women. Many are surprised by the open attitudes of an aware and knowledgeable nurse. Few are shocked; most are grateful for a tolerant and understanding person with whom to discuss their concerns.

Despite the media barrage of sexually explicit material, and the increasing incidence of sexual activity in the teenage years, many people reach adulthood sadly misinformed about human sexuality. James McCary lists some common sexual myths and fallacies:[6]

1 Simultaneous orgasms are more satisfactory than those experienced separately and are, moreover, necessary for sexual compatibility in marriage.

2 It is dangerous to have sexual intercourse during menstruation.

3 Athletic performance is diminished by sexual intercourse the night before.

4 Diminishing function of the sex glands signals the end of the sex life of both men and women.

5 A large penis is important to a woman's sexual gratification, and the man with a large penis is more sexually potent than the man with a small penis.

6 Sexual intercourse should be avoided during pregnancy.

7 The older man has no advantages over a younger one insofar as sexual activity is concerned.

8 Blacks have a greater sex drive than whites; the penis of a black male is larger than that of the white male.

9 Alcohol is a sexual stimulant.

10 Menopause or hysterectomy terminates a woman's sex life.

11 People are either totally homosexual or totally heterosexual.

12 Masturbation is known to cause idiocy, acne, and a constellation of other physical and psychological problems.

13 Vaginal-penile intercourse is the only normal method of sex relations.

14 Women who have strong sex drives, come to easy climax, and are capable of multiple orgasms are nymphomaniacs.

15 If one partner desires sex more often than the other, nothing can be done to make the couple sexually more compatible.

16 Pornography stimulates people to commit criminal sex acts.

17 The average physician is well trained and emotionally equipped to deal with his patients' sexual problems.

The young adult needs permission and information to be able to make decisions based on fact without undue influence from repressive or destructive attitudes. The myths cited above give an idea of the scope of knowledge a nurse needs to help adult clients who have concerns about sexuality. Several other chapters in this book give detailed suggestions for nursing intervention. The nurse should not expect to know everything, however, and must be willing and able to refer the client to resources which provide the answers needed. Adults who appear to have disturbances in the healthy development of sexuality might require referral to sex or marriage counselors, sex therapists, mental health clinics, physicians, social service agencies, or to other nurses with special training in a particular area.

Intervention is destructive when nurses display judgmental attitudes or present misinformation or pretend to be qualified sex counselors without adequate preparation. The nurse who has examined carefully his or her own values, beliefs, and attitudes should be able to recognize when destructive interactions occur. Nurses who are aware of sexual health needs can help each other by mutual evaluation of their interaction with patients. Nurses may imagine that they hide their true feelings but find that patients detect the hostility and conflict they attempt to conceal. A safer, more constructive approach is to confront one's "gut feelings," talk openly about these feelings, and then endeavor to alter attitudes when they interfere with good nursing care. If the nurse is unable to reconcile conflicts between "gut feelings" and "intellectual feelings," then permission is given to avoid situations which produce these conflicts. For example, if a nurse is aware that he or she has negative feelings about homosexuals, then a nurse who is comfortable with homosexuals should take over care of the homosexual patient if possible.

Pairing, mating, and building a family are tasks of the young adult based on the ability to engage in intimate relationships and the need for affection and affiliation. Commitments may vary in length, but usually sexual adjustment and fulfillment are enhanced by a close, loving relationship with another person. Relationships may be of various types. Parenthetical phrases refer to the classification of homosexuals by Bell and Weinberg.[12]

Monogamous ("close-coupled"). The couple limits the relationship to each other, either by choice or by convention. Sexual exclusivity and permanence are implied.

"Open marriage" ("open-coupled"). The couple agrees that each may seek other relationships, but the primary commitment is to each other.

Divorced or widowed. Many people who have been married previously wish to continue the sexual and emotional closeness found in a marriage. The circumstances of separation differ for these two groups and the subtle pressures brought to bear by friends and relatives also differ.

Never married ("functionals"). Society is becoming more tolerant of the single adult. Self-sufficiency and independence are seen as strengths. The stigma against single parents also has decreased, making it easier for people to have or adopt children without also being married.

Celibates ("asexuals"). A few people choose a life without sexual relationships. Various religions, institutionalization, or a fear of involvement with others can create a temporary or permanent celibacy. Self-pleasuring and fantasy are not eliminated, necessarily, and so the term *asexual* is not very precise.

The middle years are largely ignored as a period meriting study. Children are grown and responsibility for their behavior can be given up (somewhat reluctantly for some parents). Freedom to pursue life goals and to spend more time with significant others is sometimes welcomed and occasionally feared. The so-called empty nest syndrome which was thought to be the plight of the middle-aged housewife now is disappearing as the feminist movement helps women define themselves in other than reproductive terms.

CLIMACTERIC

The transition between middle age and old age takes approximately 15 to 20 years and is called the climacteric. Both men and women experience changes during this period, although only women experience menopause.

The cessation of ovarian function and subsequent reduction in estrogen production causes the menopause. Both physiological and pyschological changes are associated with menopause. The changes occur gradually. Menstrual cycles become irregular and finally cease. However, postmenopausal women continue to show effects of estrogen stimulation for as long as 25 years past menopause.[7] Women must be educated to know that they do not become totally estrogen-deficient. Science and "common knowledge" differ enormously about menopause.

A negative role change is often associated with menopause. Perhaps a woman's social worth and feminine values have been defined in terms of her reproductive capacities. After the childbearing years, she was assumed to decline in physical attractiveness, sexual desirability, and value to society. Menopause is feared because it is tangible, inescapable evidence of growing old. The "symptoms" of menopause were thought to be the result of an interaction between physical reactions and emotional responses. Menopausal symptoms apparently have an important social component:[8] if women did not expect to experience menopausal discomfort perhaps the "discomfort" would not occur.

Although a change in attitudes and expectations may have an effect on the experience of menopausal symptoms, two problems persist in American women which are unique to menopause: vasomotor symptoms such as "hot flashes" and thinning of vaginal walls. These are the only symptoms which can be relieved by estrogen replacement therapy. Contrary to popular belief, decreased estrogen does not cause the emotional changes (insomnia, anxiety, depression) which may occur at menopause. However, these problems may be exaggerated at this time for women who have had a high incidence of such symptoms during other stressful periods in their lives. According to Barber and Graber, menopausal women can be "a caricature of their younger selves at their worst."[9] Estrogen replacement will not prevent osteoporosis or increase libido. Estrogen replacement has been implicated in endometrial cancer and breast cancer.[10,11] Women must be completely informed of the risks of estrogen replacement therapy, as well as the benefits. Probably estrogen replacement therapy is helpful and not dangerous to about 10 percent of menopausal women.

Nurses can help women understand the physiological and psychological effects of menopause. Information and permission giving are vital and women may need help in interpreting feelings and experiences. Coping skills can be mobilized to assist the menopausal woman in adjusting and perhaps in seeking new and fulfilling roles. In the words of Prock:

> What needs to be pointed out to women at every stage of life is that expending and extending yourself is very exciting. You may use a known skill and attempt to stretch

it or you may develop a new skill. That is, you can utilize yourself more fully. There will be moments in any normal life where this extending and expending yourself may be the only or the biggest pleasure you have, both during a crisis and in normal times. Being in a position where your definition of self and the meaning of life and your own self-esteem all depend on other people places you in a very vulnerable position. The long haul for a woman requires maintaining a life which has *multiple anchors*. While we should all be vulnerable to the extent that we depend on others (and being loved is a great thing), we should not let our whole life depend on the love of any single person or any small group.

If she develops multiple anchors early enough, then, hopefully, a woman will not be quite as completely turned around when she is confronted with the loss of one or more of such anchors of intimate audiences.[13]

Men experience subtle changes relating to aging, but these are not the result of a decrease in testosterone production or other physiological causes. Therefore, the term "male menopause" is meaningless. Emotional and attitudinal changes do occur, however, relating to energy levels, career success, and family stress. Sexual responsiveness may decrease as a result, and this change may lead to depression, behavioral changes, and marital problems.

Although sexual processes slow down with aging (see Table 4-2), they do not stop. The maintenance of sexual response seems to be related to the regularity of sexual experience and hence the statement, "If you don't use it, you'll lose it."

Sexual fulfillment throughout adulthood and into old age is not only possi-

Table 4-2   Effects of Aging on Sexual Response Cycle (Masters and Johnson[14])

Female	Male
Excitement phase	
Lubrication is slower Lubrication amount is decreased Clitoris may be smaller	Erection is slower. Erectile firmness is decreased Increased need for direct genital stimulation
Plateau phase	
Less increase in size of vaginal canal Reduced uterine elevation	Decrease in Cowper's gland secretion Ability to maintain erection before ejaculation is increased Decreased testicular elevation
Orgasmic phase	
Shortened orgasmic phase Possible painful spasm of uterus at orgasm due to decreased estrogen	Decreased need to ejaculate Decreased ejaculatory inevitability Decreased force and volume of ejaculate
Resolution phase	
Rapid deengorgement	Rapid deengorgement Longer refractory period

ble, but likely. The feeling that older people are not interested in sex (except if they are abnormal—the "dirty old man" syndrome) is largely caused by our inability to imagine our parents or our grandparents as sexually active people. The greatest danger of such attitudes is that they tend to comprise a "self-fulfilling prophecy": if people believe that sexual interest ceases with advancing age, they will find that it does cease. Or, if sexual interest persists, people may believe themselves to be abnormal, sinful, or psychologically sick.

For some older adults, sexuality means actual sexual intercourse. For others, sexual satisfaction is achieved through physical closeness with a loved one: caressing, kissing, and holding meet needs for affection and intimacy.

Nurses and other health professionals find numerous opportunities to assist older adults with problems relating to sexuality. Many situations arise in hospitals and nursing homes which require an understanding and accepting attitude from the nurse. Especially in institutions, the privacy of individuals becomes the responsibility of nurses. The following vignette illustrates the need for nurses to be aware of the sexual needs of the older adult.

Vignette

Problem List

1 Arthritis in a 65-year-old man
2 Total hip replacement
3 Sexuality

Subjective Data

"I'm feeling so much better since my surgery. My lady friend has been coming to see me and I'd like to be more intimate with her while I'm here—sort of to try out my hip. But my roommate is so stuffy. I'm sure he'd be offended if we started fooling around on my side of the curtain."

Objective Data

Hip replacement successful. Weight bearing without difficulty. No objections from physician to sexual activity.

Assessment

Normal sexual interest. Concern about roommate probably correct. Staff will be concerned about "hanky-panky" but staff meeting may help.

Plan

1 Assure patient of the normalness of his feelings.
2 Tell patient to arrange visits with his girlfriend when the roommate is out of the room (at physical therapy, with visitors, etc.) and to use a "Do not disturb" sign.
3 Arrange a staff conference about the sexual needs of the patient.
4 Consider moving the patient to a private room.

Specifically, nurses can do the following things to help older adults with sexual problems of aging:

1 Provide a quiet, unhurried atmosphere for listening to and discussing problems.

2 Ask about sexual concerns or sex-related problems. Use a universality statement such as, "Older women sometimes worry about problems with sexual intercourse or sexual relations. Do you have similar concerns?"

3 Provide information to adults in anticipation of aging, that is, provide information before it is needed to assure realistic expectations and a positive approach to the aging problems.

4 In health care facilities, ensure privacy for all patients. "Do not disturb" signs can be used and respected if door locks are considered unsafe.

5 Help educate other nurses and physicians to understand the sexual interests and needs of older adults. Provide material to read, and be a model for open, tolerant, and accepting attitudes toward older adults.

6 Encourage the elderly to express feelings to each other and to health care providers. Feelings are to be respected.

LEARNING ACTIVITIES

1 Interview one of your parents or grandparents about their views on the changes caused by aging.

2 Discuss "Parents are the primary sex educators of their own children." Do you agree or disagree? Why?

3 What effects might media have on one's sex role? Consider television, advertising, literature, popular songs, movies, or children's books.

4 Compile a bibliography of sex education materials for parents of young children or for parents of adolescents.

5 What are "rites of passage?" What are some rites of passage in American culture?

REFERENCES

1 H. Zellweger, *Chromosomal Aberrations,* American Association for Cerebral Palsy, New Orleans Annual Meeting, 1971, p. 96.

2 J. Money and A. A. Ehrhardt, *Man and Woman, Boy and Girl,* Johns Hopkins, Baltimore, 1972.

3 E. H. Erikson, *Identity: Youth and Crisis,* Norton, New York, 1968.

4 G. Blum, A. Farly, and H. Guthals, "The Concept of Body Image and Remediating of a Body Image Disorder," *J. Learn. Disabil.* 3(9):440–447 (1970).

5 I. P. Robmault, *Sex, Society and the Disabled,* Harper & Row, Hagerstown, Md., 1978, p. 11.

6 J. L. McCary and D. R. Copeland, *Modern Views of Human Sexual Behavior,* Science Research, Chicago, 1976.

7 D. C. Gibson and K. J. Ryan. *Menopause and Aging: Summary Report and Selected Papers from a Research Conference on Menopause and Aging,* U.S. Department of Health, Education, and Welfare, Publication NIH-73-319, Bethesda, Md., 1971, p. 3.

8 S. H. Cherry, *The Menopause Myth,* Ballantine, New York, 1976.

9 H. R. K. Barber and E. A. Graber, "The Case for and against Estrogen Therapy," *Am. J. Nurs.* 75(10) (1975).

10 Ibid., p. 1769.

11   Cherry, op. cit., p. 54.
12   A. P. Bell and M. S. Weinberg, *Homosexualities: A Study of Diversity among Men and Women,* Simon and Schuster, New York, 1978, pp. 132–137.
13   V. N. Prock, "The Mid-Stage Woman," *Am. J. Nurs.* **75**(6):1019 (1975).
14   W. H. Masters and V. Johnson, *Human Sexual Response,* Little, Brown, Boston, 1966.

BIBLIOGRAPHY

Barber, H. R. K., and E. A. Graber: "The Case for and against Estrogen Therapy," *Am. J. Nurs.* **75**(10) (1975).

Bell, A. P., and M. S. Weinberg: *Homosexualities: A Study of Diversity among Men and Women,* Simon and Schuster, New York, 1978.

Blum, G., A. Farly, and H. Guthals: "The Concept of Body Image and Remediating of a Body Image Disorder," *J. Learn. Disabil.* **3**(9):440–447 (1970).

Boston Women's Health Book Collective: "Menopause," in *Our Bodies, Ourselves,* Simon and Schuster, New York, 1976.

Cherry, S. H.: *The Menopause Myth,* Ballantine, New York, 1976.

Delora, J. S., and C. A. B. Warren: *Understanding Sexual Interaction,* Houghton Mifflin, Boston, 1977.

Erikson, E. H.: *Identity: Youth and Crisis,* Norton, New York, 1968.

Gadpaille, W. J.: *The Cycles of Sex,* Scribner, New York, 1975.

Gibson, D. C., and K. J. Ryan: *Menopause and Aging: Summary Report and Selected Papers from a Research Conference on Menopause and Aging,* U.S. Department of Health, Education, and Welfare Publication NIH-73-319, Bethesda, Md., 1971.

Masters, W. H., and V. Johnson: *Human Sexual Response,* Little, Brown, Boston, 1966.

McCary, J. L., and D. R. Copeland: *Modern Views of Human Sexual Behavior,* Science Research Associates, Chicago, 1976.

Money, J., and A. A. Ehrhardt: *Man and Woman, Boy and Girl,* Johns Hopkins, Baltimore, 1972.

Prock, V. N.: "The Mid-Stage Woman," *Am. J. Nurs.* **75**(6):1019–22 (1975).

Reitz, R.: *Menopause: A Positive Approach,* Chilton, 1978.

Robmault, I. P.: *Sex, Society and the Disabled,* Harper & Row, Hagerstown, Md., 1978, p. 11.

Weideger, P.: *Menstruation and Menopause,* Knopf, New York, 1976.

Zellweger, H.: *Chromosomal Aberrations,* American Association for Cerebral Palsy, New Orleans Annual Meeting, 1971, p. 96.

Chapter 5

Atypical Sexual Patterns

Sexuality is a complex interrelation of physiological and psychological factors with society regulating and structuring behavior through sexual rules. According to Davenport:

> Sexual behavior in human societies is imbedded in a complex web of shared ideas, moral rules, jural regulations, obvious associations, and obscure symbols. The image of a human society in which sexual behavior is (or was) completely free and unfettered by socially-determined controls is pure fantasy. Such a society does not exist, and, despite so-called scientific postulations of an earlier and totally promiscuous stage in human social evolution it never did. The fundamental reasons for this are easy to find. Although human sexual behavior is directly based upon inherited biological factors, the biological bases are shaped and modified by learning in the inevitable process of maturation. Maturation is a social process as much as it is an individual learning experience. Inheritance equips the normal individual with the potentialities of adult sexual behavior but only through adequate socialization and maturation are the potentialities molded into behavior patterns that are uniform enough from individual to individual to permit sexual interaction.[1]

Sexual behavior varies from one culture to another and from one period of history to another. What is considered abnormal at one time or place may be considered normal in the next generation. In the past many terms have been used to define atypical sexual patterns including sexual deviance, perversion, sexual variance, and paraphilias. The purpose of including the material in this chapter is to provide information, to sensitize the nurse to the specific kinds of sexual behaviors for referral purposes, and to help in prevention of traumatic sexual experiences. Most nurses will not be expected to intervene higher than at the basic or intermediate level of the Sexual Health Model. A few nurses have had special education and professional experiences and are effective in therapy and research with these atypical sexual patterns.

The topics chosen for this chapter include:

1 Gender identity disorders
2 Preference for unusual sex objects
3 Atypical preference for human sexual objects
4 Behaviors focusing on atypical acts
5 Victims of atypical sexual acts
6 Contemporary controversial issues

GENDER IDENTITY DISORDERS

Since core gender identity is thought to be a continuum, and most people have a mixture of masculine and feminine characteristics, ambiguity is present even when describing gender identity disorders. According to Qualls:

> Gender identity disorders comprise a heterogenous group of disorders that involve alteration in an individual's sense of maleness or femaleness (core gender identity) and/or gender role behavior; that is, those behaviors that are dimorphic for males and females in a given culture.[2]

These disorders include transsexualism, transvestism, and various disorders of intersexuality (Turner's syndrome, Klinefelter's syndrome, adrenogenital syndrome, male pseudohermaphroditism, androgen insensitivity syndrome, and temporal lobe abnormality). According to Qualls the most severe of the core gender identity disorders is transsexualism.[3]

Transsexualism

In transsexualism there is no known discrepancy between the sex assigned at birth, the external genitals, and other measurable somatic criteria of sex. According to Money transsexualism falls within the limit of normal variation. A very few may have a chromosome abnormality, notably the 44 XXY syndrome in male transsexuals, but the majority show no chromosomal deviance. They also are in the normal range of hormonal production.[4]

Some clinicians believe that there should be more emphasis on positively reinforcing all infants for those gender characteristics that are consistent with their biological identity. Other people believe that many of those having gender identity problems have experienced an overemphasis of what is masculine and what is feminine. How the androgynous approach, which includes a comfortable mixture of what the culture labels "masculine" and "feminine," will affect gender identity developments remains a debatable topic.

Lack of gender identity development can seriously impair the individual's ability to cope with sexual relations and can reinforce patterns of isolated sexual responsiveness. According to Morgan[5] about 30 percent of the transsexual candidates who present themselves for help can be classified under the general term *homophobic*. These men are extremely reluctant to view their sexual desires for men as being homosexual because they either view homosexuality as "disgusting," "perverse," or "abnormal," have had bad homosexual experiences, or view some portion of the gay subculture as "sick." Another group, about 20 to 25 percent, are sexually ambiguous but share the diagnosis of "inadequate personality." They correctly perceive the need for a major change in their lives if they are to receive pleasure and satisfaction from human interaction but incorrectly identify their need as being the external genitalia of the opposite sex. Morgan believes that it is difficult to help the individual to see that inadequacy with a vagina may not be superior to inadequacy with a penis, except in small pockets of society where the female is expected only to look pretty while the male is expected to do something. About 10 percent of the transsexual candidates are found both clinically and psychologically to be suffering from a major mental illness, which includes paranoid schizophrenia with the delusion that he or she is of the opposite sex.[6]

The candidates for reassignment of sex are usually screened and followed for several years before surgery is attempted. The screening includes psychological testing of the core gender identity continuum. Candidates are required to live and dress in the role to which assignment is desired for a period of at least 1 year while receiving hormone therapy, electrolysis, and counseling. Taking a female hormone by the male-to-female candidates has proven to cause some irreversible changes such as penile atrophy, accumulation of fatty tissue, and the budding of breasts, making this type of evaluation a serious concern.

Transvestism (Fetishistic Cross-Dressing)

According to Stoller[7] transvestism is a condition in which a man becomes genitally sexually excited by wearing feminine garments. Some men find only one type of garment exciting (common items of clothing are women's shoes or underwear). A second type of transvestite starts with a single garment and gradually develops a need to dress completely as a woman. The transvestite regards himself as a man, does not wish to change his body, and enjoys his penis, the insignia of his maleness.

Transvestism often manifests itself when the boy masturbates near the time of puberty or adolescence. It is believed that the transvestite frequently experiences cross-dressing when others dress him in feminine apparel to reduce the boy's masculinity and humiliate him, but on subsequent occasions, he dresses himself to obtain the reverse reaction. The transvestite is always masculine, overtly enjoys heterosexual relations, and will often marry and have children.

Intersexuality

As ordinarily defined, hermaphroditism or intersexuality in human beings is a condition of prenatal origin in which embryonic and/or fetal differentiation of the reproductive system fails to reach completion as either entirely female or entirely male.[8] Hermaphroditic individuals brought up from birth uncertain as to which sex they belong may, in choosing sex objects, show varying degrees of bisexuality. Most often hermaphroditic individuals will develop an identity appropriate to the sex assignment rather than the one that is appropriate to their chromosomes, gonads, or other internal sexual organs. Thus they will usually be psychologically heterosexual regardless of the hidden biological state.[9]

PREFERENCE FOR UNUSUAL SEX OBJECTS

Fetishism

Fetishism is that condition in which genital sexual excitement is aroused by an inanimate object (e.g., pillow) or body part (e.g., hair) that is not a primary or secondary sex characteristic. Fetishism does not usually involve wearing apparel of the opposite sex as does transvestism. Fetishism is not seen very often in females. Fetishism in women may be associated with a special form of kleptomania (stealing unneeded items). According to Stoller, occasionally the woman experiences an orgasm with the act of laying hands on a particular class of object with the intent to steal.[10]

Bestiality

In bestiality, an animal is preferred as the sexual object. Occasionally, an animal is used not by preference but because of the unavailability of a human partner. Bestiality will often be practiced with some type of torture to the animal. Some couples practice bestiality, or one partner has sex with the animal and the other partner masturbates.

ATYPICAL PREFERENCE FOR HUMAN SEXUAL OBJECTS

Satyriasis and Nymphomania

Satyriasis is the need of a man to "conquer" an infinite number of women. Actually having sexual intercourse is not as important as the expressed willingness of the women. Satyriasis involves degradation because the man does not value the woman for herself as an individual. She is only a statistic in his endless amassing of numbers of subdued creatures belonging to the category of human female. *Nymphomania* is much the same, a conquering activity of women over men. The act of intercourse is not important for sexual satisfaction but to prove that members of the opposite sex are unimportant and need degradation.[11]

Pedophilia

Pedophilia is the sexual preference of men for children, in the majority of cases for children age 8 or older. It often consists of looking at a nude child or caressing the child's body and genitals and in rare instances may be accompanied by brutality. The child may be expected to masturbate the perpetrator, perform fellatio or cunnilingus, and submit to anal intercourse and/or insertion of fingers into the vagina and/or rectum.[12] According to Burgess et al.:

> Most offenders are very specific in regard to their choice of victim with respect to age, sex, and type of sexual act committed. They tend to choose either prepubertal or pubescent girls or boys with whom they focus either on the sexual areas of their victims' bodies (touching, fondling) or on their own genitals (penetration), rather than combining both. The offenders characteristically commit their offenses alone—co-defendants are atypical. Recidivism is characteristic. For some offenders the offense constitutes an exception to an otherwise law-abiding and adaptive life, whereas for others it is simply one of many life-adjustment problems. Some offenders are retarded. Some are psychotic. Most are neither. If they share any common psychological traits or characteristics, these tend to be a sense of isolation or alienation from others, an ineptitude in negotiating interpersonal relationships, deep-seated feelings of inadequacy, and a tendency to experience themselves as helpless victims of an overpowering environment.[13]

Pedophilia is a confusing phenomenon because much of the literature presents different points of view and there is very little research to support theoretical formulations. According to McCary:

> Although the Kinsey statistics show that 80% of girls who had been molested were "emotionally upset or frightened," the upset was, generally speaking, about as great as if the child had been frightened by a spider or a snake (McCaghy, 1971). Any lingering effects from the experience were probably caused by the hysterical reactions of parent or other adults to the incident.
>
> Most psychologists agree that sexual experiences at the hands of a pedophile are less traumatic to the child than to the parents. If parents can deal with such unfortunate occurrences in a controlled manner, the child will usually suffer no residual trauma.[14]

A very different philosophy is that forced, pressured, or stressful sexual behaviors committed on a person under the age of 17 may lead to physical and/or psychological aftereffects. This group of professionals believes that:

> If we are to be of help to the victim, we must understand the offenders—for the etiology of a victim's trauma lies in the offender's pathology. Only by understanding the psychological makeup of the offender, the nature of the offense, his method of operation, and his motivational intent can we fully appreciate what his victim is a victim of.[15]

The perpetrator is likely to be one who has easy access to the child whether as an outsider or a family member. According to Sgroi, "Child sexual assault by a father or father figure represents perhaps the most difficult diagnostic and therapeutic challenge in clinical practice. Under-reporting and failure to identify the situation are so widespread that there is a growing conviction among clinicians that a father or father figure is, in fact, the most common perpetrator by far.[16] According to Groth, the father would usually be classified as a regressed offender who has focused his sexual interest on peer or adult relationships. However, due to conflictual and overwhelming situational events, in a relationship or in other components of his life, the man retreats to children for sexual outlets. The other classification used by Groth is the fixated offender who has from adolescence been sexually attracted primarily or exclusively to young children.[17]

During the years 1970 to 1975, Groth and Birnbaum studied a random sample of 175 males convicted of sexual assault against children in Massachusetts. The samples divided about equally on whether they were fixated exclusively on children or had regressed from peer relationships. Female children with a mean age of 10 were victimized nearly twice as often as male children. All regressed offenders, whether their victims were male or female children, were heterosexual in their adult orientation. These offenders usually selected girls as the victim. The most predominant method of engaging the child in sexual activity by both groups was through intimidation or threat (49 percent). The next most frequent approach was through seduction or enticement (30 percent), where trickery or bribery was used for rewards or pressure from adult authority. The smallest number (20 percent) used brutal or violent attacks on the victims.[18]

Another confusing point regarding these offenders is to determine if incest or pedophilia is the term that best describes the offense. According to Groth, "Incest and pedophilia are not synonymous, since incest refers to sexual involvement with a relative, and pedophilia refers to sexual attraction to children." The major issues in pedophilia are dealing with dynamics of an individual while incest usually includes some type of family dysfunction.[19]

Incest   Often parental incest begins when there has been sexual and marital dysfunction within the marriage relationship. It is not uncommon for the mother–wife to consciously or unconsciously sanction the sexual activity of her daughter and husband. The interrelationships, dynamics, and issues of all members of the nuclear family need to be closely examined in the father-child or mother-child incest. Consequently, parental incest needs to be assessed and treated by skilled professionals, who will be highly sensitive to the possibility of creating more violent behaviors within the family constellation. Some of the psychological stresses and social pressures include divided loyalty, family and name issues, legal implications, issues of possible violent reactions and dangerousness, and reporting to child protective service and the Sex Crimes Analysis Unit.

Rape   In rape the child is forced to have nonconsenting sexual activity under duress, threat, or intimidation. Victims experience rape as a life-threatening situation.[20] Many of the same issues need to be acknowledged in rape as in incest sexual trauma. Additional stress is imposed on the child who has been raped such as emergency medical care, police interrogation, hysteria of family and other social contacts, and fear of physical harm or death.

BEHAVIORS FOCUSING ON ATYPICAL ACTS

Exhibitionism

The rewards of genital display to others is not clearly understood. In some instances this behavior seems to be a way of coping with a crisis situation or from feelings of inadequacy as a male, or anger about impotence in heterosexual relations. In other instances the exposure is a chronic behavior in which the impulse is associated with general hostility toward women. The exhibitionist does not expose himself to attract heterosexual partners. If a woman shows any interest the man will most likely flee. According to Stoller the exhibitionist is more likely than any other person practicing sexually variant activities to be caught by law enforcement officials.[21]

Voyeurism

The voyeur or "peeping Tom" is primarily interested in viewing others involved in sexual relations or in viewing a nude woman in her home. Some behaviorists separate the activity by referring to those who gain pleasure from observing sexual acts and genitalia as *scoptophilia* and those who view nudes as *voyeurism*. Other clinicians use the two terms interchangeably. This is another area in sexuality that does not have adequate experimental research to provide accurate data as to the behaviors and causative factors. Most of the writings in this area are based on clinical data or data obtained from law enforcement reports.

Sadism and Masochism

Sadism is an atypical pattern wherein sexual gratification, or at least sexual pleasure, is derived by inflicting either physical or psychological pain on the sexual partner.[22] The pain inflicted may be caused by biting, beating, scratching, whipping, choking, or by verbally aggressive acts such as insulting or abusive language. Rape may be the result of a compulsive urge of the sadist to harm others for sexual satisfaction. The sadist may be satisfied only during the act of murdering his or her victim, which for some may be a human and for others an animal.

Masochism in sexual activity is receiving sexual gratification from being physically or verbally attacked. For most masochists the area of the body to be attacked, the intensity, and the duration of the attacks must be planned and carried out precisely or these activities will not be sexually satisfying. According to Sadoff, "Masochists are most often men who enjoy being flagellated, bound, whipped, or insulted preliminary to sexual relationships." Many women make a good living using such accessories as black stockings, high black heels, leather gloves, a leather whip and other black or leather paraphernalia."[23]

Assessment of Atypical Behaviors

In order to effectively assess the client who is involved in atypical sexual behavior and/or sexual offenses, the nurse needs to determine the dangerousness of present conditions and behaviors, if destructive to self or other, and the likelihood of repetition. As noted in this chapter some atypical sexual behaviors occur alone or between two consenting adults with little or no likelihood of harming another person. Other atypical behaviors present physical and/or psychological harm to others. To make an accurate predictive analysis of most sexual offenders requires an extended period of study by a large number of highly skilled professionals. According to Ritter, "For reasons that are not clear, the first offender is usually not dangerous and there is only a 3% recidivism rate, even with no treatment at all."[24]

The responsibility of estimating danger and the likelihood of repetition is a heavy burden, for an error on the one hand could result in the needless and potentially destructive deprivation of an individual's freedom and, on the other hand, could result in further jeopardy to self and others. Because this assessment is such a heavy responsibility, most nurses would benefit from consultation and/ or referral options.[25]

Some of the treatment goals for the offender have been summarized to include four difficult tasks. First, the offender needs to be aware of and acknowledge responsibility for the activity without projecting the blame on some external factor such as intoxication, victim provocation, gang activities, or "out of my head." Second, the offender must be held responsible and accountable for the behavior. Some form of restitution is mandatory. Third, the offender and resource people must identify clues and themes to precipitating factors that occur before the offense takes place. Fourth, a change of behavior to more appropriate modes of self-expression, need gratification, and impulse control must occur.[26]

VICTIMS OF ATYPICAL SEXUAL ACTS

Victims of Rape

Sexual intercourse without consent under conditions of force or threat of violence is considered one of the most serious of sexual offenses. Statutory rape refers to the unlawful sexual intercourse between a male over the age of 16 and a female under the age of consent, depending on the state jurisdiction. Persons not not able to give consent include those who are psychotic, mentally retarded, disabled, and those whose state of consciousness has been altered by illness, sleep, drugs, or alcohol. Laws on rape differ from state to state and the nurse should be aware of the laws in the state in which she or he functions.

There is a sharp increase in reported rape and conservative estimates indicate that only one-fourth to one-third of all sexual assaults are reported. Victims fail to report the crime from the fear of physical harm, fear of parental and societal rejection, fear of having to repeatedly describe the most intimate details of the experience, from a desire to "forget" the incident, and from fear of harassment by police and legal personnel. The victim's response to the rape is influenced by many factors: relationship to the offender, the physical and emotional circumstances involved (brutality, use of weapons, threats, forced activity, the repulsiveness of the attacker, and the quality of the responses of others immediately following the rape). So often the myths and taboos concerning rape are so deeply embedded in cultural attitudes that victims are forced to cope not only with the physical and emotional problems brought forth by being raped, but also with the additional burden of irrational reactions of relatives and friends who become involved in the incident. If a person is forced to have nonconsenting sexual activity under threat, the victim will often experience rape as a life-threatening event. In the acute phase the primary feelings are expressed as fear of physical injury, mutilation, and death. Victims may express other feelings ranging from humiliation, degradation, guilt, shame, and embarrassment to self-blame, anger, and revenge.[27]

In the primary or acute stage crisis intervention provides a framework for assessment and intervention. In this stage, a thorough physical examination will determine the presence of injury, lacerations, and tears. A wet specimen of the vaginal pool and cervical mucus will help determine the presence of sperm if there has been ejaculation with vaginal penetration. Due to the high incidence of sexually transmitted disease, pharyngeal, urethral, vaginal, and rectal cultures for *Neisseria gonorrhoeae* should be performed. A urine culture for gonorrhea may also need to be obtained depending on the potential receptor sites. A baseline serologic test for syphilis should be made. A repeat at 1-month intervals three times should be performed unless prophylactic treatment is given.[28] If the victim is a woman with reproductive capabilities, the data and normality of the last menstrual period and contraceptive information are sought to determine the need to take measures to prevent pregnancy.

The psychological assessment includes the developmental stage of the client, the meaning of the event to the client, signs and symptoms of psychological disorganization, present and past coping behaviors, and situational supports. The second phase in the process of reorganization will be highly dependent on the degree of trauma associated with the incident, the success of crisis intervention, and strengths of the client and/or family. Some of the symptoms of negative reactions may include somatic complaints, nightmares, phobias, and sexual dysfunction.

Victims of Incest and Child Sexual Abuse

Child sexual abuse is defined as the involvement of dependent, developmentally immature children and adolescents in sexual activities that they do not fully comprehend, to which they are unable to give informed consent, or that violates the social taboos of family roles.[29]

According to Kempe and Kempe, the victims of incest are becoming younger and younger. The incidence of youngsters below 5 years of age increased from 5 to 25 percent of the total group seen in a large general hospital in recent years. Whether this is because the victim actually is of a younger age or whether health professionals have begun to acknowledge that this is happening and are developing more skills to deal with the problem is not resolved. Father-daughter incest accounts for approximately 75 percent of incest cases, with mother-son, father-son, mother-daughter, and brother-sister incest making up the remaining 25 percent. Society tends to be much more concerned with fathers who sleep with or manipulate the genitals of their daughters or sons than with the mothers who regularly sleep with their school-age children and sexually stimulate them.

Often incest is nonviolent and may occur without forcible penetration. Many victims of incest lack exposure for an extended period of time, which implies a high degree of disturbance within the family unit. In order to preserve the family, members will vehemently deny the incest even after it has been discovered. This type of incest is likely to go undetected by law enforcement or child protection services, with an adolescent or young adult presenting this information as an unresolved incest situation in a crisis months or years later.

In many cases Kempe and Kempe believe that the mother facilitates incest between father and daughter. "Often a very dependent mother is frantic to hold onto her man for her own needs and the financial support he provides and sees the daughter as a way of providing a younger, more attractive sexual bond with the family than she can offer."[30] This is especially true if the couple has never been sexually compatible or if the wife has become sexually unresponsive to her mate. The mother may repeatedly report the father and then drop the charges because of her ambivalence about her alternatives.

The more violent incest situations will often involve stepfathers and/or alcohol abusers and males under the age of 30. These situations are not often promoted by the mother and usually will not be of a long duration. Some of the clinical manifestations of incest in the school-age child may be detected by sudden onset of school failure, truancy, running away, weight gain or loss, provocative sexual behavior, or emotionally withdrawn behavior. In the adolescent group, the daughter may be assigned virtually all the functions ordinarily performed by a mother such as looking after the house and siblings. In these situations the nurse may wish to assess if the reassignment of the mother's function or role to the daughter is healthy.[31] As the adolescent becomes a young adult, she may become more rebellious. Some of these young women may leave home, become involved in antisocial behaviors, become involved with prostitution, become pregnant, or get married in order to escape from an intolerable family situation.

According to Sgroi, sexual assault should be suspected when gonorrhea infections (often asymptomatic) of the throat, urethra, vagina, or rectum of children are detected. Rarely will these children have any external evidence of trauma. A few will be seen for a gonorrhea infection of the eyes. The eyes are highly susceptible to *Neisseria gonorrhoeae* and may be contaminated by other than sexual contact. All other gonorrhea infections in children are acquired by having had oral-genital, genital-genital, or anal-genital contact with someone who had a gonorrhea infection. If the child's vagina or rectum is penetrated, signs of trauma may be detected during physical examination. However, many cases of child sexual assault will not be a forcible vaginal or anal penetration by the perpetrator but manipulation, fellatio, cunnilingus, or digital insertion. In suspected sexual assault the clinician is expected to report the case to child protection services and, if gonorrhea is evident, to public health authorities.[32]

CONTEMPORARY CONTROVERSIAL ISSUES

Prostitution and Massage Parlors

Prostitution is engaging in sexual activity for monetary rewards. Prostitutes may be male or female and may participate in heterosexual or homosexual activity. Generally prostitutes are young people and their clients are much older men. The prostitute may not be atypical sexually but is in a high-risk situation.

According to McCary:

> The business of prostitution has traditionally operated in three ways. There is, first, the brothel, a house in which several prostitutes (house girls) live, presided over by an older woman (the madam) who has enough money and contacts to run the house. Second is the call-girl operation; the prostitute maintains her own apartment and her customers are sent to her by the operation's management who do some screening of the clientele. Her status is therefore considered higher than that of the house girl. She is, however, discouraged from making contacts of her own because she might not properly turn over the money earned. Third is the independent prostitute who depends on certain contacts for her clients or customers—hotel employees, taxi drivers, her pimp and "the book." Books containing the names and phone numbers of long lists of men who are know to visit prostitutes are sold for large sums to women in the profession.[33]

Goldstein defines the pimp as the man who

> . . . occupies a most significant position in the life of the prostitute. He is a "functional necessity," and may be her lover, protector, teacher, employment agent, and investor all rolled into one.[34]

James and Meyerding, who compared the sexual histories of prostitutes with "normal" women, found significant differences between these two groups. Prostitutes differed in that they:

1 Learned less about sex from parents and more from personal experience
2 As children, experienced more sexual advances by elders
3 Were more often involved in incestuous relationships with their fathers
4 Generally initiated sexual activity at a younger age
5 More often had no further relationship with their first coital partner
6 Experienced a higher incidence of rape[35]

Houses of prostitution may be waning and are being replaced by other business enterprises such as the call-girl system and massage parlors. According to Goldstein, "In places such as Des Moines, Wichita, and Colorado Springs, one can find massage parlors, nude photo labs, counseling, and escort services as easily as the 'deliver-a-pizza shop.'"[36]

In a study by Farley and Davis of the masseuses of five massage parlors in a Midwestern city, 30 percent perceived the need for massage parlors as satisfying sexual needs and 20 percent responded that massage parlors reduce sex crimes and abuse in the street. The masseuses, typically 18 to 23 years old, gave their opinion regarding the rationale for the sharp increase in the number of massage parlors. The overwhelming response was money/profit (this response occurred 18 times). All remaining responses fell into eight categories such as "popularity," liberal community, bad planning, no police problems, people less inhibited, publicity, need for more love, etc. It is interesting to note that the most frequently estimated age category of the clientele was described as 40 to 50 years followed by 30 to 40 years. It was estimated that 80 percent were married. The most frequently perceived occupational category was salesman, followed by businessman, and then trucker.[37]

Speculation as to the sexual preference of some men for prostitutes includes an opportunity to engage in variant sexual practices such as fetish activities, an opportunity to have anonymous intercourse with no obligation to a relationship, exhibiting anger or boredom with a long-term relationship, proving sexual ability during a midlife identity crisis.

In recent years, there has been public concern over the increase of young males (12 to 16 years of age) engaging in homosexual prostitution with a much older male. Other communities are concerned about teens who are hooked on a life of prostitution because the "money's too good." Others get hooked on their pimp and give practically all the money to him. Some families are asking for more legal control. They claim that the social system erodes parents' authority and then offers no help when a daughter turns to prostitution.[38]

Pornography

There is widespread confusion as to what constitutes pornography and what are the differences between erotica, pornography, and obscenity. Erotica is related to eros and passionate love; pornography begins with a root meaning of prostitution; and obscenity suggests that which is offensive, foul, lurid, or disgusting. Erotica and obscenity are at opposite poles, with pornography somewhere between. The pornographic category may be viewed as "hard-core" and obscene or as "soft-core" and playful or suggestive. There has been less difficulty with knowing and acknowledging what one feels about these classifications than with being able to place art, film, speech, cartoons, and writings into distinct classifications. One of the big ethical or legal questions concerns protection of civil rights and liberties.

In the last 10 years the courts have been trying unsuccessfully to find an acceptable balance between the First Amendment, the right of freedom of speech, and what the public perceives as the dangerousness of pornography. In 1973 the Supreme Court in the case of Miller versus California offered the following definition of obscenity:

(a) Whether "the average person, applying contemporary community standards" would find that the work, taken as a whole, appeals to the prurient interest, (b) whether the work depicts or describes in a patently offensive way, sexual conduct specifically defined by the applicable state law, and (c) whether the work, taken as a whole, lacks serious literary, artistic, political, or scientific value.[39]

The "contemporary community standards" portion leaves local people the right to define what is obscenity and hard-core pornography. The small number of academic studies available suggest that there is no proven adverse effects either of short or long duration from pornography. In 1970 the Commission on Obscenity and Pornography recommended regulation of distribution of sexually explicit material to children and unconsenting adults but not to consenting adults.[40]

Some clinicians and other professionals believe that pornography can be a useful tool in obtaining satisfactory sexual experiences.

The use of sexually explicit materials (sometimes referred to as pornography) can serve a variety of important needs in the lives of countless individuals and should be available to adults who wish to have them. In this regard we find ourselves in entire agreement with the Majority Report of the President's Commission on Obscenity and Pornography.[41]

In this issue little has been settled. There continue to be strong reactions to pornography. Some women believe that pornography gives messages of violence, dominance, and conquest toward women.

Most often the conqueror is male, the victim a woman or the standard themes are focused against the female.[42]

What influence women will have in speaking out against pornography, because they believe it places women into a man's definition of sexual freedom, remains to be seen. Research is needed. Arguments without convincing research are likely to keep the subject at the emotional level and plagued with reactionary backlash from various interest groups.

Since many of these issues are created and dealt with at the local level, the nurse needs to keep in touch with local newspaper editorials, advertisements, city ordinances, and zoning laws. In some cities, the dispersal of adult theaters, adult bookstores, topless cabarets, and saloons is common. Under some city ordinances, the theater that wishes to show sexually explicit films is compelled to locate in a part of the city zoned for commercial or business purposes only. Keeping up with court decisions and city ordinances gives the nurse evidence of how a community accommodates those who believe pornography is distasteful and that it will cause social decay and those who believe that people should have an uncontrolled opportunity to indulge in pornographic movies and reading materials within the framework of the First or Fourteenth Amendments. How these concerns and issues are resolved will probably have some effect on the sexuality of the community.

Homosexuality

Although homosexuality has probably been practiced since the beginning of time, it remains a controversial issue. Kinsey and associates considered homosexuality and heterosexuality on a continuum. They found that nearly half of American males felt that they were somewhere between "exclusively heterosexual" and "exclusively homosexual." Kinsey also found that 13 percent of women and 37 percent of men claimed to have had one homosexual experience that produced an orgasm.[43,44] Over the years there has been a great deal of confusion and disagreement concerning the number and problems of persons who are homosexually inclined.

To help clear up some of the discrepancies and stereotypes and to gather some unbiased facts about homosexuality, the National Institute of Mental Health commissioned the Institute of Sex Research in Bloomington, Indiana to conduct a study of homosexuality. Bell and Weinberg were the principal investigators of the study, which was conducted in San Francisco. From data obtained from this study they proposed the following classification for homosexuals:

Close-Coupleds. These partners are closely bound together with expectations for sexual and interpersonal satisfaction and do a low amount of cruising. They are considered the happiest with self-acceptance.

Open-Coupleds. The men and women in these relationships are not happy and seek satisfaction with people outside the partnership. They have a high number of partners and sexual problems and do a high amount of cruising.

Functionals. These people resemble the "swinging singles" and seem to organize their lives around sexual activity. They cruise frequently and generally display a great deal of involvement in the gay world.

Dysfunctionals. These men and women demonstrated poor adjustment in sexual, social, and psychological aspects of their lives. They have a high number of problems and regrets about homosexuality.

Asexuals. They lack involvement with others. They report few partners, low sex appeal, low level of activity, and a fair number of sexual problems.[45]

The findings of this study should help dispel some of the negative stereotypes and the belief that homosexuals are very much alike. The great variations and the emotional approaches probably account for the many discrepancies found in the literature about homosexuality. A few of the many difficulties experienced by the women and men who choose a homosexual life-style are discussed in Chap. 6.

SUMMARY

This chapter includes material to which the general population may react more emotionally than rationally. Some behaviors involve more legal implications than health problems. A few nurses are beginning to be sensitized to the needs of the victims and offenders and are involved in treatment and research of this population. All nurses need to be aware enough to allow themselves to realize that these behaviors are actually happening in what one would consider "normal" families. From time to time some of these individuals will be in crisis and will need immediate help from skilled health professionals.

Vignette

Problem
The client is a 19-year-old student of nursing referred to the University Crisis Service by a faculty member.

Problem List

1   Signs of crisis—changing from high to poor academic performance
2   Unsafe in clinical settings
3   Cries easily
4   Sudden decision to join army

Subjective Data
"I have to leave home."
"I will be forced to leave school."
"I don't know what to do."

Objective Data
Manifestation of Crisis:

1   Drastic change in performance level
2   Preoccupied with thoughts
3   Cries easily
4   Unkempt physical appearance
5   Feelings of panic, desire to run away
6   Signs of disorganization

Assessment

1   Student in crisis about family relationships
   a   Controls and demands increasing in home from both mother and father
   b   Client has been placed in mother role since early adolescence
   c   Incestuous relationship with father since early childhood (4 to 5 years old)
   d   Sexual relationship with father becoming intolerable
   e   Father has increased alcohol drinking and threatened boyfriend with a gun about a week ago
   f   Afraid that leaving home will place a younger sister in jeopardy for incestual relationship
   g   No suicidal or homocidal plans
   h   Boyfriend does not know of incest activities. She wonders how she will respond to boyfriend sexually.

    i Client has one family friend with whom she has talked and with whom she occasionally stays over night when conditions become especially tense

    j Mother is out of the home (3 to 11 P.M.) when sexual activity takes place

Intervention

    1 Provide a safe environment with confidentiality for problem solving around the following issues:

    a Safety of the client and possible emergency housing

    b Community resources that provide client advocate services for incest victims

    c Possibility of academic failure—anticipatory planning if needed

    d Possibility of family therapy

    e Financial assistance if needed

    f Other issues that develop during session

Plan

Help client with the current crisis and refer to psychotherapist for individual or family therapy

SUGGESTED LEARNING EXPERIENCES

    1 Rank order, from the most to the least offensive, the following sexual behaviors: pedophilia, voyeurism, rape, transvestism, fetishism, prostitution, incest, bestiality, heterosexuality, homosexuality, masturbation, satyriasis, transsexualism.

    2 Imagine that in the next few months you will have clients who are being suspected of each of the following atypical behaviors: voyeurism, rape, incest, fetishism, transvestism and exhibitionism. With which of these clients will you feel comfortable in applying the nursing process? Which do you suspect you will need to refer immediately to a more highly skilled health professional? Compare and discuss your lists with classmates.

REFERENCES

1 William H. Davenport, "Sex in Cross-Cultural Perspective," in Frank A. Beach (ed.), *Human Sexuality in Four Perspectives,* Johns Hopkins, Baltimore, 1976, p. 117.

2 C. B. Qualls, "The Prevention of Sexual Disorders: An Overview," in C. B. Qualls, J. B. Wincze, and D. H. Barlow (eds.), *The Prevention of Sexual Disorders,* Plenum, New York, 1978, p. 8.

3 Ibid., p. 9.

4 J. Money, "Sex Reassignment as Related to Hermaphroditism and Transsexualism," in Richard Green and John Money (eds.), *Transsexualism and Sex Reassignment,* Johns Hopkins, Baltimore, 1969, chap. 5, p. 112.

5 A. Morgan, "Psychotherapy for Transsexual Candidates," *Arch. Sex. Behav.* 7(4):276–277 (1978).

6 Ibid.

7 R. J. Stoller, "Sexual Deviation," in Frank Beach (ed.), *Human Sexuality in Four Perspectives,* Johns Hopkins, Baltimore, 1976, p. 209.

8 John Money, "Human Hermaphroditism," in Frank Beach (ed.), *Human Sexuality in Four Perspectives,* Johns Hopkins, Baltimore, 1976, p. 64.

9 Stoller, op. cit., p. 212.

10 Ibid., p. 196.

11 Ibid, pp. 198–199.

12 Ibid., p. 201.

13 A. Burgess, A. Broth, L. Holmstrom, and S. Sgroi, *Sexual Assault of Children and Adolescents,* Heath, Lexington, Mass., 1978, p. 23.

14 McCary, op. cit., p. 347.

15 Burgess et al., op. cit, p. 24.

16 S. Sgroi in Burgess et al., op. cit., p. 133.

17 A. Groth in Burgess et al., op. cit., p. 6.

18 A. Groth and H. J. Birnbaum, "Adult Sexual Orientation and Attraction to Underage Persons," *Arch. Sex. Behav.* 7(3):175–181 (1978).

19 A. Groth in Burgess et al., op. cit, pp. 17–19.

20 Burgess and Holmstrom in Burgess et al., op. cit., p. 61.

21 Stoller, op. cit., p. 202.

22 McCary, op. cit., p. 330.

23 R. L. Sadoff, "Other Sexual Deviations," in G. B. Sadock, H. Kaplan, and A. Freedman (eds.), *Sexual Experience,* Williams & Wilkins, Baltimore, 1976, p. 433.

24 N. Ritter, "The Psychology of the Sex Offenders, Causes, Treatment and Prognosis," *Police Law Quarterly,* January 1974, p. 26.

25 A. Groth in Burgess et al., op. cit, p. 42.

26 Ibid.

27 A. Burgess and L. Holstrom in Burgess et al., op. cit., p. 43.

28 S. Sgroi, "Comprehensive Examination for Child Sexual Assault: Diagnostic, Therapeutic and Child Protection Issues," in Burgess et al., op. cit., pp. 143–156.

29 S. Kempe and C. Kempe, *Child Abuse,* Harvard University Press, Cambridge, Mass., 1978, p. 43.

30 Ibid., p. 29.

31 Ibid., p. 52.

32 S. Sgroi, "Kids with Clap: Gonorrhea as an Indication of Child Sexual Assault," *Victimology: An International Journal* 2(2):251–267 (1977).

33 McCary, op. cit., p. 363.

34 B. Goldstein, *Introduction to Human Sexuality,* McGraw-Hill, New York, 1976, p. 260.

35 Jennifer James and Jane Meyerding, "Early Sexual Experiences as a Factor in Prostitution," *Arch. Sex. Behav.* 7(1):31–41 (1977).

36 Goldstein, op. cit., p. 262.

37 F. Farley and S. Davis, "Masseuses, Men and Massage Parlors: An Explanatory Descriptive Study," *J. Sex Marital Ther.* 4(3):219–225 (1978).

38 Anita Clark, "Teen-Age Prostitute's Family Endures Agony," *Wisconsin State Journal,* November 20, 1978, p. 1.

39 J. Hyde, *Understanding Human Sexuality,* McGraw-Hill, New York, 1979, p. 507.

40 Ibid., p. 507.

41 *SIECUS Rep.* III(6):1 (1975).

42   G. Steinem, "Erotica and Pornography," *MS.,* **VII**(5), November 1978, p. 53.
43   A. C. Kinsey, W. B. Pomeroy, C. E. Martin, *Sexual Behavior in the Human Male,* Saunders, Philadelphia, 1948.
44   A. C. Kinsey, W. B. Pomeroy, C. E. Martin, P. H. Gebhard, *Sexual Behavior in the Human Female,* Saunders, Philadelphia, 1953.
45   Alan Bell and M. S. Weinberg, *Homosexualities,* Simon and Schuster, New York, 1978, pp. 217–237.

BIBLIOGRAPHY

Armstrong, E. G.: "Massage Parlors and Their Customers," *Arch. Sex. Behav.* **7**(2):117–127 (1978).
Beach, F. A. (ed.): *Human Sexuality in Four Perspectives,* Johns Hopkins, Baltimore, 1976.
Bell, A., and M. Weinberg: *Homosexualities: A Study of Diversity Among Men and Women,* Simon and Schuster, New York, 1978.
Bieber, Irving: "The Psychoanalytic Treatment of Sexual Disorders," *J. Sex Marit. Ther.* **1**(1):5–16 (1974).
Browning, D. H., and B. Boatman: "Incest: Children at Risk," *Am. J. Psychiatry* **134**:(1):69–72 (1977).
Burgess, Ann W., and L. L. Holmstrom: "Sexual Trauma in Children and Adolescents: Pressure, Sex, Secrecy," *Nurs. Clin. North Am.* **10**(3) 551–563 (1974).
Burgess, Ann W., and L. L. Holmstrom: *Rape: Victims of Crisis,* Brady, Bowie, Md., 1974.
Burgess, A., L. L. Holmstrom, and M. P. McCausland: "Child Sexual Assault by a Family Member: Decisions Following Disclosure," *Victimology: An International Journal,* **12**(2): 236–250 (1977).
Burgess, A. W., A. N. Groth, L. L. Holmstrom, and S. M. Sgroi: *Sexual Assault of Children and Adolescents,* Lexington Books, D. C. Heath and Co., Lexington, Mass., 1978.
Fensterheim, Herbert: "Behavior Therapy of the Sexual Variations," *J. Sex Marit. Ther.* **1**(1):16–29 (1974).
Fink, P. J.: "Homosexuality—Illness or Life-Style?" *J. Sex Marit. Ther.* **1**(2):225–233 (1975).
Green, Richard, and John Money (ed.): *Transsexualism and Sex Reassignment,* Johns Hopkins, Baltimore, 1969.
Green, Richard: "Sexual Identity: Research Strategies," *Arch. Sex. Behav.* **4**(4): 337–353 (1975).   *
Kaufman, I., A. L. Peck, and C. K. Taguiuri: "The Family Constellation and Overt Incestuous Relations between Father and Daughter," N. W. Bell and E. F. Vogel (eds.), *The Family,* Free Press, 1968, pp. 559–609.
Kempe, R. S., and C. H. Kempe: *Child Abuse,* Harvard, Cambridge, Mass., 1978.
Kinsey, A. C., W. Pomeroy, C. E. Martin: *Sexual Behavior in the Human Male,* Saunders, Philadelphia, 1948.
Kinsey, A. C., W. Pomeroy, C. E. Martin, and P. H. Gebhard: *Sexual Behavior in the Human Female,* Saunders, Philadelphia, 1953.
Laub, D. R., and R. Green (eds.): "The Fourth International Conference of Gender Identity," *Arch. Sex. Behav.* **7**(4):243–383 (1978).

Lloyd, Robin: *For Money or Love: Boy Prostitution in America,* Vanguard, New York, 1976.

Marmor, Judd (ed.): *Sexual Inversion,* Basic Books, New York, 1965.

McCary, J. L., and D. R. Copeland: *Modern Views of Human Sexual Behavior,* Science Research Assoc., Chicago, 1976.

Meiselman, Karin C.: *Incest,* Jossey-Bass, San Francisco, 1978.

Pomeroy, W.: "The Diagnosis and Treatment of Transvestites and Transsexuals," *J. Sex Marit. Ther.* 1(3):215–225 (1975).

Qualls, C. Brandon, J. P. Wincze, and D. H. Barlow: *The Prevention of Sexual Disorders,* Plenum, New York, 1978.

Rosenfeld, Alvin A.: "Sexual Misuse and the Family," *Victimology: An International Journal,* 2(2):226–235 (1977).

Saghir, M. T., and Eli Robins: *Male and Female Homosexuality,* Williams & Wilkins, Baltimore, 1973.

Sgroi, S. M.: "Kids with Clap: Gonorrhea as an Indicator of Child Sexual Assault," *Victimology: An International Journal,* 2(2):251–267 (1977).

Stoller, Robert: *Perversion: The Erotic Form of Hatred,* Pantheon, Random House, New York, 1975.

Zubin, Joseph, and Joan Money: *Contemporary Sexual Behavior: Critical Issues in the 1970's,* Johns Hopkins, Baltimore, 1973.

Chapter 6

Traditional and Nontraditional Life-styles: A Legal Analysis*

The law is a formal embodiment of social values, customs, and goals which regulates individuals and their interpersonal relations. As it relates to sexual practices and personal life-styles, the law provides a model of what is deemed acceptable by society. In general, the legal system contemplates a man and woman living together in a marriage relationship and engaging in procreative sexual activity. However, deviation from this legal model is inevitable because of the heterogenous nature of today's society and the tendency of the law to be behind the times. When such deviation occurs, tension is created. The individual who fails to conform to the legal model is brought face to face with the realization that his or her sexual activity or life-style is frowned upon by others. The nonconformist may also have to endure the incidents of social disapproval such as discrimination, harassment, or even criminal prosecution. On the other hand, if deviation from the legal model becomes so extensive as to indicate the predominance of new social mores, then the laws governing sexual activity and life-styles may be updated. Some of these behaviors were introduced in Chap. 5.

---

*This chapter was authored by Rebecca Fern Mims (B. A., University of Wisconsin–Madison, 1976; J. D. candidate, Harvard Law School, 1980) and Barbara Kritchevsky (B. A., Middlebury College, 1977; J. D. candidate, Harvard Law School, 1980).

This chapter will analyze the interrelationship between individuals, social values, and laws regulating sexual activity and life-styles that indirectly affect sexual health. In so doing, traditional and nontraditional sexual behavior and relationships will be discussed. Alternative life-styles, which are generally based on a nontraditional interpersonal relationship, will be highlighted.

In order to fully appreciate the extent of legal involvement in regulation of sexual activity and life-styles, as well as study various life-styles throughout the entire development of the underlying interpersonal relationships which influence health, this chapter is divided into three parts. The first part deals with actual sexual activity and explores the prohibition of certain sexual conduct. This part also considers transsexualism as an alternative life-style. The second part focuses on living-together relationships. Traditional marriage and its alternatives are compared. The legal implications of marriage are detailed and problems inherent in nonmarital cohabitation are revealed. The final part shows the effect of the dissolution of cohabitation relationships. The possibility of unmarried divorce is set forth. Custody rights of homosexuals are also detailed.

The main purpose of this chapter is to expand the awareness of traditional and nontraditional life-styles at the basic level of the Sexual Health Model. In review, the model is composed of cognitions, attitudes, and perceptions in preparation for using the nursing process. This chapter's objectives are aimed at enhancing awareness by:

1   Presenting and discussing cognitive components of the traditional and nontraditional life-styles through factual material in the form of background material and past and present laws, changes in law, and court cases
2   Presenting situations in which feelings, emotions, and attitudes have had an impact on life-style choices
3   Presenting material that will sensitize the nurse to a wide range of values on various aspects of traditional and nontraditional life-styles
4   Discussing documentation on how the law influences sexual practices and life-style choices and how sexual practices and life-style choices influence the law
5   Presenting material that will sensitize the nurse to difficulties imposed on clients and families by their life-style choices

GOVERNMENT REGULATION OF SEX AND SEXUAL ACTIVITY

Laws Affecting Consensual Sexual Activity

Sexual activity has historically been acceptable only within the marriage relationship, for the purpose of procreation. All sexual acts which could not lead to conception, and all sexual relations between unmarried people, were forbidden. Banned were all homosexual and heterosexual oral and anal sex, fornication, adultery, and bestiality. Authority for censuring nonmarital sexual relationships, especially homosexual ones, is often derived from the Bible. A verse from Leviticus is especially famous: "Thou shalt not lie with mankind as with womankind; it *is* abomination."[1] Similarly, the Ten Commandments forbid adultery[2] and Corinthians counsels, "(T)o *avoid* fornication, let every man have his own wife, and let every woman have her own husband."[3] While legal enforcement of other Biblical injunctions has long since ceased, a tone of moral condemnation pervades many of the sexual regulations in existence today. Laws regulating consensual sexual activity exist in many states, and while such conduct is rarely prosecuted, the existence of the laws is used as an excuse to limit the rights of people, especially gays, who choose to engage in sexual activity outside of marriage.

Sodomy laws are currently in a state of flux. The moralistic overtones of sodomy regulation can be detected in many of the laws on the books. Rhode Island, for example, forbids committing an "abominable and detestable crime against nature, either with mankind or with any beast."[4] Maryland's laws proscribe "unnatural or perverted sexual practices."[5] In several jurisdictions, the activity is simply called "deviate." Other states spell out the crime. Virginia's laws, for instance, provide a jail sentence for "any person (who) shall carnally know in any manner any brute animal, or carnally know any male or female person by the anus or by or with the mouth, or voluntarily submit to such carnal knowledge."[6] The location of the sodomy laws in some state penal codes is also interesting. The laws in Massachusetts, for example, are listed as "crimes against chastity, morality, decency and good order." Louisiana forbids the "crime against nature" as one of the "crimes affecting general morality."

Fewer states prohibit sodomy today than did just a few years ago. In 1974, only eight states allowed sodomous activity in private between consenting adults. Now nearly half the states have decriminalized such sodomous activity.[7] Connecticut's revised laws, for example, "adopt the basic principle that non-commercial sexual activity in private, whether heterosexual or homosexual, between consenting, competent adults, not involving corruption of the young by older persons, is no business of the criminal law."[8] Likewise Hawaii's revised criminal code "eliminates consensual sexual activity between adults in private, as a proper subject of penal law."[9] The American Bar Association and the American Medical Association are both in agreement with decriminalization of private sodomous activity between consenting adults.[10] Several states, however, forbid only homosexual activity. Texas, for instance, bans "homosexual conduct," and provides a fine "not to exceed $200" for those convicted.[11] These laws often remain on the books as a sign of legislative disapproval of homosexuality, after heterosexual sodomy is decriminalized. In still other states, sodomous activity is permitted only between married people. While many states continue to forbid harmless consensual activity, none appear to have enacted laws proscribing modes of sexual activity which could, at least in their abuse, prove harmful, such as sadomasochism. A few states, however, have prohibited the promotion of sadomasochistic material or performances.[12]

Court challenges to the constitutionality of sodomy laws are common, but frequently unsuccessful. The general position is that while sodomy laws would be unconstitutional if applied to a married couple, the states may otherwise regulate sodomous activity. The Virginia sodomy statute was upheld against a challenge brought by gay men in 1975, the deciding judge citing a Supreme Court dissenting opinion and the Bible. He noted that while marital privacy was protected, homosexuality was "obviously no portion of marriage, home, or family life." He believed that states could regulate conduct "likely to end in a contribution to moral delinquency." The United States Supreme Court affirmed the decision.[13] Before more liberal courts, some challenges have been successful. A New York judge declared that state's sodomy statute unconstitutional under the state constitution as a denial of equal protection to unmarried people and an invasion of their constitutional right to privacy.[14] A court in the District of Columbia ruled that its sodomy law "does not apply to any consensual acts between adults, whether married or single, of like or different sex."[15] The Supreme Judicial Court of Massachusetts decided that the law in that state forbidding "unnatural and lascivious" acts would be construed as inapplicable to private, consensual, adult conduct.[16] It bears noting that while prohibitions of types of sexual conduct may be permissible, it is unconstitutional to render a status criminal.[17] Thus, since there can be no crime without an act, the state of being homosexual could never be illegal.

Not only are certain sex acts illegal, but some states forbid any sexual activity between men and women outside of marriage. A number of states criminalize adultery. In the words of the New York law, "A person is guilty of adultery when he engages in sexual intercourse with another person at a time when he has a living spouse, or the other person has a living spouse."[18] Fornication, sexual intercourse when neither party is married, is illegal in over a quarter of the states. A number of states forbid cohabitation between unmarried men and women, sometimes in connection with prohibitions of fornication or adultery. North Carolina, for example, provides a penalty for those who "lewdly and lasciviously associate, bed and cohabit together."[19] In Arizona, one may not live "in a state of open and notorious cohabitation or adultery."[20] There are also assorted laws regulating the availability of sex for unmarried people. North Carolina forbids unmarried couples from sharing hotel rooms for immoral purposes or falsely registering as husband and wife.[21] Laws proscribing public sexual behavior are very common. Delaware's statute, for example, forbids committing "any lewd act in any public place or any lewd act which he knows is likely to be observed by others who would be affronted or alarmed."[22]

Prosecution for private, consensual sodomy is rare. In 1950, when sodomy laws were much more common than now, it was estimated that there were 20 convictions for every 6 million homosexual acts.[23] Courts have acknowledged that "consenting adults are prosecuted rarely if at all."[24] It has been called only "conceivable" that private consensual sodomy could ever be successfully prosecuted.[25] Informal policies not to prosecute consensual sexual activity are common.[26] The impact of having the laws on the books should not be underestimated, however. Sodomy laws indirectly sanction discrimination against their violators, in housing, public accommodations, and employment. Public indecency laws are susceptible to abuse by the police, who have a great deal of discretion in deciding which activities are indecent and when an activity will be considered public.

Arrests for consensual sexual activity are most common when the activity is semipublic. Perhaps most frequent are arrests of gay men having sexual contact in public restrooms or parks. Gay men afraid of having their homosexuality uncovered by their business associates, or for other personal reasons, may choose to obtain sexual gratification in brief encounters. Some men are married and are afraid to disturb their heterosexually accepted life-style, and seek homosexual relief in gay meeting places. Sexual encounters can take place in restrooms, gay movie houses, or parks which acquire a reputation for being likely places to find a partner. The dangers of such encounters come not only from the possibility of arrest, but from the physical danger presented by young men who prey on the gays to mug or beat them. If attacked, however, the men may well be afraid to report the crime to the police, partly from a fear of publicity and partly because the police are often unsympathetic. The problems are largely circular: society's disapproval of same-sex relationships brings people to quick semipublic encounters where they face the risk of arrest or brutality. The trauma of the arrest, especially when the person is in a sheltered and presumably safe location, can be enormous. When police raided a gay movie house in Boston and arrested six men who were masturbating or engaging in oral sex and charged them with "open and gross lewdness," a newspaper recounts that "(O)ne of the men was apparently so taken aback by the police action that he collapsed on the way to the police wagon."[27]

At times, the police resort to entrapment when attempting to arrest men for public sexual activity. Entrapment exists if the criminal design originates in the police officer's mind and the defendant is induced by the police officer to commit an offense which the defendant would not have committed without being so induced. If the police officer instigates an encounter, the defendant will usually be considered a victim of entrapment[28] and charges will be dismissed. The question of entrapment was raised in mass police arrests in a Boston library for such crimes as open and gross lewdness, indecent exposure, unnatural acts, and prostitution.

> Most of the arrests were made by . . . an "attractive young" plainclothes officer who, according to some of the men who were arrested, stood nearby the urinals "masturbating himself to encourage sexual advances." One man, who was in the men's room on legitimate business declined the officer's advances, and reported that the officer asked him, "Are you gay?" He responded, "Yes, but I'm not interested," and the officer then proceeded to arrest him.
>
> Observed in Boston's Municipal Court during the arraignments, [the officer's] statement of facts was the same for each defendant. He observed the defendant masturbating in the men's room. While some of the men agreed to the submission of facts during their arraignments (and had their cases continued without a finding for one year), others intend to press for a trial to accuse the officer of concocting nonexistent charges.[29]

The arrests may not result in convictions, such as in the above case where no findings were to be made for a year and it was expected that charges would then be dismissed if the men were not arrested again. Charges are often dismissed, especially if the judge is sympathetic and the police appear to have abused their discretion. A charge of lewd and lascivious behavior brought against a waiter who briefly sexually caressed a patron in a dimly lit gay bar and was seen by an undercover agent was dismissed when the judge determined that no one was offended by the conduct.[30] Police raids of gay bars are not common, but the knowledge that police harassment is possible could chill many from leading an openly gay life-style.

A serious problem arising from the existence of sodomy laws is that they can be used to discriminate against gays in various areas. Not only may individuals prejudiced against gays use the fact that their sex lives are often "criminal" as an excuse to discriminate against them in housing or public accommodations, but the arguments are used to defend court challenges to denials of rights because of sexual orientation. In one case, a court refused to require a student newspaper to accept a paid advertisement from an off-campus gay group. The court cited the state law prohibiting "unnatural intercourse" and the newspaper's right to remain uninvolved with illegal activity as "special reasons" supporting the decision.[31] In another case, a gay lawyer who had been arrested for sexual activity at night on a public beach was denied admission to another state's bar. The court reasoned that since sodomy was illegal, the fact that someone planned to pursue a way of life in violation of that law militated against his admission to the bar. The decision was reversed on appeal, with the court deciding that behavior in violation of accepted norms is not controlling, but relevant, in assessing fitness to practice law.[32] Now, in New York, sexual orientation is not controlling in licensing, citizenship, or admission to the bar.[33] Even when homosexuality is not used to deny admission to regulated professions, many licensing statutes rule against licensing those convicted of certain crimes; so a person convicted of sex-related crimes could be indirectly discriminated against if the arrest were discriminatory.

Responding to these problems, many communities are passing antidiscrimination ordinances which include protection against discrimination based on sexual orientation. As of early 1979, 43 communities had banned discrimination against gays generally or specifically in city hiring practices.[34] Cities with such ordinances include San Francisco and Berkeley in California, Detroit in Michigan, and Washington, D.C. At least five cities have passed such ordinances since the publicized repeal of one in Dade County, Florida. The rights of gays in nursing homes is protected on the state level in Michigan.[35] Several public officials have expressed their beliefs that sexual orientation is irrelevant in employment and that the needs of the gay community need public attention. New York City's mayor, Edward Koch, banned discrimination against gays in city hiring. Boston Mayor Kevin White appointed a liaison to the city's gay community and former Pennsylvania Governor Milton Shapp formed the Pennsylvania Council on Sexual Minorities. Just as the existence of sodomy laws can encourage discrimination, the repeal of those laws and presence of antidiscrimination legislation can have positive repercussions. A court in Oregon ruled that a gay man had the "good moral character" necessary to be admitted to citizenship. The judge looked to the repeal of Oregon's sodomy laws and to Portland, Oregon's policy not to discriminate against gays in employment in deciding that the community regarded homosexuality "with tolerance, if not indifference."[36]

Discrimination against gays is also being voluntarily banned in the private sector. According to a survey by the National Gay Task Force, 121 of the nation's largest industrial corporations state that they do not discriminate on the basis of sexual orientation in hiring and promotions. Companies on the list include AT&T, IBM, Ford, General Electric, and General Motors.[37]

Transsexuals

Transsexualism questions society's heretofore unchallenged assumption that human beings can be classified into two clearly identifiable and distinct sexes.[38] Transsexuals believe that their biological sex and their gender identity do not match; they desire, and sometimes obtain, sex reassignment operations to rectify this imbalance. Due to the importance of sex as an identifying and classifying factor, and the relative infrequency of transsexualism, there are few determined ways of dealing with the legal implications of sex reassignment, and transsexuals are left in a state of limbo.

The few states which have considered the problem of changing sexual designation on such basic identification as birth certificates have reached varying decisions. Illinois and Louisiana have statutory provisions allowing alteration of birth certificates to reflect a change of sex and over a dozen states have permitted sex to be changed on birth certificates.[39] New York, however, determined that birth certificates should be historically accurate and that chromosomal sex is determinative.[40] As more states are faced with the difficulty on a legislative level, they will probably choose to follow either the New York or Illinois example. Practicality would seem to indicate, and commentators recommend, that the Illinois practice be accepted.[41] Sexual appearance plays a major role in daily activities while chromosomal sex is not a consideration to the average person. It appears much less difficult to receive such everyday identification as a driver's license in a new name and sexual identity.[42]

The question of an individual's sex can become relevant in many areas of life. For example, a transsexual could face difficulties obtaining property left to him in a will, if the property had been left to a daughter who now has a male name and is, to all appearances, a son.[43] Sexual identity is especially relevant in marriage. Many transsexuals do marry and proof of sex is generally not required to obtain a marriage license. The difficult questions arise if one party wishes to annul the marriage, arguing that he or she has really married someone of the same sex. If a married person had a sex change operation then, to all appearances, two persons of the same sex would be married. In a state in which chromosomal sex was considered determinative, it would appear that a woman could marry a male-to-female transsexual, since they would be of biologically different sexes. Faced with difficulties such as this, a state would have to decide whether to use one definition of sex for all determinations, or to retain chromosomal determination for birth certificates and allow sexual appearance to govern in other areas.

Transsexuals whose behavior patterns make it likely for them to come into contact with the police face special threats from the criminal law. Some jurisdictions have laws prohibiting, or use vagrancy statutes for punishing, transvestism. Such statutes are often applied to transsexuals.[44] One statute prohibiting a person from appearing in public in the clothing of the other sex was declared unconstitutional as applied to preoperative transsexuals.[45] It is also suggested that transsexuals carry permits from their doctors explaining the reasons for their dress.[46] Legal sexual relations can also be problematic for transsexuals. Preoperative transsexuals having sexual relations with a person of their biological sex are arguably subject to the prohibitions on homosexuality, even though they consider the sex heterosexual. Police can entrap transsexuals seeking sexual encounters. In one case, a sympathetic judge described the transsexuals' sexual needs while ruling that the police's entrapment by initiating encounters was "so unfair and shocking" as to deprive them of due process of law and that subjecting them to arrest and detention was cruel and unusual punishment. He explained that, due to the risk of violence and humiliation:

> Transsexuals, in seeking sexual interchange with other human beings must often rely on the "street" encounter which is brief, impersonal, and which minimizes the risks of discovery. The transsexual thus must approach the making of sexual arrangements only with extreme caution—he or she will become involved only with those who express a particular interest in him or her.[47]

LIVING TOGETHER: IN MARRIAGE AND OUT

Finding a Place to Live

People who choose to live together, but who do not constitute a conventional family unit, may discover that they cannot settle wherever they desire. A significant portion of the residential land in this country has been zoned for the sole use of the traditional family. Zoning ordinances which define the family unit in terms of relation by blood, marriage, or adoption and which limit the use of prime residential land to single families, have the effect of excluding innovative domestic life-styles from much of suburbia.[48]

Since permissible zoning is related to objectives such as protecting public safety, preventing overcrowding. and facilitating adequate provision of transportation, sewerage, water, and public schools,[49] zoning ordinances designed to achieve social conformity may eventually prove vulnerable to constitutional attack in the courts. In the meantime, however, various courts have upheld zoning ordinances which exclude nontraditional living groups from residential areas. In *Palo Alto Tenants Union v. Morgan,* a California court upheld the exclusion of a communal group from an area zoned as a single family residential neighborhood. Although the communal group insisted that they were living together as a family, the court did not recognize the group as a family.

The traditional family is an institution reinforced by biological and legal ties which are difficult, or impossible, to sunder. It plays a role in educating and nourishing the young which, far from being "voluntary," is often compulsory. Finally, it has been a means, for uncounted millenia, of satisfying the deepest emotional and physical needs of human beings. A zoning law which divided or totally excluded traditional families would indeed be "suspect."

The communal living groups represented by plaintiffs share few of the above characteristics. They are voluntary, with fluctuating memberships who have no legal obligations of support or cohabitation. They are in no way subject to the State's vast body of domestic relations law. They do not have the biological links which characterize most families. Emotional ties between commune members may exist, but this is true of members of many groups. Plaintiffs are unquestionably sincere in seeking to devise and test new life-styles, but the communes they have formed are legally indistinguishable from such traditional living groups as religious communities and residence clubs. The right to form such groups may be constitutionally protected, but the right to insist that these groups live under the same roof, in any part of the city they choose, is not.[50]

The same people who are excluded from certain residential areas due to their noncomformist life-style may also find it difficult to rent a house or apartment. No doubt many landlords will simply refuse to rent to communal living groups. "It has been stated that the commune raises images in the average middle class American mind of 'wild sex-dope-rock-filth orgies.'"[51] Generally, there will be nothing that can be done through the legal process to prevent such discrimination, unless a statute prohibiting discrimination in housing on grounds such as sex, marital status, and sexual orientation exists in the jurisdiction and is enforced.

Who Can Get Married

Our society defines marriage according to the Judeo-Christian ideal: marriage is a union of two single individuals, of opposite sexes, each of whom promises absolute fidelity to the other.[52] Thus, while marriage is considered a fundamental civil right,[53] it must conform to the traditional pattern. In one writer's words:

> Generally, it is assumed that individuals in a free society have the right to marry whomever they choose. The fact is, however, that the right to marry varies from state to state and depends upon the existence of the requisite mental capacity and the fulfillment of certain qualifications such as age, physical well-being, gender, and blood relationship of the parties.[54]

Marriage is viewed as an institution in which society is legitimately interested. The state is said to have an interest in supporting stable marriages as the foundation of the family and society and a consequent right to regulate the marriage contract and the parties to the marriage. The state exercises its control over the relationship by regulating the licensing of potential couples and requiring certain forms of solemnization.[55]

One basic tenet of legal marriage is that the partners be of opposite sexes, an idea stemming to some degree from the belief that marriages are formed to have and to raise children. So far, no gay couples have succeeded in court fights to gain the right to marry. A court in Minnesota dismissed a challenge to the restriction of marriage to heterosexual couples, ruling that marriage is a union of persons of opposite sexes and that there is no constitutional right to marriage.[56] A court in Washington state ruled that the state's Equal Rights Amendment did not require permitting homosexual marriages.[57] In California, a legal advisory opinion held that even though all consensual sexual activity was permitted in the state and the state laws did not specifically require that marriage be between members of opposite sexes, no marriage licenses would be given to homosexual couples. A clerk responsible for issuing marriage licenses said that he received about one inquiry a week from gay couples.[58] Although some commentators argue that the Equal Rights Amendment should require legalizing gay marriages,[59] the common belief is that it will not do so.[60] Thus, although gay couples apparently have managed to obtain marriage licenses and some ministers will perform ceremonies for gay couples,[61] legal marriages for same-sex couples are not forseeable in the near future.

Other restrictions on marriage emphasize various traditional aspects of the institution. Bigamy and polygamy are prohibited, emphasizing the fact that marriage is a union of only two individuals. Bigamy is outlawed by statute in most states.[62] As extra emphasis, some states criminalize bigamy and provide that no individual who has a living spouse can obtain a marriage license.[63] Not only can a person not have two spouses, then, but communal living arrangements cannot be legally legitimated. The belief that spouses should promise total fidelity is enforced through statutory criminalization of adultery and making adultery grounds for divorce.

Some marriage regulations aim to guarantee enduring relationships and the breeding of healthy children who will not become the responsibility of the state. People are not permitted to marry until they reach a certain age set by the state; sometimes they may marry younger if they have compelling reasons or have received parental consent. The laws aim to protect against divorces which are feared if a couple marries too young.[64] The common law prohibited the mentally disturbed from marrying, and that prohibition has been carried into the laws of various states.[65] The restricted categories are defined by such terms as "idiots," "insane," "imbeciles," and "feebleminded." These persons are kept from marrying out of a fear that they will not understand the marriage contract or that they will not be able to care for their children. In some states, they can marry if they demonstrate that they cannot procreate.[66] Other worries about the health of the children born of the marriage can be seen in the restrictions on marriage by persons suffering from hereditary insanity or advanced pulmonary tuberculosis. In some states, again, individuals who suffer from these disabilities but who cannot reproduce are permitted to marry.[67] As science learns to detect genetic disorders, some states require premarital screening. In Kentucky, sickle cell anemia must be tested for; some states are considering requiring similar checks for Tay-Sachs disease.[68] Premarriage medical testing is not a totally new phenomenon, as some states require the prospective spouses to be screened for contagious venereal disease.[69] A concern for the health of the offspring, as well as deference to moral and religious taboos, underlies the prohibition of marriage between close relatives. Marriages between parents and children and brothers and sisters are universally forbidden. First cousins are permitted to marry in some states, and virtually all the states allow marriages between more distant relatives.[70] Occasional restrictions on marriage appear to lack any clear purpose and are largely unenforceable. Washington state, for example, will not allow a "common drunkard" to marry.[71] Some of these restrictions may be dated and vulnerable to court challenges. Nevertheless, their presence reinforces the notion that marriage is a union between two persons, but one in which the government is an omnipresent and very interested third party.

Traditional Marriage

Marriage is an agreement between two parties, husband and wife, which is enforceable by law. For this reason, marriage is often defined and discussed as a contract. The term *contract* implies that the conditions of the relationship are subject to bargain and agreement between the parties. The terms of the traditional marriage contract, however, are imposed by law. The man and woman in a traditional marriage do not define the terms of their legal relationship, nor do they often know what terms the law imposes. The only agreement between the couple is whether to marry. Upon marriage the couple enters a predetermined legal arrangement.[72]

The marriage arrangement imposed by law obscures the woman's separate identity. Historically, a woman became a legal nonperson upon marriage. According to Blackstone:

> By marriage, the husband and wife are one person in law; that is, the very being or legal existence of the woman is suspended during marriage, or at least is incorporated and consolidated into that of the husband: under whose wing, protection, and cover, she performs everything; and is therefore called . . . a feme-covert; . . . and her condition during her marriage is called her coverture. Upon this principle, of a union of person in husband and wife, depend almost all the legal rights, duties and disabilities that either of them acquire by the marriage.[73]

As an incident to the doctrine of coverture, the woman by marriage lost the power to make a will, retain her wages, sue and be sued, manage and control her land, own personal property, make enforceable contracts, and choose her own domicile.[74] Under old law, a wife was given no more legal status than a child.

Today when a couple marries, they enter a legal relationship which has its roots in the historical doctrine of coverture. Although the woman's separate identity is no longer extinguished upon marriage and a married woman now retains her civil and property rights, it is still traditional for the wife to assume her husband's surname and his domicile.

A woman is not expressly required by law to adopt her husband's surname. Nonetheless, society encourages the name adoption and the law facilitates and reinforces the practice. If a woman does conform to the traditional practice of assuming her husband's surname, the mere use of his name effects a legally binding name change. Other name changes may require a court proceeding. Moreover, certain states' laws require a married woman to use her husband's surname when registering to vote, obtaining driver's licenses, or running for election.[75] Although the recent trend is to invalidate these laws when challenged in the courts, they still exist on the books of many states.[76]

In most states, the wife's domicile follows her husband's. When a woman marries, she automatically assumes her husband's domicile no matter where she resides or what she intends her legal residence to be. Therefore, the woman who chooses to live in a different state from her husband's state of domicile may lose certain rights and privileges in her home state. Generally, a person cannot vote, run for office, serve on juries, receive free or lowered tuition at a state school, pay taxes, or register a car in a state other than her domicile.[77]

The traditional marriage contract prescribed by law assumes that the husband will provide support in return for the wife's domestic and child care services. In all states, the husband is obligated by law to provide support for both his wife and children. However, the husband is required to provide only the necessities. The husband has no duty to support his wife in the style which he can afford or which would be reasonable in view of his financial situation. Also, the legal system is often reluctant to enforce the husband's support obligations due to an attitude that the courts should not get involved in domestic quarrels.[78]

The legal system both assumes and reinforces the wife's role as domestic servant and child rearer. The services a man can legally expect from his wife were enumerated by the Superior Court of Connecticut in *Rucci v. Rucci:*

> The status and rights of the husband resulting from the marital relationship . . . include the husband's right to the services, society, companionship, and conjugal affection of his wife; and it naturally follows that she has a duty "to be his helpmate, to love and care for him in such a role, to afford him her society and her person, to protect and care for him in sickness, and to labor faithfully to advance his interests." Likewise, she must perform "her household and domestic duties . . . without compensation therefor. A husband is entitled to the benefit of his wife's industry and economy."[79]

Federal income tax law encourages a wife to assume the traditional role of homemaker. The tax law operates to discount the economic rewards from a married woman's work outside the home. Aggregation of dual income in a family creates a strong work disincentive for potential or actual secondary family earners. The secondary earner's first dollar of income is effectively taxed at the primary earner's highest rate. Moreover, a married couple with only one income can take advantage of income splitting provisions of the federal tax law. With income splitting, the couple's aggregated income is divided in half, the marginal rate of taxation for half the income is determined, and the couple's total tax liability is computed as twice the tax on one-half the income. With the highly progressive tax rates of the federal income tax system, income splitting provides a substantial tax benefit for the one-income family. For two-income families, especially those in which the wife's income is roughly equivalent to her husband's, the benefits resulting from income splitting are negligible or even nonexistent.[80]

The tax structure further discourages married women from working by failing to provide a substantial deduction for child care and housekeeping expenses. And, because the actual cost of paying others to do housework is great and because there is no tax cost in doing it herself, the housewife is often deterred from entering the work force.[81]

Under the traditional marriage contract, the wife is expected to provide sexual services for her husband. Criminal law buttresses this provision of the contract by failing to protect the wife from rape by her husband. In all states but Oregon, New Jersey, Iowa, and Delaware, a man who lives with his wife cannot be charged with raping her. The theory is that by marrying her husband, the wife has consented to all of his sexual advances. Even in the states where it is a crime to rape your wife, it is doubtful whether convictions under this law will ensue. In a recent Oregon case, which attracted national attention, John Rideout, accused of raping his wife, was found not guilty.[82]

The failure of the criminal law system to deter wife beating reflects a legal tradition of abandoning the wife to her husband's control and domination. Historically, a husband had the legal right "to beat his wife severely with scourges and sticks" for some misdemeanors and "to use moderate chastisement" for other transgressions.[83] Today the prevailing view is that wife beating amounts to the crime of assault and battery.[84] However, laws prohibiting wife beating are not effectively enforced. Perhaps most instances of wife beating are never reported to the police.[85] And many of the reported incidents are never prosecuted. Public prosecutors often dismiss wife-beating cases, thus revealing an attitude that such cases do not belong in the criminal courts. Of the Washington, D.C., prosecutor's office, it has been said, "The job of the office is to prosecute criminal cases, and not to psychoanalyze the disturbed, reorder family affairs, or threaten or cajole the obstinate."[86] Finally, the few cases of domestic violence which do reach the courts result in few sentences. Accused wife beaters are handled by the judiciary with lectures, threats, permissive referrals to social service agencies, or unsupervised probation. Such measures accomplish little in the reduction of recidivism.[87]

Upon marrying, a couple enters a partnership in which the law and society in general deem the woman to be the subservient partner. Such a realization may come as quite a shock to a woman who never bargained for such a role in her marriage. Social pressures to conform to the traditional role of submissive wife and obedient homemaker come as less of a surprise than the extent to which the law legitimizes such a role. Coming to grips with her lowered status as a wife may be a painful experience for a woman and may create tension in the marriage relationship.[88]

Nontraditional Contracts within Marriage

Recently a number of couples have expressed dissatisfaction with the traditional marriage contract. The rebellion has taken the form of a large number of couples making a commitment to live together without entering into formal marriage with all of its legal implications. Other couples who do not wish to live within the traditional marriage contract imposed by law are experimenting with writing their own marriage contracts.

The theory behind the marriage contract is that the couple will enter a formal marriage but substitute their own contract for the traditional marriage contract imposed by law. The contract is negotiated by the couple and fashioned to fit the couple's own needs and life-style. Possible topics to be included in the contract are

Aims of and expectations for the relationship
Duration of the contract
Property division
Financial arrangements
Housework
Personal and interpersonal relations
Plans for children
Religion
Provisions for wills and inheritance
Relations with others outside the contract relationship
Method of resolving disagreements
Procedures for changing the contract
Provision of money damages for breach of the contract
Provision for dissolution of the contract and the relationship.[89]

The actual experience of negotiating a marriage contract may be a healthy exercise of communication for a couple. Such an experience may foster openness in a relationship and enable the two to explore their views on various issues and expectations for the relationship. In addition, a written marriage contract can serve as a useful aid in periodic evaluation of the relationship. The couple could occasionally consult their contract to determine to what extent they have accomplished their goals and lived up to their expectations as articulated in the contract. Of course, the contract should not be allowed to stifle growth and changes within the relationship; there should be a procedure for modifying terms of the contract as people and conditions change.

Vignette: A Nontraditional Marriage Contract

Brad, a graduate student of nursing, and Cindy, a law student, are planning to marry this spring when they both graduate. The following are excerpts from their marriage contract.

Finances   Brad and Cindy both expect to be working after graduation. Viewing their relationship as a partnership, they wish to contribute most of their earnings for joint use. However, realizing that each has interests which the other does not share, Brad and Cindy may both set aside $1500 from their earnings for personal expenses or savings. The remaining earnings will be placed in joint checking and savings accounts. Each may make any necessary or desired expenditures from these accounts, except that any expenditure over $150 requires the approval of both Brad and Cindy.

All property (e.g., house, car) that can be held by title will be bought and held jointly. If possible, all credit and loans will be obtained in both names.

Both Brad and Cindy have outstanding debts for student loans. These debts will be paid from the joint account. This provision may be altered if either Brad or Cindy discontinues employment.

Household Arrangements   Since Brad loves to cook, he is responsible for cooking all meals the two will eat at home together. Brad will also do the grocery shopping. Cindy will be responsible for doing the dishes and the laundry. Living quarters will be cleaned jointly. If, for some reason, one is unable to meet his or her household obligations, the other will assume the tasks and will be discharged from an equivalent amount of work in the near future.

Children   Brad and Cindy currently plan on having two children. However, Cindy would like to establish herself in her profession before assuming the responsibility of motherhood. She will not endeavor to have children until approximately 4 to 5 years in the future.

Cindy will take a leave of absence from her work for each pregnancy. She will remain home with the baby until it is old enough for day care services (at least 6 months). When at home, Brad will assist in child care. If a child is ill or for some reason needs a parent at home after Cindy resumes her job, Brad will assume this responsibility if possible.

Religion   Although religion is not important to Brad, Cindy is active in the Lutheran church. Cindy will be responsible for the religious upbringing of the children. Brad agrees to attend church with the family at least once a month.

Residence   Brad and Cindy will move to Cincinnati after graduation and the wedding to commence employment. Although they plan on remaining in Cincinnati indefinitely, Brad and Cindy realize that career or other reasons may render a move desirable. Unless a move is absolutely essential for career or health reasons, all moves will be by mutual agreement. If one partner agrees to a move which is less favorable to him or her, then he or she will be permitted to select the area in the new city in which they will live.

Surnames   Cindy has agreed to take Brad's surname as her middle name, retaining her own surname as a last name. The children will assume Brad's surname and may be given Cindy's surname as a middle name.

Sexual Relations and Birth Control   Sexual relations between the two are subject to the consent of both Brad and Cindy. Both agree to forego sexual relations with any other partner. Cindy will assume responsibility for birth control. Any unwanted pregnancy may be terminated upon Cindy's decision.

Resolving Disagreements   Brad and Cindy will attempt to resolve their disagreements on their own. However, if a conflict continues unresolved, they both agree that they will seek professional guidance (e.g., marriage counseling).

Alteration of the Contract   This contract is subject to renegotiation upon any material change of circumstances.

Most contracts are enforceable in the courts. Hence, if one party fails to comply with a term of a contract, then the other party may sue in order to force compliance or in order to obtain monetary compensation for the damages resulting from the breach. However, enforcement of marriage contracts in the courts presents some problems. Generally courts have been reluctant to interfere in disputes involving the domestic arrangements of married couples. The judiciary has also been unwilling to enforce terms in marriage contracts that alter the essential elements of the traditional marriage contracts, which provide for the exchange of the husband's support for the wife's services.[90] As a result of these two standards, there have been court decisions refusing to enforce agreements to obtain a divorce, to refrain from sexual relations, to refrain from cohabitation, not to have children, to exclude children of the wife's prior marriage from the household, to bind the husband to reside in a particular location, to permit the wife to choose the marital domicile, to raise children in a particular religion, to relieve the husband of his obligation to support his wife, to limit the husband's liability for support in the event of separation or divorce, to keep the husband's mother in the household indefinitely, and to have the husband pay his wife for his care.[91]

As a practical matter, the courts' refusal to enforce the provisions in the contract relating to the ongoing marriage may prove to be inconsequential. Most contractual disputes which are serious enough to result in litigation are also serious enough to result in termination of the relationship. And the courts do tend to enforce antenuptual and marriage contract provisions which provide for division of property rights and alimony upon divorce.[92] Moreover, most couples will not depend on courts to enforce their marriage contract, but will instead rely upon self-enforcement. When irreconcilable differences arise, the couple may wish to seek advice and perhaps arbitration from a neutral party or guidance from a trained professional.

Contracts in Lieu of Marriage

Contracts in lieu of marriage can be used to provide some structure and stability for relationships in which traditional marriage is unwanted or impossible. Such contracts provide a method of legitimizing gay couples' relationships and "group marriages." For heterosexual couples who desire more flexibility in their relationship than the traditional marriage contract permits, contracts in lieu of marriage provide an alternative.

Contracts in lieu of marriage may deal with many issues which are also provided for in marriage contracts. However, couples writing contracts within marriage can always depend on the traditional marriage contract to fill in gaps in their own agreement. A contract in lieu of marriage, on the other hand, will be the only legal tie between its writers. Although domestic relations law provides support and property arrangements upon the dissolution of a marriage, no such protection is afforded by law upon the dissolution of a living-together arrangement. Therefore, people writing contracts in lieu of marriage should consider including provisions dealing with support, property settlement, and inheritance. Enforcement of contracts in lieu of marriage cannot be guaranteed and depends upon the law of the state.

Vignette: A Contract in Lieu of Marriage

Terry, a high school social studies teacher, and Pat, a professional tennis player, have been living together for several months. Being deeply in love and hoping to remain together indefinitely, they wish to formalize their relationship. The following are excerpts from their contract in lieu of marriage.

Property and Support Pat and Terry will retain separate ownership of all property brought into the relationship. They both agree to contribute one-half of their annual incomes for their joint expenses. Any property purchased with funds from this joint fund will be owned jointly. Property purchased with separate funds will be owned solely by the purchaser.

If for any reason Pat or Terry discontinues work, the other will assume all household expenses. If necessary, each will help pay any unanticipated expense (such as medical bills) incurred by their partner.

Relations with Others outside the Contract Relationship Although Pat and Terry's primary commitment is to each other, occasional sexual involvement with others is not prohibited. It is hoped that such outside involvement will be kept to a minimum.

Pat and Terry agree that they may each take separate vacations to visit relatives, old friends, etc.

Termination of the Relationship Prior to termination of the relationship, both parties agree to participate in three conciliation sessions with a mutually acceptable third party. If after conclusion of the three sessions, one or both parties desires termination, it will occur immediately. Upon separation, both will keep all separate property and all jointly owned property will be divided equally.

If at the time of separation either Pat or Terry is unemployed and incapable of self-support, the other will assume the responsibility for support until self-sufficiency is achieved or until a year has expired, whichever period is shorter.

Death Both parties agree to write wills leaving all of their property to the other in the event that death should occur while this agreement is in effect. After termination of this agreement and division of the jointly held property, neither party will have any obligation to provide for the other in a will.

DISSOLVING THE RELATIONSHIP

Property Settlement and Support upon Termination of Unmarried Cohabitation

Judicial enforcement of contracts in lieu of marriage must be available if provisions for support and property settlement upon dissolution of the cohabitation relationship are to be meaningful. If these provisions cannot be enforced in the court, then people living outside of marriage cannot rely on their contracts to provide the protection and security upon dissolution of the relationship which domestic relations law fails to accord nonmarital partners.

Until recently, courts would not enforce contracts between unmarried cohabitants. It was argued that such contracts were unenforceable as illegal contracts for prostitution. Another impediment to the enforcement of the contracts was the general doctrine that no contract is made unless each party contributes something of economic value to the other. Since the courts refused to assign any economic value to domestic services, many contracts between cohabitants were found to be invalid.[93] In a 1976 case, the Supreme Court of California overcame the objections to enforcing contracts between unmarried cohabitants and held valid contract provisions disposing of property and providing for support upon the termination of unmarried cohabitation. The case involved actor Lee Marvin and Michelle Triola Marvin, who had been living with him for 7 years. Michelle brought suit to enforce an alleged oral contract under which she was entitled to one-half the property which had been acquired during the period in which they lived together and to support payments. Michelle argued that she had given up her career as a singer in order to contribute to the relationship her skills as a companion, homemaker, housekeeper, and cook. The court found that such services were of sufficient value to uphold the formation of a contract.[94] Moreover, "The fact that a man and woman live together without marriage, and engage in a sexual relationship, does not in itself invalidate agreements between them relating to their earnings, property, or expenses."[95]

Although the *Marvin* case applies only in California, other states have followed suit and allowed property settlements and support arrangements upon termination of unmarried cohabitation.[96] Many states are expected to reach similar results in the near future. It is expected that the new principles developed will apply not only to heterosexual couples, but also to gay couples and perhaps communal living groups. Hence, the prospect of "unmarried divorce" looms large.

The fact that the average couple living together outside of marriage has not written a contract will not absolutely preclude enforcement of property settlements and support arrangements when the two terminate their relationship. Contracts can be oral and informal. Moreover, contracts are often implied from the conduct of the parties. Should the conduct and circumstances of the cohabitants lead to the logical conclusion that they intended for there to be support obligations and property settlements when the relationship was ended, then such provisions will be applied by the courts. Contracts between cohabitants can also be implied by a court regardless of the intentions of the two. If one partner would be unjustly enriched and the other unfairly harmed by the termination of the cohabitation without support and property provisions, then a court may simply order such remedy as fairness dictates.[97]

With all the methods available for finding a property and support contract between two cohabitants, it may soon prove impossible to dissolve a nonmarital relationship without one party having to relinquish property or pay alimony to the other. Such a result would eliminate some of the freedom that the living-together arrangement has heretofore afforded. Two people living together for some time may soon find it difficult to maintain a no-strings-attached living arrangement. Once again the legal system seems to be contracting the scope of possible life-styles.

Property and support in the dissolution of traditional marriage will not be covered since nurses will have life experience or contacts to obtain this material according to the state in which they practice.

Custody

The important but vexing decision of custody has to be made at the dissolution of any relationship in which children are involved. Since most children are born within traditional marriages, custody usually becomes an issue at divorce. The court, applying articulated case law and statutory standards, must decide whether the mother, father, or a third party will gain custody of the children. Until this century, fathers had a virtually absolute right to the children of their marriage. "This paternal presumption, essentially irrebuttable, stemmed from English common law which viewed children as the servants of their fathers; the father was entitled to the child's services in return for which the father owed the duty of maintenance and support."[98] As time went on, the mother gained greater rights to her children. First, the mother was given preference during the "tender years" of the child's development, as psychological theories stressing the importance of the mother–child bond developed. A marked preference for maternal custody had come into the law by the 1950s. It was encouraged by a duty imposed on fathers to support all their children regardless of custody and a belief that the mother's place was at home with her offspring.[99]

The general view today is that both parents have an equal right to custody, with a possible preference for the mother in the child's infancy. Today, "All rules and preferences yield before the 'polar star,' the paramount standard in child custody proceedings, the welfare or 'best interests of the child.'"[100] In practice, this means that the mother will almost always gain custody, unless she is shown to be unfit. It is estimated that the mother gains custody in at least four out of five divorce cases.[101] Custody can also be raised in the courts if a parent or third party petitions for a change in an existing custody order, which may be granted if there has been a "material change of circumstances."[102] States also have various statutory provisions authorizing the state to assume custody of children if no parent is properly caring for them.[103]

It is not difficult to see how a judge being asked to determine a child's "best interests" could be easily swayed by personal prejudices and beliefs about child rearing. "Unfortunately, the 'best interest of the child' formulation, while high-tone and well-intended, is devoid of substance. A 'child's best interest' comprises any and all of the deciding judge's child rearing prejudices."[104] The degree of discretion vested in the judge is large and it is increasingly likely that personal prejudices will guide a decision as the issues become more controversial.

> When a parent asserting a right to custody, continuation of parental rights, or visitation privileges deviates in a highly noticeable way from society's norms, the degree of subjectivity with which a judge comes to a final decision is frequently escalated. In some instances the degree of abhorrence or sympathy that a judge feels for an embattled parent can cause the judge, obviously or artfully, to disregard

statutory or common-law standards and to avoid even the pretext of a genuine attempt to discover how the best interests of the child might be served.[105]

Many types of parents can be injured by abuses of judicial discretion. The retarded may be hurt by judicial assumptions that they cannot cope with the responsibilities of child rearing, mentally ill people may be declared to be unstable or unable to control even their own lives, and prisoners lose control of their children while they are incarcerated and may have to fight to prove fitness to regain custody.[106] Although parents suffering from these disabilities may be misunderstood and underestimated, it is unlikely that any are subject to the prejudice and moralistic dislike felt for people who live alternative life-styles and wish to retain custody of their children.

The crucial factor in determining the child's best interests is the relative fitness of the parents. Many factors are involved in a determination of fitness; factors reaching into all considerations of the parent's health, home environments, and the child and parent's preferences. Included as considerations are the reasons for the termination of the marriage and the parents' sexual conduct.[107] Because of the many prejudices that a judge may have against those who indulge in extramarital sexual activity, "a mother desiring custody is well advised to practice a conventional 19th century life-style."[108] Of course, this will often be neither desired nor practical, and any deviations from perfect chastity may be used to attack the parent desiring custody, usually the mother. One mother lost custody on the grounds that her children were exposed to an "immoral and improper atmosphere" when she cohabited with a man.[109] Another mother was able to retain custody over an attack that her communal life-style was inappropriate for child rearing.[110] And a father was able to keep custody which was challenged because he married a bisexual woman.[111] Especially vulnerable in custody cases are lesbian mothers, of which there are an estimated 1½ million in the United States.[112]

Lesbian mothers face numerous problems in obtaining and keeping custody of their children. If discovery of the mother's lesbianism was a reason for the divorce, she will be at a disadvantage, since the party who is not at fault in a divorce is often given preference in custody. While homosexuality is usually not a legal ground for divorce, it is often treated as being "at fault." The gay mother whose lesbianism was not known by others prior to the divorce must make the difficult decision of whether to acknowledge her sexual orientation at the original custody hearing or to keep it secret and risk having her custody challenged if it is later discovered. A mother who recognizes her lesbianism after her divorce may have to keep her new life-style concealed or else risk attacks on her fitness as a parent. Many lesbian mothers may feel that they have been forced to decide between keeping their children and pursuing their chosen life-style.

Once an openly lesbian mother comes into contact with a judge, her treatment in court will depend to a degree upon the individual judge's views on homosexuality. Some judges believe that lesbianism is a vice for which the woman should be punished by the loss of her child.[113] Other judges may assume that lesbians are immoral persons and thus unfit mothers.[114] The mother's lesbianism is seen as relevant not only to a determination of her fitness as a mother but also to the question of the child's best interests. The three concerns most often articulated by the courts are that a child may become homosexual if raised by homosexual parents, that a child's development may be affected by parental "proselytizing" of the gay life-style, and that a child may be stigmatized by having a homosexual parent.[115]

The lesbian mother who attempts to assert her custody rights in court cannot predict her likelihood of success; cases have been decided on both sides of the issue. To some extent, then, entering court is a gamble for the lesbian mother. In one case in which the lesbian mother was denied custody,[116] the simple fact that the mother was a lesbian ultimately decided the issue. Other courts have proven more sympathetic to lesbian custody rights. In Washington, two lesbian lovers were permitted to keep their children if they lived separately. The husbands moved for a change of custody when they learned that the women had moved into apartments across the hall from each other and that the mothers' relationship had been publicized in a movie and book. The judge decided that there had been no material change in circumstances and that the women could live together and keep their children.[118] In an unusual case in Colorado, the court awarded custody to the deceased mother's lesbian lover in preference to the child's aunt. The Court decided that the woman's sexual preference "was not related to her ability to parent the child," that the child was the most important person in the lover's life, and that the continued relationship between the woman and child was essential to the child's development.[119] In a Michigan case, the court reversed a lower court decision that the children of a lesbian couple should be placed in foster homes. The court said there was no true evidence that the women's relationship rendered their home unfit for their children.[120] "This is the first case in which acknowledged lesbian mothers were permitted both to retain custody of their children and to live together in a loving relationship."[121]

Cases involving gay fathers are less common than those involving lesbian mothers but the results are subject to many of the same influences. A father whose wife said he was gay was permitted to retain custody of his sons, but the court placed conditions on this decision; it required that no other man live in the family home to guard against "possible pernicious influences."[122] In another case, the court ruled that while it would be unconstitutional to deprive the gay activist father of visitation rights solely on grounds of his homosexuality, limitation of visitation was here in the children's best interests and was needed to protect them from unnecessary exposure to a possibly deleterious environment.[123] In one other interesting case, a court did not require a change of custody when the mother became a man through a sex reassignment operation. The court ruled that it would be improper to base the decision solely on the sex change, and decided that the situation did not endanger the children's moral or emotional development.[124]

Men who have fathered children out of wedlock are another group which has traditionally been denied custody or input in the raising of their children. They have been presumed to be unstable and uninterested in their children's development. Courts historically were insensitive to their interests, even when a man had admitted paternity and thus obviated the questions of proof raised in paternity suits. The rights of unwed fathers are beginning to be recognized; in 1972 the Supreme Court decided that a state could not take children from an unwed father on the mother's death without a hearing and finding of unfitness.[125] In a unique case the donor of sperm which artificially inseminated a woman whom he knew but had not married was granted rights to visit the child.[126] As with other groups who are not traditionally considered proper custodians because they live and desire children outside a marriage relationship, unwed fathers face a difficult battle to attain any role in their children's development.

In conclusion, this chapter may create conflict between what one values, what one thinks is right or wrong, and the various viewpoints presented in this material. What one values, what one considers right and wrong, need not be changed. But the process of affirming what one believes, of choosing from alternatives after considering the consequences, and of allowing others (clients) to do the same is the core concept of awareness.

LEARNING ACTIVITIES

1 Rank the life-style choices below in order of preference and give the rationale for your first and last choices. Share your choices within a group of 8 or 10 members.

    a   Traditional marriage
    b   Communal living with partner swapping
    c   Communal living with no partner swapping
    d   One-to-one relationship with opposite sex; living together with no contract
    e   One-to-one relationship with opposite sex; living together with contract
    f   One-to-one relationship with same sex; living together with no contract
    g   One-to-one relationship with same sex; living together with contract
    h   Divorced with children
    i   Divorced without children
    j   Singles—many relationships with opposite sex
    k   Singles—many relationships with same sex

2 Review the vignette of an example of a marriage contract. Write a contract for you and a significant person in your life or fantasize the person and write a contract. Discuss your contract with "the significant other" or with someone who is likely to express values different from yours.

REFERENCES

1   Leviticus, 18:22.
2   Exodus, 20:14.
3   I Corinthians, 7:2.
4   General Laws of Rhode Island, secs. 11-10-1 (Bobbs-Merrill, Indianapolis, 1970).

5   Annotated Code of Maryland, Art. 27, sec. 554 (Michie Supp., 1978).

6   Code of Virginia, Annotated, sec. 18.2-361 (Michie Supp., 1978).

7   The states which have totally eliminated sodomy laws, although not all eliminations are yet in effect, appear to be Alaska, California, Colorado, Connecticut, Delaware, Hawaii, Indiana, Illinois, Iowa, Maine, Nebraska, New Hampshire, New Jersey, New Mexico, North Dakota, Ohio, Oregon, South Dakota, Vermont, Washington, West Virginia, and Wyoming.

8   Connecticut General Statutes Annotated, Commission Comment to sec. 532-65 to sec. 532-81, 1971 (West, 1972).

9   Hawaii Revised Statutes, Commentary on secs. 707-733 to 735 (1976).

10 Norman Dorsen, Paul Bender, and Burt Neuborne, *Political and Civil Rights in the United States,* vol. I, 4th ed., Little, Brown, Boston, 1976, p. 1013.

11 Texas Penal Code Annotated, sec. 21.06; sec. 12.23 (Vernon, 1974). Other states which criminalize only homosexual conduct are Arkansas, Kansas, Kentucky, Missouri, and Nevada. Montana forbids "deviate sexual relations," which a comment defines as including homosexuality and bestiality.

12 E.g., Colorado Revised Statutes, sec. 18-7-101 and sec. 18-7-102 (1974).

13 *Doe v. Commonwealth's Attorney,* 403 F. Supp. 1199 (E.D. Va., 1975), aff'd mem., 405 U.S. 901 (1976).

14 *In Re P.,* 92 Misc. 2d 62, 400 N.Y.S. 2d 455 (1977).

15 *U.S. v. Doe,* (D.C. Superior Ct., Feb. 21, 1973). Reported in *Criminal Law Reporter* **12**(25):2531 (1973).

16 *Commonwealth v. Balthazar,* 318 Mass. 473, 318 N.E. 2d 478 (1974).

17 *Robinson v. California,* 370 U.S. 660 (1962).

18 New York Penal Law, sec. 255.17 (Consolidated Laws Service, 1977).

19 General Statutes of North Carolina, sec. 14-184 (Michie, 1969).

20 Arizona Revised Statutes Annotated, sec. 13-1409 (West, 1978).

21 General Statutes of North Carolina, sec. 14-186 (Michie, 1969).

22 Delaware Code Annotated Title 11, sec. 1341 (Michie, 1975).

23 Committee on Forensic Psychiatry of the Group for Advancement of Psychiatry, Report no. 9, Psychiatrically Deviated Sex Offenders 2 (1950). Cited in Robert J. Fisher, "The Sex Offender Provisions of the Proposed New Maryland Criminal Code: Should Private, Consenting Adult Homosexual Behavior be Excluded?" *Maryland Law Rev.* **30**(2):91, 95 (1970).

24 State v. Lair, 62 N.J. 388, 301 A. 2d 748 (1973).

25 J. A. Bryant, Jr., "Annotation: Consent as Defense in Prosecution for Sodomy," *Am. Law Rep.,* 3d **58**:636–655. (1974).

26 Dorsen et al., op. cit.

27 "Boston Police Raid South Station Cinema," *Gay Community News,* Jan. 20, 1979, p. 1, col. 1.

28 "Annotation: Entrapment to Commit Sexual Offense," *Am. Law.* 2d, **52**:1194–1202 (1957).

29 "Nearly 50 Charged after Increase in Arrests at Boston Library," *Gay Community News,* March 25, 1978, p. 1, col. 1.

30 *Campbell v. State* (Fla, Sup. Ct, March 31, 1976), *Criminal Law Reporter* **19**(5):2114 (1976).

31 *Mississippi Gay Alliance v. Goudelock,* 536 F. 2d 1073 (5th Cir., 1976).

32 *In Re Kimball,* 40 A. 2d 252, 339 N.Y.S. 2d 302 (1973), reversed 33 N.Y. 2d 586, 347 N.Y.S. 2d 453 (1973).

33 *In Re P.,* 92 Misc. 2d 62, 73, 400 N.Y.S. 2d 455, 463 (1977).

34 "Troy, New York Bans Discrimination in Hiring Practices, *Gay Community News,* Jan. 20, 1979, p. 1, col. 1.
35 "Michigan Has New Law," *Gay Community News,* Jan. 6, 1979, News Notes, p. 2, col. 3.
36 *In Re Brodie,* 394 F. Supp. 1208 (D. Ore., 1975).
37 "Corporations Surveyed," *Gay Community News,* Jan. 6, 1979, News Notes, p. 2, col. 3.
38 "Transsexualism, Sex Reassignment Surgery, and the Law," *Cornell Law Rev.* **56**(6):964–965 (1971).
39 Ibid., pp. 994–995.
40 Gail Brent, "Some Legal Problems of the Post-Operative Transsexual," *J. Fam. Law* **12**:407–410 (1972–73).
41 Ibid. See also, "Transsexuals in Limbo: The Search for a Legal Definition of Sex," *Maryland Law Rev.* **31**(3):243 (1971).
42 "Transsexualism, Sex Reassignment Surgery, and the Law," op. cit., pp. 1000–1002. Also Brent, op. cit., pp. 406–422.
43 "Transsexuals in Limbo," op. cit., p. 247.
44 Ibid., p. 251.
45 *Criminal Law Reporter* **23**(15):2346 (1978).
46 "Transsexualism, Sex Reassignment Surgery, and the Law," op. cit., p. 990.
47 *U.S. v. Collins* (D.C. Superior Ct., Criminal Division, March 12, 1975), *Criminal Law Reporter* **17**(1):2013–2014 (1975).
48 "Burning the House to Roast the Pig: Unrelated Individuals and Single Family Zoning's Blood Relation Criterion," *Cornell Law Rev.* **58**(1):138 (1972).
49 "Excluding the Commune from Suburbia: The Use of Zoning for Social Control," *Hastings Law J.* **23**:1459 (1972).
50 *Palo Alto Tenants Union v. Morgan,* 321 F. Supp. 908 (N.D. Cal., 1970).
51 "All in the Family: Legal Implications of Communes," *Harvard Civil Rights Civil Liberties Law Rev.* **7**(2):393 (1972).
52 Lenore J. Weitzman, "Legal Regulation of Marriage: Tradition and Change. A Proposal for Individual Contracts and Contracts in Lieu of Marriage," *California Law Rev.* **62**:1230 (1974).
53 *Skinner v. Oklahoma,* 316 U.S. 535 (1942); *Loving v. Virginia,* 388 U.S. 1 (1967).
54 Carol A. Fuller, "Washington's Statutory Restrictions on Marriage: Ripe for Legislative Review," *Gonzaga Law Rev.* **12**(3):403 (1977).
55 Ibid., p. 404.
56 *Baker v. Nelson,* 291 Minn. 310, 191 N.W. 2d 185 (1971), appeal dismissed 409 U.S. 810 (1972).
57 *Singer v. Hara,* 11 Wash. App. 247, 522 P. 2d 1187 (1974).
58 "News Notes: California—Marriage—Homosexual Couples," *Fam. Law Rep.* **2**(27):2461 (1976).
59 "The Legality of the Homosexual Marriage," *Yale Law J.* **82**:573–588 (1973).
60 Ibid., p. 584, quoting Senator Birch Bayh speaking in the Senate on the effect of the proposed Equal Rights Amendments.
61 "News Notes: Maryland—Women's Marriage," *Fam. Law Rep.* **1**(34):2598 (1975).
62 Weitzman, op. cit., p. 1230.
63 E.g., New York Penal Laws, secs. 255.10 and 255.15 (Consolidated Laws Service, 1977).
64 Fuller, op. cit., p. 407.

65 Ibid., pp. 417–418.
66 Ibid., p. 417.
67 Ibid., pp. 415–416.
68 Ibid., pp. 419–420.
69 Ibid., p. 413.
70 Ibid., pp. 410–412.
71 Ibid., pp. 412–413.
72 Barbara Allen Babcock, Ann E. Freedman, Eleanor Holmes Norton, and Susan C. Ross, *Sex Discrimination and the Law: Causes and Remedies,* Little, Brown, Boston, 1975, p. 561.
73 William Blackstone, *Commentaries on the Laws of England,* vol. 1, Dawsons of Pall Mall, London, 1966, p. 430.
74 Babcock et al., op. cit., p. 562.
75 Ibid., p. 582.
76 Wendy Webster Williams, 1978 Supplement to Babcock et al., *Sex Discrimination and the Law: Causes and Remedies,* Little, Brown, Boston, 1978, pp. 173, 174.
77 Weitzman, op. cit., pp. 1175–1177.
78 Babcock et al., op. cit., p. 623.
79 *Rucci v. Rucci,* 23 Conn. Supp. 221, 224, 181 A. 2d. 125, 127 (Super. Ct., 1962).
80 Babcock et al, op. cit., pp. 737–740.
81 Ibid., pp. 740–741.
82 *The Family Law Reporter* **5**(8):2164 (1979).
83 Blackstone, op. cit., pp. 432–433.
84 "Assault and Battery," in *American Jurisprudence,* 2d ed., vol. 6, Lawyers Cooperative, Rochester, N.Y., 1963, p. 41.
85 Terry Davidson, *Conjugal Crime: Understanding and Changing the Wife Beating Pattern,* Hawthorn, New York, 1978.
86 Raymond I. Parnas, "Prosecutorial and Judicial Handling of Family Violence," *Criminal Law Bull.* **9**(9):735 (1973).
87 Ibid., pp. 747–748.
88 Jessie Bernard, "Marriage: Hers and His," *Ms. Magazine,* December 1972, pp. 46, 47–49, 110, 113.
89 Weitzman, op. cit., pp. 1250–1253.
90 Ibid., pp. 1269–1270.
91 Babcock et al., op. cit., pp. 636–637.
92 See *Posner v. Posner,* 233 So. 2d (Fla. S. Ct., 1970); *Volid v. Volid,* 6 Ill. App. 3d 386, 286 N.E. 2d 42 (1972); *Unander v. Unander,* 506 P. 2d 719 (Ore. Sup. Ct., 1973); *Buettner v. Buettner,* 89 Nev. 39, 505 P. 2d 600 (1973).
93 Carol S. Bruch, "Property Rights of Defacto Spouses Including Thoughts on the Value of Homemakers' Services," *Fam. Law Q.* **10**:106–114 (1976).
94 *Marvin v. Marvin,* 18 Cal. 3d 660, 557 P. 2d 106, 134 Cal. Rptr. 815 (1976).
95 *Marvin v. Marvin,* 557 P. 2d 113 (1976).
96 *Carlson v. Olson,* 256 N.W. 2d 249 (S. Ct. of Minn., May 1977).
97 "Property Rights upon Termination of Unmarried Cohabitation: Marvin v. Marvin," *Harvard Law Rev.* **90**:1708 (1977).
98 Rena K. Uviller, "Fathers' Rights and Feminism: The Maternal Presumption Revisited," *Harvard Women's Law J.* **1**(1):112 (1978).
99 Ibid., pp. 113–114.
100 R. H. Basile, "Lesbian Mothers I," *Women's Rights Law Rep.* **2**(2):12 (1974).

101 Nora Laverman, "Non-Marital Sexual Conduct and Child Custody," *U. Cincinnati Law Rev.* **46**:6534 (1977).

102 "The Law and the Problem Parent: Custody and Parental Rights of Homosexuals, Mentally Retarded, Mentally Ill and Incarcerated Parents," *J. Fam. Law* **16**:797 (1978).

103 "Custody and Homosexual Parents," *Women's Rights Law Rep.* **2**(2):21 (1974).

104 Uviller, op. cit., p. 124.

105 "The Law and the Problem Parent," op. cit., p. 797.

106 Ibid.

107 Basile, op. cit., p. 13.

108 Ibid.

109 *Ahlman v. Ahlman,* Nebraska Sup. Ct., May 28, 1978, *Fam. Law Rep.* **4**(42):2677 (1978).

110 *In Re Daub* (Wash. Super. Ct., Snohomish City, September 16, 1975), *Fam. Law Rep.* **1**(48):2834 (1974).

111 *Anonymous v. Anonymous,* N.Y. Sup. Ct., N.Y. City, December 9, 1977, *Fam. Law Rep.* **4**(9):2124 (1978).

112 Nan D. Hunter and Nancy D. Polikoff, "Custody Rights of Lesbian Mothers: Legal Theory and Litigation Strategy," *Buffalo Law Rev.* **25**:691 (1976).

113 Basile, op. cit., p. 7.

114 Ibid., p. 13.

115 Ibid., p. 15.

116 *Townend v. Townend,* Ohio C. P. of Portage County, March 14, 1975, *Fam. Law Rep.* **1**(48):2830 (1975).

117 "The Law and the Problem Parent," op. cit., p. 801.

118 *Schuster v. Schuster* and *Isaacson v. Isaacson* (Wash. Super. Ct. King City, September 3, 1974), *Fam. Law Rep.* **1**(1):2004 (1974).

119 *In Re Hatzopoulos* (Colo. Juv. Ct., Denver City, July 8, 1977), *Fam. Law Rep.* **4**(6):2075 (1977).

120 *People v. Brown,* 49 Mich App. 358, 212 N.W. 2d 55 (1973), in "Custody and Homosexual Parents," op. cit., p. 19.

121 "Custody and Homosexual Parents," op. cit., p. 19.

122 *A v. A,* 514 P. 2d 358 (Ore. Ct. App. 1973), ibid., p. 24.

123 *In Re. J., S., & C.* (N.J. Superior Ct. Chancery Div. Bergen City, July 26, 1974), ibid., pp. 24–25.

124 *Christian v. Randall,* 33 Colo. App. 129, 516 P. 2d 132 (1973), in Hunter and Polikoff, op. cit, p. 703.

125 *Stanley v. Illinois,* 405 U.S. 645 (1972).

126 *C.M. v. C.C.* (N.J. Juv. and Dom. Relations Ct., Cumberland City, August 18, 1977), *Fam. Law Rep.* **3**(45):2690–2692 (1977).

Chapter 7

Taking a Sexual History

As nursing continues to expand in scope, taking the health history has become part of the role of the nurse in assembling a complete data base on each client. The sexual history is as important a component as the review of systems, and requires as much skill to obtain. The objectives of this chapter are

1 To provide and to discuss the rationale for taking a sexual history,
2 To provide guidelines for taking a sexual history,
3 To provide convenient, short sexual history forms for use with children and adults,
4 To discuss referral for clients who request help with sexual concerns,
5 To discuss the sexual history as a teaching device for clients.

The nurse who is comfortable with his or her own sexuality will soon discover that clients are surprisingly willing to discuss sexual concerns. It is necessary that the client first become aware that sexuality is a topic that is appropriate for discussion with the nurse, and that the discussion will be confidential. The questions in the sexual history provide both nurse and client with a way to begin the discussion of sexual concerns.

A sexual history gives the client permission to discuss questions and concerns, either at the present or in the future. Often a client may appear disinterested or may refuse to discuss sexuality when the topic is first approached by the nurse. Later this same client may have many questions to ask and will bring them up when he or she is ready.

Sometimes a simple statement is all that is required to begin the sexual history. Sometimes a more extensive interview is required in order to accurately determine the nature of the problem. Specific techniques of questioning and strategies for teaching must be altered to meet the developmental needs of the individual. Nurses must be aware of their own limitations and must avoid purposeless gathering of intimate information. Similarly, the inexperienced nurse must avoid attempting to provide therapy; if the client requests help, the nurse is responsible for suggesting resources and providing encouragement to the client.

THE BASIC LEVEL

The sexual history interview begins with a "universality statement." The content of the statement varies with the individual client's age and life situation. For example, with an adolescent, one might say, "Many kids have questions about sex. Some wonder about venereal disease or about kissing or about relationships with friends. What kinds of questions or concerns do you have?" Several subtle messages are conveyed by this opening: (1) It is normal to have questions: lots of people do; (2) questions can be simple (kissing) or complicated (relationships); (3) the nurse is willing to talk about sex, is fairly comfortable with the topic, and assumes that the client has questions.

Young adults may have questions or concerns about contraception, homosexuality, or masturbation; middle-aged adults may be concerned with menopause or physical changes; older adults' questions might include physical limitations or social restrictions on sexual activity. Regardless of developmental level, most clients have some questions which they may or may not be willing to share.

Why might a client deny concerns even when concerns are present? Perhaps the nurse's discomfort with sexual discussion is evident, despite efforts to appear at ease. Maybe the level of trust in the practitioner is not yet high enough for the client to confide in the nurse. The client may feel that the nurse is rushed or not really interested. Maybe the client simply is so surprised by the openness of the question that the client is unable to remember any questions.

If the client says that he or she has no questions, accept this answer and do not continue questions about sexuality. An appropriate response is, "That's fine that you haven't any questions now. If there is ever a sexual concern you'd like to talk about, I will be happy to discuss it with you." The nurse may think, based on other cues or prior knowledge, that the client does have a sexual problem. Remember that the client is the one who can best decide when he or she is ready to discuss these issues with the nurse. By merely asking the basic level question, the nurse gives permission to the client to bring up sexual questions at a later time.

If a question or concern is presented, listen to the entire problem. Sometimes what may seem to be the question is not the question at all. The nurse, by clarifying terminology, sequences, and details, can identify the concern. Encourage the client to describe the situation using terminology that is most comfortable for the client (not necessarily terms which are most comfortable for the nurse). The concern may not be a specific problem at all but may be an opportunity for the client to "check out" with a health professional something that was heard or read about. The client may be "testing" to see whether the problem shocks the nurse. Perhaps all that is necessary is the assurance that the client's sexual activity is normal and acceptable.

Following identification of a problem, question, or concern, the nurse must decide whether he or she is competent to give information or suggestions. If the nurse is unsure, the client will feel insecure about the answer. If the technique or information given is wrong, the client suffers and the trust relationship between client and nurse is damaged. Therefore the inexperienced nurse must consider referral of the client to a more skillful counselor or may be able to find out the answer and report back to the client. Remember, wrong information is worse than no information.

INTERMEDIATE LEVEL (ADULT)

The sexual history form may be included as part of an initial health history. More than basic knowledge in the area of human sexuality is required, since many of the questions are designed to help in the identification of sexual problems. Not all questions are appropriate to all age groups, so the nurse must adapt the questions to meet the special needs of the particular client.

Ideally, the nurse knows the questions to ask without needing to refer to a written sheet. However, it is also acceptable to have the written questions available. Quick notes may be taken if necessary, but avoid extensive writing, which is time-consuming. The client also may wonder if what is being written down may appear in future medical records. Prior to asking the questions, be sure of a quiet, private place to talk and enough time for client education. Assure the client of the absolute confidentiality of the interview. Information recorded in the medical chart is carefully protected but is, of course, open to the client if he or she should wish to read it.

Begin on the basic level with a universality statement. It may be helpful to the client to know why sexual health is included in the health history. The nurse might say, "An important part of many people's lives is their sexual health. Sometimes physical health affects sexual health or vice versa. I'd like to ask some questions about your sexual health that will help me understand another important part of you."

The questions for adults are shown in Fig. 7-1. All questions are optional, and the nurse must assess the readiness of the client as the history taking progresses. Assure clients that if they choose not to answer a particular question, such a response is perfectly acceptable. The nurse may decide to skip some questions or to ask additional questions. This form merely provides a guideline of suggested questions.

1 When you were a child, how were your questions about sex answered (where did your sexual information come from)? (Appropriate for adolescents.)

When you were a teenager, how were your questions about sex answered? (Appropriate for adults.)

2 How did you first find out about sexual intercourse (how babies are made)? (Appropriate for adolescents and young adults.)

3 How would you describe your current sexual activity?

4 What, if anything, would you change about your current sexual activity?

5 At this time in your life, how important is a sexual relationship to you?

6 Do you have any concerns about birth control?

7 Do you have any health problems that, in your opinion, affect your sexual health or happiness?

8 Are you taking any medicines that, in your opinion, affect your sexual health or happiness?

9 Is there anything about these questions that you would like clarified or explained?

Figure 7-1 Sexual history (adult). *(Developed by M. Swenson.)*

Vignette

Based on data gathered during a sexual history interview, the following problem and progress note was added to the record of Suzanne, a 20-year-old woman who has come in to the family planning clinic for a premarital examination.

Problem List

1 Desires contraception
2 Fear of first intercourse

Subjective Data

My fiancé and I have been petting a lot, but we've never made love, partly because I don't want to get pregnant and partly because I'm scared it will hurt.

Objective Data

Somewhat anxious but able to respond well to questions. Pelvic examination reveals intact hymen and normal vagina and internal organs.

Assessment

Virgin whose anxiety regarding first intercourse is normal. Expect no physical problems with penetration.

Intervention

Given prescription and instructions for oral contraceptions (see problem 1). Discussed ways of reducing anxiety on honeymoon (a glass of wine before bed, adequate foreplay, use of sterile water-soluble lubricant—given tube of K-Y jelly); need for time to learn about own and partner's responses.

Plan

Return visit scheduled in 2 weeks; will bring fiancé. Discussion with Suzanne to cover external genital anatomy using a mirror. Suggest reading basic information on sexual response as found in Chap. 3 of this book.

INTERMEDIATE LEVEL (CHILD)

There are many reasons for interest in the sexual history of a child. One of the greatest benefits, however, may be the education of the parent which can take place during the interview. Subtle messages are conveyed which include that (1) children are sexual, (2) children normally ask questions about sex, (3) children need to know about reproduction, masturbation, menstruation, and nocturnal emissions (taking into consideration the child's age and developmental level), and (4) parents sometimes have difficulty coping with the sexuality of their children.

The interview begins on the basic level with a universality statement. For example, ''Many parents are concerned about sex education of their children. It will be helpful for me to know a little about your child's sexual history and what you have already thought about in connection with sexual health education.''

The questions are given in Fig. 7-2. Again. a parent may choose not to answer some of the questions. The nurse must assure the parent that it is all right to skip a question.

Most parents are not threatened by gentle questioning and are willing to discuss their concerns regarding their children's sexuality. However, as before, if the parent wishes not to answer any questions, that choice certainly is acceptable. Be sure to indicate that questions are welcome at any future time.

The form for the child may be adapted for questioning the child directly. The questions must be changed to accommodate the developmental level of the individual child, and the nurse must use utmost sensitivity in phrasing the questions, making special effort to use an understandable vocabulary. Using a book to read together and discuss is one way to base questions. *Where Did I Come From?* is an excellent example of a book that is simultaneously humorous and accurate. It is appropriate for children aged 4 to 10 or 12. The older child with more sophisticated knowledge might also appreciate *Show Me,* although this

1 How have you answered your child's questions about sex?

2 Who else does your child ask about sex?

3 How old was your child when you first talked about reproduction (intercourse, how babies are made)? Does your child know about menstruation? Erections? Wet dreams?

4 Describe your child's sexual activity:
   a When he or she was younger.
   b Now.
   c What changes do you expect in the next year?

5 Is there anything you would change about your child's sexual activity?

6 Do you have any concerns about your child's relationships with friends or with family members?

7 Is there anything you think your child needs to or wants to know that you are unable to discuss with him or her?

8 Would you like help from someone in discussing that difficult area?

9 Do you have any questions about your own sexuality, sexual activity, or sexual health?

Figure 7-2 Sexual history (child). *(Developed by M. Swenson.)*

book is sexually explicit and should not be used without prior approval from the parents.

Questions could include the following:

1 Did you find out anything new from this book about sex?
2 What other questions do you have?
3 Who can you talk to about your questions or go to if you need any help?

Vignette

Freddie is 8 years old.

Problem List

1 Normal growth and development
2 Immunizations
3 Sex education

Subjective Data

Expresses willingness when asked if he would like to read a book with nurse and his mother.

Objective Data

Normal growth and development. Freddie's mother is about 5 months pregnant. Freddie curious about book he saw on nurse's shelf.

Assessment

Freddie needs to discuss pregnancy and may have other questions relating to sexuality. His mother feels uneasy about bringing up the subject of sex and needs role model to learn how to be "askable."

Intervention

Read *Where Did I Come From?* together. Freddie learned to use word "penis" and was interested that the baby inside his mother moved and had fingernails. Questions about umbilical cord, twins, and "how does the baby get out?" were answered, using book and drawing pictures. Freddie says he will ask his mother if he thinks of any questions.

Plan

Ask for questions again at next visit; encourage mother to continue discussion at home and to include father as well.

ADVANCED LEVEL

No nurse, regardless of educational level, can function safely as a sexual therapist without specialized training in a supervised clinical setting. This training may take several months to several years. It is more than a weekend workshop or a single college course or one supervised interview. The training involves intensive reading, long hours of clinical work, interaction with an experienced therapist, and practice in caseload management. Crisis intervention and psychotherapeutic models are incorporated, as well as behavior modification and specific sex therapy techniques. The American Association of Sex Educators, Counselors, and Therapists publishes lists of certified professionals whose education, background, and experience qualify them as sex therapists.

Dr. Jack Annon[1] suggests the following guidelines for taking a sexual problem history prior to brief therapy:

1 Description of current problem
2 Onset and course of problem
    a Onset (age, gradual or sudden precipitating events, contingencies)

  b Course (change over time: increase, decrease, or fluctuation in severity, frequency, or intensity; any functional relationships)
3 Client's concept of cause and maintenance of problem
4 Past treatment and outcome
  a Medical evaluation (specialty, date, form of treatment, results, currently on any medication for any reason?)
  b Professional help
  c Self-treatment (type and results)
5 Current expectancies and goals of treatment (concrete or ideal)[2]

Knowing the focus of a sexual problem history can enable the nurse to prepare the client for entry into sexual counseling or therapy. By knowing the kinds of questions that may arise in discussion with a therapist, the nurse can help prepare the client for coping with the interview. Anticipatory guidance in this situation means explaining to the client why sexual counseling might be helpful, what information the counselor might need to know, what kind of results might be obtained, and how much time and energy it might require. The more preparatory information a nurse can provide, the less likely that the client will be frightened or threatened by the idea of sexual therapy.

Many people fear sex therapy. Myths and misconceptions abound: sex therapy is only for "perverts," sex therapy gets too personal, sex therapy is threatening or demeaning, and so on. If the nurse who refers the client feels confident and optimistic about the results of counseling by a competent professional, this feeling will encourage the client to seek help. Of course, success is not guaranteed: the client (and sex partner, if possible) must want help and must be willing to accept some responsibility for the investment of energy and attention. Some sexual counselors offer a sliding fee scale, based on ability to pay. Some insurance policies provide full or partial coverage for psychological counseling of this nature. It is especially helpful to have a list of available counselors or clinics, including fee schedules if possible. Together the referring nurse and client can decide where help can most easily and appropriately be found.

SUMMARY

Nurses are becoming more aware of the sexual concerns of their clients and are including teaching human sexuality in their routine health promotion. The sexual history provides a convenient way to begin the discussion of sexuality with a client, and the information obtained becomes a valuable part of the data base. In addition, the sexual history enables the nurse to assess areas in which a particular client needs further teaching or needs referral to appropriate helping resources.

Self-assessment is the key to effective intervention in the realm of human sexuality. Clients need to know that information they receive is accurate, is not obscured by judgmental attitudes, and is kept confidential. Under these conditions the discussion of sexual concerns will contribute to a trusting rapport between client and nurse.

LEARNING ACTIVITIES

1 Role-play taking a sexual history in dyads in class. Focus on use of terminology, assurance of privacy and confidentiality, and clarification of "client's" response.

2 Select a friend, relative, or client. Tape-record a sexual history, then later construct a problem list and a client assessment.

3 Discuss the following questions in a small group:
   a Is taking a sexual history an invasion of the client's privacy?
   b What should a nurse do if he or she is too embarrassed to introduce the topic of sex?
   c How would you respond to a client who is very uncomfortable with the discussion of sexuality?

SUGGESTED READING

Annon, J. S.: "Brief Therapy," in *The Behavioral Treatment of Sexual Problems,* vol. I, Enabling Systems, Honolulu, 1974.

Fleischhauer-Hardt, Helga: *Show Me,* St. Martin's, New York, 1975.

Green, R.: "Taking a Sexual History," in *Human Sexuality: A Health Practitioner's Text,* Williams & Wilkins, Baltimore, 1975.

Mayle, Peter: *Where Did I Come From?* Lyle Stuart, Secaucus, N.J., 1973.

Roznoy, M.: "Taking a Sexual History," *Am. J. Nurs.* **76**(8):1279–1282 (1976).

REFERENCES

1 J. S. Annon, "Brief Therapy," in *The Behavioral Treatment of Sexual Problems,* vol. I, Enabling Systems, Honolulu, 1974.

2 Ibid., pp. 100–101.

Chapter 8

Physical Examination with Sexual Health Teaching*

The gynecologic examination of the female patient is most appropriately viewed as a component of a complete physical examination, especially if a data base is being obtained or questions related to the general health of the client need to be answered. Unfortunately, the physical examination of the breasts and the female genitalia is frequently given insufficient time or is referred to another health provider. Commonly, this is a reflection of the examiner's discomfort rather than that of the client. The nurse can use the gynecologic examination for data collection beyond physical findings. Additional history can be obtained. Also, the examination is an excellent client teaching opportunity. When women are given permission and the time to discuss the structure and function of their bodies, an exchange of information takes place that is rewarding to the client and the health provider: the client may remember information she was unable to recall during the history and she may feel that this is a more comfortable time to ask questions. The learning aspect of the physical examination can be enhanced if the client agrees to having her sexual partner present during the examination.

Before performing gynecologic examinations, the nurse should be well aware of his or her comfort level with the content area. Nurses also need to recognize the scope of their ability in interpretation of the findings. Referral or

*By Judith Bautch, R. N., M. S. N. Associate Clinical Professor, University of Wisconsin; Clinical Nurse Specialist/Practioner, University Hospitals and Clinics.

consultation may be necessary. Information from the client's history will be important for interpreting physical findings, directing the examination, and determining specimens that should be obtained. Therefore, the sexual history should be obtained first.

This chapter has been specifically designed to provide the nurse with the following:

1 Procedure for performance of gynecologic examinations
2 Procedure for performance of examinations of male genitalia
3 Interpretation of normal physical findings
4 Suggested information for patient education

This chapter discusses the procedure for a complete examination of the genitals with associated teaching. An examination this complete is not always necessary nor appropriate. The nurse will decide which components of the examination are necessary based on the reason for the examination and approved procedure in the clinical setting.

Before the physical examination is begun, the nurse should discuss with clients exactly what will be done during the examination. This should include what specimens are likely to be taken and the positioning and the sensations they will experience. The female patient should have an opportunity to decide if she would like to "participate in the examination" by using a mirror to observe the examination. She should also decide either alone or with her sexual partner regarding participation. Partners enjoy a moment of privacy from the examiner to discuss the examination and decide about joint participation.

PREPARATION FOR THE GYNECOLOGIC EXAMINATION

The examination room should be warm and have adequate lighting. If the patient can hear voices from adjoining rooms or the hallway, there will be no assurance that discussion during her examination will not be heard by others. Measures should be taken to ensure that the examination will not be interrupted by other persons or the telephone.

Equipment and supplies should be available, functional, and within reach of the examiner. The routine gynecologic examination requires the following:

Patient gown
Drape (optional)
Hand mirror
Flashlight
Vaginal speculum (warmed) (Fig. 8-1)
Clean examination gloves
Water-soluble lubricant
Adjustable light
Stool for examiner

If laboratory specimens are required, the following may be needed:

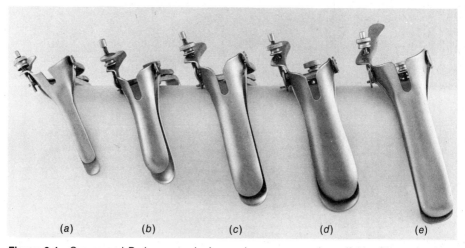

Figure 8-1 Graves and Pederson vaginal specula are commonly available. Size varies from small to large: (*a*), (*c*), and (*e*) Pederson; (*b*) and (*d*) Graves.

Sterile cotton-tipped applicators (for cytology and preparation of cultures and smears)
Thayer-Martin culture plate (for gonorrhea cultures)
Glass slides and cover slips (for cytology and microscopic examination)
Potassium hydroxide 10% solution (for smear for fungus)
Normal saline solution (smears for *Trichomonas*)
Spatula with rounded and bifid ends (cytology)
Fixative solution (for preparing cytology slide)

The client should be instructed not to douche or use any vaginal medications, creams, or jelly during the 24 hours prior to her examination. She should empty her bladder just prior to the examination. The patient should be asked to use a gown and remove all clothing. If the stirrups on the examination table are not padded, the client will be more comfortable if she is allowed to leave her shoes on. (Sheepskin stirrup pads are available, or folded towels can be used.)

EXAMINATION OF THE BREASTS

The breast examination (Table 8-1) is an ideal time for the nurse to determine if the client has adequate information and proper technique to perform monthly self-examinations. If the patient says she does her own examinations, the nurse can ask her when it is in the menstrual cycle and to demonstrate her technique. If she performs her examination 1 week after her period starts and the technique is good, there is excellent opportunity to reinforce the client's practices. If the technique is improper or incomplete, proper methods can be taught. (Most commonly, women neglect to visually inspect their breasts.) If the patient needs teaching, the nurse can demonstrate the technique and ask the patient to repeat the demonstration. Excellent pamphlets are available to be given to clients to

Table 8-1 The Breast Examination

Procedure	Suggested comments to client	Interpretation of findings
Inspection		
The client sits at the foot of the examination table in adequate lighting. The gown is removed to the waist. Breasts are inspected for symmetry, contour, lesions, evidence of inflammation, dimpling, orange-peel appearance, nipple retraction, inversion, deviation, or discharge.	The breast examination should be done 1 week after your period begins. (Women who do not have a period select a timed monthly event to help them remember.) Inspection is a very important part of your monthly examination. A good place to do it is in front of a mirror or where you can see both breasts simultaneously. Inspect for size, asymmetry (more than usual), lumps, nipple changes, discharge, skin changes, or changes in breast contour. You will quickly become the best expert in what your breasts look and feel like. If you should find a change or mass, it is appropriate to consult your health professional soon, but do not assume it is cancer. Examinations and/or tests will need to be done.	Estrogen levels during this time are lower and the breasts will be less engorged and tender. The consistency of breast tissue changes through the cycle, especially if there is fibrocystic disease. One breast is usually larger or more pendulous than the other. An increase in difference is abnormal. An underlying lesion may be suspected if abnormalities are identified.
The nurse should demonstrate these maneuvers to the client. Inspect as above.	Now raise both arms straight over your head. Inspect your breasts for the same things you did before. Turn your torso to the side in front of your mirror so you can see all parts of your breast. Place your hands on your hips. Press your hands into your hips. This muscle contraction causes your breasts to become more erect. Inspect them as you did before.	Same as above.
In some patients with very large or pendulous breasts, have patient extend her arms and lean forward.	Place your hands in front of you—now lean forward.	Same as above.

Palpation

The patient is lying on the examination table. A small pillow is placed under the shoulder on the side of the breast to be examined. Arm on same side is placed under the head. Remove gown to expose breast to be examined. Elevation of the shoulder allows the breast to spread more evenly over anterior chest. If the client has small breasts, she can be taught to do self-palpation in either a sitting position or lying down. Some women like to perform breast examinations while they are in the tub or shower.

If areas of thickening or the ribs are palpated by the examiner, the client should be helped to identify the same normal findings.

Repeat same procedure on other side.

It is important that you examine your breasts regularly and in a systematic manner. Use the "flats" of your fingers and gently and with a rotating motion compress breast tissue between your fingers and ribs. "Inch" your way around the breast examining a small area at a time. The breast can be thought of as a clock. Proceed in clockwise fashion, spiraling toward the areola. Go around the breast as many times as necessary to examine all areas. Compress the area around the nipple (areola) and observe for discharge. Compress nipple between thumb and index finger. Look for discharge.

Clients commonly misinterpret ribs or the ridge of tissue at the inferior border as a "lump." Important to include the "tail" of the breast which extends from the upper outer quadrant into the axilla. Normal pre-menopausal breast tissue is smooth and firm in consistency. During ovulation breast tissue may become tender and engorged. During pregnancy breasts enlarge and become more tender. There may be increased pigmentation of areola. After pregnancy breasts may retain some increased size and pigmentation. With aging breast tissue becomes less elastic and may become "ropy" or "stringy" in consistency. Breasts may become more pendulous without estrogen stimulation.

help them remember the technique at home. Some women find self-examination of their breasts objectionable, but will allow another individual (e.g., husband) to be taught the examination. Responsibility for breast self-examination should be given only to those women who are comfortable with the procedure and trust themselves. Women who are uncomfortable doing their own should be sure to have a yearly one by their health professional.

THE PELVIC EXAMINATION

The client is placed in the dorsolithotomy position, with her feet in stirrups (Table 8-2). If the patient wishes to participate in her examination, the head of the examination table is raised to 45 degrees with a pillow behind her head. She is given the mirror and flashlight and the examiner makes certain that the patient is able to visualize her genitalia. While this may be an uncomfortable position to assume, some clients express feeling "less vulnerable" in this position and appreciate being able to have eye contact with the examiner. The drape obstructs the client's view so it is not used unless some form of draping is necessary for warmth or for the psychological comfort of the woman. If the client does not wish to participate in her examination, the head of the table can be raised to 30 degrees. The traditional draping procedure for the dorsolithotomy position can be used. The drape between the client's knees is lowered to the abdomen. This enables the client to have eye contact with the examiner and the examiner can observe the client's facial expressions during the examination.

EXAMINATION OF THE MALE GENITALIA

The general principles related to the gynecologic examination in women that were discussed at the beginning of this chapter are appropriate for the male genital examination (Table 8-3). The examination consists of inspection and palpation components and no special equipment or supplies are needed unless cultures are necessary. If the examiner is female, it is appropriate that gloves be worn to decrease tactile stimulation during the examination. It is important for the examiner to discuss with the client prior to the examination the possibility of him having an erection. This should be described as a normal, although somewhat embarrassing, occurrence.

BIBLIOGRAPHY

Anthony, C. P., and N. J. Kolthoff: *Textbook of Anatomy and Physiology,* Mosby, St. Louis, 1975.
Bates, Barbara: *A Guide to Physical Examination,* Lippincott, Philadelphia, 1974.
Green, Thomas H., Jr.: *Gynecology Essentials for Clinical Practice,* 3d ed., Little, Brown, Boston, 1977.
Malasanos, Lois, et al.: *Health Assessment,* Mosby, St. Louis, 1977.
Sherman, Jacques L., and Sylvia K. Fields: *Guide to Patient Evaluation,* 3d ed., Medical Examination, Garden City, N.Y., 1978.

Table 8-2 The Pelvic Examination

Procedure	Suggested comments to client	Interpretation of findings
Inspection	Examination of the external genitalia	
The client is given the hand-held mirror and instructed in its use. The examiner sits on a stool in front of patient with light directed toward vulva. Touch the internal thigh of the patient with one or both gloved hands. This will prepare the patient for touching more sensitive areas.	Hold the mirror at arm's length between your legs so you can see your vulva. It is difficult to do, but it will help you relax if you allow your legs to fall as far apart as you can. The first thing I am going to do is to inspect the areas of your external genitalia (vulva). I will point out structures as I go.	For a review of anatomy see Chap. 3, Figs. 3-3 to 3-6.
Inspect area for excoriation, parasites, nits, edema, skin lesions, or changes in pigmentation.	This is your mons, the pad over your pubic bone. The hair distribution (escutcheon) is normal for a female and I do not see any skin changes or lesions.	Female escutcheon is an inverted triangle in shape. Sparse hair toward umbilicus is normal. Pubic hair is sparse in adolescence; full, curly, and coarse in adulthood; thinning and graying with age.
Inspect as above.	The mons extends downward and forms the large lips (labia majora) which are covered on the outside with hair. The labia majora and the covering of hair function as a protection for the more-sensitive inner structures. Inside the labia majora are the small lips (labia minora). They are like folds of skin directly surrounding the vaginal opening.	Asymmetry of the labia minora without inflammation is a common finding. The mucous membranes of the labia are dark pink and moist. Labia in a nulliparous client closely approximate. After vaginal delivery labia tend to remain open. Labia of a premenopausal woman will have a full appearance. Postmenopausal labia may appear atrophic and pale.
Separate the labia. Labia can be held apart with one hand while structures are identified and pointed out to the patient. It may be helpful to use a cotton-tipped applicator as a pointer.		
Retract hood of clitoris. Inspect for edema, lesions, collection of secretions.	The labia minora meet near the mons to form the hood for the clitoris. The clitoris in the female is analogous to the male penis. It varies in size among individuals and is a site of pleasurable sensation. It becomes engorged and slightly erect with stimulation. Sometimes it is too sensitive to touch directly.	The hood of the clitoris should easily retract. Clitoris is not greater than 1 cm wide and 2 cm long.

143

Table 8-2 The Pelvic Examination (continued)

Procedure	Suggested comments to client	Interpretation of findings
Inspect urethral opening for discharge or signs of inflammation.	Just below the clitoris is the urinary meatus. The area between these structures is the vestibule. The paraurethral glands (Skene's) open into the urethra but they are not normally visualized.	The urinary meatus may be star-shaped. Signs of inflammation or discharge are abnormal. Skene's gland ducts are not normally visualized.
Inspect for any obvious vaginal wall relaxation.	The large opening is the introitus to the vagina. Within the introitus is the maidenhead (hymen). It is always present but changes from its initial form as a circle of tissue around the vaginal opening. It can be (perforated) opened in many ways in addition to intercourse. Some examples might be participating in athletics, biking, and possibly the use of tampons.	Intact (virginal) hymen will appear as a thin circular membrane around the introitus with an opening at the center. A partially intact hymen may appear crescent-shaped. More commonly portions of hymenal ring appear as tags or flaps of tissue, the same color as the vagina and labia.
Inspect ductal area for inflammation or discharge. Area over gland inspected for erythema or edema.	The Bartholin s glands are located behind and to the sides of the vagina. Their ducts open into the vagina. They cannot be visualized but they play an important ro e by secreting a lubricating fluid during sexual intercourse.	Bartholin's glands or ducts are not normally visualized. Signs of inflammation or discharge at ductal opening or area of edema over the gland is abnormal.
Inspect for episiotomy scar. Inspect area for external hemorrhoids. Using the medical term with the definition provides the client with correct terminology for discussing her body.	The fourchette is the fold of skin below the vagina where the labia come together. The perineum (perineal body) is this muscular area from the vagina to the anus. It is in this area that an incision (episiotomy) is made to prevent tearing of tissues during a vaginal delivery. At the lower area of the perineum is the terminal end of the intestine (anus).	Inspect as above.

Palpation
Palpate mons, labia

Use water to lubricate index finger of hand that will be internal hand. Lubricating jelly invalidates laboratory specimens. (Texts differ in opinion regarding which hand should be internal vs. external. Examiner should use most comfortable method, use it consistently, and work toward perfecting skills.)

I am palpating the vulva for any masses. Is there any tenderness anywhere?

Tissues should be soft, without masses or tenderness.

Separate labia with external hand. Insert index finger into vagina and identify location of cervix. Question for tenderness. Gently "milk" the urethra from inside the vagina to the external orifice. Any discharge from urethra or Skene's ducts should be observed and cultures obtained.

I am inserting one finger into your vagina to locate your cervix. Any tenderness?
Then I will compress the urethra to look for signs of inflammation. (When normal findings are elicited the client should be told.)

The cervix feels similar to the cartilage on the end of the nose. Determining the location of the cervix will be helpful later during the speculum examination. Tenderness with palpation of the cervix is abnormal and indicates inflammation. Discharge from the urethra or Skene's ducts is abnormal.

Gently insert index and middle fingers into vagina. Palpate perineal body for consistency or scarring. Have client tighten pelvic muscles against fingers to assess strength of pubococcygeus muscle.

I'm now inserting two fingers into the vagina and feeling the perineal muscle for strength—now squeeze down on my fingers. Use the same muscles that are used when you try to stop urination (Kegal's maneuver).

Perineal body with good muscle strength will feel firm, smooth, and rounded. After episiotomy, area feels thinner and more fibrotic. Weakened vaginal musculature may decrease sexual satisfaction of both partners. (This method is only an estimate of strength, and more objective measurement methods are available.)

Palpate posterolateral vaginal area between thumb on exterior and index and middle finger on interior of vagina for Bartholin's gland enlargement or tenderness.

At the posterior sides of the vagina I'm palpating the Bartholin's gland.

Gland not normally palpable. Tenderness indicates inflammation.

Spread the internal fingers laterally. Ask the client to perform the Valsalva maneuver.
Observe for incontinence of urine, urethrocele, cystocele, rectocele, enterocele, or uterine prolapse.

My fingers are holding the vagina open. Push down as if you were to have a bowel movement. This is when I am looking for any weakening or relaxation of the vaginal wall or muscles.

Normally there is slight movement of vaginal tissues. Protrusion of vaginal wall is abnormal. In uterine prolapse the cervix protrudes through the vagina to or through the introitus.

Table 8-2 The Pelvic Examination (continued)

Procedure	Suggested comments to client	Interpretation of findings
	Examination of internal genitalia (Fig. 8-2)	

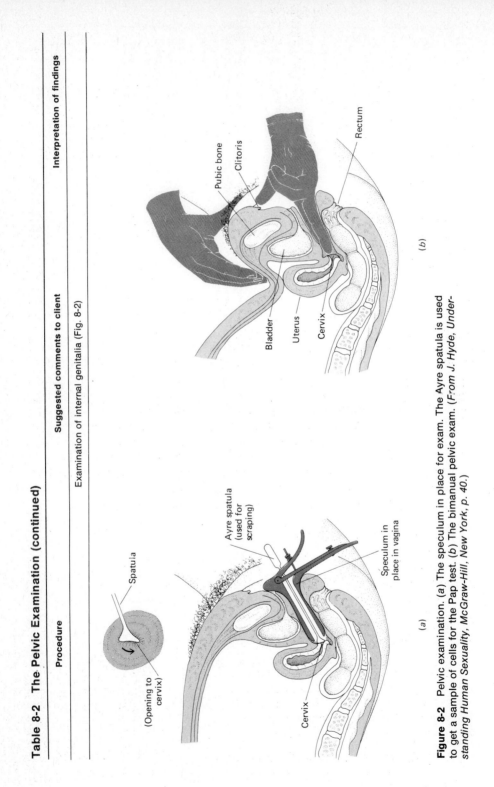

Figure 8-2 Pelvic examination. (a) The speculum in place for exam. The Ayre spatula is used to get a sample of cells for the Pap test. (b) The bimanual pelvic exam. (*From J. Hyde, Understanding Human Sexuality, McGraw-Hill, New York, p. 40.*)

Inspection

If not done earlier, allow the client to see the speculum in both open and closed position (Speculum has been warmed.) Touch internal aspect of thigh with speculum to ensure body temperature. (This procedure necessary only with a metal speculum.)

Separate the labia with the thumb and middle finger of external hand. The index finger can be used to guard the anterior aspect of the introitus against pressure or bumping with the speculum.

Place the blades of the speculum between index and middle finger with the thumb over the handle end.

Insert the speculum at an oblique angle into the vagina (i.e., sides of blades directed toward two and eight o'clock) toward the area where the cervix was palpated earlier. Insert speculum approximately 5–6 cm or until the fingers rest against the labia. Rotate blades to transverse position. Use the internal hand on the handle of the speculum to maintain a posterior pressure. With the internal hand, open speculum blades to visualize the cervix. Tighten the screw to keep blades open.

Obtain specimens for cytology, culture, or slides for microscopic examination.

Assist the client to visualize the cervix. The light from the flashlight held by the client is directed onto the mirror and reflected onto the cervix and vagina. The examiner's adjustable light can be repositioned and used in same manner. (This allows the client one free hand.) The examiner will be aware of the structures visible to the client because they will "light up" with the reflected light.

I will insert the speculum into the vagina in a closed position and when it is in all the way I will open the blades to allow visualization of the lower part of the uterus (cervix) and vagina. How is this for temperature?

You will feel a pressure sensation. If you feel pain, let me know.

The speculum is in now. I am going to open the blades. You will feel pressure. . . .

A simple maneuver, but women often verbalize appreciation of a warm speculum.

The anterior aspect of the vagina is very pressure sensitive. Most of the discomfort of the speculum examination can be prevented by carefully avoiding pressure anteriorly. The posterior aspect tolerates pressure well.

This prevents the blades from opening and pinching sensitive vaginal tissue.

It is not uncommon to be unable to visualize the cervix during the first attempt. Withdraw the speculum partially and reinsert as done previously. A more posterior direction is usually necessary.

The vagina prior to menopause is a highly distensible, laterally rugated tube which is 7-8 cm long. The mucous membrane lining is pink and moist. After menopause there may be fewer or no rugae; the membranes become drier and easily friable. The nulliparous cervix extends into the vagina 1-3 cm. It is 2-3 cm in diameter, round, smooth, and the same pink color of the vagina. A bluish discoloration of the cervix is a sign of pregnancy (Chadwick's sign). It becomes more pale postmenopause. After pregnancy the cervix diameter can

Table 8-2 The Pelvic Examination (continued)

Procedure	Suggested comments to client	Interpretation of findings
		enlarge to 5 cm and the cervical os increases from a nulliparous round 3–5 mm to an uneven lateral slit variable in length. A common benign finding is a cervical eversion. This occurs when the red, vascular, columnar epithelium and the pink squamous epithelium meet on the ectocervix rather than the endocervix. This appears as a red, smooth ring around the os, different from an erosion which appears rough, irregular, and easily friable. A cervical-eversion appearance can be created if pressure from speculum blades opens the cervical os.
	The cervix looks like a doughnut or pink rubber ring. The opening in the center is the os.	
	Discuss findings and interpretation with the client.	The characteristics of vaginal secretions are influenced by phase of the menstrual cycle, vaginal flora, and desquamation of epithelium. The amount varies, consistency ranges from watery to mucoid, and color from clear to milky white. A malodorous discharge is abnormal.
After the cervix is inspected and specimens obtained, the blades of the speculum are partially closed. As the speculum is withdrawn, the blades are rotated to complete inspection of the vagina.	I am inspecting the walls of the vagina as I am removing the speculum.	
This completes the inspection of the internal genitalia. The light (accessory) can be turned off. If the patient desires, the head of the examination table can be lowered to 30 degrees. This will facilitate the bimanual examination.		

Palpation

The examiner stands in front of the client. The index and middle fingers of the internal hand are well-lubricated. The thumb is abducted and ring and little fingers are flexed on palm. The labia are separated with the external hand and the examining fingers, closely approximated, are gently introduced into the vagina. The fingers should enter the vagina in the vertical plane with pressure exerted toward the posterovaginal wall. When the fingers are in the vagina, the hand is supinated. The palmar pads of the fingers are more sensitive than the tips or posterior surface and should be used for palpation. The vaginal walls are palpated for tenderness, masses, or relaxation. The cervix is identified and assessed for consistency, size, contour, mobility, and tenderness. All surfaces of the cervix are palpated. The anterior, posterior, and lateral fornices are palpated for tumors, scars, or tenderness.

The index finger is gently inserted into the external os of the cervix. The external hand is placed on the abdomen at the level of the umbilicus. Firm pressure is used to bring the pelvic contents toward the internal hand and held in position for palpation by the internal hand. In addition to assessing for size, shape, tenderness, consistency, and mobility, an evaluation of uterine position is made.

I am putting my fingers into the vagina. Again, you will feel pressure but should not feel pain. If you are able to relax, the examination will be more comfortable and provide more complete information. This is the last procedure of the examination and it has two parts: abdominovaginal and rectovaginal. You may have some discomfort as I turn my hand. I am paying special attention to the size, shape, position, consistency, and mobility of the uterus. I will also try to feel your ovaries. Ovaries are not always felt.

I'm using my hand on your abdomen to hold the uterus against the examining hand.

Share findings with the client as the examination progresses.

It is difficult to perform an adequate bimanual examination if the woman is obese or is tense and has rigid abdominal musculature.

The cervix feels similar to the tip of the nose. It should be firm, smooth, nontender, and freely mobile in any direction 1–2 cm. The cervix becomes soft in pregnancy and hardens with tumors.

The external os should admit a finger to 0.5 cm. Identification of the cervical os helps the examiner determine the position of the uterus.

The nulliparous uterus is pear-shaped 6–8 cm long, 3–4 cm wide, and 2–2.5 cm in anteroposterior diameter. After pregnancy the uterus may remain enlarged 2–3 cm in any dimension. The uterus should be smooth, firm, moveable in all planes, and without tenderness. The uterus may lie in several positions: midposition, anteverted, or retroverted. A uterus in an anteverted position can also be anteflexed (flexed upon itself). A retroverted uterus can also be retroflexed.

Table 8-2 The Pelvic Examination (continued)

Procedure	Suggested comments to client	Interpretation of findings
Palpation of the adenexal areas is done by directing the fingers of the internal hand anteriorly and into the lateral fornices. The external hand is placed below the iliac crest on the same side. Both hands are in a slightly cupped position and move downward and medially, allowing tissues to "slip" through hands. Palpate for ovary size, shape, symmetry, masses, areas of tenderness. Same procedure on other side.	The ovaries are located to the sides of the uterus. They are small and not always felt. As the ovary slips through my hands, you will experience a very brief "twinge" of discomfort. This is normal. The fallopian tubes are very small and not normally felt.	The ovary is 3 × 4 cm, sensitive, and mobile. The ovulating ovary may increase in size to 6 cm. This will be a unilateral finding. It is abnormal to find a prepuberal or postmenopausal ovary greater than 4 cm in any diameter. Fallopian tubes are not palpable.
Further lubrication of the glove may be necessary. The rectovaginal examination is accomplished by placing the index finger in the vagina and the middle finger into the rectum. The client is asked to perform a Valsalva maneuver to relax the anal sphincter for easier insertion of the finger. The rectovaginal septum is palpated for masses or relaxation. The posterior fornix is examined for masses. The rectal walls are palpated for masses.	This may be uncomfortable to you. Push down as if you were having a bowel movement. I will put one finger in the vagina and another in the rectum.	The rectovaginal examination is mostly confirmatory. However, this is the only way in which a retroverted uterus can be palpated.
This completes the pelvic examination. The patient is provided with tissues for removal of lubricating jelly. She is assisted to a sitting position and allowed to dress.	The examination is complete. You might like to wipe yourself off. Be sure to move your buttocks to the head of the table before you sit up. There is nothing under you now.	If a stool specimen is to be examined for blood, gloves should be either changed or washed between abdominovaginal and rectovaginal examinations because of the possibility of false-positive results.

Table 8-3 Examination of Male Genitalia

Procedure	Suggested comments to client	Interpretation of findings
Inspection The client either stands with the examiner seated on a stool in front of him or is lying on the examination table. Clothing from the waist to the knees has been removed.		For a review of anatomy see Chap. 3, Figs. 3-1 and 3-2.
Observe hair distribution. Inspect skin for chancres, parasites, nits, excoriation, tumors, or other lesions. Important to inspect all areas of penis and scrotum.	I'm looking at the hair distribution (escutcheon) and checking the skin for any lesions or changes. The penis consists of three parts: anteriorly are two corpora cavernosa and posteriorly the corpus spongiosum, which contains the urethra. These three ''tubes'' extend the length of the shaft of the penis. The corpus spongiosum enlarges and forms the head (glans) which also covers the ends of the corpora cavernosa. The ridge (corona) forms where the glans attaches to the shaft of the penis. The skin on the penis is normally thin and loose. The portion that extends beyond the corona over the	The male escutcheon is a triangle with the apex toward the umbilicus. The scrotum is covered with some hair but none is present on the penis. Hair is sparse in adolescence, dense in middle years, and thinning and graying with age. Skin of the penis and scrotum is thin and darker than the rest of the body.
If prepuce is present, retract and inspect area of corona for collection of secretions.	glans is the foreskin (prepuce). A circumcision is the surgical removal of the prepuce. If it is present, it should retract freely to allow for proper cleansing. The size of the nonerect penis is highly variable among men and is not a reflection of sexual functioning. There is little difference among men in the size of the erect penis.	The prepuce should retract easily. A phimosis is present when the prepuce will not retract over the glans. A paraphimosis exists if the prepuce is retracted but cannot be placed over the glans.
Inspect the urethral meatus for signs of inflammation or discharge. It should be located at the tip of the glans.		Urethral inflammation or discharge is abnormal. A discharge should be cultured. Hypospadias is a condition in which the urethral meatus is located more proximally and on the ventral surface of the penis. An epispadias exists when the urethral opening is on the dorsal aspect of the penis.
Clients worry that an abnormality will be found. The examiner should share findings as the examination proceeds.	The scrotum consists of a muscular sac covered with loose skin. It has two compartments. Each contains a testis, the epididymis, and the vas deferens.	The testes are supported in the scrotal sac by the dartos muscle and the spermatic cord. The left is usually lower than the right. With age the dartos muscle relaxes and the scrotum becomes more pendulous.
Palpation Palpate the length of the penis for lesions. Apply anteroposterior pressure to the glans. This will open the meatus. Observe discharge or inflammation. (The client can be instructed to do this.)	I am palpating for any lesions. Some men develop painless lesions in the soft tissues.	Penile discharge is abnormal. If infection is suspected or the client complains of discharge, cultures should be obtained.
	Hold the glans between your thumb and forefinger. Squeeze gently. This is a method to check for discharge.	
If it is necessary to obtain a specimen, ''milk'' the penis from the base to the glans by grasping with thumb and index finger. With gentle pressure ''strip'' tissues between fingers. (The patient can be instructed to do this.)		

Table 8-3 Examination of Male Genitalia (continued)

Procedure	Suggested comments to client	Interpretation of findings
Grasp the scrotum in midline using the index and middle fingers of the right hand in a scissorslike motion. The right testis will be stabilized by the examiner's right hand. Bimanual examination is now possible using the palpating surfaces of the left fingers. Palpate for size, contour, masses, tenderness of the testes. The scrotal sac contents are also examined for presence of fluid, hernias, masses. Repeat procedure for left using opposite hands.	Now I will examine each of the testes, the epididymis, and the spermatic cord. The testes are sensitive to pressure but not tender. Let me know if you feel discomfort. The vas deferens (seminal duct) is part of the passageway for sperm from the testes into the abdominal cavity and eventually out through the penis. The male sterilization procedure (vasectomy) involves cutting the vas deferens, making sperm transport impossible.	The testes are firm but not hard, ovoid-shaped, approximately 4 cm long, 2.5 cm in anteroposterior diameter, and 2 cm wide. On the posterolateral aspect of the testes is the epididymis which is soft and crescent-shaped. As it extends upward to the upper pole of the testis it enlarges. This area is called the head of the epididymis. The epididymis is, in fact, a series of small tubes which come together to form the vas deferens (seminal duct) which forms a passageway into the abdominal cavity through the inguinal canal. A fibrous covering encloses the vas deferens, blood vessels, lymphatics, and nerve supply from the scrotum into the abdominal cavity. This is called the spermatic cord. It is palpated as a firm nontender cord.
Some health professionals feel it is advisable to teach the client to examine his own testes for early detection of testicular cancer. This is felt especially important in high-risk populations (i.e., history of undescended testicle at birth).	Your testes and scrotum feel normal. Now I'd like you to learn to examine yourself. This is an important way to find an early cancer if it should occur. You can learn what your testes feel like. Then, if changes occur, it is appropriate that they be brought to the attention of your health professional. Several kinds of nondangerous, benign changes can occur. If you detect a change, don't assume cancer. The large egglike structure is the testis. To the side and back is a soft piece of tissue, the epididymis. The cord or ropelike structure is the spermatic cord. Compare one side to the other. They should be equal. Sometimes the left testis is lower than the right because of a longer cord. The muscle in the scrotal sac also reacts to temperature and reflexes, elevating the testes on one side or the other. When you palpate the testes pay special attention to the firm but not hard texture. Also the contour is even and smooth. Any changes should be reported.	
The index finger is well-lubricated. The finger is placed over the anus and the patient is instructed to bear down. The finger is inserted into the rectum toward the umbilicus. The prostate gland is palpated for size, contour, consistency. Identify right and left lobes and midline fissure. Also palpate for seminal vessicles.	The last part of the examination involves the prostate gland. This necessitates doing a rectal examination. If you will lean over the examination table, you can rest your head on your arms on the table. Push down as if you were having a bowel movement. That will relax the sphincter and make the finger insertion less uncomfortable. The largest portion of the seminal fluid volume is secreted by the prostate gland. It is normally palpable. It is common for the gland to enlarge in older men and that may cause problems with urination.	This maneuver will cause the external sphincter to relax and allow more comfortable insertion of the finger. The prostate gland measures 4 × 3 cm on its palpable surface. The entire gland weighs 5–10 g. The prostate gland is located anterior to the rectum. It is smooth, firm, and rubbery in consistency. The right and left lobes should be symmetrical. The borders of the two lobes should be palpable as well as the midline fissure. The median lobe is anterior and not palpable. The prostate, although palpable through the thin rectal wall, should not protrude into the rectum. Prostatic enlargement is common in the elderly.

Table 8-3 Examination of Male Genitalia (continued)

Procedure	Suggested comments to client	Interpretation of findings
Palpate for the seminal vessicles which are in the area upward and lateral to the prostate.		The seminal vesicles are not usually palpable, but they may be felt as slightly corrugated structures.
The patient is provided with tissues for removal of lubricating jelly. He is instructed to put on his clothes.	This is the end of the examination.	

Part Three

Reproductive Decision Making

Chapter 9

Contraception

SEXUALITY, REPRODUCTION, AND DECISIONS

Men and women in a civilized society can make rational sexual decisions based on information about available choices. Family planning specialists, sex educators, and health professionals direct much energy toward providing information about the advantages and disadvantages of reproductive choices, especially in regard to contraceptive methods and pregnancy options. Unfortunately, not all people operate on the same decision-making model, and as a result, some professionals are frustrated and angered by the decisions made by clients. A decision that seems rational to a family planner may seem irrational to a client and vice versa. Decisions about sex, contraception, pregnancy, and abortion are heavily influenced by factors such as religion, culture, money, education, and age.

For the purposes of this chapter, a few assumptions are proposed:

    1 Both men and women make decisions about sexual intercourse, contraception, and pregnancy.

    2 Men and women may decide not to use contraception, even though they do not want a child.

    3 Decisions about birth control must be remade every time there is a change in sexual partners.

   4   A pregnancy can be unplanned and unwanted, unplanned and wanted, planned and unwanted, or planned and wanted.

   Several theories have been proposed to explain why women have unplanned pregnancies. The traditional family planning viewpoint is that women become pregnant because of ignorance of contraceptive methods or because of a lack of access to contraceptives. A "psychological" explanation is that women have an "instinctual" desire to be pregnant or that the pregnancy reflects an affiliative need or the replacement of a personal loss. Kristin Luker[1] recently proposed that women make rational decisions not to use contraception even though they do not want to have a baby. Some health practitioners believe that the male partners in an attempt to prove masculinity exert a strong influence on women not to use a birth control method and not to seek abortion.

   These various explanations will be examined in this chapter. Perhaps none of them completely explains the reproductive behavior of men and women. However, some suggestions for pragmatic intervention by nurses will be presented because nurses in many fields of practice are called upon to assist in the decision-making process. Reproductive decisions cannot be divorced from the sexuality of the decision makers; hence, the nurse must be aware of the sexual nature of human beings in order to adequately assist them in making these decisions.

Contraceptive Information

Family planning agencies exist to help women and men learn about contraceptive choices and make decisions about the spacing and number of children. The solutions seem relatively simple at first: explain the risks and benefits of each method, allow the person to choose a method, teach the specific method of choice, and help the person obtain the chosen supplies or devices. Of course, nothing is this easy in real life. Men and women have personal biases about particular contraceptives. Medical contraindications eliminate some choices. The sexual relationship, emotional atmosphere, and financial considerations affect the decision. Instructions are misunderstood or disregarded or forgotten. However, probably most of the women who are sure they want to prevent pregnancy do accurately and consistently use effective methods of birth control.

   Others lack sufficient knowledge about effective contraception. Old wives' tales and the well-meaning (although inaccurate) advice of family and friends can masquerade as birth control information. People who lack knowledge may be those people who do not expect to have have sexual intercourse or those who have not truly confronted their sexuality. Public information programs, school programs, and family planning education services in the community are geared to the needs of people who have inadequate information about birth control.

   Access to contraceptive services is a factor in their use. Financial barriers are common, as are age limits and legal constraints; therefore, minors and the poor are most likely to be affected by problems of access. Some states still have statutes prohibiting provision of contraceptives to adolescents without parental consent. Some areas lack clinic facilities for people unable to afford a private physician. Similar constraints apply to access to abortion facilities and adoption services.

Both men and women are affected by a pregnancy. Some are pregnant because they make a decision to have a child, because they made no decision about having a baby, or because they took a chance and risked a pregnancy even though they do not want a child.

Some people make no decisions about sexuality and reproduction. They do not see themselves as sexual beings or consider the possibility of a sexual relationship resulting in a pregnancy; therefore, they do not feel they need to know anything about birth control methods. Some of these people become pregnant and have babies, some do not. The unplanned pregnancies occasionally are welcomed, sometimes are merely tolerated, and often are totally unwanted.

Some women who use no method are aware that they are taking chances. They gamble intercourse against a possible pregnancy and have made a decision not to contracept. These women simply (or not so simply) decide not to use a birth control method even though they are aware they might get pregnant.

Why do these women choose to take such an enormous risk? Perhaps because the costs of contraception are high. Not financial costs necessarily, since most birth control methods cost less than, say, smoking cigarettes. (Most birth control methods are considerably safer than smoking as well.) Certainly contraception is cheaper than abortion or a term delivery. But the emotional costs can be high. Can the relationship withstand a discussion of a possible pregnancy? Are the partners able to share their feelings about sexuality?

The social costs also can be high. Is the woman, especially if she is young or unmarried, comfortable enough with her family doctor to tell him or her she needs a birth control method? And what if her parents find out? Parental consent is required by some physicians, making access to contraception difficult unless clinic facilities are available.

And health costs can be high. Not all women can safely use the birth control pill or the intrauterine device. If they cannot use the pill, some women say, then they will not use anything at all. Other methods are just "too much hassle."

The relative cost of a possible pregnancy, then, might seem low by comparison and the evaluation could be conscious or unconscious.

"If I get pregnant, I'll just get married. I was going to get married anyway."

"I love kids and I always wanted a large family. Might as well start now; going to college isn't that important anyway."

"When you have as many kids as I do, one more doesn't make much difference."

"My mother said if I had a baby she'd take care of it for me."

And the most common of all:

"I never thought it would happen to me."

To have or not to have children involves several important, separate decisions. The first is whether or not to recognize one's sexual self. Some people are unaware that healthy sexuality demands decisions: one must recognize sexual feelings in oneself and others, must be aware of the consequences of intercourse, must understand some of the anatomy of oneself and one's partner, and must accept responsibility for one's actions. Such complex knowledge as this can be learned from parents, from many excellent books, from sex educators and counselors, and from developmental experiences. Sexuality has many dimensions, including the need to learn gender identity (knowing you are male or female), to learn sex role behavior (acting like a male or a female), to learn intimacy and affection, to learn to be accepting of one's own body, and to learn a sexual value system. Ignorance, not knowledge, stimulates inappropriate decision making.

After a person has become aware of himself or herself as a healthy, sexual human being, the next decision is whether or not to have intercourse. The social, emotional, cultural, and religious risks and benefits must be considered carefully. Too often, this crucial decision is made on impulse at the spur of the moment. Sometimes no decision is made at all, and "things just happen." A person who has made no decision is extremely vulnerable to coercion and pressure from others, and may end up with a result he or she will regret.

Some benefits of a sexual relationship might be that intercourse is pleasurable, is an expression of love, produces desired pregnancy, and bonds the couple together. Risks might include a sexually transmitted disease, an unwanted pregnancy, a social nonacceptance (especially for unmarried people), or emotional vulnerability.

People should never have sexual intercourse if they do not want to. This "right to say no" includes young teens, adults, and the elderly. It includes children, the mentally and developmentally disabled, and married people.

If intercourse occurs, an additional decision arises: whether or not to conceive a child. If the person or couple decides they do not want a baby at this time, they usually seek some sort of contraceptive method. Sometimes they ask friends, or read magazines, or simply go to the drugstore and look around. Friends and family frequently provide well-intentioned, although erroneous, information. Others seek help at a birth control clinic such as Planned Parenthood or from their family doctor. This professional advice sometimes is misinterpreted or forgotten, leaving the person still at risk for pregnancy. Usually, however, a reliable contraceptive method such as the condom, foam, diaphragm, intrauterine device (IUD), birth control pills, or natural family planning will effectively prevent pregnancy. A tangential chain of decision making precedes the choice of a contraceptive method. Both men and women can be actively involved in the decision about which method to use.

Many women want to use the birth control pill, but others want information about IUDs, diaphragms, and natural family planning. Men continue to use condoms, although the use has decreased as other methods have gained popularity. More and more men and women elect permanent sterilization when their families are complete. Some even choose sterilization before they have had children at all, or after having only one child.

If a pregnancy that is unplanned and unwanted does occur, more decisions must be confronted. Many women find that the decision of whether or not to continue the pregnancy is the most agonizing choice they will ever make. Fortunately for women and men in the United States, they do have this choice. Abortion is legal in all 50 states during the first trimester.

If abortion is not the chosen solution to an unwanted pregnancy, or if the abortion decision is made too late, another agonizing decision remains: whether or not to place the unwanted child for adoption. Adoption is infrequently chosen as a solution.

Model for Sexual Decision Making

The proposed model begins with a hypothetical woman who has not experienced sexual intercourse (Fig. 9-1). The first decision involves her own sexual self, sexual identity, and sexual feelings. Does she choose to recognize these feelings? Is she sexually aware of herself? Is she able to see herself in a sexual relationship now or in the future? If the active decisions promote sexual experience, she might have sexual intercourse or might not, depending on opportunity, partner's feelings, and other factors. She may also make a conscious decision to abstain from intercourse. If the active decisions deny sexuality, intercourse may or may not occur, again depending on circumstance. Those who make no decisions are vulnerable to pressure and coercion and may engage in intercourse even if they do not really want to.

She may, if she wishes, decide to engage in sexual intercourse or she may decide to avoid intercourse. These are active decisions, requiring an assessment of risks and benefits based on knowledge, attitudes, and beliefs. She may also make a passive decision (which is accomplished by simply not making any decision at all and by ignoring the option to make an active decision).

A woman who decides to have intercourse must then decide whether she wants to get pregnant at this time. If she does not want to get pregnant, and if she has knowledge of and access to contraceptive services, she can subsequently decide to use a birth control method. (The process of deciding precisely which method to use is discussed in another part of this chapter. A separate and complex chain of decision making is undertaken at this point.) If she decides against intercourse, she may or may not think about the use of a contraceptive method. Some women maintain abstinence; others do have intercourse, by "accident," and probably do not use a birth control method. Again, ignoring the options may frequently result in a passive decision.

For all women, intercourse either occurs or it does not. Some women get pregnant and some do not. The model demonstrates that a pregnancy can occur if no decisions are made about intercourse, babies, or birth control as well as if active decisions are made at each "trigger point."

Once a pregnancy has occurred, new decisions regarding carrying to a term delivery are considered. Some women find they want the baby even though the pregnancy was unplanned and unwanted. Others may find their life situation

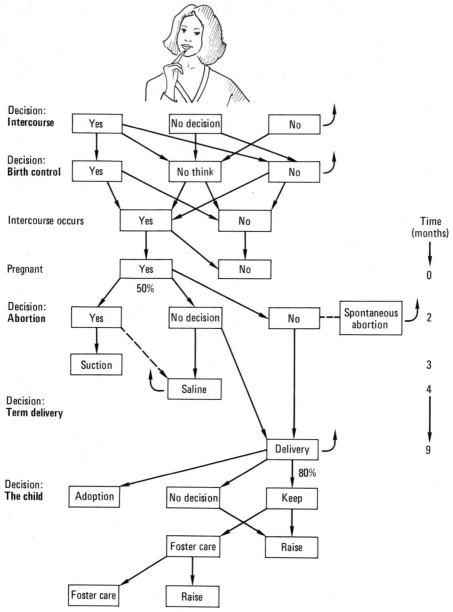

Figure 9-1 Chain of sexual decision making. *(Developed by M. Swenson.)*

changed in the interim, causing a planned pregnancy to result in an unwanted baby.

The occurrence of pregnancy introduces a time factor into the decision-making scheme. Abortion decisions must be made in the first or possibly second trimester. If the pregnant woman makes no decision to seek an abortion, she soon loses that option: a nondecision is a decision nevertheless.

Some pregnancies will terminate in spontaneous abortions. Whenever a woman ceases to be pregnant, she reenters the decision-making model and must decide again whether or not to have sexual intercourse. As a matter of fact, the initial decisions probably are remade or rethought (or continue to be ignored) at each intercourse episode, and certainly with each new partner.

Term delivery occurs if the woman consciously and actively chooses this option. It also occurs if she makes no decision at all about her pregnancy outcome. The birth of the baby initiates new decisions for the mothers of unwanted infants. Some will choose to place the baby in an adoptive or foster care setting. Some will choose to keep the baby and raise it as a single parent. Some women will marry either before or after the birth. If the mother makes no active decision to give up the child, she keeps the child: again, a nondecision is a decision. Many teenage girls become premature parents by default; they never made any decisions at any of the trigger points on the model.

The Nurse and Sexual Decisions

Providing assistance to people who wish to make decisions is a primary nursing task. Nurses in public schools, higher education, physicians' offices, public health agencies, and hospitals have nearly limitless opportunities to help people make decisions. Nurses can (1) point out options, reviewing the risks and benefits ("pros and cons"); (2) provide accurate information about each choice; and (3) help the person accomplish the decided-upon goal.

The intercourse decision is affected by fear of pregnancy, conflict with religious or moral values, age, cultural or peer group influence, respect and concern for oneself and others, individual sexual needs, availability and suitability of a partner, and access to an appropriate place for intercourse. Many teenagers struggle with all these factors and solicit help from adults whom they trust in order to clarify values.

The decision regarding the number of children to bear affects not only the sexually active woman but also her children, her partner, her parents, and society as a whole. For the family, economic, psychological, and social effects occur. The woman's own life is dramatically affected in terms of education, career, and marriage. If her partner participates in the decision regarding children, his influence can be enormous.

The child and potential siblings are affected by the age of the mother, the spacing of the children, and the ability of the mother to provide care. Very young adolescents tend to bear low birth weight babies, who in turn have greater incidences of neurological and intellectual impairments. Having children very close together is physically difficult for the mother and frequently means she is unable to spend sufficient time or energy in caring for her children.

The world population seems little affected by whether or not one particular woman has one particular child. But if she has two or three, and each of them has two or three, and so on, very large numbers soon are reached. Few people die these days before they are truly elderly. It is not uncommon to see photographs of four or even five generations of daughters seated together. Having one child has far-reaching results.

Nurses must assist people at each "trigger point" in the chain of sexual and reproductive decision making. Education programs we provide for high schools should emphasize that no one should ever have a sexual relationship if it causes emotional discomfort. Everyone also has the right to be a virgin without harassment from others. Many teenagers need to be reminded that abstinence—i.e., not having sex—is normal, and healthy, and perfectly OK. They need to know there is *no* perfect form of contraception except abstinence. As a matter of fact, the majority of teens is *not* sexually active in high school. They also need to know that contraceptive methods are available to teens and that most unwanted pregnancies can be prevented.

Nurses instruct couples and individuals about the many effective methods of birth control and then help them to choose the method best for them. Many people equate birth control with birth control pills and are truly surprised to learn that there are lots of different ways to keep from getting pregnant. A yearly pelvic examination, breast examination, Pap smear, and VD test help women protect their reproductive health.

A woman or a couple facing an unplanned pregnancy must make many additional choices: How to tell the partner/parents? Have the baby? Have an abortion? Keep the baby? Get married? Stay single? Adoption? Foster care? Most married women continue the pregnancy and keep the child. If they make no active decision to have an abortion, they will have a baby. For some, the decision to terminate or to continue a pregnancy may be the first important decision they ever made. Problem-pregnancy counseling with an emphasis on informed decision making is provided by nurses.

About half the unmarried teens choose abortion, the other half mainly keep the baby whether or not they marry. Very few women choose adoption despite common knowledge that infants are very quickly adopted by carefully screened people who desperately desire a child. There is considerable pressure, especially among teen peers and partners, in favor of keeping the baby.

Many unwanted children are born because the parents avoided decisions or because the decisions made were based on false information. Every child has a right to be welcomed and wanted. Every parent has a responsibility to provide the best possible care for each potential child. There are many choices if only we learn to make honest, informed, and rational decisions.

Finally, nurses must filter out their own opinions and judgments from the counsel they give. Nurses must listen to themselves and to each other as they talk with clients in order to identify those subtle points where objectivity ends and persuasion begins. Nurses are responsible only to delineate options, to provide accurate information about risks, benefits, and procedures, and to assist in implementation of goals. Nurses do not make the decisions and are not responsible for the decisions clients make.

ABSTINENCE

The only "perfect and risk-free" form of birth control is abstinence from sexual intercourse. Individuals or a couple may consciously avoid intercourse because of the fear of an unwanted pregnancy or lack of access to or knowledge about contraception. People may refrain from intercourse for moral or religious reasons. The continence might be only situational or may be cultural or traditional. There are, of course, no physical side effects. As a form of contraception, however, this method places strain on a sexual relationship and therefore on the entire relationship. For most couples, it is impractical except for short periods. But some individuals may find abstinence to be a useful way to control conception.

Adolescents must be given information about abstinence. The majority of teenagers are probably not sexually active. Nurses may need to acknowledge to teens and others that not to have sexual intercourse is perfectly healthy and normal if that is the client's preference. Although all people are sexual, being sexually active is not necessary to maintain health or even to maintain sexual health. Abstinence from intercourse does not always need to include abstinence from other forms of sexual expression such as oral-genital sex or masturbation. Again, the nurse has a responsibility to "legitimize" these practices for clients. This goal may be accomplished by the nonjudgmental attitude of the nurse as abstention is seriously discussed, by encouraging the client to feel comfortable with the choice of abstinence, and by acknowledging that not having sexual intercourse is a normal, natural way for some people to be themselves.

Vignette

The client is a 16-year-old woman.

Problem List
1 Sex education
2 Family conflicts
3 Borderline diabetic

Subjective Data
"My boyfriend and I are really close. We're even thinking of maybe getting married. We like to neck and pet and fool around, but we're scared to have intercourse because I might get pregnant. Actually, I don't think we're ready for sex. At least, I'm not. But sometimes I worry that getting so physical with each other isn't a good thing. I mean, is it healthy and normal to not actually go all the way? Could it make me frigid later or anything?"

Objective Data

Virgin, not using any contraceptive method. Has made mature decisions in the past about her own health.

Assessment

Needs reassurance of naturalness of her feelings. Needs information on sexual response cycle, permission "not to have sex," and information on birth control should be available in case it is needed later.

Intervention

Explained that petting and mutual masturbation to orgasm are normal alternatives to sexual intercourse. Given pamphlet on birth control methods. Given some positive reinforcement for taking the time to think about such important issues and to make thoughtful decisions.

Plan

Discuss again at next visit, especially about her possible need for contraceptive and sexually transmitted disease information.

COITUS INTERRUPTUS

Also known as the withdrawal method or "pulling out," this method is probably the most widely used by teenagers. The male partner simply removes his penis from the woman's vagina before ejaculation occurs. To be able to accomplish this, the man must be able to control ejaculation to a considerable extent so as to be able to predict when it will occur. Self-control is essential, since the temptation to continue intercourse "just this once" is hard to resist for most couples. Probably the greatest risk results from sperm which are present in the earliest preejaculate from the Cowper's glands. The sperm contained in this fluid are just as capable of impregnating a woman as the sperm contained in semen. The woman can get pregnant even if the man never ejaculates within her, since the sperm can move (via flagellating tails) up into the uterus. There are no contraindications to this method; the possible side effect is frustration, especially for the woman. However, if cunnilingus or masturbation is used to allow orgasm for the woman, the method, though relatively ineffective, is better than no method. It is easily available to any couple at any time, costs nothing, and has no medical contraindications.

PERIODIC ABSTINENCE

The rise of the women's movement and recent evidence of side effects of other birth control methods have given renewed attention to the various methods of fertility awareness. The several variations of the "rhythm method" all strive to help a woman identify her most fertile time of the menstrual cycle (ovulation and the time just before and just after). She then abstains from sexual intercourse during this time. For women whose periods are regular, and therefore predictable, the rhythm method may be fairly effective in the prevention of unwanted pregnancy (somewhere between 15 and 40 percent of users will get pregnant using this method).[2] There are three variations of the rhythm method, and a woman may use any combination of these or may use only one of the techniques for predicting ovulation.

The most commonly used method, and the one most often misused (especially by adolescents), is the calendar method. Misinformation about this method abounds: "I only have sex just before and just after my period when it's absolutely impossible to get pregnant." Many teenagers have erroneous ideas regarding the calendar method, and any explanation of the method with clients must be very precise. Women need to know that the more irregular their periods, the less effective the method. Women need to know that the method requires careful record keeping on their menstrual cycles over a period of time (about a year). The abstention time for some might approach 2 weeks and possibly longer. Basically, the woman must figure what was her longest cycle ever and her shortest cycle ever (in the last 2 years or so). Since most women ovulate 11 to 14 days before their next period, and since both the longest and shortest cycles must be considered, the time of abstinence occurs 11 days before the shortest cycle to 11 days before the longest cycle. Additionally, since sperm and ova live for a day or two, this extra time must be added to the continent time. Obviously, the method is complex if it is used correctly, and most women will appreciate help from a health professional in figuring out the "safe" times of the month.[3,4]

The second variation of the rhythm method is the basal body temperature system. It is somewhat more reliable in the prediction of ovulation. The woman must be able to read an oral thermometer, and must take her temperature every morning before she gets out of bed. A small but discernible rise in the body temperature occurs on the day the ovum is released. Continence is maintained until the higher temperature has been held for 3 days. Nurses can be very helpful to women using this method by teaching thermometer reading, by helping the woman make a chart on which to keep her daily temperature recordings, and by helping the woman analyze the data after a month or two of daily recordings. Obviously, an illness which causes a fever confuses the temperature record.

Third, the nurse can instruct the woman in the cervical mucus method.[5] This method was developed by Evelyn and John Billings and was tested on hundreds of women in Australia. The technique is based on the fact that vaginal mucus changes during the menstrual cycle in ways women can learn to recognize.

Vignette

Client is 34 years old, married, and has six living children at home.

Problem List

1   Health promotion
2   Wants no more children
3   Marital conflict

Subjective Data

I don't want any more kids—the ones I have are driving me crazy. Besides, we can't afford any more. My husband doesn't believe in birth control and he won't let me use anything. He doesn't believe in sterilization either. We don't even have sex all that often—I avoid it most of the time. So what can I do? Just keep on having the babies I don't want?

Objective Data

Client is crying, wringing her hands. Is here alone because husband refuses to come in for a consultation. Last two deliveries were premature. Family lives at poverty level, but does not qualify for welfare assistance since the husband lives in the home.

Assessment

Needs information on natural family planning so that at least she can avoid sexual intercourse during her most fertile part of the cycle. Needs support for limiting family without contributing to already-present marriage problems. Could benefit from further counseling alone if husband cannot be persuaded to participate.

Intervention

Taught calendar method of periodic abstinence.

Plan

Encourage her to share knowledge of method with her husband if she is ready to do so. Arrange return visits as necessary (probably every 3 months) to help with record keeping and calendar blocking out. Continue to urge family therapy and/or sex counseling.

Sexuality affects and is influenced by the rhythm methods in various ways. The couple must first be willing to curtail spontaneous desire for intercourse on fertile days. This will be an easier task for some than for others, and for this reason the method will be more effective for some couples. If the couple wishes, noncoital sexual activity is helpful in reducing frustration. However, not everyone likes or is comfortable with mutual masturbation or oral-genital sex. Nurses who are aware of sexual options will be comfortable in giving permission to clients to engage in noncoital sexual relations.

The fear of possible pregnancy is inhibiting to many couples. If either partner is preoccupied with anxiety, responsiveness is reduced. Simply acknowledging this problem may increase a client's comfort. Perhaps sharing anxieties with another person, especially someone using the same method, may provide some emotional support and encouragement.

CONDOM

Condoms (also known as "rubbers," "safes," "baggies," or prophylactics) usually are made of thin latex or animal tissue. They may be smooth or ribbed, lubricated or dry, brightly colored or transparent. The sheath covers the erect penis and prevents ejaculate from entering the woman's vagina. Condoms are readily available, easy to carry, and simple to use. Condoms (and possibly diaphragms) are the only birth control method which also prevents the spread of sexually transmitted diseases. The condom is unrolled over the penis by either partner. (Many men find they are sexually "turned on" when their partner puts on the condom for them.) The tip must not balloon with trapped air; space must be left at the end for collecting ejaculate. The rim of the condom must be held in place by one of the partners when the penis is withdrawn from the vagina. (If not held, the condom may slip off or may remain in the vagina, spilling the sperm and risking pregnancy.)

Sporadic use, condoms which fall off or break, and failure to apply the condom soon enough probably account for the 15 to 20 percent failure rate.

There are no contraindications or side effects with condom use. Some women find the increased friction of the latex sheath to be sexually stimulating; other women may need to use a nonpetroleum-lubricant contraceptive cream, foam, or jelly, or prelubricated condoms to reduce the "pull" on vaginal tissues. Some men complain of reduced sensation, perhaps because they have been told by other men to expect this "shower with your socks on" effect. Other men, who have been able to escape this cultural bias, may find eroticism in using a condom, particularly if the partner also finds the condom sexually stimulating. Recent advertising has been oriented toward just such a goal.

FOAM

Spermicidal foam, when inserted into the vagina, covers the cervix and forms a barrier against penetration by sperm. Foam is easily obtained, simple to use, fairly inexpensive, and safe from side effects. Used by itself, foam is about 70 percent effective. Foam can be used to back up several other contraceptive methods to increase their effectiveness. Foam and condoms, used together and used perfectly, are about as effective as the birth control pill used perfectly. Foam can be used as an adjunct to an IUD, especially in the first few months and at midcycle. Women are advised to use foam and/or condom during the first month that they are on the oral contraceptive pill (Fig. 9-2).

Foam is contained in a can or large vial. The user inserts the foam intravaginally using an applicator. Foam can be inserted 30 minutes before intercourse so long as the woman remains lying down. If she gets up and walks around, the liquefied foam will drip out and protection will thus be reduced. One large or two small applicators full of foam protect for one episode of intercourse; subsequent intercourse requires reapplication of foam.

Aside from occasional skin sensitivities (usually resulting in itching or a rash), there are no contraindications to or side effects from foam. If a woman experiences vaginal irritation from one brand of foam, she should try other brands before concluding that she is "allergic to foam."

Disadvantages of foam include the following: (1) Materials must be assembled and used prior to each intercourse. (2) Foam does not taste good at all and may even have an anesthetic effect on oral mucous membranes. Therefore, couples who engage in oral-genital contact will need to use foam after this activity. (3) Some men believe that the stimulating friction of the walls of the vagina is reduced by foam. (Other couples find the lubricating effect of foam to be pleasurable and helpful.) (4) Insertion of foam requires some genital touching. Women who feel very inhibited about touching or manipulating their genitals may find foam unacceptable for this reason.

Advantages are the following. (1) No medical consultation is required for

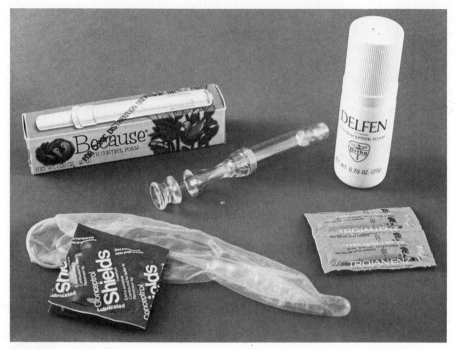

Figure 9-2 Nonprescription contraceptive methods. *(Photograph by Carmen C. Carter.)*

use of foam. This fact makes foam a reasonable choice for teenagers, vacation-ers, and people who fear physicians or who do not have access to health care. (2) Foam does not change any natural chemical balance in the woman's body. Her menstrual periods, ovulation, and vaginal pH are essentially unaltered. (3) There need be no "waiting period" after foam use before attempting a desired preg-nancy. (4) There is some evidence that use of foam may reduce the incidence of vaginitis. This effect may be due to the antiseptic properties of foam. (5) Couples using foam need no additional artificial lubricant.

FOAMING VAGINAL SUPPOSITORY

After several years of use in West Germany, the foaming vaginal suppository has only recently been available in the United States. Prior experience has led family planners to view vaginal suppositories as ineffective. However, data avail-able on the suppository seems to indicate that it will be a successful contracep-tive choice for some couples. The suppository uses both barrier and spermicidal mechanisms and therefore probably is similar in effectiveness to foam. The suppository can be inserted up to 1 hour prior to intercourse, an advantage for some sexual relationships. No applicator or shaking is required, allowing inser-tion to be unobtrusive. The woman must be able to use her finger to insert the suppository into the vagina. Many women note a warmth resulting from the foaming action which is not unpleasant and for some may be erotically stimulating. Male partners also feel the warmth. Further research on this method is pending.

DIAPHRAGM

The diaphragm is a soft latex or rubber dome over a circular rim of flexible steel. Size varies from 35 to 95 cm in diameter. It is worn internally by the woman and forms a barrier in front of the cervical opening to the uterus. The diaphragm must be used with spermicidal cream or jelly (*not* Vaseline or other petroleum-based lubricants, since these will deteriorate the rubber and will not kill sperm). The spermicide is applied to the concave side of the diaphragm, with a small amount rubbed around the rim. The diaphragm is flexed and inserted in the vagina in the manner of inserting a tampon. When properly fitted and placed, the diaphragm lies between the pubic bone and the posterior fornix of the cervix (Fig. 9-3).

The diaphragm is an intercourse-linked method. The user must be able to connect the contraceptive need with the act of sexual intercourse, must have and know how to use the diaphragm, and must be willing to use it. If the woman is uncomfortable with the idea of touching her labia, vagina, and cervix, the method is not appropriate for her. A woman whose background reflects sexual repression and inhibition may feel that manipulating her genitals is "bad" or "dirty" and will not be able to insert the diaphragm or position it properly.

The spermicide used with the diaphragm may help provide needed lubrication during intercourse; the jelly is "wetter" than the cream but the cream has a more perfumed, less medicinal odor. Neither cream nor jelly tastes good; therefore if cunnilingus is practiced, it should take place before the diaphragm is inserted. Nurses should warn clients about the taste of spermicidal preparations.

A properly fitting diaphragm will not be felt by either partner. However, vigorous sexual activity with woman on top may dislodge the diaphragm and expose the cervix. Since orgasm also causes the vaginal barrel to enlarge and

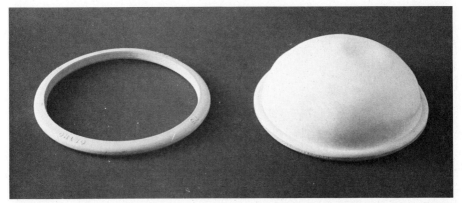

Figure 9-3 Diaphragm fitting ring and diaphragm of comparable size. *(Photograph by Carmen C. Carter.)*

lengthen, an occasional check of position is a good idea. The client who understands the sexual response cycle may be a more knowledgeable diaphragm user. The nurse may discuss the sexual response cycle as part of routine contraceptive teaching.

Since the diaphragm must be inserted before intercourse, it must be related to intercourse by the user. However, foreplay is not necessarily interrupted for diaphragm insertion, since the device can be positioned as long as 2 hours before intercourse. The pleasurable postintercourse period also is not interrupted: the diaphragm must be left undisturbed for 6 to 8 hours after intercourse. The only point at which the method affects sexual activity directly is when more than one intercourse experience occurs. Additional spermicidal cream or jelly must be inserted into the vagina before additional penile-vaginal intercourse. Applicators are included with the tubes of the spermicidal products.

Vignette

Client is an 18-year-old woman.

Problem List

    1   Health maintenance and health promotion
    2   Contraceptive needs
    3   Migraine headaches

Subjective Data
"Jerry and I are here because neither of us wants a baby right now. We're engaged, but we probably won't get married for a couple of years, at least 'til Jerry finishes school. We've used rubbers a few times, but Jerry doesn't like how they feel."

Objective Data
Couple here together at their own request. Sexually active: intercourse 2 to 3 times per week.

Assessment
At risk for pregnancy. Susan not a candidate for oral contraceptives due to history of migraine headaches. Mature, caring relationship appears stable. Unlikely Jerry will use condoms.

Intervention
Instructed in all methods including costs and benefits. Couple decided to use diaphragm with contraceptive cream. Relationship of diaphragm to sexual response cycle explained.

Plan
Schedule diaphragm fitting with return to clinic in 1 week to check placement. Invite couple to return for consultation whenever necessary. Reevaluate satisfaction with method in 3 to 6 months.

INTRAUTERINE DEVICE (IUD)

The IUD was introduced in this country about 1960, although it had been used in other countries long before that. Currently, about 15 million women throughout the world use IUDs to prevent pregnancy.[6] It is a metal and/or plastic device

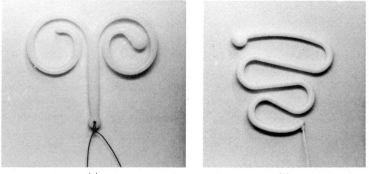

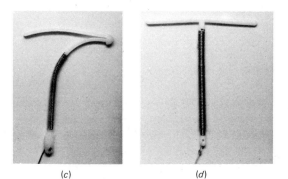

Figure 9-4 Types of IUDs. (*a*) SAF-T coil. (*b*) Lippes loop. (*c*) Copper 7 device. (*d*) Copper T device. *From J. Clausen et al., Maternity Nursing Today, 2/e, McGraw-Hill, New York, 1976, p. 238.)*

which is inserted into the uterus through the cervical os (Fig. 9-4). How the IUD prevents pregnancy remains somewhat of a mystery. It may be that the IUD prevents fertilization by increasing the speed of the ovum through the fallopian tubes or by immobilizing sperm. Implantation of a fertilized ovum might be prevented by uterine inflammation or by mechanical action of the IUD against the uterine wall. Copper-containing IUDs may alter intrauterine chemistry or interfere with estrogen absorbtion in the endometrium. Progesterone-containing IUDs probably make cervical mucosa "hostile" to penetration by sperm, just as progesterone-containing oral contraceptives do.

Before insertion, the woman must be free from vaginal infection and must have an essentially normal Pap smear. The uterus is sounded prior to insertion to minimize risk of perforation. Ideally, the IUD is inserted while the woman is having her menstrual flow: the cervical os is somewhat relaxed then, the menstrual blood masks bleeding from the IUD insertion procedure, and the practitioner can be fairly certain that the woman is not pregnant. (Some practitioners suggest IUD insertion instead of the "morning-after pill" as a means to prevent implantation of a fertilized ovum.[7])

The IUD, although a very effective birth control method, has some side effects, possible complications, and contraindications. The older the woman, the better she tolerates an IUD. The woman with an IUD does not have to connect intercourse and contraception in her mind, nor does she need to remember anything on a daily basis (except to check monthly for the string). The woman who is unwilling to check her cervix for the presence of IUD strings will not know whether her IUD is in place. Many women need to be taught how to differentiate between vaginal and cervical tissue. Nurses may find that some women react to the task of checking IUD strings with repugnance. The idea of putting one's finger deep into the vagina makes some women feel guilt or shame associated with feelings about masturbation. The nurse, by giving information and by giving permission, can assist women to master this skill, to feel more comfortable about vaginal touching, and can help them to learn about their bodies at the same time.

Some women find the heavier, longer periods and the increased cramping associated with the IUD to be intolerable, while others find little or no change in their menstrual pattern and may even find that cramping is reduced. The IUD does not appear to change hormones or body chemistry.

IUD users may find that their birth control method influences their sexual lives. The major complication of the IUD is infection. Women with multiple sexual partners are at a greater risk for the development of vaginal and cervical infections, particularly gonorrhea, and hence may be at greater risk of developing IUD complications as a result. Occasionally a woman with an IUD finds she is having delayed menstrual bleeding which is heavy and accompanied by severe cramping. It is possible that such a situation could be the result of early spontaneous abortions caused by the IUD. The woman who is opposed to abortion may want to change to another method if her IUD is causing these symptoms.

ORAL CONTRACEPTIVES

Two types of oral contraceptives are currently in use in the United States. The "combination pill" is a steroid preparation consisting of synthetic estrogen and synthetic progesterone. Taken in high, consistent doses, these hormones prevent the release of FSH (follicle-stimulating hormone) from the anterior pituitary gland. Ovulation is suppressed in the absence of FSH (Fig. 9-5).

Secondary contraceptive effects of the combination pill are the result of progestin, which causes the cervical mucus to become "hostile" to penetration by sperm. Progestin also stimulates changes in the endometrium which discourage implantation if an ovum were to be successfully released and fertilized. The combination of primary and secondary contraceptive effects prevents nearly 100% of possible pregnancies if the pill is taken consistently and correctly.

Combination pills are packaged in either 21- or 28-day containers. Actually, only 21 days are active pills; the remaining 7 are "reminder pills"—placebos which assist the woman to count the days properly between 21-day cycles. Also, many woman can remember to take pills more correctly if they take a pill every

Figure 9-5 Oral contraceptives (combination pills) in 28-day packages. *(Photograph by Carmen C. Carter.)*

day. Withdrawal from the active pills causes a decline in blood levels of the hormones and results in simulated menstruation.

The alternative pill, the "mini-pill," contains only progestin. These pills are taken every day (there are no "reminder pills" or any "week off" the pill) and contain little or no estrogen. Contraceptive effects of the progestin-only pill include stimulation of thick cervical mucus which is difficult for sperm to penetrate, slowed movement of ova through the tubes, impaired implantation of fertilized ova, and inhibition of ovulation.

Many side effects of the birth control pills can affect sexuality (Table 9-1). Oral contraceptives can cause depression, fatigue, and a reduced libido and thus can directly influence sexual responsiveness. Other changes, such as weight gain, complexion changes (chloasma), and increased irritability, can adversely affect self-image and subsequently affect sexuality. Some side effects of the pills can enhance sexuality: the spontaneity afforded by a non-coitally linked method, possible breast enlargement, and improvement in acne are examples of such effects. Some women note an increase in libido while on oral contraceptives. Vaginal lubrication may be either increased or decreased by the pill. Some sex therapists are so convinced that the birth control pill can affect sexual responsiveness that they will not accept a couple for therapy unless the woman has been off the pill for at least 6 months.

Table 9-1   Side Effects of Oral Contraceptives

Estrogen-related effects		Progestin-related effects	
Excess	Deficiency	Excess	Deficiency
Nausea/vomiting	Nervousness	Acne	Late breakthrough
Dizziness	Irritability	Increased	bleeding and
Weight gain	Hot flashes	appetite	spotting
Headache	Early and midcycle	Fatigue	Delayed onset of
Breast tenderness	bleeding	Change in libido	period
Uterine cramps	Decreased amount	Hair loss	Heavy menstrual
Edema	of menstrual flow	Virilization	flow
Leg cramps	Missed periods	Decreased length	Menstrual cramps
Leukorrhea		of menstrual	
Chloasma		flow	
Contact lens		Oily scalp	
problems		Headaches	
Thrombosis		Hypertension	
Hypertension		Jaundice	
		Decreased vagi-	
		nal lubrication	

"MALE PILL"

Until very recently, there always has been more interest in female methods of contraception than in male methods. Perhaps this is because our culture believes that women are ultimately responsible for birth control, or because male researchers are threatened by the idea of reducing or curtailing the fertility of men. Probably the most significant reason for the concentration on the female oral contraceptive was pressure from feminists for the development of a method of birth control that was reliable, relatively safe, and "hassle-free." No similar pressure has been present in the past for the development of a "male pill." Also, female reproductive function is easier to disrupt, since only one ovum per month is produced in contrast to the constant production of sperm by men. Sperm movement, fertilization, and implantation all occur within the female body, and all of these processes may be interrupted only within the female.

However, research into fertility avoidance for men has increased in the past few years. A possible male contraceptive pill includes a combination of a low dose of testosterone plus progesterone. This pill would induce infertility while replacing the deficient testosterone (to avoid the undesirable side effects of low testosterone in men). Although this idea is being investigated, it may be several years before it will be available.

Methods of reversing vasectomy (either by surgical means or by use of a "faucet" which, when placed in the vas deferens, could be turned off or on) are being studied. Immunology may have some possibilities, although the problem of prolonged and possibly permanent sterility remains.

The best male method of temporary birth control currently available is the condom.

INJECTION

Not available (in 1979) in the United States, "the shot" is use by approximately 1 million women in 64 other countries.[8] The effectiveness of long-acting progesterone injections approaches that of combination oral contraceptives.

Contraindications are the same as the contraindications to the combination pills. The injection lasts for 3 months. Side effects such as irregular menstrual periods, delayed return of fertility, decreased libido, weight gain, and headaches may occur and are potentially disruptive to a woman's sexuality.

Since the injection is coitus-independent, it could be the method of choice for adolescents (particularly those who would have trouble remembering pills and hiding them from disapproving parents). Any woman who wants the effectiveness of the pill without having to deal with daily medication might consider the injection. Mentally retarded or mentally ill women might be protected from pregnancy more successfully by the injectable progesterone.

The sexual implications of the injection parallel the implications for users of oral contraceptives. The injection may cause very irregular bleeding or may cause cessation of bleeding entirely. Women may find this situation enhances their sexual relationships (no need to abstain at time of bleeding) or detracts from sexual enjoyment (worry about pregnancy when no cyclic bleeding occurs).

STERILIZATION

Sterilization, "permanent birth control," is finding increased popularity in this country as well as in the world. The increased use of surgical sterilization procedures may be the result of a combination of factors: worry about side effects of effective temporary contraceptive methods such as the pill and IUD, changes in the cultural definition of masculinity as measured by the number of children fathered, the "population explosion," and the increased costs of raising children in the world today. Four to five million people have elected permanent sterilization in this country; about three-quarters of these are men.[9] Voluntary sterilization is legal in all the states, although individual physicians and hospitals may refuse to do the procedure for reasons ranging from religious ethics to judgments regarding the age of the client, the number of children he or she might have already, and the absence of spousal consent.

Sterilization may be done by surgical and nonsurgical methods. Nonsurgical means are used infrequently and may include immunological, hormonal, irradiation, and other medical methods. These contraceptive techniques are uncommon and are insufficiently tested.

Surgical contraceptive measures are most frequently used. The operation for women varies; for men, vasectomy is the primary technique. No matter which method is employed, the practitioner must spend much time and energy before the procedure in explanation and clarification. The client or couple must understand, unequivocally, that the operation cannot be reversed. Many people, when faced with a change in life situation, desire to have the sterilization "undone." Careful presurgery discussion should include these or similar questions:

1 Were you to separate from this current partner, would you want more children with another partner?
2 If some tragedy occurred, and your present children were killed or taken from you, would you want more children?
3 If your income increased a great deal, would you want more children?

Vasectomy and tubal sterilization do not affect hormone secretions and hence do not affect libido. Some studies suggest that circulating antibodies are present in vasectomized men; but the effect of these antibodies is still unclear.[10] However, changes in sexuality may occur for a variety of subtle reasons. Sexual excitation and orgasm are unchanged, yet feelings about oneself as a sexual person may be altered by sterilization (Fig. 9-6).

After sterilization, women continue to menstruate as before. The ovaries function and the uterus, vagina, and clitoris are unchanged. Since she no longer need fear an unwanted pregnancy, a woman may find herself more responsive and less inhibited during lovemaking. She may also experience a feeling of loss and depression, especially if she tended to define herself in terms of her ability to bear children.

Men, particularly those whose self-definition depends on their ability to keep women "barefoot and pregnant," may have sexual problems following a vasectomy. (These same men may refuse consent for their wives' tubal sterilization.) The man who has problems with primary or secondary impotence may be threatened by the mere idea of surgery on the genitals. Men with difficulties such as these probably should not have a vasectomy until the existing problem is resolved.[11] Freedom from the worry of pregnancy allows most men with vasectomies to engage in sexual intercourse with even greater enthusiasm than before. Perhaps the best person to help a man who is anxious about the effects of vasectomy on sexual performance is a man who already has had a vasectomy.

Sterilization, like babies, has both improved and destroyed marriages—but cannot be counted on to produce either result. Sterilization may make a good relationship better or may make a poor relationship worse. Some relationships may be unchanged by sterilization.

CHOOSING AND USING A METHOD

Clients who seek a contraceptive method may already know the method they prefer. Even if the client says, "I know I want the pill so you don't need to go through explanations of the other methods," the nurse is obligated to briefly describe all the contraceptive choices. Written material which provides facts about the various methods must also be provided. The client simply may be unaware that other forms of contraception are available besides the birth control pill. The client might not realize the difference between a diaphragm and an IUD.

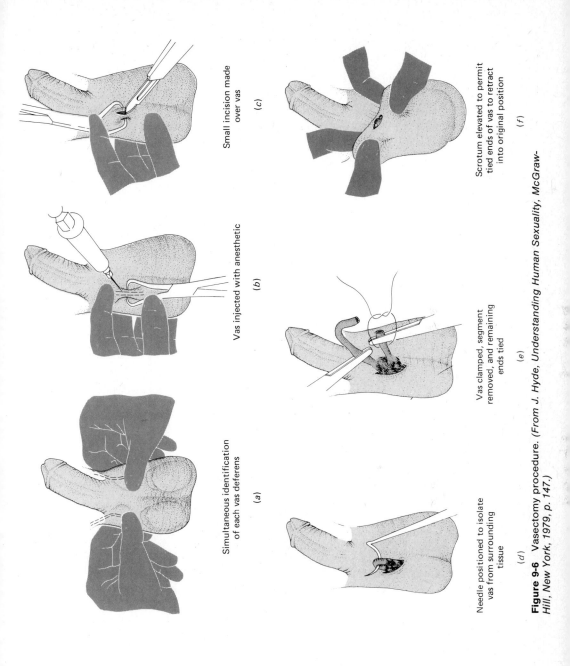

Simultaneous identification of each vas deferens

(a)

Vas injected with anesthetic

(b)

Small incision made over vas

(c)

Needle positioned to isolate vas from surrounding tissue

(d)

Vas clamped, segment removed, and remaining ends tied

(e)

Scrotum elevated to permit tied ends of vas to retract into original position

(f)

Figure 9-6 Vasectomy procedure. *(From J. Hyde, Understanding Human Sexuality, McGraw-Hill, New York, 1979, p. 147.)*

Medical contraindications may prohibit clients from obtaining their method of first choice.

The right to decline use of a method must be protected. The client may change his or her mind at any point in the decision process. Five minutes after the IUD is inserted, it must be removed if the client wishes. Two weeks after starting the pill, the client may choose to stop. Nurses in these situations must present facts about the consequences of a decision change, but must be careful to avoid giving advice or passing judgment.

If a client does discontinue use of one contraceptive method, the nurse must again provide information about choices. A woman who stops taking the pill should be told more than, "You need to use another method of birth control if you still want to prevent pregnancy." Detailed descriptions of other methods and a reevaluation of her life situation will be beneficial in making a new contraceptive choice.

Nursing interventions continue throughout the process of contraceptive decision making. The client who is aware of his or her sexual self and who acknowledges that present or prospective intercourse may lead to an unwanted pregnancy needs information about birth control choices. The nurse provides unbiased factual information and helps the client assess contraceptive options in the light of the sexual history and the relative costs and benefits of birth control and pregnancy. Clients may need additional information and help to obtain the method they decide to use, and later may need support and/or assistance in using the method (Fig. 9-7).

Nurses in all settings may assist clients in these areas. The public health nurse, school nurse, office or clinic nurse, pediatric and obstetrics practitioner, and psychiatric or gynecologic nurse are particularly likely to come in contact with clients who desire to limit, space, or prevent pregnancies. The alert nurse can pick up cues from clients which lead to a discussion of contraception.

Clients need information both about methods available and about how to obtain the method they choose. Nurses can refer to physicians or to birth control clinics such as Planned Parenthood for contraceptive methods which require medical supervision. Specific instructions in "drugstore methods" are necessary for some clients to use their method correctly. Some women need assistance with making a temperature chart, with learning to read a thermometer, or with taking care of their diaphragm. Instructions, side effects, and warning signs may need to be reviewed. Clients can easily be confused during their initial, perhaps rushed, visit to a doctor or clinic. The following problem might not have occurred if a follow-up appointment or public health nursing referral had been made.

Vignette

Problem
Vaginal infection
Subjective Data
"I've got a terrible discharge down there. I've had it for a month or so and it just gets worse and worse. Now I can hardly sit down let alone have sex. I got a diaphragm

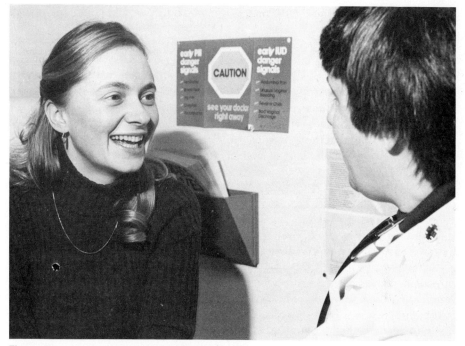

Figure 9-7 The nurse practitioner discusses risks and benefits of each contraceptive method with the patient. *(Photograph by Carmen C. Carter.)*

here a month or so ago and when the doctor put it in he never told me to take it out, so I never did take it out and it's still in there, I guess."

Objective Data
Foul-smelling mixed bacterial infection. Diaphragm in place.

Assessment
Client believed diaphragm was permanent. Perhaps got confused between diaphragm and IUD. Needs *very* careful instructions, probably in writing, to help with next method chosen.

Intervention
Medication for infection after diaphragm removal.

Plan
Reinstruct in all methods. Help client choose a new method or perhaps use diaphragm again with better instructions. Refer to public health nurse for follow-up and assistance with method.

Accessibility to health care in this country depends, among other factors, on the client's age, ability to pay, and distance from a facility. Adolescents may legally obtain contraceptive information and supplies without parental consent; however, individual physicians or clinics may refuse to serve a minor for fear of litigation. A nurse in public schools or other settings may be able to refer teenage clients to sympathetic practitioners. Local family planning and Planned Parenthood clinics usually serve clients regardless of age, marital status, or ability to pay. Many have "walk-in" arrangements in which a client may be seen without an appointment.

Nurses in a doctor's office may be responsible for helping private clients decide upon and successfully use a method. Never assume that the client can read printed directions, especially package inserts which are written in difficult-to-understand medical terms. Doctors may have schedules which do not permit sufficient time spent with clients in education, decision making, and evaluation of a method; therefore, the nurse assumes primary responsibility in this area.

After starting a method, women often have questions or concerns when at home. They may be reluctant to appear unsure or be afraid to ask a "stupid question." Telephone calls to and from a client are an excellent means of evaluating use and satisfaction with the contraceptive method. No question is too ridiculous and all concerns must be treated with serious consideration.

If the nurse is doubtful that the client fully understands the method or if there are other considerations that need close supervision, referral may be helpful. The clinic or office nurse can enlist the aid of a public health or school nurse to help the client. A family-planning nurse initiates a referral to the primary physician when preexisting medical conditions may affect contraceptive use. Nurses in ambulatory settings and emergency rooms may discuss birth control information with episodic clients and refer them for help in obtaining and using a method. Secondary-based nurses, especially those in pediatrics and postpartum, may have many contacts with patients or family members who desire contraceptive information and services.

In all these cases, nurses must first be aware of sexuality, both in themselves and in their clients. The very young adult, the middle-aged person, and the aged may need and want information on how to prevent unwanted pregnancy. Clients are not always courageous enough to ask without first having been given the opportunity. The nurse first must be aware enough to be "askable."

> Contraception is practiced in order to enjoy sexual relations without suffering the consequences of unwanted reproduction.[11]

Agencies, educators, organizations, and parents frequently seek to separate sexuality from birth control. Family planning groups tend to emphasize the social and health benefits of limiting family size, while public institutions are likely to give lip service to sex education but to specifically prohibit birth control education.

Reasons for ignoring the sexual implications of birth control are cited by Stycos.[11] Parents and schools often believe that people, particularly adolescents, will increase sexual activity if the fear of unwanted pregnancy is eliminated. Thus information about birth control for adolescents has been much more difficult to obtain than education about reproduction, venereal diseases, and "illegitimate" babies. Western religion has tended to define sexuality as evil unless it is for procreation and is within the marriage bond. Health professionals and the advertising industry always have been more willing to publicly discuss intimate personal hygiene relating to bowel regularity, underarm and genital odors, and menstrual difficulties than to publicly acknowledge that humans have sexual feelings regardless of age, condition, or setting. An honest, nonjudgmental reason for providing contraceptive information is to allow sexual intercourse to be joyfully free from anxiety about subsequent unwanted pregnancy. Contraceptive technology has made more liberated sexuality possible. It is the responsibility of aware health professionals to present this psychological advantage of contraception along with the health, social, and financial advantages.

LEARNING ACTIVITIES

1 View available films: *Hope Is Not a Method* and *Modern Methods of Birth Control* and discuss their appropriateness for various client groups.
2 Discuss the following:
   a Implications of nurse's bias on contraceptive counseling.
   b Group trends versus community or client population trends.
   c Will a woman who has had an elective tubal sterilization procedure have fewer symptoms during menopause than a woman who retained her childbearing capacity until menopause?
   d Discuss the more effective the contraceptive, the greater the risks.
   e How do you feel about Christopher Tietze's[12] statement that the safest form of fertility control is the diaphragm backed up by abortion?
   f If you had a choice in choosing a contraceptive for a client, which of the following criteria would be most important to you?
      1 No side effects
      2 No deaths
      3 Acceptable to both partners
      4 Very effective in preventing pregnancy
   g Which of the criteria above would most influence your contraceptive choice for *yourself?*
   h Discuss the statement by Stycos[11] that contraception is a means of enhancing and encouraging sexual pleasure.

REFERENCES

1 Kristen Luker, *Taking Chances: Abortion and the Decision Not To Contracept,* University of California Press, Berkeley, Calif., 1975, p. 32.
2 R. A. Hatcher, G. K. Stewart, F. Guest, R. Finkelstein, and C. Godwin, *Contraceptive Technology: 1976–1977,* Irvington Publishers, New York, 1976, p. 91.
3 Boston Women's Health Book Collective, "Birth Control," in *Our Bodies, Ourselves,* Simon and Schuster, New York, 1976, Chap. 10.
4 M. Nafziger, *A Cooperative Method of Natural Birth Control,* The Book Publishing Co., Summertown, Tenn., 1976.
5 E. L. Billings, J. J. Billings, and M. Catarinich: *Atlas of the Ovulation Method,* Liturgical Press, Collegeville, Minn., 1974.
6 Hatcher, op. cit., p. 65.

7   Ibid., p. 62.
8   Ibid., p. 59.
9   B. Goldstein, "Abstinence and Contraception" and "Sterilization, Abortion and Artificial Insemination," in *Human Sexuality,* McGraw-Hill, New York, 1976.
10 Joseph E. Davis, "Vasectomy," *AJN* **72**(3):511 (1972).
11 H. Edey, "Sterilization," *N.Y. Med.* **26**(8):339–343 (1970).
12 J. M. Stycos, "Desexing Birth Control," *Fam. Plann. Perspect.* **9**(6):286–292 (1977).
13 Christopher Tietze and Sarah Lewit, "Legal Abortion," *Scientific American* **236**(1):27 (1977).

BIBLIOGRAPHY

Byrne, D., and L. Byrne: "Contraception and Family Planning," in *Exploring Human Sexuality,* Thomas Y. Crowell, 1977, Chap. 9.

Cherniak, D., and A. Feingold: *Birth Control Handbook,* Montreal Health Press, Montreal, 1974.

Delora, J. S., and C. A. B. Warren: "Contraception, Sterilization, and Abortion," in *Understanding Sexual Interaction,* Houghton Mifflin, Boston, 1977, p. 404 and 407.

Fischman, S. H.: "Choosing an Appropriate Contraceptive," *Nurs. Outlook* **15**:28–31 (1967).

Gagnon, J. H.: "Physical Health and Sexual Conduct," in *Human Sexualities,* Scott, Foresman, Glenview, Ill., 1977, Chap. 19.

Huxall, L. K.: "Today's Pill and the Individual Woman," *MCN: Am. J. of Matern. Child Nurs.* **2**:359–363 (1977).

Katchadourian, H. A., and D. T. Lunde, "Contraception," in *Fundamentals of Human Sexuality,* Holt, 1972, Chap. 6.

McCary, J. L.: "Birth Control," in *Human Sexuality,* Van Nostrand, Princeton, N.J., 1973, Chap. 14.

Sandberg, E. C., and R. I. Jacobs: "Psychology of the Misuse and Rejection of Contraception," presented at the 37th Annual Meeting of the Pacific Coast Obstetrical and Gynecological Society, Kauai, Hawaii, November 1970, printed in *Am. J. Obstet. Gynecol.* **110**:227–242 (1971).

Chapter 10

Pregnancy

Pregnancy is a crisis period for most women and their partners whether it be planned or unplanned, wanted or unwanted. Caplan states that pregnancy is like puberty and menopause in that pregnancy is a period of increased susceptibility to other stresses, a period of altered behavior, disequilibrium, and emotional upset.[1] During pregnancy, a woman has to cope with more problems, and with new problems, at a time when her capacity to deal with any stress is altered.[2]

In most cases, pregnancy is undeniable proof that a man and woman have been sexually active and have had intercourse. For some women (especially young adolescents) and for their families, it is the fact of intercourse that is hard to accept, not the fact of pregnancy. ("I'm not upset that she's pregnant, but I'm mad that she's been screwing around.") Pregnancy can be used to prove a consummated marriage, to prove the masculinity of the partner, or to prove the femininity of the woman. Pregnancy may be sought as a means of improving or ensuring a sexual relationship. Whether for better or worse, pregnancy does alter the dyad relationship as well as other family relationships.

Falicov states that " . . . for many women, motherhood may represent a supreme test and a proof of one's womanhood, bringing a fuller and more mature acceptance of one's femininity. Furthermore . . . women commented that the period of pregnancy seemed to aid in shedding traces of one's timidity in relation to bodily function and to augment intimacy in the marital interaction as well as prompt some abandonment of one's girlishness."[3] Being pregnant changes one's social status from child to adult.

PSYCHOSEXUAL CHANGES

Sexual desire and sexual responsiveness change during a pregnancy. Masters and Johnson believe that sexual responsiveness and frequency of intercourse decrease during the first trimester due to psychological factors. During the second trimester, sexual desire increases, perhaps due to increased pelvic congestion. The third trimester, the authors believe, brings another decline in interest and response because of physical factors or fear of harm to the baby.[4]

Other studies by Solberg et al.[5] and by Pasini[6] found a gradual decline from first to third trimester, especially in primiparae. Solberg's study showing a decrease in frequency of sexual intercourse in the second and third trimesters cited the following reasons for the decrease: 46 percent physical discomfort, 27 percent fear of injury to the baby, 23 percent loss of interest, 17 percent awkwardness of coital positions, 6 percent reasons extraneous to pregnancy, 4 percent loss of attractiveness, 17 percent recommendations of people other than the physician, and other reasons, 15 percent.

In the Falicov study, tension and vaginal tightness were reported in the first trimester, as well as a fear of miscarriage. In the midtrimester, fatigue, breast tenderness, and genital discomfort contributed to a decrease in sexual activity. Women in the third trimester were more relaxed, but did report a decrease in coitus even if their physicians said nothing about stopping, because they had heard or read that they should stop "for the sake of the baby."[7] Pasini also points out that a positive feeling about the pregnancy promotes a good sexual relationship during the pregnancy; a negative attitude can contribute to a reduction in sexual desire and responsiveness.[8]

Whether or not sexual interest is increased, the pregnant woman probably does have strong needs for loving attention and especially for physical intimacy.

Tolor and De Gazia, in a study of 216 pregnant women, found that all the subjects had a greatly increased desire for body contact with their sexual partner. Changes in location of erogenous zones also were reported.[9] As the woman's body changes, her feelings about her sexual attractiveness may be altered. The physical alterations during the first trimester (swollen breasts, nausea, vomiting, and fatigue) may be heightened by psychological conflicts about the pregnancy.[10] She needs assurance from her partner that she is still sexually desirable.

However, the partner may also be experiencing psychological and physical changes. Some men have symptoms of nausea, vomiting, backache, and fatigue which reflect sympathetic concern for the woman or a need to be involved in the pregnancy. The phenomenon is called *couvade*. If the woman becomes engrossed in herself and her unborn child, the partner may feel abandoned and lonely. "He may find himself going outside the home for comfort and understanding, becoming interested in a new hobby, or getting involved with his work.

This may also be the time of the husband's first extramarital affair."[11] Men may view the pregnant woman as glowingly beautiful or as disgusting. She may become more sexually desirable or may arouse sexual revulsion or may even be frightening to her partner in her new image. His worry or self-consciousness about the fetus may impair his ability to function sexually.

INTERCOURSE DURING PREGNANCY

For most women, sexual intercourse and orgasm are safe during pregnancy and should be discussed and recommended by the nurse. Some couples seem to need only simple information and permission to be sexual during pregnancy. Physiological, psychological, and anatomical barriers to sexual pleasure can be discussed freely with both partners in an attempt to anticipate potential problems. Couples need to know about vascular changes which affect the breasts and pelvic region and which may increase sensitivity. As the woman's abdomen increases in size, changes in coital position or in mode of sexual pleasuring may be helpful. The nurse can suggest side by side, rear entry, or female superior positions if the "missionary position" is uncomfortable. Couples may need permission to use hand or mouth stimulation as an adjunct to intercourse. (Cunnilingus is perfectly acceptable so long as the partner does not blow air into the vagina. Fatal air embolism can occur as a result in pregnant women, since air can enter the placental circulation.[12,13])

Penile-vaginal intercourse should be encouraged for pregnant couples except in the following situations:[14]

1   There is a history of early miscarriage. Abnormal fetal development, maternal disease, and endocrine defects are the most frequent causes of first trimester spontaneous abortion. If multiple miscarriages have preceded the present pregnancy, the couple may decide to refrain from intercourse in an attempt to influence the outcome of the pregnancy. They will need support in this decision as well.

2   The woman has fibroids, uterine abnormalities, or cervical incompetence. Careful prenatal supervision is essential in order to recognize early cervical shortening or dilation. If cervical banding is done to tighten the cervix, intercourse may be resumed.

3   There is evidence of premature rupture of the amniotic membranes. Intercourse could introduce bacterial infection.

4   There is unexplained vaginal bleeding. Any vaginal bleeding is considered abnormal in a pregnancy. One serious cause of bleeding can be placenta previa, which in turn causes hemorrhage and threatens both fetal and maternal life. Until the cause of bleeding is determined, intercourse should be stopped.

5   There is abdominal pain. Impending labor, either premature or term, can be signaled by pain.

Although there is no reliable evidence that the uterine contractions caused by female orgasm lead to premature labor, women with a history of premature delivery should be cautioned against orgasm (but not against intercourse) during the last 6 to 8 weeks before term. The uterus contracts throughout the antepartum period, but the sensitivity seems to increase as term approaches.[15]

Women and their partners can be encouraged to use other forms of sexual expression as well as coitus. Cuddling, kissing, manual stimulation, body massage, and other kinds of lovemaking should not be ignored during pregnancy (or at any other time).

A few women will engage in intercourse despite their negative feelings about it simply out of fear that their husbands might be unfaithful if sex is withdrawn. These couples need extra counseling, preferably together, for help in discussing feelings and arriving at mutually acceptable compromises.

POSTPARTUM SEXUALITY

Just as myth, tradition, and Victorian attitudes have affected sexual expression during pregnancy, sexuality after pregnancy also is affected. "No sex for 6 weeks before delivery and for 6 weeks after" seems to be such common advice that it rarely is questioned. The reasons for postpartum abstinence vary from fear of pain to fear of another pregnancy. The resumption of intercourse may be delayed because of fatigue and preoccupation with the new infant, because of absence of desire, because of breast sensitivity, postpartum depression, or performance anxiety.

If an episiotomy (Fig. 10-1) was performed at delivery, it usually is healed completely in 2 weeks, and intercourse can be comfortably resumed. If no episiotomy was done, intercourse may be resumed at any time. A woman who fears pain may seek to avoid intercourse long after the incision has healed and may need permission to try nongenital lovemaking prior to returning to coitus.

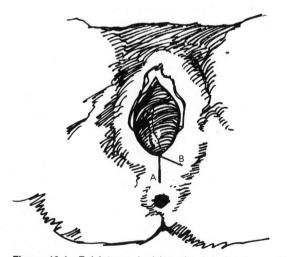

Figure 10-1 Episiotomy. Incision site A is for the median episiotomy and site B is for the mediolateral. *(From J. Clausen et al., Maternity Nursing Today, 2/e, McGraw-Hill, New York, 1976, p. 238.)*

Some women desire a more rapid return to intercourse. Women whose husbands wanted sexual gratification were found by Falicov to resume intercourse earlier than women whose husbands were disinterested in sex.[14]

In resuming intercourse, some couples may feel "out of practice" and perhaps need to go through a period of adjustment and exploration similar to what they first experienced when they initiated their sexual relationship.

The lubrication of the vagina may be decreased due to lowered systemic estrogen in nursing mothers, and an artificial lubricant such as estrogen cream, contraceptive foam or jelly, surgical gels, or saliva can be recommended to increase comfort and pleasure. Breast milk may be released at the point of orgasm in uncontrollable spurts. Women and their partners who are prepared for this phenomenon will find it less embarrassing or frightening. Some women find that the experience of breast feeding causes heightened breast sensitivity.

Nurses are sought out by women for discussions of sexuality and pregnancy. Unfortunately, many nurses are not well informed about the physiological and psychosexual rationale for the advice they give to women during pregnancy. Furthermore, many nurses simply are too embarrassed to provide more than vague references and implied explanations. Quirk and Hassenein interviewed obstetrical nursing instructors about what they taught students. One reason given for postpartum abstention until the 6-week checkup was to prevent pregnancy until the physician could provide contraceptives.[16] Surely these nurses were knowledgeable enough to discuss birth control methods with women and to help them use a nonprescription method until the physician could offer the medical options of the contraceptive pill and the IUD (intrauterine device). Most likely, the nurses avoided such intimate discussions because of personal discomfort and embarrassment.

Nurses must be able to discuss not only family planning during the postpartum, but more intimate topics as well. Women need to talk about changes in their sexual feelings, about the sexual interest of their partners, about their fear of injuring themselves, about their fear of having a "stretched-out vagina" which will no longer satisfy their partner, and about their altered physical appearance. None of these worries is simple, nor can any be discussed in a vague manner. None can be dismissed as "minor problems" which will work out by themselves. Men and women need honest and direct communication from knowledgeable care givers during the antepartum, intrapartum, and postpartum periods.

GUIDELINES FOR NURSES

1 Take a sexual history. A sexual history taken early in the pregnancy will provide baseline information about the sexual experience and expectations of the woman and her partner.

2 Include the partner whenever possible. Potential fathers can be included in consultations and can be present during the pelvic examination. He can feel the woman's uterus and hear fetal heart tones. He can be present not only during labor but during delivery as well. (Some hospitals now are allowing fathers to be present during cesarean deliveries.) He can be encouraged to ask

questions, vent his fears and frustrations, and be instructed in ways to help the woman cope.

3 Give permission to be sexual during and after pregnancy. Encourage sexual intimacy and nongenital lovemaking as well as intercourse.

4 Give specific suggestions whenever appropriate. Suggestions may include changes in coital position, foreplay, and the inclusion of manual and oral stimulation.

Vignette

Problem List

1 Health promotion
2 Desires contraception
3 Three months' postpartum
4 Dyspareunia

Subjective Data

"The baby is fine. I just stay home and take care of her all day, but I'm still tired at night. We've been having a problem with intercourse ever since she was born, though. It hurts me a lot, like I was being ripped apart inside."

Objective Data

Normal pelvic examination. Delivery was normal—no forceps. Uncomplicated and well-healed episiotomy. No infection or other gynecologic abnormalities. Pelvic examination did not cause discomfort.

Assessment

Painful intercourse may be caused by psychological factors or by reduction in lubrication (dyspareunia).

Plan

1 Discuss problem with both partners.
2 Suggest longer foreplay, use of additional lubricant, and change in position to allow more control by female partner over depth of penile thrusting.
3 Explore possibility of discord caused by infant's influence on marriage. Is mother able to get away from baby now and then? Does baby interrupt lovemaking?
4 Reevaluate in 1 to 2 weeks after couple has tried suggestions. If no improvement, refer for sexual therapy to a qualified therapist or counselor.

INFERTILITY

As defined by Novak and Novak, infertility is "the inability to initiate the reproductive process on the part of the couple who have desired and attempted to reproduce for a reasonable length of time."[17] The chances of conceiving a child are affected by the ages of the partners, the frequency of intercourse, and the length of intercourse exposure. Age of peak fertility for men and women is the middle twenties and the decline after that is quite gradual. If intercourse occurs about four times per week, conception is likely to occur within 6 months.

Infertility is differentiated from sterility: infertility is relative difficulty in conceiving but conception probably is possible with specific suggestions, techniques, or surgical or medical intervention. Sterility is absolute inability to achieve conception, and usually is irreversible. Approximately 15 percent of couples will experience infertility and probably 5 to 10 percent will remain sterile.[18]

Infertility is a problem with multiple causes. Some general causes include nutritional deficiencies; fatigue; tobacco, alcohol, and drug abuse; and sexual ignorance relating to douching and coital position. Impotence in the male or vaginismus in the female are obvious causes which sometimes are overlooked. Genital anomalies and endocrine system dysfunction can lead to infertility, as can diseases such as endometriosis, mumps, and sexually transmitted infections. The long-term effects of the oral contraceptive pills and the IUD are not known to influence fertility, but this possibility is being studied. Other research involves immunology and cervical mucus-sperm incompatibility.

Management of the infertile couple requires sensitivity and perceptiveness on the part of health care providers. The history and physical examination begin the evaluation. The information discussed during this phase can be intensely personal, and hence be quite threatening and upsetting. The entire relationship must be scrutinized, including the couple's coital practices, feelings about pregnancy and parenting, and their sexual self-confidence. Since a large part of the self-concept of some men and women is represented by the ability to have a child, the inability to conceive can have serious implications for the identity and adequacy of the individuals involved.

Physicians and nurses cooperate in identification of infertility. Many women find that they can relate more easily to another female; male nurses can be very helpful to men with infertility problems. Nurses in family planning clinics, obstetricians' offices, family practice situations, and in public health departments will find that questions about infertility arise frequently, especially if the nurse is "askable" and knowledgeable about sexual matters.

After the couple has embarked upon an investigation of their infertility, counseling becomes even more vital. Couples may experience stress in their relationship because their sexual encounters cannot help but be focused on conception. The joy of sexual intimacy can be diminished by the intensity of desire for a pregnancy. For some couples, a group counseling experience may be beneficial. Men, especially, may feel relief at finding other males in a similar situation, and may be reassured that their masculinity need not be threatened by infertility. Nurses can help couples remember to find pleasure in each other, even if conception does not occur. Nurses function as friend and confidante for women who feel inadequate because they are unable to "give him a baby." The woman's self-image as a feminine and desirable person may need considerable support.

Alternatives

Adoption Couples who are unable to conceive a child have other options which will enable them to become parents. Adoption is the choice most frequently made. Even though the "perfect adoptable child" (newborn, white, with no defects) is rarely available, adoption agencies do place mixed-racial, handicapped, and older children with eager parents. Nurses assist these couples by facilitating communication with adoption agencies and by helping couples adjust to their new role as parents.

Artificial Insemination Conception which takes place outside the female body is a relatively recent phenomenon ("test tube babies"). However, collection of semen for artificial insemination has been known about and practiced for hundreds—or perhaps thousands—of years. Even the *Talmud,* the Jewish book of laws, mentions the process. Because of confidentiality restrictions, it is difficult to estimate the number of conceptions accomplished by artificial insemination. An estimated 250,000 people in the United States alone might be the result of artificial insemination.

Usually, AI (artificial insemination) is used when the male partner has a low sperm count, nonmotile sperm, or is infertile. AIH is the term used when the husband's own semen is used alone. AID is the term used when the husband's semen is mixed with donor semen. Donors are anonymous and usually are students in professional schools who are screened carefully for genetic history, appearance, intelligence and educational background, and perhaps even religion. The purpose of the screening is to attempt to conceive a child who resembles the husband.

The husband or donor masturbates to collect a specimen of semen. The specimen is used immediately or is preserved by freezing. Frozen sperm are stored in so-called "sperm banks" and may be capable of fertilization for an indefinite period of time. A man facing sterility from radiotherapy or chemotherapy or from an elective vasectomy might want to preserve his sperm to enable him to father children later.

Many legal questions surround artificial insemination, particularly in regard to the legal rights of children conceived in this manner. So far courts have ruled that the child is the legitimate offspring of the couple, and that the husband is responsible for child support as he would be for any other child. The California Supreme Court ruled in 1968 that a sterile father who consented to artificial insemination with donor semen for his wife had to pay child support after a divorce and that the AID child was not the product of an adulterous marriage.

Since the ability to father a child is tied so closely to the self-image of some men, they are unable to participate in or even agree to the artificial insemination of their wives. For others, ethical or religious sanctions inhibit them.

LEARNING ACTIVITIES

1 Interview a woman in an antepartum clinic or on a postpartum unit in a hospital. Ask her about sexual changes during pregnancy; her partner's reactions; medical, nursing, and "nonprofessional" advice she may have received; and her expectations for the immediate future.

    2 Discuss with the following pregnant women your interventions relative to sexuality:

        a A 16-year-old black woman who is having her second child.

        b A 30-year-old primipara who has a million questions about sex.

        c The young married woman who believes pregnancy has caused her to become frigid.

        d The 40-year-old grandmultipara who plans to have a tubal sterilization after this delivery.

    3 How do various cultures view pregnancy? Ask or read about American Indian, chicano, rural poor, upper-middle-class white, urban black, Oriental, and European cultures.

REFERENCES

1 G. Caplan, "Psychological Aspects of Maternity Care," *Am. J. Public Health* **47**:25–31 (1597).

2 M. Roznoy, *Prediction of Patient Behavior during Abortion,* unpublished master's thesis, University of Wisconsin, May 1975, p. 6.

3 C. J. Falicov, "Sexual Adjustment during First Pregnancy and Postpartum," *Am. J. Obstet. Gynecol.* **117**(7):991–1000 (1973).

4 W. H. Masters and V. E. Johnson, *Human Sexual Response,* Little, Brown, Boston, 1966.

5 D. A. Solberg, J. Butler, and N. M. Wagner, "Sexual Behavior in Pregnancy," *N. Engl. J. Med.* **288**:1098 (1973).

6 W. Pasini, "Sexuality during Pregnancy and Postpartum Frigidity," in John Money and Herman Musaph (eds.), *Handbook of Sexology,* Excerpta Medica, Amsterdam, 1977, p. 887.

7 Falicov, op. cit., pp. 994–996.

8 Pasini, op. cit., p. 890.

9 A. Tolor and P. V. De Gazia, "Sexual Attitudes and Behavior Problems during and following Pregnancy," *Arch. Sex. Behav.* **5**(6) (1976).

10 M. A. Friedrich, "Psychological Changes during Pregnancy," *Contemp. Obstet. Gynecol.* **9**:29 (1977).

11 W. H. Masters and V. E. Johnson, op. cit.

12 H. Benjamin, "Case of Fatal Air Embolism through an Unusual Sexual Act," *J. Clin. Psychopathol.* **7**(4):815–820 (1946).

13 J. Butler and N. Wagner, "Sexuality during Pregnancy and Postpartum," in Richard Green (ed.), *Human Sexuality,* Williams & Wilkins, Baltimore, 1975, p. 143.

14 Falicov, op. cit., p. 999.

15 R. C. Goodlin, D. W. Kelter, and M. Raffin, "Orgasm during Late Pregnancy," *Obstet. Gynecol.* **38**:916 (1971).

16 B. Quirk and R. Hassenein, "The Nurse's Role in Advising Patients on Coitus during Pregnancy," *Nurs. Clin. North Am.* **8**:501–507 (1973).

17 E. Novak and E. R. Novak (eds.), *Textbook of Gynecology,* Williams & Wilkins, Baltimore, 1952, p. 657.

18 S. J. Behrman and R. W. Kistner, "A Rational Approach to the Evaluation of Infertility," in *Progress in Infertility,* Little, Brown, Boston, 1968, p. 3.

BIBLIOGRAPHY

Behrman, S. J., and R. W. Kistner: "A Rational Approach to the Evaluation of Infertility," in *Progress in Infertility,* Little, Brown, Boston, 1968, p. 3.

Boston Women's Health Book Collective: *Our Bodies, Ourselves,* Simon and Schuster, New York, 1976.

Caplan, G.: "Psychological Aspects of Maternity Care," *Am. J. Public Health* **47**:25–31 (1957).

Clausen, J. P., M. H. Flook, and B. Ford: *Maternity Nursing Today,* McGraw-Hill, New York, 1977.

Dickason, E. J., and M. O. Schult: *Maternal and Infant Care,* McGraw-Hill, New York, 1975.

Falicov, C. J.: "Sexual Adjustment during First Pregnancy and Postpartum," *Am. J. Obstet. Gynecol.* **117**(7) (1973).

Goldstein, B.: *Human Sexuality,* McGraw-Hill, New York, 1976.

Goodlin, R. C., D. W. Kelter, and M. Raffin: "Orgasm during Late Pregnancy," *Obstet. Gynecol.* **38**:916 (1971).

Green, R. (ed.): *Human Sexuality,* Williams & Wilkins, Baltimore, 1975.

Lytle, N. A.: *Nursing of Women in the Age of Liberation,* Brown, Dubuque, Ia, 1977.

Masters, W. H., and V. E. Johnson: *Human Sexual Response,* Little, Brown, Boston, 1966.

Novak, E., and E. R. Novak (eds.): *Textbook of Gynecology,* Williams & Wilkins, Baltimore, 1952, p. 657.

Pasini, W.: "Sexuality during Pregnancy and Postpartum Frigidity," in John Money and Herman Musaph (eds.), *Handbook of Sexology,* Excerpta Medica, Amsterdam, 1977, p. 887.

Quirk, B., and R. Hassenein: "The Nurse's Role in Advising Patients on Coitus during Pregnancy," *Nurs. Clin. North Am.* **8**:501–507 (1973).

Roznoy, M.: *Prediction of Patient Behavior during Abortion,* unpublished master's thesis, University of Wisconsin, May 1975, p. 6.

Chapter 11

Abortion

Abortion is defined as the termination of pregnancy before the fetus is able to survive on its own. Dickason and Schult suggest the following classifications:[1]

I Spontaneous (involuntary) abortion
  A Threatened
  B Inevitable
    1 Complete
    2 Incomplete
    3 Habitual
  C Missed or retained
II Induced (voluntary) abortion
  A Legal
    1 Therapeutic (performed for medical reasons)
    2 Elective
      a Menstrual regulation
      b Dilation and evacuation (aspiration abortion)
      c Hypertonic injection (saline abortion)
      d Prostaglandin
      e Hysterotomy
  B Illegal
    1 Criminal
    2 Self-induced

SPONTANEOUS ABORTION

Sometimes called a miscarriage, an involuntary abortion creates physical and emotional difficulties for a woman. If the pregnancy was planned and a baby eagerly anticipated, the loss can be overwhelmingly sad. If the pregnancy precipitated major life changes (getting married, quitting a job), the frustration will be great. If the woman defines herself in terms of her childbearing capacity, a spontaneous abortion may lead her to feel inadequate and incompetent.

An estimated 41 percent of all pregnancies are spontaneously aborted.[2] In the past, hormones [DES (diethylstilbestrol)] were administered to avert a threatened abortion. The subsequent dangers of this therapy now are known, and chemical intervention is undertaken rarely. The current philosophy is wait-and-see, with occasional surgical action such as Shirodkar procedures to delay early delivery in a woman with "incompetent cervix." A threatened abortion sometimes can be averted if the woman rests at home until the abnormal vaginal bleeding ceases. Intercourse is proscribed for at least 2 weeks after the bleeding episode is over.

If the abortion becomes inevitable, no successful intervention is available. The helplessness and hopelessness of a woman awaiting an inevitable sponta- neous abortion can be agonizing for the woman, for health care givers, for the woman's family, and for her partner. The attitudes of nurses and physicians may be easily misinterpreted by the woman. The care giver may mean well and say, "The abortion is inevitable and there is nothing we can do to stop it. A spontaneous abortion usually is caused by a fetal defect, so perhaps it is better if the baby is not born. You can always try again." However, the woman may think that the doctor or the nurse simply does not care, is insensitive to the grief involved, and is refusing to do anything to help. It is far more helpful to recognize the anticipatory grieving that occurs and to provide sympathetic support. The potential parents can be encouraged to mourn in whatever way they choose, including crying or anger or apparent indifference to help.

The health care team must remember that the mourning for a miscarriage might be as intense as for a stillbirth and perhaps is more difficult to reconcile because the woman has lost something she never really "owned." The grieving process will be similar to that following the loss of a child, and the couple will need perceptive support from the nurse to cope constructively.

A missed or retained abortion may require a dilation and curettage or a saline procedure to induce labor. In these instances, the danger of infection, uterine perforation or hemorrhage, and clotting disturbances (disseminated inter- cellular coagulation) greatly increases the risk to the woman. Nursing interven- tion includes not only supportive physical care, but perceptive, sensitive, and sympathetic listening. The nurse should be especially alert to a reaction resem- bling postpartum depression after a spontaneous abortion. The hormonal changes are similar, and the possibility of this crisis should be considered carefully.

After an involuntary abortion, couples may be in conflict about whether or not to seek another pregnancy. The desire for a baby may be overshadowed by the need to avoid another emotionally painful experience. If no genetic, anatomic, or hormonal cause can be determined for the miscarriage, the couple should be advised to use a contraceptive method such as a diaphragm or foam for several months while the endometrium is rebuilding. During these months, the couple has time to work through feelings of guilt, mourning, and frustration and to reestablish sexual intimacy. When they feel ready, the couple may discontinue the contraception and pursue another pregnancy.

INDUCED ABORTION

Medical Aspects

Voluntary interruption of pregnancy involves safe, legal procedures done in a physician's office, a free-standing clinic, or a hospital. The earlier in a pregnancy that abortion is performed, the fewer are the medical, economic, and emotional risks. First-trimester abortion is legal in all 50 states since 1973. Pregnancy tests (which detect the presence of human chorionic gonadotropin in urine as an indication of pregnancy) are only reliable at about 2 weeks past the first missed menstrual period. Many women, especially those with irregular periods, wait even longer to find out whether or not they are pregnant, perhaps as long as 3 or 4 months. As a result these women have very little time to spend in decision making regarding abortion. Help from qualified counselors during the critical time of decision is invaluable to many women. This help may range from sympathetic listening as the pregnant woman "thinks out loud" to active intervention in pointing out advantages and disadvantages as part of creative problem solving. The feelings of partners, parents, and peers may exert great influence on the woman as she struggles to decide what to do. Nurses should include these significant others in counseling if possible; however, it is important that the woman not be coerced by them into making a decision with which she herself is not comfortable. Studies have found that women who have the support of a parent, partner, or friend had more positive postabortion reactions than women who faced abortion alone.[3,4]

Techniques of Abortion

Menstrual Regulation/Menstrual Extraction (0 to 6 Weeks from Last Menstrual Period) A woman who has had unprotected intercourse, who has been the victim of rape, or who experiences early symptoms of pregnancy may seek an abortion before a pregnancy test can be performed accurately. Endometrial aspiration can be performed in a physician's office without any cervical dilation or anesthesia. Aspiration of the uterine lining is accomplished by use of a narrow, flexible plastic tube which is inserted into the uterus. Gentle suction is applied by mechanical pump or by manual use of a large syringe. The procedure is quick and pain medication is seldom necessary.

One disadvantage of this early method is that it is difficult to determine if the fetal and placental parts have been totally removed. Retained tissue or even a retained pregnancy is possible, which may necessitate a second procedure.

Another disadvantage is that the procedure might have been done when the woman was not actually pregnant. For this reason, many physicians require a positive pregnancy test before doing any abortion procedure. Recent advances in the technology of very early pregnancy determination may precede an increase in very early endometrial extractions.

Dilation and Evacuation (D and E) (7 to 12 Weeks from Last Menstrual Period) This procedure is usually performed in a clinic or hospital setting, although it may be done safely in a physician's office as well. A flexible or rigid plastic cannula is passed through a dilated cervix into the uterine cavity. Suction is applied by machine and the contents of the uterus are withdrawn. After suctioning, the clinician may check the interior of the uterus with a standard curette for remaining tissue. Risks of this 5- to 15-minute procedure include perforation of the uterine wall, hemorrhage, and infection. Most women, although they experience cramping with the abortion procedure, need little or no analgesia. Some clinics use an oxytocic to promote uterine involution and/or a muscle relaxant such as Valium (Fig. 11-1).

The vacuum aspiration abortion is the most commonly used procedure. Of the 1 million abortions performed yearly in the United States, about 80 percent are of this type in the first trimester of pregnancy.

Dilation and Curettage (D and C) (8 to 12 or 15 Weeks since Last Menstrual Period) The D and C abortion is a procedure similar to the D and C done to correct hypermenorrhea and menstrual irregularity. Before aspiration abortion was recognized as a safer procedure, most first-trimester abortions were done by D and C. The risks of perforation, hemorrhage, and infection are greatest for the "late D and C"—abortion done at 12 to 15 weeks after the last menstrual period. The cervix is dilated, usually with the assistance of local anesthesia (paracervical block). The contents of the uterus are removed using a standard curette. The woman may be offered local or general anesthesia, and may require a longer recovery period than the suction abortion.

Intraamniotic Saline or Urea Instillation (Saline Abortion, Prostaglandin Abortion, "Salting Out," Late Abortion) (16 to 24 Weeks from Last Menstrual Period) After the sixteenth week of pregnancy, the intrauterine cavity can be located and a hypertonic solution such as 20% saline, or urea, infused. The solution causes the death of the fetus, which is then expelled by the process of labor. In the case of prostaglandin infusion, the fetus is not killed by the solution, but does not usually survive the stress of delivery. The fetus is not viable outside the uterus. The contractions of the uterus may be augmented by oxytocics which are administered intravenously. The process takes 12 to 48 hours and must be done in a hospital, since risks associated with this procedure (infection, hemor-

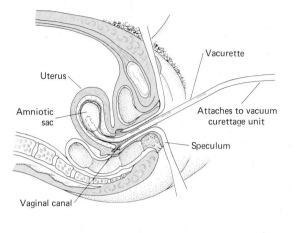

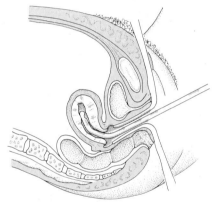

Figure 11-1 Aspiration abortion. (*From J. Hyde, Understanding Human Sexuality, McGraw-Hill, New York, 1979, p. 151.*)

rhage, retained placenta or retained tissue, and water intoxication) are higher than for first-trimester abortions.

Hysterotomy (after 10 Weeks from Last Menstrual Period. Very Rarely Used) Like a cesarean delivery, hysterotomy is major surgery. General anesthesia usually is used and the woman spends several postoperative days in the hospital. As with all other abortion procedures, future fertility is unaffected; however, future deliveries may be done by cesarean section.

NURSING INTERVENTION

Since 1973, the number of patients undergoing abortion procedures has risen to nearly 1 million per year. The only surgical procedure performed more frequently is tonsillectomy. Consequently, the number of nurses who care for patients before, during, and after abortion also has increased tremendously.

The goals of nursing intervention are summarized by Harper et al. as follows:[5]

1 Promote recovery.
2 Minimize physical complications.
3 Minimize psychic sequelae.

To these are added:

4 Avoid giving a lecture about sex, pregnancy, or birth control.
5 Promote emotional growth through creative problem solving.
6 Assist with planning subsequent pregnancies by providing contraceptive information and supplies.

Depending on the age of the pregnant woman, her decisions and her behavior may be heavily influenced by her peers, her parents, and her sexual partner. The nurse must be aware that these significant others may be coercive or destructive influences, even though they may believe themselves to be considering the woman's best interests.

For example, a young teenager may suffer criticism from peers for choosing to terminate a pregnancy. Adolescents may see babies as "fun" and motherhood as the quickest route to adulthood. Rarely are the long-term consequences of childbearing and childrearing considered fully.

The teenager may be concerned about the feelings and wishes of her parents, even before her own. Her parents may be struggling with their own feelings of failure, their despair over their daughter's lost virginity and lost innocence, their anger at the boy involved, and their feelings that abortion is wrong even though abortion is the only choice. The conflict over the morality of abortion frequently is more difficult for parents than for daughters. This situation may be explained by the realization that adults remember the time when abortion was a criminal act and was always a dreadfully dangerous and shameful undertaking. Adolescents today have grown up in a time when legalized abortion has made the procedure safe, uncomplicated, available, and morally acceptable to the majority of the population.

Many parents take comfort in talking with a nonjudgmental nurse about these conflicting feelings. They may be relieved to discover that many other parents have faced similar situations and have made similar decisions.

A major problem faced by many parents is the issue of punishment. Judeo-Christian ethics and Victorian attitudes have led many to believe that a woman should "pay" for the sin of sexual pleasure by bearing the consequences (a child). In this frame of reference, abortion seems "too easy" because no punishment is involved. Counselors and nurses in abortion facilities have frequently had a parent say privately, "Don't make this abortion too easy for my daughter. I want her to suffer a little so she will learn a lesson from this experience." The professional may find such an attitude infuriating, but if the

Figure 11-2 (*Cartoon by Bill Sanders. Courtesy of The Milwaukee Journal.*)

tremendous conflict reflected in these remarks is remembered, the nursing response can be helpful and even growth producing. The nurse can point out that the abortion is an important event regardless of whether it causes physical pain, that adolescents learn from such experiences, and can make better adult decisions as a result (Fig. 11-2).

The partner of a woman exerts great influence on her decisions. The partner who abandons the pregnant woman rejects her not only as a woman but also as a potential mother. Some men abandon women who choose abortion because the men are opposed to abortion. The opposition may be religious or moral in origin, but may also reflect a "macho" ethic wherein masculinity is measured in number of children sired. The woman, abandoned, pregnant, and considering abortion, may find herself angry with all men and may find difficulty in establishing future relationships with men.

Supportive male partners can be a great help to a woman throughout the abortion experience. The reaffirmation of the relationship establishes a basis for planning future pregnancies. These men usually cooperate with contraceptive decisions made by the woman and can be helpful to her in coping with possible residual guilt or postabortion sadness.

Vignette

Susan, age 15.

Problem List

1 Saline abortion
2 Emotional immaturity
3 Desires contraception

Subjective Data

"I want to get on the pill to regulate my periods. I don't plan to have sex anymore until I get married. We used to have sex about once a week, but I'm going to stop now. Sex is yucky and just causes a lot of trouble."

Objective Data

Susan's boyfriend is with her constantly. Observed by night nurse to be petting heavily in hospital bed before saline instillation.

Assessment

Susan may have unrealistic expectations about her self-control. Boyfriend seems insistent about sex.

Plan

1 Initiate discussion about human sexuality with Susan and her boyfriend. Concentrate on giving information and permission.

2 Instruct in contraceptive methods. Encourage them to make a choice "just in case."

3 Reassess at 3-week checkup:
   a Relationship with boyfriend
   b Feelings about sex, self-respect
   c Feelings about abortion
   d Reaction to contraceptive method

PREPARING NURSES ABOUT ABORTION

Basic nursing education rarely prepares nurses to be effective care givers to patients seeking abortion. Schools of nursing may be reluctant to place students in abortion clinics because of the controversial nature of the abortion issue. Few fully qualified and willing instructors are available, and the clinical supervision in such an emotionally charged situation is time and energy consuming. Nevertheless, nursing students, both graduate and undergraduate, benefit from a clinical experience with women undergoing an abortion. The instructor in this situation must be very comfortable with abortion and abortion procedures, since students often feel very uncomfortable during this kind of learning experience. A description of one program follows.

An elective clinical placement (on a unit where second-trimester abortions were done) was offered to nursing students at a large midwestern university. The objectives for students were as follows. Each student:

1 Describes how personal philosophy (values, beliefs, and perceptions) affects nursing practice in working with individuals and families in the abortion clinic.
   A Verbalizes own philosophy about relevant issues such as population control, eugenics, women's rights, when does life begin, and other legal and ethical problems). Discusses the impact of values on the care provided.
   B Identifies differing cultural views regarding unwanted pregnancies and discusses how these views may affect nursing practice.
   C Demonstrates ability to identify when personal philosophy is in conflict with that of the patient or the patient's family.
   D When personal philosophy is in conflict with that of the patient, develops appropriate strategies for dealing with such conflicts which may be growth producing for the patient and family.
2 Applies principles of crisis theory to patient care situations.
   A Observes patient behavior and coping. Analyzes this data within a framework of patient's level of development in order to assess and plan for nursing intervention.
   B Assesses decision-making abilities of the patient and family, including alternatives to be considered. Nursing care assistance will be given to help the patient carry out the decision most effectively.
3 Applies principles outlined by Johnson to specific patient care situations.[6]
   A Explains rationale for patient preparation before a stressful procedure.
   B Explains rationale for "emotional support" to a patient under stress.
   C Plans intervention and anticipates any problems in patient support during stressful procedures.
   D Evaluates intervention with patient and faculty, based on identified problems of patient care.
4 Uses communication skills, both verbal and written, to facilitate coordination of patient care.
   A Uses problem-oriented system to account for care and evaluation in written form.
   B Participates in conferences with patient and with staff to assess and evaluate nursing care.
   C Demonstrates an awareness of the importance of coordinated care by working effectively with other health team members.
   D Assesses need for community nurse referral before patient is discharged, and initiates referral when appropriate. Referral will include a statement of the nursing problems identified, the patient's hospital course, and short- and long-term goals.
5 Uses knowledge of human sexuality and contraception when appropriate.
   A Participates in patient conferences and collects and analyzes data regarding patients' knowledge of contraception to plan for intervention and instruction regarding available methods of birth control.
   B Participates in patient discussion groups and offers information regard-

ing human sexuality in relationships when patient indicates a desire for this information.

6 Applies knowledge of fetal growth and development in the examination of the products of conception.

A Points out significant features of fetus which verify its gestational age.

B Examines the placenta and determines whether it is intact following delivery.

C Using the framework on grief and mourning outlined by Elisabeth Kübler-Ross[7] assesses patient's need to see the fetus, and allows this experience to occur if appropriate. Data pertinent to making this decision are collected from the patient herself, from an analysis of her situation, and from the responses of other patients in similar situations. Consultations with faculty and/or staff is suggested for the student who may have to deal with this experience.

Students met individually with the instructor during the week before their scheduled clinical experience. The student's personal goals were discussed and clarified, the student was encouraged to read reference material available in the library, and feelings and attitudes about abortion were explored. Students were expected to be able to discuss issues such as sexuality, contraception, and family crisis dynamics, since these questions probably would arise and need assessment, intervention, and evaluation by the student.

The saline induction procedure was used, and the patients were in the hospital approximately 3 days. The students spent an average of 18 hours with their patients over those 3 days. They participated in initial physical examinations, counseling interviews, the saline instillation, care of the patient during "labor," delivery of the fetus, postabortion counseling, contraceptive and sexuality education, and nursing referral to local community resources.

Objective 6 caused students great stress. The instructor used several techniques to minimize the shock experienced by students viewing an aborted fetus. First, a verbal description of the fetus was introduced, along with scale drawings of fetal growth and development. If another patient aborted before the student's assigned patient, this fetus was examined first. The instructor was careful to handle the fetus gently and to approach the examination in a quiet, dignified, and scholarly manner. The developmental stage of the fetus was determined by observation of characteristics such as hair, genitalia, and size.

Later, when the student's assigned patient delivered a fetus, the student was able to focus on support to the woman, and to deal with the fetus in a matter-of-fact, nonemotional way while with the patient. When examining the fetus with the instructor, students were able to express feelings of relief, sadness, and sometimes, confusion. Students were also better able to cope with questions from the woman regarding the sex of the fetus (a frequently asked question), the condition of the fetus, and what happened to the fetus after it was expelled.

Several days later, in a postclinical conference, students had reestablished emotional equilibrium. They were reflective, sobered, and surer of their feelings about pregnancy, abortion, and sexuality.

Evaluations submitted by the students contained comments like these:

"I got really involved, not just intellectually."
"I learned a lot about adolescents, their parents, and sex."
"My attitudes about abortion are not as absolute as I had thought."
"I feel shaken and exhausted, but also feel very positive."
"I faced some questions about sexuality by taking care of this patient who is my own age."
"Some of my half-formed opinions and attitudes became whole."
"I wish I knew more about human sexuality. That's mostly what my patient and her mother and her boyfriend needed to talk about."

ILLEGAL ABORTION

Since 1973, the number of deaths caused by abortion has decreased enormously. Rarely do emergency rooms treat women for incomplete criminal or self-induced abortion, in contrast to the years before abortion was declared legal. Nevertheless, women still seek to terminate their pregnancies by taking drugs such as quinine, cod liver oil, and milk of magnesia, by falling down stairs, and by using caustic douches.

A recent unprecedented court case involved a woman who attempted a self-induced abortion by using a knitting needle. When she was unsuccessful and sought medical help, she was arrested for attempted criminal abortion. This was the first time the woman herself was charged with illegal abortion; previously the abortionist alone was charged. The woman was found "not guilty by reason of insanity."[8]

If antiabortion forces succeed in returning abortion to illegality, women will again seek abortions from unqualified, insensitive, expensive criminal abortionists.

POSTABORTION INTERVENTION

The feelings of a woman when an abortion is over range from relief to depression. She may feel pride in having made and carried through an important decision. She may experience brief depression associated more with sadness over a loss than with regret or guilt. She may need help in her relationships with her parents and/or her sexual partner. She may find that sex is repulsive or frightening and may avoid a sexual relationship in order to avoid emotional pain. She may be very worried about her future fertility; some women seek another pregnancy in a conscious or unconscious attempt to prove reproductive ability.

The nurse's first responsibility is to become aware of the concerns of the patients, to be sensitive to their physical and emotional needs, and to recognize his or her own attitudes and beliefs about abortion.

Giving information includes an explanation of the procedure using salient features in the environment of the clinic to describe what will be happening. Leventhal and Johnson note in their research on the preparation of patients for traumatic procedures that patients should be told in descriptive detail what they will see, hear, taste, smell, and feel during the procedure.[5] If possible, instruments such as a speculum, dilators, and suction curette should be seen and handled by the patient. Ideally, the procedure room should be toured. The patient should meet the practitioner who will be performing the abortion ahead of time. According to Friedman et al., " . . . abortion presents a double challenge because it is both the termination of a pregnancy and a surgical procedure, and any surgery causes a complex of feelings related to invasion of the body."[9]

Women must be told what to expect before, during, and also after an abortion. Written information, in addition to verbal preparation, is helpful.

Permission is given to be frightened, to feel worried, and afterward, to feel sad and relieved. Women must be encouraged to ask questions, to ask for help from the nurse, to ask for pain medication, and to ask to be left alone if they desire privacy.

Specific suggestions include ways of coping with the stress of a pelvic examination and the abortion itself (relaxation techniques, breathing exercises, hand holding). After the procedure, suggestions include ways to reduce breast tenderness, contraceptive methods, and ways to deal with curious friends and relatives.

Some women will require more extensive intervention in the postabortion period. Referrals to local public health nurses, to social service or mental health consultants, and to local physicians might be appropriate in some cases. Continuing therapy is necessary for women with severe psychological sequelae to abortion; fortunately, such is rarely the case. Overall, the vast majority of women emerge from the abortion experience emotionally stronger and more healthy than before their decision to seek abortion.

REFERENCES

1 E. J. Dickason and M. O. Schult, *Maternal and Infant Care,* McGraw-Hill, New York, 1975, p. 411.
2 Bishop and Richards, in E. R. Novak, G. S. Jones, and H. W. Jones, *Novak's Textbook of Gynecology,* Williams & Wilkins, Baltimore, 1975, p. 641.
3 M. B. Bracken, M. Hachamovitch, and G. Grossman, "The Decision to Abort and Psychological Sequelae," *J. Nerv. Ment. Dis.* **188**:154–161 (1972).
4 M. Roznoy, Prediction of Patient Behavior during Abortion, unpublished master's thesis, University of Wisconsin, 1975.
5 M. W. Harper, B. R. Marcom, and V. D. Wall, "Abortion: Do Attitudes of Nursing Personnel Affect the Patients' Perception of Care?" *Nurs. Res.* **21**(4) (1972).
6 J. Johnson, "Effects of Accurate Expectations about Sensations on the Sensory and Distress Components of Pain," *Soc. Psychol.* **27**:261–275 (1973).
7 E. Kübler-Ross, *On Death and Dying,* Macmillan, New York, 1969.
8 Garrett, B., "An American Tragedy," in *Louisville Today* **3**:32–38 (January 1979).
9 C. M. Friedman, R. Greenspan, and F. Mittleman, "The Decision-Making Process and the Outcome of Abortion," in R. Kalmar (ed.), *Abortion: The Emotional Implications,* Kendall/Hunt, Dubuque, Ia., 1977.

BIBLIOGRAPHY

Arney, W. R., and W. H. Trescher: "Trends in Attitudes Toward Abortion 1972–1975," *Fam. Plann. Perspect.* **8**(3):117–124 (1976).

Bracken, M. B., M. Hachamovitch, and G. Grossman: "The Decision to Abort and Psychological Sequelae," *J. Nerv. Ment. Dis.* **188**:154–161 (1973).

Clancy, B.: "The Nurse and the Abortion Patient," *Nurs. Clin. North Amer.* **8**(3):469–478 (1973).

Cronewett, L. R., and J. M. Choyce: "Saline Abortion," *Am. J. Nurs.* **71**:1754–1757 (1971).

Friedman, C. M., R. Greenspan, and F. Mittleman: "The Decision-Making Process and the Outcome of Therapeutic Abortion," *Am. J. Psychiatry* **131**:1332–1337 (1974).

Hatcher, S. L.: "Termination of Pregnancy," in N. Y. Howells (ed.), *Modern Perspectives in Psycho-Obstetrics,* Brunner-Mazel, New York, 1972.

Osofsky, H., and J. Osofsky (eds.): *The Abortion Experience in the United States,* Harper & Row, New York, 1973.

Roe v. Wade, 93 Supreme Court 705 (1973), 41 USL Week 4213 (No. 70-18. January 22, 1973).

Roe v. Bolton, 93 Supreme Court 705 (1973), 41 USL Week 4233-4240 (No. 70-18. January 22, 1973).

Part Four

Sexuality and Health Disruptions

Chapter 12

Psychosexual Effects of Change

To become more effective in providing sexual health care, the psychosexual dynamics of those experiencing health disruptions need special attention. This chapter provides background material and presents some of the complex psychosocial and psychosexual interactions that influence sexuality of individuals and families experiencing changes in health. The concepts and behaviors that are presented are not unique to a particular health condition but may be experienced by persons with a wide variety of physical and/or mental health disruptions. The objectives of this chapter are:

    1 To present and discuss psychosocial and psychosexual responses to health disruptions
    2 To emphasize that each person, with any type of health change, presents unique personal characteristics and responses that may require specific attention for successful health care and/or satisfactory adaptation

    The selection of psychosexual concepts and responses for this chapter is based on input from staff nurses, students, and instructors regarding recognition, acceptance, understanding, and offering of therapeutic nursing interventions for clients with a wide variety of health disruptions. These responses may arise with the clients and families that are discussed in the following seven chapters. These same concepts will also apply to clients and families with many other types of health disruptions including arthritis, amputations, cerebrovascular disease, kidney failure and transplants, blindness, deafness, developmental disabilities, paralysis, and disfigurements. The psychosexual responses chosen for discussion are:

1 Importance of sex in illness
2 Disturbance of sexual self-concept
3 Coping with loss
4 Vulnerability in developmental and situational crises
5 Choosing alternatives
6 Aggravation of preexisting problems
7 Sexual acting out
8 Sexual relationship issues
9 Affective changes

IMPORTANCE OF SEX IN ILLNESS

Sexuality is a major aspect of the human experience in both health and illness. An individual's emotional and psychological adjustment to a chronic illness or handicap is somewhat dependent on past experiences, present resources, and the hope of remaining a whole person, including a sexual person.

Sexual attitudes, values, and understanding influence one's perception of self. Each individual attempts to resolve conflicts between personal sexual identity and the stress that is created by a particular illness or handicap. Some disruptions in health create specific physical and emotional vulnerabilities. The degree and influence of a health disruption on sexuality vary, depending on a variety of factors revolving around self, family, psychosocial environment, and professional or treatment resources.

Some individuals are able to make needed psychological and physiological changes and combat negative feedback—hence, maintain their full humanity. However, these individuals may need to fight a constant battle to keep themselves and family members from denying their needs, desires, rights, and responsibilities of their humanity, including all aspects of sexuality. Significant others—families, staff of social institutions, and health personnel—have a tendency to treat the person with a chronic illness or handicap as asexual. The more severe the health condition, the more likely the individual will avoid, or be forced to deny, the need for sexual expression. The concept of asexuality is communicated to the client by the lack of opportunity for sexual expression in the hospitalization and rehabilitation processes. Some clients express needs by making sexual advances toward the nurse. Common testing behaviors include direct and indirect verbal exchanges about sex, making body contact with the nurse, and fondling or exposure of genitalia. Other clients are too inhibited to express needs but internalize a negative sexual self-image and feelings of self-worth.

DISTURBANCE OF SEXUAL SELF-CONCEPT

Self-concept, self-esteem, and self-dignity are components of sexuality. How bodily functioning influences these concepts is related to impressions and experiences learned from nonsexual as well as sexual activities. The complexity of these relationships is demonstrated by the following questions.

1 Why does a health disruption, major or minor, prompt a loss of sexual self-worth for some and not for others?
2 What are the dynamics that change the perception of one's maleness or femaleness?
3 What is the relationship between a health condition and sexual desire?
4 How do forced sex role changes affect the client, partner, and family?
5 Can the loss of a previous sexual identity become the primary problem of disability?
6 Can a number of forced sexual changes become assets rather than liabilities?

These are but a few of the many possible questions, and the answers are complex, requiring exploration and study of each situation. In problem solving sessions the nurse initiates and provides the facilitative expertise to help the client explore and understand the troublesome issues. The client supplies the goals and information that are unique to each individual. The next few paragraphs discuss issues that the nurse needs to understand in order to be effective in facilitating problem solving with clients who are experiencing a disturbance of self-concept and self-esteem.

Usually a drastic change in the dependent state, required during hospitalization or bouts of long illness, decreases self-worth and can have an adverse effect on the sexual self-concept. Threats to nurturing can also result from hospitalization, especially if the hospitalized individual is attached to many tubes and machines that prevent touching by loved ones.

For many people, sexuality can be the key factor in maintaining the sense of wholeness and self-worth which is threatened by prolonged or serious illness and dependency. Encouragement to develop compensating mechanisms to reengage in social, sexual, and work opportunities helps maintain or reestablish a positive self-image. Sexuality may be the main catalyst for rehabilitation.

For others, a chronic illness or handicap from birth may prevent the development of a positive sexual image. It is understandable that delays and abnormalities in physiological development take their toll on sexuality. These people are often forced to engage in a very different life-style from their peers. Dependencies on others for treatments, medications, and transportation are basic realities for many in this population. These differences and forced dependencies are likely to be extremely difficult during adolescence when peer identification and support may be needed to master independence from parents. Another difficulty experienced by an adolescent with a developmental disability or chronic health condition is the likelihood of parents being overprotective. Peers may not be helpful to the teenager with health problems since the development of a positive self-concept normally requires tremendous effort, energy, and resources and nothing is left over for helping others.

Most people of all ages have many concerns and insecurities about their body. It is especially difficult to like and accept a body that functions poorly and looks different. Feedback often comes from strangers in statements like "What courage you have" or "what happened to you?" Help can come from the nurse by making an effort to condition the client to realize that there will always be insensitive people who have little understanding of the feelings of the handicapped or ill person.

Other manifestations of a chronic illness and/or disabilities that create difficulties in establishing or maintaining a positive sexual identity are feelings of inadequacy and embarrassment; growth retardation with the secondary sexual characteristics being slow to appear (e.g., cystic fibrosis); threat of health status deteriorating with pregnancy (e.g., leukemia); possibility of genetic risks of reproduction (e.g., diabetes); possibility of infertility (e.g., cystic fibrosis); body disfigurement or malformation (e.g., burns or colostomy); pain (e.g., rheumatoid arthritis); physical limitations (e.g., quadriplegia or paraplegia); threat of an early death or lack of partners for sexual experimentation (e.g., cerebral palsy or developmental disability). The complexity of sexuality is noted again when there is often no identified relationship between the severity and number of the above factors and the development or maintenance of a positive self-image. For example, a young woman with leukemia may consider her sexuality and sex as being her greatest attribute even though many of the above factors are in operation and apparent to her and her companions.

For some individuals, one of the greatest concerns and difficulties evolves from a required or forced shift in sex roles. Sex roles provide culture scripts by defining the rules in definitive terms for each social class, age group, ethnic group, work group, and health status. Even though sex roles are in transition, with men's roles and women's roles becoming more symmetrical, there are still many people unable to gracefully accept or acknowledge a forced change due to a deteriorating health status. However, for others a needed change may be hastened, or dictated, by a disruption in health. Some people and some relationships accept and grow from a forced change. Those practicing their beliefs arising from the women's movement may have already challenged the typical stereotypic sex role behaviors and having to shift sex roles for health purposes may not be as troublesome for these families.

The concept of self-worth is a composite of feelings, values, and experiences that come from the affection and approval of other people and from feedback on having an effect on the physical or social environment. Variables which help most people feel self-worth can be reinforced if the health professional involves the client in problem solving. Involvement in their own health care helps clients retain control over the events in their lives, acknowledges their influence on others, and provides opportunity for a sense of competence and mastery. Coping with loss is one of the first tasks necessary to maintain a positive sexual identity.

COPING WITH LOSS

An immediate reaction to physcial trauma, whether a chronic disease process, loss of body part, loss of body function, or surgical change in body structure, is expressed in grief and related mourning behavior. Loss of a body part, a valued healthy state, or an important body function activates mourning reactions, which can be adaptive in preventing complete breakdowns of the ego. The more valued body parts, or body functions, require a great deal of effort and energy to compensate for the physical loss and accompanying loss of self-esteem. In this society most people have been socialized to believe that intact sexual anatomy and functioning are necessary for a positive sexual identity. Consequently, the person with physical debilitation needs to cope with several types of losses. The reactions to loss of sexual functions or a change in a specific sexual identity are influenced by previous sexual experience, present values and attitudes, existing personality, mental health status, experience and capacity for dealing with change and loss, available resources, and the type and health of support systems. Loss of an old familiar symptom as a result of surgery or medical intervention can result in unpleasant feeling states when the symptom has provided degrees of secondary gain and control over aspects of the environment. Lindemann, Engle, Bowlby, and Schoenberg have described an orderly sequence for the normal mourning process. Most of these authors agree that there are several different phases or stages of mourning behaviors. The names and descriptions of behaviors may be slightly different with each author.

Initially, the individual is still attached to the original object. At times, there is still a hope of regaining all or part of the lost function; these feelings alternate with severe separation anxiety. Denial is the most common psychological process for most people in the first phase. Comfort, reassurance, and sympathy may not be appreciated since the loss has not been internalized as a reality by the bereaved individual. For many people realization of the loss takes place in the second phase and the individual will become depressed and feel hopeless, restless, or apathetic. Crying is often helpful and is used as communication to others. Once the significance and reality of the loss is realized and grieved over, a reorganization takes place. Finally, with resolution, the third phase, comes a reinvestment in life with the realization of the loss. Different activities, a different focus on life, and change in attitudes and values are often acquired after the loss of a body part, body function, or a healthy status.[1]

Having identified stages of mourning, the nurse needs to be cautioned that there is no "recipe" or "right way" for individuals to mourn a loss. There are several types of grieving reactions, including inhibited, delayed, prolonged, absent, or anticipatory. Each of these modifications may serve an adaptive function for individuals who have not engaged in the usual three-phase mourning process. For example, it is unrealistic to expect an older person to change patterns of mourning that have been successful or provided a needed secondary gain.

Shock, denial, depression, anger, fear, and anxiety are common emotional reactions to loss associated with a health disruption that alters sexuality. The amount of energy expended on these emotional states has a direct impact on sexual functioning. According to Kaplan, it is possible that the physiological and endocrine changes that accompany severe depression, stress, and fatigue states contribute to a loss of sexual motivation by affecting the central nervous system and the neurotransmitters and by lowering the available androgen supply.[2]

Some people deal with loss by throwing themselves into activity rather than experience the pain. They will find a series of substitutes such as overindulgence in work or travel, hobbies, alcohol or other drug dependence, and promiscuousness. Persistent unaccustomed patterns of sexual practice or drug dependence suggest that emotional reactions to a loss are becoming pathological.

Since nurses have been accustomed to dealing with loss, this material is meant only to sensitize the nurse to a different kind of loss which is so easily overlooked or undernoted. Many nurses have been socialized to think of health care in terms of life and death issues and not in terms of sexuality. It may be very difficult for the nurse to empathize with a patient who has more concern about the ability to have an erection than the surgical removal of cancer that will prolong his life expectancy.

According to Cole:

> For some, disability offers an opportunity to better understand one's self. Reassessment of one's own ingrained attitudes is often not undertaken by most adults. The average person may have little reason to reassess his sexuality since 'it all seems to be working pretty well for me.' Reasons to do so usually arrive on the wings of crisis, disruption, and pain. Only when the old rules are changed and the solutions of the past no longer apply do some begin to re-examine the foundations of their sexuality.[3]

Imagine yourself with chronic renal failure and secondary impotence or with multiple sclerosis and incontinence. In that imaginary world one may find compelling reasons to reexamine the notions that a beautiful body or a stiff penis are essential to a satisfactory sex life. The exploring mind may perceive some of the richness of sexuality and sexual relationships which may have been hidden behind society's well-known external symbols of maleness and femaleness, of desirability and acceptability.

Just how far this reconsideration of sexuality may carry a person is an individual matter, but in spite of the liabilities imposed by a handicapping condition, it may contain the potential for enrichment. Some disabled people report that they might have overlooked this potential for enrichment had they not become physically disabled.[4] Coping with loss is likely to be more difficult for those already experiencing developmental or situational crises.

VULNERABILITY IN DEVELOPMENTAL AND SITUATIONAL CRISES

During some developmental phases, particularly adolescence and old age, the sexuality of an individual is easily insulted. It is during adolescence that the sex drive becomes stronger and more demanding. Adolescence is the beginning of sexual object finding and experimentation. Mood swings move from feelings of depression to euphoria concerning body and relationship changes. This is a time for the development of psychosocial intimacy, which often depends on a firm sense of identity. The slightest additional stress during this period may interfere with experimentation, aggressive impulses, sex behaviors, and continuity in the sense of self. Chronic illness, physical handicaps, and body disfigurement add to the other stresses and threaten the adolescent's sense of being in control of the body and its function. Developmental impasse or misperception of body images is often noted in some clinical syndromes such as anorexia nervosa and obesity. Failure of sexual functioning and the denial of sexual feelings may result from the many stresses experienced by teenagers with health disruptions.

The declining years also bring a number of physiological and psychological changes that affect sexuality.

According to Comfort:

> Old folks stop having sex for the same reasons they stop riding a bicycle—general infirmity, thinking it looks ridiculous, no bicycle, and perhaps most pernicious, acceptance of the social image of the dirty old man and the undesirable older woman.[5]

Opposition to sexuality in the aged arises from adult children who view their aged parents' normal urges for intimacy and romance as a threat. The negative attitude of the children toward their parents holds much more strongly for the mother than for the father, which then generalizes to all elderly females. Consequently, thwarted sexuality may contribute to the depression that is often diagnosed as involutional or a depressive reaction to physical illness.[6] Situational crises are experienced by all age groups and have the potential of threatening sexuality. Divorce, death of a spouse, and loss of job increase the pressure of coping with a health disruption or disability. Besides the developmental and situational crises, other variables may influence the alternatives available following a change in health status.

CHOOSING ALTERNATIVES

Alterations in identity, expression, options, and practices are likely to occur following a change in health status. These alterations have the potential of restricting or broadening sexuality for the client and significant others. To maintain status quo would be the choice of many, but they find that a significant change in health status does not allow them this choice.

After a disruption in health, the client may be forced to take stock and then make an effort to face society's proper "masculine" or "feminine" image, expressions, and behaviors. The abandonment of traditional sexual options can create a new freedom to form a new identity. This identity may evolve from a whole new gestalt formed to define personal and social sexuality with a change in sexual expressions, options, or practices. The change may revolve around self-fulfillment with a new freedom from social conformity. Men may find themselves more tolerant or even enjoying less pressure to be masculine. Men may not have the option of being the principal breadwinner and can become actively involved in exploring new directions for their lives. Roles and options may be chosen from personal preferences for the first time in their lives. Partners and families will also need to change to accommodate the temporary or permanent sexual alterations.

Some people feel a great pressure from self or significant others to maintain the status quo during and after a disruption in health. Others are able to restrict sexuality through the emphasis on the "right way" and the "sickness" of certain sexual options. Social mores or religious dogma may prove helpful to those choosing sexual restrictions.

Sudden deprivation of sexual strokes from others may force some alteration in sexual expression. Masturbation and self-pleasuring are major changes for some people. The comfort level of experimentation is a clue to managing successful alterations in sexuality. Resolution for each client and family will often depend on the willingness to change and to accept change from others. Nurses have many opportunities to help an individual or couple explore new options, clarify their values, discuss the pros and cons of specific alternatives, and help couples to feel good about their choices. For some clients there is a need to emphasize that sexual activity need not be equated with orgasm or genital sexual intercourse. Couples can be counseled in various ways of giving and receiving pleasure and sharing intimately with each other. Some couples will experience additional stress due to preexisting problems with sexuality.

AGGRAVATION OF PREEXISTING PROBLEMS

It is unrealistic to believe that all presenting sexual problems, complaints, and dysfunctions of the chronically ill began with a specific disruption in health. With the "healthy" population not being so "healthy" regarding sexuality, many of the problems will be exacerbations and will not have originated from a particular illness or disability. Recently, when a man with paraplegia was asked about his sex life, he answered by saying, "It wasn't any good before the accident—do you think the accident will improve it? It has only one way to go." This client is somewhat exceptional in his perceptions and openness regarding his previous sexual experiences. For reasons already discussed, many people have a difficult time acknowledging that they have ever experienced sexual difficulties and it is very easy to forget "exactly how it was" before an illness or handicap. It is much easier to remember the "good old days" and place the responsibility for sexual difficulties on a disease process.

Some sexual difficulties would have emerged with any type of additional strain to client or relationship. The dysfunction or problems of the partner can also surface and provoke additional stress for the client or be interpreted as the client's problem. Problems should be suspected with acting out behaviors of either partner.

SEXUAL ACTING OUT

With so much emphasis placed on a young, beautiful body, it is not difficult to understand that the uncertainty of regaining health and controlling mortality can result in destructive sexual behaviors. Some of these behaviors may be classified as sexual promiscuity. Fleeing from familiar environments and having many unsatisfying sexual affairs is not uncommon for young people when prognosis is poor. A young woman with Hodgkin's disease or leukemia with a poor prognosis may try controlling mortality by becoming pregnant. Under such conditions a therapeutic abortion may be required, which could be destructive to both physical and mental health status.

An older person with body changes that threaten integrity may act impulsively and marry a younger person to recapture youth and health. After the honeymoon and the life savings are squandered, there are additional problems.

Isolation and long hospital stays restrict sexual activity. Often an attractive nurse or physician will become the love object in a transference reaction. The client may be interested only in testing sexual functioning and desirability. Nurses and physicians can use labels such as "dirty old man" or "man chaser" or they can realize that most of these behaviors come from deprivation and can help the patient problem solve to obtain appropriate ways of meeting sex needs. For example, a weekend at home or a visit from a special partner with appropriate privacy should be a standard option for everyone.

Some clients have never been strong in controlling impulses. Some families, social institutions, and nurses reinforce impulsivity. Sexual advances may be disapproved but they do prevent boredom and provide excitement or attention. People who have not learned impulse control in relating to others will not likely change without planned and systematic professional help.

Other people wish to control all interpersonal interaction and environments and find that illness and the hospital culture leave them only one choice—offensive sexual advances. Once an offensive sexual behavior begins, nurses commonly respond by leaving the room, using punitive measures, avoiding the patient, displaying anger by verbal or physical methods, or accepting the advances as an ego inflator. These interactions can become destructive to patient, nurse, and other staff members. In dealing with sexual acting out, firm limits that neither encourage the behavior nor reject the patient are needed. The patient should be offered other methods of control and be encouraged to talk about feelings and concerns.

Sexual acting out behaviors, or those perceived by the staff as such, can cause great difficulty for nurses who have not examined their own sexual fears, anxieties, feelings, and repulsions. For example, masturbation may be a very appropriate means of satisfying sexual needs, but the anxiety of staff members may engender feelings of fear and guilt.

In summary, acting out sexuality comes from a variety of needs and personality problems which include deprivation, lack of impulse control, anxiety, need for control, attention, ego needs, or from the perceptions and biases of the staff. Acting out, along with other issues, may prove to be difficult for some sexual relationships.

SEXUAL RELATIONSHIP ISSUES

Sexual relationships are considered important to various individuals for very different reasons, depending on attitudes, value systems, and past experiences. A sexual relationship may be used primarily to fulfill the following purposes: procreation; orgastic response; bolstering ego and self-esteem; experimentation with different life-styles or sexual preference; manipulating others; caring, pleasuring, sharing, and loving a "special" person; meeting peer, family, or societal expectations; satisfying physical sexual needs; friendship; combating hopelessness and loneliness; meeting partner needs or expectations; aggression and hostility toward values of significant others. Often the primary purpose will be accompanied by secondary purposes or secondary gain from the relationship. Also, the primary purpose may not be understood or there may be several equally important purposes that form the rationale for the sexual relationship. The major cultural attitudes and values may be strongly entrenched into right and wrong categories which show up in many aspects of the individual's behavior, even though they are verbally denied.

Sexuality of a client must be evaluated in terms of the rationale, desire, and patterns of relating to others. If a person has a great many inhibiting sexual attitudes, there is a high probability that there will be difficulty in change and less options for beginning or reestablishing sexual relationships following a change in the health status. Furthermore, a chronic illness, physical disability, or handicap will likely produce additional complications for self-image because of decreased mobility, neurological impairment of the sex organs, and chronic pain and discomfort. The importance of communication between the client and partner cannot be overemphasized. Communication and an understanding partner will often help in compensating for the loss of a healthy body.

If the client and partner have major conflicting expectations of each other and of the relationship, then there is a high probability that there will be serious adjustment problems following any type of stressful event. The relationship may have always functioned rather superficially or on the borderline of incompatibility. The added stress may hasten a break in the relationship that would have normally occurred over time.

Nurses need to make an effort to keep from indicating a personal preference of sexual practices for client relationships. The inclination to place judgmental evaluation on the type and purpose of sexual relationships is learned from values derived from family, church, and society. For many nurses the learned controls, prohibitions, and regulations of sexuality during their own childhood produce major conflicts in the acceptance of various types of sexual relationships and life styles of their clients. Some nurses report difficulty in being therapeutic with relationships that choose extramarital relations and those including a third party for sexual purposes. Nurses need to be cognizant that sexual attitudes and needs vary according to age, race, social class, religion, and psychological development. Also, a few partners will enjoy the increased dependency needs of the ill person and encourage the continuation of dependency behaviors much longer than may be helpful to the client. Other partners will feel trapped and have urges to flee. Some may need to mourn the loss of a healthy sexual partner. For a variety of reasons already discussed, in health disruptions affective changes tend to affect sexuality of clients and relationships.

AFFECTIVE CHANGES

Feelings and emotional responses will often change with major health disruptions. These changes are evident in behaviors, feeling states, and interpersonal responses. The affective changes discussed below are reactive depression and anxiety states.

In reactive depression the precipitating factor is a specific traumatic event or loss. A sense of emptiness and physical distress are natural responses to a substantial loss. Grief for over 1 year is generally classified as a reactive depression. All types of depression, reactive, neurotic, and psychotic, take a toll on libido. The incidence of depression is about twice as high in women as in men. Usually there is a low self-evaluation; the person sees himself or herself as deficient in attributes that are important to self and to society. These attributes include health, beauty, intelligence, and achievement.[6] The affective manifestations include sadness, loneliness, hopelessness, and helplessness.

According to Kaplan:

> The pain of depression extinguishes libido, makes the person resistant to arousal, and may actually impair the physiological vasocongestive sexual response. Erection in the male is especially vulnerable to depression. There is some evidence to indicate that endocrine, as well as psychological factors may play a role in diminished sexuality of depressed patients.[7]

Loss of sexual interest and sexual satisfaction is often a symptom of those clients who are depressed, angry, or guilt-ridden. The depressed person may be so self-punitive and low in energy that there is no sexual activity for extended periods of time. Others may not decrease activity but have less pleasure or orgasmic capacity. Orgasms may become painful or there may be an uncomfortable tenseness of the muscles. Depression may be masked by somatic complaints which can be an acceptable means of seeking help.[8] Occasionally a major treatment goal for these clients is to prevent decompensation toward hypochondriasis. Encouraging the client to suppress self-depreciating fantasies, unmasking the guilt feelings or sense of rejection, and offering cognitive input toward reality can be therapeutic in clinical management of depression. After anger and guilt are dealt with, the client may be ready to focus on new interests and different activities to gain positive feelings about self. Antidepressants may be useful in chronic neurotic depression but are often less helpful to those experiencing reactive depression.

Anxiety that accompanies acute stress can also cause a temporary decrease in sexual interest. However, most people do not focus much attention on a temporary sexual decline during acute stress. Usually, the loss of libido will gradually subside as the anxiety decreases. A few people increase sexual activity to help cope with the precipitating stress by releasing emotional energy. Some clients use sex to allay anxiety, which allows them temporary relief from their problems.

In summary, it seems appropriate to emphasize that an individual with a minor or major health disruption may experience all or none of the psychosexual responses discussed in this chapter. It seems equally important to emphasize that nurses are not omnipotent; they cannot hide, take away, or give back sexuality to those they serve. However, nurses can help clients and families who are experiencing a disruption in health to understand and appreciate their sexuality, take responsibility for it, make choices based on information, and be relatively free from fear about their sexuality.

Vignette

Problem

Carolyn A., a 28-year-old married woman, complained of "not desiring sex anymore." Robert A., spouse, 29, has begun to have erectile difficulties during the last few weeks.

Subjective Data

1 Decline of sexual relationship in the past 2 years
2 Successful coitus not more than once a month during the past year
3 No masturbatory activity by either partner
4 Robert is a spasmodic user of alcohol and other drugs to enhance self-esteem
5 Neither partner wishes to take the responsibility of initiating sex due to fear of failure of performance or by being rejected by the other partner
6 Both partners feel guilty about the birth of a child with a severe congenital deformity, 2 years ago

Objective Data

1 Married 5 years
2 No treatment of endocrine disorders, chronic disease, or dyspareunia
3 Physical and genital examinations normal

4   Birth of a child with developmental disability 2 years ago
5   Using the "pill" as contraceptive

Assessment

1   Reactive depression (Carolyn)
2   Disturbance of sexual self-concept (Robert)
3   Psychological conflict in relationship resulting in decreased libido (Carolyn) and erectile difficulty (Robert)

Plan

1   Permission and guidance for Carolyn and Robert to discuss the following:
    a   The meaning of the birth of a child with a developmental disability
    b   Loss of the fantasized normal infant
    c   The guilt and anger toward the infant and each other
    d   What were the things that attracted them to each other and when did those things stop happening or feeling good?
    e   The goals for the relationship at this time
    f   Their willingness to try to understand each other's feelings and to make necessary changes to enhance the relationship
    g   The perception of each partner as to the major obstacle or obstacles in obtaining their own sexual gratification
    h   Each partner defines own rights and responsibilities regarding this sexual relationship—have them determine if they have ever been compatible. If not compatible, the nurse can offer information or suggestions on how they might wish to change
2   Information
    a   Review the normal reactions to grief and loss.
    b   Review the basic anatomy and physiology of both male and female.
    c   Give readings or show films to demonstrate how stress and conflict may affect the sexual response cycle.
3   Specific suggestions
    a   Have this couple practice giving and receiving positive and negative feedback to help reduce hostility and feelings of worthlessness.
    b   Use a film like *Reaching Orgasm* to promote an awareness of the different methods of creating positive sexuality in sexual activity.
    c   Place less emphasis on performance and more on determining what "feels good" during each sexual experience.
    d   Take turns in the initiation of sexual activity and of giving and receiving learned pleasuring behaviors.

Evaluation

Is the original problem still a concern for Carolyn and Robert? (Evaluation is a continuous process and the plans may change as the needs of the clients become more clearly defined.) Plans will be revised after the couple talks about the birth of the child to determine if there is unresolved grief that is affecting the sexual relationship.

Has the couple ever been compatible? Determine if increased sexual gratification results in an increase in positive feelings toward each other. If the couple is committed to improving the relationship, there may be a need for additional counseling to work on ways to handle stress and improve communication.

LEARNING ACTIVITIES

1   Sexual self-concept: Each member of a small group (12) constructs a collage of pictures that emphasizes their own sexual self-concept. The collages are shared, with a short explanation or a period of questions from other group members. After the exercise, each person sharing the collage has a few minutes of quiet time, then each group member makes a written comment that best describes the sexual self-concept of each member of the group.[9]

2   Each member of the group fantasizes having a specific health disruption (e.g., kidney failure, blindness, paralysis). Then the members select the three psychosexual responses that they believe would affect them most. Each member shares the rationale for their choices.

REFERENCES

1   L. A. Hoff, *People in Crisis,* Addison-Wesley, Menlo Park, Calif., 1978, p. 190.
2   Helen S. Kaplan, *The New Sex Therapy,* Brunner-Mazel, New York, 1974, p. 76.
3   T. Cole and S. Cole, "The Handicapped and Sexual Health," *SIECUS Rep.* **IV**(5):3 (1976).
4   Ibid.
5   Alex Comfort, "Sexuality and Aging," *SIECUS Rep.* **IV**(6):1 (1976).
6   M. A. Sviland, "Helping Elderly Couples Become Sexually Liberated," in J. LoPiccolo and L. LoPiccolo (eds.), *Handbook of Sex Therapy,* Plenum, New York, 1978, p. 352.
7   Kaplan, op. cit., p. 475.
8   Roger Spencer and David Raft, "Depression and Diminished Sexual Desire," *Med. Aspects Hum. Sexual.* **11**(8):51–61 (1976).
9   R. Kaplan, L. B. Meeks, and J. S. Segal, *Group Strategies in Understanding Human Sexuality,* Brown, Dubuque, Ia., 1978, p. 40.

Chapter 13

Pharmacologic Modification of Human Sexuality*

Throughout recorded history there has been interest in identifying substances that would enhance sexual interest, performance, or pleasure. Likewise, there is evidence in early literature of awareness that some agents impair sexual functioning. Only recently has there been both the technology and a social climate conducive to the application of methods of scientific inquiry to questions about drug effects on this significant area of human behavior. Concomitantly clinicians have begun to recognize an obligation to detect adverse drug effects on sexual function and to inform clients of current knowledge about drug effects that may enhance or impair sexuality.

Considering the complex interaction of mind and body in sexual behavior, incuding the interplay of hormones and the biogenic amines in mediating central and peripheral nervous systems and gonadal cellular receptors, it is conceivable that many, if not most, drugs can affect sexual function. The majority of these effects are secondary to the drugs' therapeutic and adverse effects: The patient whose condition is markedly improved by a medication is more likely to be interested in sexual activity. However, if the drug results in an adverse effect,

*This chapter was authored by Ginette A. Pepper, R.N., M.S., an assistant professor at the University of Colorado School of Nursing, Denver, Colorado.

such as nausea which occurs with many therapeutic agents, potential for sexual arousal and enjoyment is decreased.

In addition to these indirect effects a growing number of drugs which directly influence sexual functioning have been identified; these agents are the primary focus of this chapter. No drug will act the same way in every person who takes it, and this is particularly true of sexual effects where the interaction between psychological and physical factors is so important. The occurrence and magnitude of a sexual reaction to a drug will depend on individual variables, such as dose, route and duration of administration, psychological conditioning, physical and emotional health status, and environmental setting. On the cellular level the hormonal status, balance between the excitatory and inhibitory biogenic amines, and underlying autonomic tone may alter drug effects. As a result there will be wide variability in drug effects on sexuality.

The purpose of this chapter is to give an overview of current knowledge related to sexual effects of agents used to treat diseases and of social drug use. The therapeutic use of drugs to alter sexual function is also presented.

BARRIERS TO RESEARCH

There are very few well-controlled studies of the effects of drugs on human sexual function. Many of the reports in the literature are anecdotal or impression-istic case reports and few meet the rigorous criteria of double-blind crossover methodology which characterizes the most reliable studies in pharmacology. Recently, however, studies on the sexual effects of drugs have increased both in number and quality, but there still remain significant barriers to research in this area.

Currently, the most common methodology used to assess the sexual effects of a drug is the three-generational feeding study on laboratory animals.[1] The drug is placed in the diet of the animals continuously for three consecutive generations and the effect of the drug on libido, potency, number of offspring, and breeding cycles is recorded. However, these studies may have limited applicability to humans. McEwen and his associates[2] have demonstrated that steroid hormones have markedly different effects in the monkey and the rat; other species-specific reactions should be anticipated. A well-publicized example of such differences is the drug parachlorophenylalanine, which was purported to be an aphrodisiac because it increased the mounting and copulation behavior of the male rat,[3] but which has no comparable effect on humans when administered alone.[4]

One of the major problems in researching the effects of drugs on sexual function is to differentiate the placebo effect from the actual effects of the drug. This phenomenon was first identified in controlled drug studies on various drugs, where it has been noted that the inert agent used in the control group will exert some pharmacologic activity against the condition for which it is tested. There is evidence that there is a significant placebo effect whenever drugs are tested for effects on sexuality.

Well-controlled studies are difficult to design in this area of pharmacologic research. Adequate and reliable reporting by subjects is problematic. Even the most easily quantifiable parameters (such as serum testosterone levels) are influenced by numerous variables which may be impossible to control. Due to the number of interacting variables, it is often difficult to identify causal relationships. Particularly with social drugs it may not be easily discernible whether the drug use causes or is caused by the sexual behavior or dysfunction, or whether both the behavior and the drug use are related to some other personality or social variables. With agents used to treat diseases it is necessary to define whether sexual effects are due to the drug or to the underlying disease.

A goal of pharmacologic research is to identify the risk-benefit ratio of therapeutic agents. In this manner the risks, in terms of adverse effects, are weighed against the efficacy of the agent. However, when sexual effects are considered, either as "risk" (as with drugs that inhibit sexual function as a side effect) or as "benefit" (when drugs enhance sexual function), interpretation of this ratio will depend on the value system of the interpreter. For example, one physician may feel that the benefit of an antihypertensive medication in terms of prolongation of life makes the impotence that the drug may cause a tolerable adverse effect. The patient or another physician might disagree, like the man who observed, "I won't live longer if I take the drug; it will only seem longer!" Likewise some researchers feel that minor risks which may accompany drugs to enhance sexual enjoyment are acceptable, while those with a different philosophy would not accept any risk in what they would consider nonessential drug use. Differences in interpretation of the same research data often reflect these philosophic variations.

Another curiosity of the published research and scientific literature is that drug effects on female sexual functioning have been largely ignored. Some proposed explanations for this situation are the following: (1) the female sexual response is much more difficult to measure and quantify than the male response; (2) women may fail to voluntarily report sexual effects of drugs; (3) the male-dominated medical and scientific communities may be disinterested or uncomfortable with the topic; or (4) there are fewer drug-related sexual dysfunctions in women.[5]

When reviewing reports of drug effects on sexual function, it is important to keep in mind all of these significant methodological problems which are barriers to research. Because studies on this topic are so often reported in the public press, the clinician often must guide the client in interpretation and analysis of these findings.

GENERAL MECHANISMS OF DRUG EFFECTS

Most of the drugs which have been reported to directly affect sexual functioning probably act through one or more of a limited number of mechanisms. These mechanisms can be central or peripheral.

Biogenic Amines

There is evidence that the primary neurohormone in mobilizing sexual behavior is dopamine, while serotonin is the major inhibitor.[6] Hence dopamine-receptor blockers (such as the phenothiazines) and drugs that deplete dopamine (such as reserpine) interfere with central control of sexual function. Likewise drugs that depress serotonin concentrations in the brain could be expected to stimulate sexual function (e.g., parachlorophenylalanine or PCPA).

Autonomic Nervous System

Peripheral effects of drugs may be expressed through autonomic nervous system function. Erection, vaginal lubrication, and clitoral engorgement are mediated through the parasympathetic (cholinergic) nervous system through dilation of arterioles and compression of veins. Parasympatholytic or cholinergic blocking drugs have the capacity to cause impotence in the male. Table 13-1 lists some drugs with anticholinergic effects which could theoretically interfere with sexual function. However, most of these drugs exert other effects on sexual functioning which are probably more significant than the anticholinergic ones.

Generally drugs which stimulate the parasympathetic nervous system are not used to stimulate sexual function due to their many unpleasant side effects. However, cholinesterase inhibitors, particularly physostigmine and the organophosphates (found in insecticides), increase libido as part of a symptom complex which includes excessive dreaming, insomnia, jitteriness, mental confusion, headache, and visual hallucinations.[7]

Orgasm and ejaculation are primarily a function of the sympathetic (adrenergic) nervous system. Drugs, such as antihypertensive agents, which block α-adrenergic receptors, inhibit the release of the neurotransmitter norepinephrine, block the adrenergic neuron, or serve as a false neurotransmitter, can interfere with potency and orgasm. The "dry" ejaculation (absence of semen with otherwise normal orgasm) reported with some of these drugs has been attributed to bladder neck dysfunction due to lack of sympathetic tone, resulting in retrograde

Table 13-1   Drugs with Anticholinergic Effects

Category	Examples
Antihistamines*	Chlorpheniramine (Chlor-Trimeton), diphenhydramine (Benadryl)
Antihypertensives	Clonidine (Catapres), methyldopa (Aldomet), trimethaphan (Arfonad)
Antispasmodics	Methantheline (Banthine), propantheline (Pro-Banthine), isopropamide (Darbid)
Antiparkinsons	Trihexyphenidyl (Artane, Tremin), biperiden (Akineton), benztropine (Cogentin)
Belladonna alkaloids*	Atropine, scopolamine
Psychotropics	Chlorpromazine (Thorazine), thioridazine (Mellaril), haloperidol (Haldol), prochlorperazine (Compazine), thiothixene (Navane)
Tricyclic antidepressants	Imipramine (Tofranil), amitriptyline (Elavil)
Others	Disopyramide (Norpace)

*Common ingredients in cold and sleep preparations sold over the counter.

emission of the semen into the bladder. However, Kedia and Markland[8] studied nine men receiving the antihypertensive guanethidine, and found no evidence of retrograde ejaculation in postmasturbatory urine samples. They conclude that with some drugs the phenomenon of dry ejaculation may be due to α-adrenergic blockade affecting contractility of the ductus deferens, ampulla, and seminal vesicles, so as to produce temporary aspermia, rather than due to retrograde ejaculation.

Both sympathetic and parasympathetic nervous system function are impaired with ganglionic blocking drugs, since ganglia are found in both divisions of the autonomic nervous system. As would be expected, drugs of this type used to treat hypertension have been implicated in impotence in men and impaired sexual function in women.

Sex Hormones

The gonadal hormones, typified by testosterone in the male and estrogen and progesterone in the female, are involved in the sexual differentiation of the fetus, as well as the development of sex organs and secondary sex characteristics at puberty and the maintenance of the sex organs, gametogenesis, and pregnancy during adult life. These effects, caused by the influence of these substances on peripheral receptors, evidence only a part of the complex functions of the hormones. While the hypothalamic-pituitary-gonadal axis in the control of sex hormones is fairly well understood, the role of the limbic system and other cerebral connections needs additional elucidation. Recent evidence in laboratory animals indicates that estradiol and testosterone exert direct effects on specific regions of the brain that influence sexual behavior.[9] While sexual behavior seems not to be dictated by hormones in humans to the extent that it is in animals, drugs which alter hormone balance do influence human libido and sexual function.

Paradoxically, androgens, produced primary by the adrenal but also in the ovary, are apparently more important than estrogens in maintaining sexual drive in the female, as well as in general body growth and pubic and axillary hair formation.[10] The functions, if any, of the very small amounts of endogenous estrogens normally found in the male have not been elucidated, but the therapeutic levels of exogenous estrogens and progestins used to treat some cancers decrease libido in men.

General Central Nervous System Effects

Drugs which stimulate or depress the CNS (central nervous system) can affect sexuality, particularly libido, enjoyment, or disinhibition. This is the mechanism postulated for anxiolytics, narcotics, and a number of social drugs. Obviously the expectations of the person taking these drugs may profoundly affect the expression of CNS effects.

ADVERSE EFFECTS OF THERAPEUTIC AGENTS

With few exceptions the effects of therapeutically useful drugs on sexual function are adverse. Possible exceptions include the steroidal hormones, clomiphene, levodopa, bromocriptine, amphetamines, and thyroxine, which will be discussed in later sections. Table 13-2 summarizes the sexual effects of therapeutically useful drugs.

Drugs Used in Cardiology

Antihypertensives Of the many therapeutically indicated drugs which cause sexual dysfunction those used to treat hypertension are among the most significant. Because most of these agents work by modifying the effects of the sympathetic nervous system, they have been implicated in failure to reach orgasm in women and interference with ejaculation in men. This is complicated by the fact that there is increased incidence of sexual dysfunction in untreated hypertensive men.[11]

Frequently cited as causing failure to ejaculate is *guanethidine (Ismelin),* an antihypertensive which works by depleting and preventing the release of norepinephrine at sympathetic postganglionic nerve terminals. Up to 60 percent of the men taking this drug report "dry sex," while a few report impotence.[12] One study indicates that the men usually experience normal orgasm in spite of the failure to ejaculate.[8] While it is possible, based on this mechanism of action, that this drug could also influence the sexual functioning of the female, no such reports have been published. Lower doses of guanethidine are less commonly associated with sexual effects.

The primary antihypertensive action of *methyldopa (Aldomet)* is a central hypotensive and behavioral depressing effect which occurs when methyldopa (chemically similar to dopa, a precursor of dopamine) reaches the CNS, where it is converted to α-methylnorepinephrine. This similarity to the metabolism of dopamine may explain the reported sexual effects of methyldopa in doses of 500 to 2000 mg/day which include failure of erection, ejaculatory failure and decreased libido in men, and decreased libido and rare galactorrhea in women.[12,13] These adverse effects begin within a few days of the commencement of therapy and disappear within 2 weeks after the drug is discontinued.[14] The incidence of sexual dysfunction with methyldopa is reportedly between 2 and 33 percent,[1] being greater at doses greater than 1500 mg/day. Mental depression has also been attributed to methyldopa.

Reserpine has long been associated with reports of adverse effects on sexual function. No longer recommended for routine use as an antihypertensive medication due to mental depression which may be precipitated by this agent, reserpine exerts its hypotensive effect by decreasing dopaminergic transmission and by blocking transport of norepinephrine into storage vesicles in terminal sympathetic synapses and decreasing the norepinephrine available to the receptor. Reported effects include erectile difficulties, decreased emission, and delayed ejaculation in males and decreased libido in females,[15,16] although to what extent sexual effects are secondary to mental depression is unknown.

The lower incidence of sexual dysfunction reported with *clonidine (Catapres)* may be due to the fact that there has been less clinical experience with this newer agent, which acts centrally to reduce blood pressure by decreasing the sympathetic outflow from the medulla.[14] This drug also causes urinary retention

Table 13-2   Therapeutic Agents Affecting Sexual Function

Drug		
Class	Examples	Common therapeutic uses	Effect on sexual response
Cholinesterase inhibitor	Physostigmine	Glaucoma (topical)	Increase libido
Antihypertensive	Phenoxybenzamine (Dibenzyline)	Preoperative management of pheochromocytoma, shock (research)	Inhibit ejaculation, "dry" ejaculation
	Methyldopa (Aldomet)	Hypertension	Inability to maintain erection, ejaculatory failure, decrease in libido (men and women), galactorrhea (rare)
	Guanethidine (Ismelin)	Hypertension	Ejaculatory failure, erectile dysfunction (rare)
	Reserpine	Hypertension, Huntington's chorea	Decreased libido, decreased emission, "dry" ejaculation, erectile dysfunction, bizarre erotic dreams, depressive psychosis
	Propranolol (Inderal)	Hypertension, angina, arrhythmias, thyrotoxicosis, pheochromocytoma, migraine, familial tremor, others	Erectile dysfunction
	Clonidine (Catapres)	Hypertension	Erectile dysfunction
Diuretic	Spironolactone (Aldactone)	Hypertension, congestive heart failure, fluid retention, used for potassium-sparing effects with other diuretics	Impotence, amenorrhea, gynecomastia
	Thiazides: hydrochlorothiazide (HydroDiuril), chlorthalidone (Hygroton)	Hypertension, congestive heart failure, fluid retention, renal failure	Impotence

Table 13-2 Therapeutic Agents Affecting Sexual Function (continued)

Class	Drug Examples	Common therapeutic uses	Effect on sexual response
Antipsychotic	Thioridazine (Mellaril), chlorproma-zine (Thorazine), chlorprothixene (Taractan), promazine (Sparine), prochlorperazine (Compazine), tri-fluoperazine (Stelazine), triflupro-mazine (Vesprin), perphenazine, (Tri-lafon), fluphenazine (Prolixin), haloperidol (Haldol), piperacetazine (Quide)	Schizophrenia, depression, pruritus, nausea, various neurological syndromes	Inhibition of ejaculation, failure to ejac-ulate, erectile dysfunction, changes in libido, decreased sperm count, amenorrhea, galactorrhea, gyneco-mastia, decreased serum testosterone
Antidepressant	Tricyclic antidepressants: imipramine (Tofranil), desipramine (Norpramin, Pertofrane), amitriptyline (Elavil), protriptyline (Vivactil)	Endogenous depression, enuresis in children	Delayed ejaculation, ejaculation fail-ure, changes in libido, erectile dys-function, delayed orgasm in female
	MAO inhibitors: tranylcypromine (Parnate), phenelzine (Nardil), par-gyline (Eutonyl), isocarboxazid (Marplan)	Depressive states	Delayed ejaculation, impotence, ejacu-lation failure, delayed orgasm in females, increased libido (due to improved condition?)
	Lithium (Lithonate, Lithane)	Manic depression	Erectile impotence
Anxiolytics, sedatives, hypnotics	Chlordiazepoxide (Librium), diaze-pam (Valium), oxazepam (Serax), barbiturates, meprobamate (Equanil, Miltown), many others	Anxiety, sexual dysfunction, muscle spasm, insomnia, preprocedural medication	Increased and decreased libido, ejacu-lation failure, amenorrhea, galactor-rhea, decreased testosterone levels
Ganglionic blockers	Mecamylamine (Inversine), Tri-methaphan (Arfonad)	Hypertensive crisis	Erectile impotence, failure of ejacula-tion, decreased emission
Amphetamines	Methamphetamine (Ambar, Desbutal), chlorphentermine (Pre-Sate), fenfluramine (Pondimin), di-ethylpropion (Tenuate, Tepanil), phendimetrazine (Plegine), dex-troamphetamine (Amodex, Benze-drine, others)	Anorectics, CNS depression, hyperkinesis in children, narcolepsy	Impotence, changes in libido, women more often develop decreased libido

Category	Drug	Use	Effect
Steroids	Estrogens	Oral contraceptives, replacement in deficiency states, menopause, osteoporosis, dysmenorrhea, prostatic cancer, suppression of lactation	Depression, increased libido in women, decreased libido in men
	Progestins	Oral contraceptives, dysmenorrhea, endometriosis, infertility	Decreased libido in men and women
	Androgens and anabolic steroids	Replacement in deficiency states, postpartal lactation suppression, anemia, protein anabolic agent, osteoporosis, contraceptive in men, breast cancer	Increased libido in men and women, in women: hirsutism, amenorrhea, clitoral enlargement
Antispasmodics	Methantheline (Banthine), propantheline (Pro-Banthine), isopropamide (Darbid)	Peptic ulcer, functional gastrointestinal disturbances	Impotence
Cytotoxic	Alkylating Agents, antimetabolites plant alkaloids, antitumor antibiotics	Cancer, psoriasis	Amenorrhea, decreased spermatogenesis, sterility, decreased libido, impotence
Antilipemic	Clofibrate (Atromid-S)	Hyperlipoproteinemia	Impotence
Antiparkinsonian	Levodopa (L-dopa, Dopar, Larodopa)	Parkinsonism	Increased libido, increased sexual feelings
Other	Trimeprazine (Temaril),	Pruritus	Inhibition of ejaculation, gynecomastia, galactorrhea, menstrual irregularities
	Disulfiram (Antabuse)	Alcoholism	Rare impotence
	Aminocaproic acid (Amicar)	Hemophilia, coagulopathies	Inhibition of ejaculation

and gynecomastia, indicating anticholinergic and hormonal effects as well.[16] While no effects on the female have been reported, the incidence of erectile difficulties and other effects similar to methyldopa have been reported in recent studies to be at 14 to 24 percent, and many clinicians feel that the frequency of dysfunction with clonidine is comparable to that with methyldopa.[16] Since patients who experience sexual dysfunction may discontinue the drug, they should be warned that a potentially dangerous rebound hypertension accompanied by restlessness, insomnia, and headache will occur if the drug is abruptly discontinued.

Recently erectile dysfunction related to *propranolol (Inderal)* has been reported.[17,18] A β-adrenergic blocker, propranolol has been used to treat hypertension, angina, arrhythmias, thyrotoxicosis, and other disorders. The sexual effects, which are not included in the package insert, may be from a blockade of central dopaminergic stimulation.[1] In a study of 95 men taking 120 mg/day or more the incidence of erectile dysfunction was 5 percent.[19] There has been insufficient experience with the recently released β_1 blocker, metapropranolol (Lopressor), to ascertain if it will have similar effects.

The α -adrenergic blocker, *phenoxybenzamine (Dibenzyline),* has few therapeutic uses, because its use as an antihypertensive is limited by nausea. Therefore, the inhibition of ejaculation[20] is primarily of academic importance, since it is theorized that α blockade causes this effect in other therapeutic agents. Ganglionic blocking agents, such as mecamylamine (Inversine) and trimethaphan (Arfonad), are currently reserved for the treatment of hypertensive crisis. Therefore, the potential effects of these drugs on sexual function (see Table 13-2) are of little clinical significance.

One ethical question which arises regarding the sexual effects of drugs used in hypertension is whether the patient should be told of these adverse effects when the drug is prescribed. While the doctrine of informed consent would dictate that the patient be told, there is also the risk that the anxiety about the potential effects may contribute to or even induce their occurrence. Many clinicians therefore recommend that the patient not be told of the potential effects on sexual functioning, but that subsequent follow-up be structured to encourage the patient to report any adverse changes in sexual functioning. It is unlikely that impotence is drug-induced if the patient experiences an erection upon awakening in the morning. Often patients experiencing sexual dysfunction with one antihypertensive drug may recover sexual function when placed on another drug, even if it is known to cause sexual dysfunction in other patients. When drug-induced sexual dysfunction occurs, the patient should be reassured about the cause and reversibility of the effect.

Diuretics   Several diuretics including *spironolactone (Aldactone), chlorthalidone (Hygroton),* and other thiazides, especially *hydrochlorothiazide (HydroDiuril),* have been associated with adverse effects on sexual function.[14] Chlorthalidone occasionally causes impotence.[13] Spironolactone, an inhibitor of the adrenal steroid, aldosterone, has caused a reversible amenorrhea in women and gynecomastia and impotence in men.[13,21,22]

Antiarrhythmic   The new antiarrhythmic drug *disopyramide (Norpace),* which has other anticholinergic side effects, has been reported in a single case report to cause impotence. This condition was reversible when the dosage was adjusted downward from the initial 300- to 400-mg/day level.[23]

Drugs Used in Psychiatry

Like the antihypertensive agents, drugs used to treat psychiatric disorders have considerable potential to adversely affect sexual function. These drugs may cause an improvement in sexual functioning as well, due to the generally improved psychological condition.

Antipsychotic Drugs   Many of the psychotropic drugs have α-adrenergic blocking properties, as well as anticholinergic action, and thus impair sexual function. Equally important is the effect upon the reticular activating system, the limbic system, and other higher centers, which reduces sensory input, interest in the external world, and thereby inhibits sex-related drives.[24] There are three classes of antipsychotics: phenothiazines, thioxanthenes, and butyrophenones. While there is similarity in the effects on sexuality with each group, the incidence of the various adverse effects differs.

Phenothiazine administration has been correlated with inhibition of ejaculation, "dry" ejaculation, erectile difficulties, and decreased responsiveness in women, as well as galactorrhea, amenorrhea, and gynecomastia.[1,13] Impairment of erectile response has been attributed to blockade of cholinergic transmission, while ejaculation inhibition may be due to a central dopamine blockade, as well as a peripheral α-adrenergic blocking effect.[25] The endocrine effects such as gynecomastia, amenorrhea, and nonpuerperal lactation result from depression of the hypothalamus and resulting decrease in several releasing factors and in prolactin inhibiting factor, which causes an increase in lactogenic hormone.

Thioridazine (Mellaril) is the most commonly implicated of the phenothiazines in causing sexual dysfunction. Kotin and associates[26] reported that as many as 60 percent of males on this drug experience adverse effects on sexual function: 44 percent of 57 males experienced erectile difficulties, while 49 percent had impaired ejaculation. In the same study only 25 percent of the men taking other phenothiazines, such as chlorpromazine (Thorazine), trifluoperazine (Stelazine), and promazine (Sparine), experienced sexual dysfunction and one of four women reported a decrease in libido and less satisfying orgasms. Sexual dysfunction with thioridazine and other phenothiazines is well documented in the literature for all age groups including adolescents.[27-29]

The butyrophenone, haloperidol (Haldol), in high doses has caused impotence and impaired libido. The thioxanthenes, thiothixene (Navane) and chlorprothixene (Taractan), also cause impotence and failure to ejaculate, but the latter is less commmon with these drugs than with the phenothiazines.[16]

Antidepressant Drugs   There are three distinct types of antidepressants: tricyclic antidepressants, MAO (monoamine oxidase) inhibitors, and lithium carbonate. The tricyclic antidepressants, such as imipramine (Tofranil), amitriptyline (Elavil), and protriptyline (Vivactil), are chemically very similar to the phenothiazines and may induce sexual dysfunction through similar mechanisms. Even with low doses delayed ejaculation, failure to ejaculate, changes in libido, erectile dysfunction, and delayed orgasm in the female have been reported.[1,30] There are no good studies on the incidence of these effects, but only one case of sexual dysfunction in women has been reported.[31]

The mechanism of the sexual effects of monoamine oxidase inhibitors such as pargyline (Eutonyl), tranylcypromine (Parnate), and isocarboxazid (Marplan) may be a decrease in norepinephrine for release during sympathetic stimulation or the formation of a false neurotransmitter.[16] Erectile impotence, ejaculatory difficulties, and difficulty achieving orgasm in the female have been reported.[13]

Vinarova and associates[32] noted impaired potency in 10 percent of men receiving lithium carbonate for manic depression. This is probably due to a decrease in dopaminergic activity caused by lithium.

Anxiolytics, Sedatives, and Narcotics   While these agents could potentially alter sexual function when employed in usual doses for normal therapeutic indications, the sexual effects are most apparent in the abuse situation. Therefore, these agents will be covered in the section on social drugs.

Drugs Used to Prevent Pregnancy

No drug has a more profound effect upon the sexuality of both males and females than the oral contraceptive. Due to the high efficacy of "the pill," it has been possible to separate sexuality from reproduction, allowing persons to realize and express this facet of the human experience.

While there has generally been little research on the effect of drugs on the sexual functioning of the female, the effects of oral contraceptives are a notable exception. The pill is usually a combination of estrogens (commonly ethinyl estradiol or mestranol) and progestins (commonly norethindrone, dl-norgestrel, or ethynodiol acetate). However, the "minipill" and the long-acting injectable contraceptives contain only progestins and the postcoital or "morning-after" contraceptives contain only an estrogen, diethylstilbestrol. In the female estrogens are thought to increase libido while progestins reportedly decrease libido.[33] Studies with oral contraceptives show variable results from decreased libido in 20 percent of those taking the drug to increased sexual activity during the second half of the menstrual cycle, attributed to absence of the normal luteal peak of progesterone secretion at this time.[34,35] The effects are probably very individualized with freedom from the worry about pregnancy increasing sexual enjoyment for many women[36] and decrease in libido, probably secondary to mood depression, affecting other women. While pill users complain about loss of libido 4.5 times more often than nonusers, there is at present no good evidence that it is caused by the pill.[37]

Other contraceptives, such as the spermicides in foams and jellies, have caused dyspareunia (painful intercourse) when the woman is hypersensitive to the chemical in the spermicide. This effect ceases when the chemical is no longer used.

The problem of developing an effective contraceptive for the male is complicated by the biology of spermatogenesis, which is a continuous process, rather than the single surge of gonadotropic hormone in midcycle typical of the female. Estrogens and progestins will interfere with spermatogenesis by suppressing output of LH (luteinizing hormone), but also cause gynecomastia and decreased libido. The synthetic steroid danazol combined with testosterone, a combination presently under research investigation, does deter spermatogenesis without affecting libido. The bis (dichloroacetyl) diamines demonstrated effective and reversible antispermatogenesis by direct action on germ cells, but were abandoned when an incompatibility with alcohol (Antabuse-like reaction) was noted. Cytotoxic drugs were ruled out as male contraceptives due to a mutagenic potential. Much research is presently focused on drugs that would act indirectly on sperm by interfering with epididymal transport and function; the epididymis is the location for maturation of the sperm. No effective male contraceptive is anticipated for a number of years.[38]

Miscellaneous Drugs

The effects of the *cytotoxic drugs* used to treat neoplasms include infertility related to amenorrhea in women and decreased spermatogenesis in males. No reliable studies to evaluate the common assumption that these antineoplastic drugs decrease libido and potency have been published.[1]

Due to the strong anticholinergic action attributable to the ganglionic blocking properties of their quaternary ammonium chemical structure, the *antispasmodic drugs,* which are prescribed for their vagolytic effect in peptic ulcer disease, also have caused impotence.[13,16] Agents in the category include *methantheline (Banthine), propantheline (Pro-Banthine),* and *isopropamide (Darbid).* The antipruritic, *trimeprazine (Temaril),* which is chemically similar to the antipsychotics, elicits similar adverse changes in sexual function: galactorrhea and menstrual irregularities.[13] *Disulfiram (Antabuse),* which causes illness when alcohol is ingested and is therefore used in alcoholics to cause alcohol aversion, has resulted in transient impotence.[1,13]

One study[39] reported several cases of inhibition of ejaculation in hemophilic patients administered *aminocaproic acid (Amicar).* This effect was reversible within 6 hours after the drug, an inhibitor of fibrinolysis, was administered prior to dental procedures.

Clofibrate (Atromid-S), used to reduce blood lipoproteinemia, has caused an impotence which was reversible within 4 weeks after the drug was stopped, but returned when the drug was resumed.[40] No effects of this agent upon sexual functioning of women have been reported.

Merely because no effects for a given therapeutic agent upon sexual functioning have been reported in the literature does not necessarily mean that the drug is without these effects. The clinician must constantly be on the lookout for previously undetected or idiosyncratic reactions. When the patient is receiving a drug implicated in sexual dysfunction, it is important to take a good history at each contact and to work with the patient in drug selection and dosage adjustment to achieve an optimal risk-benefit ratio.

SOCIAL DRUGS

A variety of pharmacologic agents, referred to as social drugs, are self-prescribed by the public to enhance general performance, to decrease inhibitions in social situations, or for their euphoriant effects. Some of these agents are so common that the user is not even cognizant that he or she is self-administering a drug. Some are used specifically for reputed effects on sexual function.

Legal Drugs

The three major socially approved drugs in Western society are caffeine, nicotine, and alcohol. *Caffeine* is widely available in medications (e.g., over-the-counter analgesics, cold preparations, and stimulants) and in beverages (e.g., coffee, tea, cola drinks, and cocoa). Chemically it is a methylated xanthine, as are theophylline and theobromine, which are found in tea and cocoa, respectively. Pharmacologically it is a CNS stimulant. Many psychotropic effects have been attributed to caffeine, including stimulation and suppression of sexuality. The average cup of brewed coffee contains 85 mg caffeine per 150 ml. Doses of 50 to 200 mg result in increased alertness, decreased fatigue, lessened drowsiness, and a feeling of improved physical activity. This might be expected to increase sexual interest in the person who otherwise might have been too fatigued. Pleasant or unpleasant hyperesthesia (increased sensitivity to sensory stimuli) can occur with caffeine intake and could enhance sexual pleasure or responsiveness. Higher doses (200 to 500 mg) may produce headache, tremor, and irritability, with the effects of a dose taken in a beverage persisting 2 to 3 hours.[41-43]

Advertising in the mass media has systematically attempted to link cigarette smoking to sex appeal and, more recently, to liberation in the female. The neurotransmitter receptors at autonomic ganglia and at skeletal muscle are referred to as *nicotinic receptors* because the alkaloid nicotine mimics the effects of the physiological neurotransmitter acetylcholine at both sites. Nicotine exerts a biphasic effect of initial stimulation at the ganglia, resulting in increased blood pressure, respiratory rate, and gastrointestinal motility and secretions, followed by a ganglionic blockage with reversal of these effects. Effects persist for about an hour after smoking a cigarette. Habitual users show few of these effects of nicotine in tobacco smoke. Therefore, while the nicotinic effects on both sympathetic and parasympathetic ganglia could theoretically produce effects on sexual function, no evidence of this has been presented. Any effects of nicotine—or the more than 500 other substances found in cigarette smoke—appear to be from the social symbolism of rebellion and liberation which might also carry over into sexual expression.[43,44]

Despite much research on alcohol, little has been elucidated about the effects of alcohol on sexual behavior beyond what Shakespeare expressed in the play *Macbeth* (Act 2, Scene 3) through the gatekeeper speaking to Macduff:

> Lechery, sir, it provokes and unprovokes; it provokes the desire but it takes away the performance; therefore, much drink may be said to be an equivocator with lechery.

One must not forget that in spite of appearances of stimulation, alcohol is pharmacologically a CNS depressant. Disinhibition may result in an increased sexual desire but performance can be impaired. In animals alcohol causes a prolongation of erection time, increased latency to the first mount, intromission, and ejaculation, but fewer intromissions to achieve ejaculation. At blood alcohol levels associated with loss of the ejaculation reflex, dogs maintained interest in receptive females in spite of the inability to complete copulation. The estrous cycle of female animals is disrupted by alcohol, but the sexual response of the female animal to alcohol administration has not been reported in the literature.[45] Actually, little research upon the effects of alcohol on the human female sexual ressponse has been done.

Impotence has been observed in at least 8 percent of men with prolonged heavy use of alcohol, half of whom regained sexual function after several months of abstinence from alcohol. Lemere and Smith[46] postulated that alcohol may destroy the neurogenic reflex that mediates erection, which is reasonable considering the multiple neurotoxic manifestations in alcohol abusers. In these men the sexual desire persists in spite of the erectile dysfunction. Secondary impotence has been found to be more highly associated with excessive alcohol consumption than with any other factor. The initial failure to attain or maintain an erection in men of all ages often occurs when the man is under the influence of alcohol.[47]

Illicit and Illegal Drugs

Research studies have shown a consistent positive correlation between illicit drug use and sexual activity. Goode[48] questioned college students and found a relationship between the use of marijuana and other drugs and indices of sexual activity (frequency of sexual activity, age of first experience, and total number of partners). Those who used drugs were more likely to be sexually active, more frequently and with more partners, and to have begun sexual activity earlier. However, this does not necessarily mean that drugs incite sexual activity, as has been asserted by some. Rather, both are probably related to other social or personality variables.

Likewise, the fact that those who inject drugs have more sexual dysfunction than those who take them orally[49] may not be due to the effects of the drugs, but related to the degree of personality deviation more commonly found in this group. Bartholomew[50] reported the observation of several cases of "orgastic pleasure" from the process of drug injection itself; he postulates that this conditioned response may complicate the treatment process. Some researchers suggest that those with sexual dysfunction use drugs as a substitute for sexual activity.

A very common reason cited by young adults for drug use is to enhance the sexual experience, but conscious sexual problems seldom contribute to addiction. Enhancement of sexual enjoyment is a strong reinforcer of drug use, but sexual dysfunction is commonly tolerated as a side effect of drug use.[49]

As all of this points out, it is difficult to unravel the complex interrelationship between drug use and human sexual behavior. Nowlis[51] suggests that research involving these two factors should be considered from four distinct points of view: (1) the effect of drug use on the subjective and objective sexual behavior; (2) the effect of sexual behavior and sexual experiences upon drug use or repeat drug use; (3) associations and correlations in the ways in which these two phenomena tend to occur together in daily life, in the life histories of the person as a child, adolescent, and adult, in clinical and criminal records, etc.; and (4) instances in which an attribute of one is identified as an equivalent of an attribute of the other, as in the statement that injection of heroin causes a "pharmacologic orgasm." Certainly more research is needed in each of these areas and definition of questions from a single point of view might help to clarify what so often now seems to be conflicting findings from one study to another.

Problems in researching the effects of illicit and illegal social drugs upon sexual function are compounded by the restrictions upon these agents and legal sanctions against drug users. Therefore, our knowledge about these agents is based primarily on retrospective reports of those in drug treatment programs or anonymous reports of current users rather than upon controlled studies. The fact that there is no quality control on street drugs means that neither the user nor the researcher can be sure of the dosage level or even the identification of all components of the drug. Table 13-3 summarizes the reputed effects of the social drugs, but these limitations and the fact that environment and psychological expectations can modify the effects should be kept in mind when referring to the table.

Narcotics   The effects of narcotics on sexual function has received intense study. In the male there is an inhibition of both desire and potency. Ejaculation time for one group of addicts was increased while on heroin from a former mean of 8.7 minutes to 44.2 minutes.[52] These men report decreased frequency of intercourse, poor quality of orgasm, difficulty achieving orgasm, fewer nocturnal emissions, decreased frequency of masturbation, and decrement in general level of desire. As many as half of the male addicts may be impotent.[53]

Morphine inhibits release of hypothalamic and pituitary hormones, thereby decreasing gonadotropins. Testosterone probably stays within normal range, although some studies do show decreased testosterone levels. The decrease in gonadotropins may be due to the sedative effects of the narcotics.[1,15,49]

Women on heroin and other narcotics may initially experience the disinhibition that occurs with low doses of most CNS-depressant drugs, but chronic users usually have decreased libido, apathy, and even antipathy toward intercourse. They report decreased sexual sensation during intercourse and fewer orgastic experiences.[49] Inhibition of the output of thyrotropin and gonadotropin from the

Table 13-3 Effects of Social Drugs on Sexual Function

Drug	Usual effect on libido		Usual effect on performance	
	Male	**Female**	**Male**	**Female**
Alcohol	Increased, disinhibition	Increased, disinhibition	Impotence, delayed ejaculation, chronic: impotence	Negligible effect until severely depressed
Heroin	Decreased	Decreased, some experience disinhibition, others apathetic or antipathetic. Lack of sexual pleasure	Delayed ejaculation, decreased quality of orgasm, difficulty reaching orgasm. Decreased gonadotropic hormones. Withdrawal—spontaneous erection and ejaculation. Often premature ejaculation when drug-free. Narcotic antagonists may have "aphrodisiac" effect	Decreased sexual sensation, decreased proportion of orgastic coital experiences. Decreased gonadotropic hormones result in amenorrhea, infertility, spontaneous abortion. Withdrawal—increased excitability, spontaneous orgasm
Methadone	Improved, but less than drug-free	Same as male	Same as heroin but less marked. Low plasma testosterone on higher doses	Same as heroin but less marked

241

Table 13-3 Effects of Social Drugs on Sexual Function (continued)

Drug	Usual effect on libido		Usual effect on performance	
	Male	Female	Male	Female
Sedatives and hypnotics: Meprobamate (Miltown, Equanil), diazepam (Valium), chlordiazepoxide (Librium), secobarbital (Seconal), pentobarbital (Nembutal), other barbiturates, methaqualone (Quaalude)	Varies. Decrease with chronic abuse	Often increased from disinhibition. Decreases with chronic abuse	Failure to ejaculate (rare). Decreased gonadotropins and impaired performance with barbiturates	Disinhibition may improve performance and enjoyment. Females show greater preference for sedative drugs
Hallucinogens: Lysergic acid diethylamide (LSD), mescaline, phencyclidine (PCP), psilocybin, peyote	Usually decreased, sex is incidental. Very selective in choice of partner, shared experience. Many hallucinogens inhibit libido	Same as male	Prolonged coitus. Delay orgasm. Orgasm is "explosive." Heighten sensory awareness, more distractable. Sense of timelessness. Increased enjoyment. May cause impotence	Similar to male

Drug				
Amphetamines	Marked increase, especially intravenous. Chronic use may decrease. Initial "rush" is orgastic experience	Often decreases interest and responsiveness, but may increase	Prolonged erections. Delayed orgasm or multiple orgasm. Heightened enjoyment. May cause impotence	May become more sexually agressive. Less favorable than males. Apathy or antipathy toward sex in chronic users
Cocaine	Increase. Chronic sustained use leads to decreased sex drive	Usually increases. Decreases with chronic use	Enhance planned sex. Increase enjoyment. Delay ejaculation	Similar to male, no sex differences noted. Facilitate orgasm
Marijuana	Increased with small doses (disinhibition). Decreased with larger doses	Same as male	Effect dose-related—enhanced orgasm, improved tactile awareness, improved interpersonal experience, greater awareness of sexual organs with low dose. Chronic use may decrease testosterone, cause impotence, infertility	Similar to male, few sex differences noted. Some women report feelings of depersonalization
Amyl nitrite	Usually no effect	Usually no effect	Delay ejaculation. Prolonged or heightened orgasm. Used by homosexuals. May relax sphincters for anal sex	Usually no effect

pituitary probably causes the amenorrhea, decreased fertility, and increased rate of spontaneous abortion found in addicts.[54]

During withdrawal women may often report increased excitability and spontaneous orgasm,[49] while men may have spontaneous erection and ejaculation. The "aphrodisiac" quality of narcotic antagonists formerly reported by addicts is probably due to precipitation of this withdrawal effect.[55,56]

While addicts do not seem to have more sexual problems prior to addiction than the general population, there is a high incidence of premature ejaculation reported in the postwithdrawal drug-free period.[55] Normal function usually returns within a year of abstinence.

Those on methadone maintenance programs report similar problems as when on other narcotics, but the effects are less dramatic. Females report less effect than men from either heroin or methadone.[55] Methadone may cause plasma testosterone to fall below normal levels, especially when there is also alcohol use.[49]

Sedatives and Hypnotics   This group of CNS depressants includes some of the most widely prescribed medications in the United States at the current time: diazepam (Valium) and chlordiazepoxide (Librium). Also included are the barbiturates, meprobamate (Miltown, Equanil), and methaqualone (Sopor, Parest, Quaalude), which was reputed by the drug culture to have some mystical sexual properties. There is no reason to believe that any one of this group of drugs has any unique sex-enhancing qualities. All may result in disinhibition, permitting expression of repressed sexuality. In a study of 70 polydrug users Ungerer et al.[57] found that individuals who prefer sedatives are higher in sex guilt than those who prefer stimulants or individuals with no definite preference. Another study[58] revealed that more females take decrement-producing drugs such as the barbiturates and anxiolytics. Considering usual child-rearing practices for males and females with respect to sexuality, it is reasonable that women, who may experience more guilt and inhibition related to sexual behavior, would choose sedative drugs either to suppress the guilt associated with sex or to suppress the sexual behavior that precipitates the guilt. However, there are insufficient data to establish a causal relationship.

Like morphine barbiturates depress the output of the pituitary gonadatropins; other sedatives also may inhibit pituitary tropic hormones.[59] One reported case of failure to ejaculate has been caused by chlordiazepoxide (Librium); when the drug was withdrawn the problem resolved but returned when the drug was readministered.[60]

Barbiturates are viewed less favorably than other drugs in this class by some drug abusers, especially by men who may note decreased libido and performance and reduced discrimination in selection of partner.[49]

Hallucinogens   There are numerous substances used for their ability to provoke hallucinations. LSD (lysergic acid diethylamide) and mescaline are the most common of these used to augment sexuality. However, results may be variable since drugs sold on the street often have numerous drugs and impurities combined with them. These drugs have been lauded as aphrodisiacs and enhancers of sexual behavior.

In male rats there is a predictable dose-response curve with LSD; small doses accelerate sexual behavior while larger doses completely disrupt sexual behavior.[61] Humans report that sexual intercourse under the influence of LSD is an intensified experience with heightened sensory awareness and deeper appreciation. There is a sense of timelessness and orgasm is delayed. Both mescaline and LSD are sympathomimetic drugs. Men and women report an "explosive" orgasm and heightened enjoyment.[49]

On the other hand, LSD does not stimulate libido in the sense that it incites the user to sexual activity; sex is often a matter of chance and sexual thoughts are often irrelevant or displaced by other preoccupations. There is an increased selectivity in choice of partner and environment. Psychological state and individual factors, more than some inherent property of the drug, seem to determine whether sexual intercourse occurs when the person takes a hallucinogen.[49]

Amphetamines Pharmacologically amphetamines are CNS stimulants and sympathomimetic drugs. There appear to be distinctions between males and females in the effects of these drugs upon sexual function, although there is inadequate well-documented information in the literature on all aspects of amphetamine effect on sexuality. Animal studies indicate that lower doses of amphetamine accelerate male sexual behavior.[62]

Use of smaller oral doses of amphetamines seems to have little effect in human drug abusers, while larger intravenous doses appear to be a distinct aphrodisiac, especially in the male.[15,49] The initial "rush" which occurs when the drug is injected intravenously, described as a visceral numbness and tingling likened to a diffuse orgasm, is caused by sympathetic hyperactivity. Dopaminergic activity could explain the sexual stimulation that may cause the woman to be more sexually aggressive.[15] The prolonged erections, delayed ejaculation, or increased capacity for repeat orgasm common in the male is hard to explain in this sympathetic drug, but may be due to an increased distractibility to external stimuli. Some cases of amphetamine use can be traced to self-treatment of premature ejaculation.[49] Some drug users report impotence and penile shrinkage.[63]

Men generally tend to judge the effect of this drug on sexual functioning positively, while women are less favorable; some female chronic users of amphetamines are apathetic or antipathetic toward sexual activity. Greaves[63] found sexual disturbances, dissatisfaction with current sexual activity, and promiscuity among chronic amphetamine users, although the males were more favorable toward the drug than the females in this group as well. It has been hypothesized that chronic users substitute amphetamines for sexual activity, but Greaves felt that both drug use and sexual disturbances resulted from a common personality variable and were not substitution or causally related factors.

Amphetamine drugs are commonly prescribed as anorectics to decrease appetite and promote weight loss. Impotence and changes in libido (increase and decrease) have been reported for therapeutic oral doses of these drugs.[13]

Cocaine The resurgence of popularity of cocaine is probably due to increased law enforcement of amphetamine restrictions and the growing reputation of cocaine as a sexual stimulant. While classified by the government as a narcotic, it is pharmacologically a CNS stimulant similar to the amphetamines. Its euphoriant effects are probably due to inhibition of reuptake of brain amine transmitters. Cocaine has a biphasic effect of mood elevation followed by depression.[41] It enhances libido, performance, and sexual pleasure, delays ejaculation, and promotes orgasm. Chronic sustained usage will result in loss of sexual drive and decreased performance.[64]

Marijuana Derived from the *Cannabis* plant, marijuana is closely associated with sexuality for many of the millions of users in America. The active ingredient, δ-9-tetrahydrocannabinol, has some qualities of the hallucinogens, of the CNS depressants, and of the CNS stimulants. Generally the user feels that sexual performance and enjoyment is enhanced by marijuana. Aphrodisiac qualities have been claimed for cannabis derivatives throughout its long history. As many as 30 percent of those who use marijuana give sex as the reason for starting to use it.[61] Increase in libido is thought to be due to disinhibition and the subjective impression of slowing of time that accompanies marijuana may make the orgastic experience seem to extend for many minutes. However, these effects occur only at small doses. At moderate doses, the reaction may be similar to alcohol with increased libido, but decreased ability to perform. At large doses the individual may become so preoccupied with the personal experience that both libido and performance are impaired.[65] Decreased sexual activity at high doses is found in animals.[66,67]

Characteristics ascribed to sexual activity under the effects of marijuana include enhanced awareness of sexual pleasure, new pleasurable qualities of orgasm, enhanced sexual fantasy, increased sensuality of tactile sensation, enhanced interpersonal sexuality, more responsive partners, and greater awareness of internal organs.[51] However, more recently a number of young women have taken exception to the notion that marijuana enhances the interpersonal relationship, feeling that often the primary experience of the man is with the drug rather than within the relationship.

While there has been some question about the methodology and replicability of the study, Kolodny and associates[68] found decreased testosterone levels in chronic heavy users of marijuana, as well as two cases of impaired potency. Gynecomastia has also been noted in male chronic marijuana users.[69]

Amyl Nitrite One of the most recent additions to the catalogue of social drug use is amyl nitrite, which is widely used as a sexual stimulant, especially among homosexual males. These ampules were originally designed for use as a fast-acting vasodilator in anginal attacks. Reported subjective effects include an enhanced orgasm which may also be more prolonged.[70] This effect may be due to the giddiness caused by a drop in blood pressure from general vasodilation. Another advantage that has been suggested is that relaxation of the sphincters may facilitate anal sex. With the exclusion of those with serious cardiovascular disease, the primary adverse effects would seem to be headache and possible loss of erection. Few women report any effect of use of this drug.

DRUGS EMPLOYED TO MODIFY SEXUAL RESPONSE

Literally thousands of agents, such as the pith from a pomegranate tree, testicles of various animals, musk, and nail clippings, have been used to alter sexual function.[71] Only those that are the subject of enduring myths and misconceptions and those that are currently being widely studied will be presented in this discussion (Table 13-4).

Aphrodisiacs

The term aphrodisiac is employed for a drug that (1) arouses sexual desire, (2) increases performance, and (3) increases enjoyment. Several of the social drugs might meet one or more of these criteria in some people, provided that proper

Table 13-4 Therapeutic Modification of Sexuality

Drug	Reputed effect	Proposed mechanism
Anxiolytic [e.g., diazepam (Valium)]	Increase sexual desire and participation	Decrease anxiety, disinhibition
Cantharides (Spanish fly)	Aphrodisia	Irritation of bladder, penile and clitoral engorgement. Dangerous drug
Nux vomica	Aphrodisia	Excitation of CNS, potent poison (strychnine)
Parachlorophenylalanine (PCPA)	Aphrodisia	Synergistic with testosterone in man. Inhibits brain serotonin. Numerous side effects
Yohimbine	Aphrodisia	α-Adrenergic blocker vasodilator
Levodopa (L-dopa, Dopar)	Aphrodisia	Dopaminergic, clinical improvement in disease
Cyproterone acetate	Sexual suppression	Antiandrogenic effects, decrease sexual activity
Saltpeter (potassium nitrate)	Sexual suppression	Mild diuretic action, but no direct inhibition of libido or performance proved
Gonadotropins Human chorionic gonadotropin (HCG), luteinizing hormone releasing hormone (LHRH)	Cure impotence, stimulate sexual function	Improve fertility. Increase output of testosterone. Central stimulation of sexuality (?)

dosage and a complementary environment are included. However, expectations still play an important role in human aphrodisia.

A drug which has held a centuries-long reputation as an aphrodisiac is *cantharides,* also called Spanish fly because it is derived from certain insects. Actually a potentially lethal drug which is an irritant, it causes irritation of the urinary tract, resulting in urgency of urination, and occasionally persistent erections and clitoral engorgement. No stimulation of sexual behavior has been noted in laboratory animals administered cantharides; in fact a majority of the animals died.[72]

Nux vomica, from the dried ripe seeds of the *Strychnos nuxvomica* tree, contains about 40 percent strychnine, which produces excitation of the CNS and, at high doses, increased muscle tone. No good evidence of its usefulness as a sexual stimulant has been reported.[1]

Another plant derivative, *yohimbine,* has been employed as an aphrodisiac. It is an α-adrenergic blocker chemically related to reserpine. No differences between control and yohimbine-treated rats were found in study of the sexual organs or frequency of erections.[72]

While *PCPA (parachlorophenylalanine)* alone was not found to have similar aphrodisiac properties in men as in male rats, a controlled study of 16 men suffering from illness and with complaints of sexual deficiency indicated that PCPA and testosterone administered conjointly exhibited a clear aphrodisiac effect. However, such treatment is limited by side effects of PCPA, but other inhibitors of serotonin synthesis may prove to have therapeutic usefulness.[73]

An increase in sexual function has been noted in 25 to 35 percent of those taking *levodopa* (L-dopa, Lopar) for parkinsonism with increased libido, sexual dreams, and sexual activity occurring in males and females.[1] Increased dopaminergic stimulation in the hypothalamus would provide a feasible rationale for these findings, but the clinical and psychological improvement of the patient cannot be disregarded as a factor. Ten impotent males without parkinsonism who received levodopa had increased frequency of spotaneous erection, but not adequate to successfully complete sexual intercourse. Two of the ten reported increased libido.[74] Currently it is not clear how much, if any, real aphrodisiac effect levodopa possesses.

Drugs to Suppress Sexuality

In recent years there has been considerable research directed at suppressing sexuality, particularly deviant forms of sexual expression. In military institutions, prisons, and boarding schools it has long been rumored that *saltpeter* (potassium nitrate) was added to food to suppress sexual arousal. Saltpeter has a mild diuretic action, but no direct effects on sexual interest or capacity for performance have been documented. Several types of diuretics (see previous discussion) have been implicated in impotence, but there is currently no reason to believe that this is true of saltpeter.

Methods of suppressing the sexuality of the male sex offender which have been studied include administration of estrogens, progestins, and phenothiazine tranquilizers (e.g., benpendol or thioridazine) which alter endocrine balance.[75-78] A very effective agent used in Europe is the antiandrogen *cyproterone acetate,* which has proven effective in decreasing sexual thoughts, sexual activity, plasma testosterone, and erectile response in convicted male sexual offenders and in male and female neuropsychiatric patients.[79-81] A number of significant legal and technical problems, as well as ethical concerns, arise out of this proposed form of treatment.[82,83]

Sexual Dysfunction in the Male

The initial concern in the treatment of any sexual dysfunction is the diagnosis of its cause. Male sexual dysfunctions sometimes amenable to pharmacologic treatment are premature ejaculation, retrograde ejaculation, and impotence. The primary treatment of these conditions is psychotherapy, with drug treatment merely serving an adjuvant role. For example, drugs which inhibit ejaculation may be helpful in the management of premature ejaculation. Chlorpromazine (Thorazine), thioridazine (Mellaril), and chlorprothixine (Taractan) and other antipsychotic drugs with α-adrenergic blocking qualities may be of benefit in some cases. However, their anticholinergic actions may adversely effect potency so they should be used with caution.

Retrograde ejaculation is most commonly the result of a neurologic lesion such as spinal cord injury, cancer resection with nerve destruction, or diabetic neuropathy. The antihistamine brompheniramine (Dimetane) and the α-adrenergic agent synephrine have been used to overcome parasympathetic stimulation of the bladder sphincter and thereby reverse retrograde ejaculation.[84-86]

Impotence is the most troublesome and prevalent problem, particularly in the aged, where it is present in 75 percent of men over 60.[87] Causes of impotence may be psychogenic, organic, or drug-related. Atherosclerosis may cause organic impotence in many older men and may be diagnosed with vasodilators.[88]

For a drug-related impotence the drug should be eliminated or changed to an alternative agent. If this is not feasible, the lowest effective dose and psychological support for the couple are important. Lording[87] emphasizes that both partners should be involved in management, even if the problem is organic.

Impotence associated with hypogonadism is treated with long-acting testosterone esters such as testosterone propionate, testosterone enanthate, or testosterone decanoate. The drug is usually administered parenterally every 1 to 4 weeks. In the future subcutaneous implants should become more widely available. Oral testosterone forms usually are not used as they are rapidly metabolized by the liver and are therefore poorly effective. Androgens can cause polycythemia due to stimulation of erythropoietin which increases red cell production. Salt and water retention and elevated cholesterol are other adverse effects to note. Since prostatic tumors may be stimulated by testosterone, the elderly patient should be evaluated carefully for prostatic enlargement.

In cases where impotence, infertility, and sometimes galactorrhea are associated with elevated serum prolactin, bromocriptine (Parlodel) may restore potency. In Europe this drug, an ergot alkaloid which is a dopamine-receptor agonist in the CNS and an inhibitor of prolactin secretion, is being heralded as a panacea for sexual dysfunction and infertility. Few studies support this assertion and the drug can cause neurologic side effects.[89-91]

Other clinicians and researchers have recommended the use of other endocrine or gonadotropic hormones alone or in various combinations with testosterone to treat hypogonadal impotence and the impotence associated with aging. Teter[92] recommended testosterone and estrogens, attributing good results to vasodilation caused by the estrogens. Kupperman[93] found that human chorionic gonadotropin with testosterone after the climacteric decreased testicular atrophy and impotence and increased libido. Other drugs which interact with the pituitary-testicular axis, such as clomiphene (Clomid), a female fertility drug, and luteinizing hormone releasing hormone, have been recommended; increased libido and potency have been reported with their use.[94-97] Considerably more research is needed before the place of these agents in the treatment of impotence is clarified.

A combination of nux vomica, yohimbine, and methyltestosterone was marketed under the name Afrodex, recommended for use in impotence. Numerous research projects were conducted on the product and analysis of the many studies representing over 10,000 cases indicated that the drug was 1.7 to 5.4 times more effective than the placebo.[98-100] However, review of the data analysis reveals a significant placebo effect.[1] The product was removed from the market in 1975 by the Food and Drug Administration on the grounds that efficacy for substances that it contained had not been established.

In a double-blind study Jakobovits[101] found a favorable response in 78 percent of the 100 cases of impotent men using a methyltestosterone/thyroid combination. Further study of this method of treatment is needed. While use of androgens in nonhypogonadal men over 50 is controversial, many clinicians support it for its general anabolic effects, allaying of anxiety, and placebo effect.[102]

Sexual Dysfunction in the Female

Pharmacologic management plays a small role in sexual dysfunction of the female, since psychotherapy is a primary treatment modality. Anxiolytic drugs, particularly the benzodiazepines, have been used for their disinhibiting effect in the treatment of sexual frigidity,[103] but the abuse potential of these drugs dictates that they play a minor role in treatment of sexual problems.

Hormonal replacement for the menopausal woman is a common practice, although this approach is being challenged by those who feel the practice may be dangerous. Obviously the woman who experiences dyspareunia from atropic vaginitis is a candidate for local or systemic estrogens. Those who experience an improved sense of well-being and sexual responsiveness with estrogen replacement should probably not be deprived of these benefits, although the problems associated with uterine bleeding, the risk of thrombophlebitis, and possible links to cancer of the uterus should be explained to the woman.

Greenblatt[10] has recommended low-dose androgens for the elderly woman with decreased libido, to replace decreasing adrenal androgens.

An understanding of the potentially profound effects of therapeutic agents and social drugs upon human sexual function, as well as some of the issues in the treatment of sexual dysfunction, is essential for the nurse clinician. By the same token the nurse must appreciate how very limited is our ability to control or even to accurately predict these profound effects.

SUMMARY

Currently there is inadequate knowledge about the effects of specific pharmacologic agents on sexual functioning because there are significant barriers to research of the problem. Furthermore, numerous individual factors can alter how drugs' sexual effects are manifested.

Most drugs have the potential to indirectly affect sexual function in the human by causing clinical improvement in the patient's condition or by eliciting adverse effects which interfere with sexual activity or interest. The mechanism of action of those drugs known to directly alter sexual function is usually through (1) alteration of the levels of the biogenic amines, especially dopamine and serotonin, in the CNS; (2) enhancing or blocking of the parasympathetic or sympathetic divisions of the autonomic nervous system; (3) changes in hormone balance; or (4) general stimulation or depression of the CNS.

Therapeutic agents which commonly affect adversely human sexual function include several antihypertensive and antipsychotic drugs. Social drugs which can enhance or impede sexuality, depending upon dosage level and chronicity of use, include alcohol, narcotics, sedatives, LSD, amphetamines, marijuana, and cocaine. Substances presently under investigation as aphrodisiacs for use in sexual dysfunctions are PCPA, levodopa, and testosterone, alone or in combination with other hormones such as thyroid, luteinizing hormone releasing hormone, and human chorionic gonadotropin. Tables 13-2, 13-3, and 13-4 summarize the sexual effects of pharmacologic agents.

SUGGESTED LEARNING EXPERIENCES

1. Give the historical perspective (see Chap. 2) of the religious and social values underlying the following observations.
    a. Far less is known about the effects of drugs upon the sexual functioning of women than of men.
    b. Today illicit social drugs are an accepted part of sexual expression for many people.
    c. Some women taking oral contraceptives experience increased libido while some others experience decreased libido.
    d. Recently there has been an increased quantity and quality of research on drug effects on sexuality.
    e. Individual variables profoundly affect the expression of the sexual effects of drugs.
2. Select two of the observations above and postulate an "old myth" and a "new myth" related to each. (See examples in Chap. 2.)

3. On a sheet of paper write the following column headings: (a) Alter Biogenic Amines, (b) Affect Autonomic Nervous System, (c) Alter Hormone Balance, and (d) General CNS Stimulation or Depression. Write the name of each drug or drug group discussed in this chapter in the appropriate column(s). Compare your list with that of classmates and discuss any discrepancies by giving the rationale for your classification.

4. Counseling and teaching are important components of the nursing role in drug therapy. In a small group role-play the following situation to identify how the nurse could best manage the drug problem.

A 38-year-old black male taking methyldopa (Aldomet) for hypertension reports to the nurse practititioner for the first follow-up visit after the drug was initiated. He had not been informed of the potential adverse sexual effects. The nurse's role in the clinic is to ascertain therapeutic effectiveness, incidence of adverse reactions, and patient compliance and to refer any problems requiring medication adjustment to the physician.

5. Organize a class debate on one of the following topics. Research the legal, ethical, and technical (e.g. patient compliance, methods of drug administration, etc.) aspects of the topic.

    a. Resolved that sex offenders with more than one conviction should be required to undergo castration or to take an antiandrogen to suppress sex drive as a requirement for parole.

    b. Resolved that persons with indications for drugs that may affect sexuality should be informed of these effects prior to the drug order.

REFERENCES

1 S. J. Stohs, "Drugs and Sexual Effects," *U.S. Pharmacist* **3**(10):51–68 (1978).

2 B. S. McEwen, speaking at the Annual Meeting of the Society for Neuroscience, St. Louis, 1978, reported in *Chem. Eng. News* **56**(47):26 (1978).

3 A. Tagliamonte, P. Tagliamonte, G. L. Gessa, and B. B. Brodie, "Compulsive Sexual Activity Induced by *p*-Chlorophenylalanine in Normal and Pinealectomized Male Rats," *Science* **166**:1433–1435 (1969).

4 F. Sicuteri, "Serotonin and Sex in Man," *Pharmacol. Res. Commun.* **6**:403–411 (1974).

5 L. Dennerstein and G. D. Burrows, "Sexual Side Effects of Drugs," *Med. J. Aust.* **2**:26 (1977).

6 G. M. Everett, "Amyl Nitrite ("Poppers") as an Aphrodisiac," in M. Sandler and G. L. Gessa (eds.), *Sexual Behavior: Pharmacology and Biochemistry,* Raven, New York, 1975b, pp. 97–98.

7 S. Ehrenpreis, "Parasympathetic Drugs and Cholinesterase Inhibitors," in M. B. Wiener, G. A. Pepper, G. Weissman, and J. Romano (eds.), *Clinical Pharmacology and Therapeutics in Nursing,* McGraw-Hill, New York, 1979.

8 K. Kedia and C. Markland, "The Effect of Pharmacological Agents on Ejaculation," *J. Urol.* **114**:569–573 (1975).

9 R. L. Moss, speaking at the Annual Meeting of the Society for Neuroscience, St. Louis, 1978, reported in *Chem. Eng. News* **56**(47):26 (1978).

10 D. J. Greenblatt and J. Koch-Weser, "Gynecomastia and Impotence—Complications of Spironolactone Therapy," *J. Am. Med. Assoc.* **223**:82 (1973).

11 C. J. Bulpitt, C. T. Dollery, and S. Carne, "Change in Symptoms of Hypertensive Patients after Referral to Hospital Clinic," *Br. Heart J.* **38**:121 (1976).

12 M. A. Riddinough, "Preventing, Detecting, and Managing Adverse Reactions of Anti-Hypertensive Agents in the Ambulant Patient with Essential Hypertension," *Am. J. Hosp. Pharm.* **34**:465–479 (1977).

13 N. L. Story, "Sexual Dysfunction Resulting from Drug Side Effects," *J. Sex Res.* **10**(2):132–149 (1974).

14 *Medical Letter,* "Clonidine (Catapres) and Other Drugs Causing Sexual Dysfunction," **19**(20):81–82 (1977).

15 L. E. Hollister, "Drugs and Sexual Behavior in Man," *Life Sci.* **17**:661–667 (1975).

16 L. C. Mills, "Drug-Induced Impotence," *Am. Fam. Phys.* **12**(2):104–106 (1975).

17 J. W. Hollifield, K. Sherman, R. VanderZwagg, and D. G. Shand, "Proposed Mechanisms of Propranolol's Antihypertensive Effect in Essential Hypertension," *N. Engl. J. Med.* **295**:68–73 (1976).

18 S. G. Warren, D. L. Brewer, and E. S. Orgain: "Long-Term Propranolol Therapy for Angina Pectoris," *Am. J. Cardiol.* **37**:420–426 (1976).

19 S. C. Warren and S. G. Warren, "Propranolol and Sexual Impotence," *Ann. Int. Med.* **86**:112 (1977).

20 J. F. Ricordon and G. Walkers, "Effects of Phenoxybenzamine in Shock Due to Myocardial Infarction," *Br. Med. J.* **1**:155 (1969).

21 D. J. Greenblatt and J. Koch-Weser, "Gynecomastia and Impotence—Complications of Spironolactone Therapy," *J. Am. Med. Assoc.* **223**:82 (1973).

22 J. Levitt, "Spironolactone Therapy and Amenorrhea," *J. Am. Med. Assoc.* **211**:2014–2015 (1970).

23 D. J. McHaffie, A. Guz, and A. Johnston, "Impotency in a Patient on Dysopramide," *Lancet* **1**:859 (1977).

24 A. Dotti and M. Reda, "Major Tranquilizers and Sexual Function," in M. Sandler and G. L. Gessa (eds.), *Sexual Behavior: Pharmacology and Biochemistry,* Raven, New York, 1975, pp. 193–196.

25 R. T. Segraves, "Pharmacological Agents Causing Sexual Dysfunction," *J. Sex Marital Ther.* **3**:157–176 (1977).

26 J. Kotin, D. E. Wilbert, D. Verburg, and S. M. Soldinger, "Thioridazine and Sexual Dysfunction," *Am. J. Psychiatry* **133**:82–85 (1976).

27 M. Green, "Inhibition of Ejaculation as a Side Effect of Mellaril," *Am. J. Psychiatry* **118**:173 (1961).

28 J. J. Jeffries, "Piperacetazine-Induced Failure to Ejaculate," *Can. Psychiatry Assoc. J.* **19**:322–323 (1974).

29 H. R. Greenberg and C. Carrillo, "Thioridazine-Induced Inhibition of Masturbatory Ejaculation in an Adolescent," *Am. J. Psychiatry* **124**:991–993 (1978).

30 J. E. Nininger, "Inhibition of Ejaculation by Amitriptyline," *Am. J. Psychiatry* **135**(6):750–751 (1978).

31 J. D. Couper-Smartt and R. Rodham, "A Technique for Surveying Side-Effects of Tricyclic Drugs with Reference to Reported Sexual Effects," *J. Int. Med. Res.* **1**:473–476 (1973).

32 E. Vinarova, O. Uhlif, L. Stika, and O. Vinar, "Side Effects of Lithium Administration," *Activ. Nerv. Suppl. (Praha)* **14**:105–107 (1972).

33 R. A. Hatcher, G. K. Steward, F. Guest, R. Finkelstein, and C. Godwin, *Contraceptive Technology, 1976–1977,* 8th ed., Irvington, New York, 1976, pp. 49–51.

34 B. N. Herzberg, K. C. Draper, A. J. Johnson, and G. C. Nichol, "Oral Contraceptives, Depression, and Libido," *Br. Med. J.* **3**:495–500 (1971).

35 J. R. Udry and N. M. Morris, "Effect of Contraceptive Pills on the Distribution of Sexual Activity in the Menstrual Cycle," *Nature* **227**:502–503 (1970).

36 M. Roland, *Progestagen Therapy,* Charles C Thomas, Springfield, Ill., 1965, p. 55.

37 C. R. Kay, "Oral Contraceptives—The Clinical Perspective," in G. Carattini and H. W. Berendes, *Pharmacology of Steroid Contraceptive Drugs,* Raven, New York, 1977, p. 10.

38 D. W. Fawcett, "Prospect for Fertility Control in the Male," in M. C. Diamond and C. C. Korenbrot (eds.), *Hormonal Contraceptives, Estrogens and Human Welfare,* Academic, New York, 1978, pp. 57–71.

39 B. E. Evans and L. M. Aledort, "Inhibition of Ejaculation Due to Epsilon Amino-caproic Acid," *N. Engl. J. Med.* **298**:166–167 (1978).

40 J. Schneider and H. Kaffarnik, "Impotence in Patients Treated with Clofibrate," *Atherosclerosis* **21**:455–457 (1975).

41 B. J. Kirkstone and R. A. Levitt, "Stimulant and Antidepressant Drugs," in R. A. Levitt (ed.), *Psychopharmacology: A Biological Approach,* Wiley, New York, 1975, pp. 231–238.

42 P. E. Stephensen, "Physiologic and Psychotropic Effects of Caffeine on Man," *J. Am. Diet. Assoc.* **71**(9):240–247 (1977).

43 E. Leavitt, *Drugs and Behavior,* Saunders, Philadelphia, 1974.

44 H. E. Crisswell and R. A. Levitt, "Cholinergic Drugs," in R. A. Levitt (ed.), *Psychopharmacology: A Biological Approach,* Wiley, New York, 1975, pp. 97–100.

45 C. Kornetsky, *Pharmacology: Drugs Affecting Behavior,* Wiley, New York, 1976, pp. 153–154.

46 F. Lemere and J. W. Smith, "Alcohol-Induced Sexual Impotence," *Am. J. Psychiatry* **130**:212–213 (1973).

47 W. H. Masters and V. E. Johnson, *Human Sexual Response,* Little, Brown, Boston, 1966, p. 67.

48 E. Goode, "Drugs and Sexual Activity on a College Campus," *Am. J. Psychiatry* **128**:1272–1276 (1972).

49 D. Parr, "Sexual Aspects of Drug Abuse in Narcotic Addicts," *Br. J. Addict.* **71**:261–268 (1976).

50 A. A. Bartholomew, "Two Features Occasionally Associated with Intravenous Drug Users," *Aust. N. Z. J. Psychiatry* **7**:206–207 (1973).

51 V. Nowlis, "Categories of Interest in the Scientific Search for Relationships (i.e. Interactions, Associations, Comparisons) in Human Sexual Behavior," in M. Sandler and G. L. Gessa (eds.), *Sexual Behavior: Pharmacology and Biochemistry,* Raven, New York, 1975, pp. 93–96.

52 G. Leon and H. Wexler, "Heroin Addiction: Its Relation to Sexual Behavior and Sexual Addiction," *J. Abnorm. Psychol.* **81**:36–38 (1973).

53 Leavitt, op. cit., p. 316.

54 S. S. Stoffer, "A Gynecologic Study of Drug Addicts," *Am. J. Obstet. Gynecol.* **101**:779–783 (1968).

55 J. Mintz, K. O'Hare, C. O'Brien, and J. Goldschmidt, "Sexual Problems of Heroin Addicts," *Arch. Gen. Psychiatry* **31**:700–703 (1974).

56 O. S. Ray, *Drugs, Society, and Human Behavior,* rev. ed., Mosby, St. Louis, 1974.

57 J. C. Ugerer, R. J. Harford, F. L. Brown, and H. D. Kleger, "Sex, Guilt and Preferences for Illegal Drugs among Drug Abusers," *J. Clin. Psychol.* **32**:891–895 (1976).

58 K. R. Mitchell, D. M. Mitchell, and R. J. Kerby, "Note on Sex Differences in Student Drug Usage," *Psychol. Rep.* **27**:116 (1970).

59   R. E. Wilcox and R. A. Levitt, "The Depressants," in R. A. Levitt (ed.), *Psycho-pharmacology: A Biological Approach,* Wiley, New York, 1975, pp. 145–185.

60   J. M. Hughes, "Failure to Ejaculate with Chlordiazepoxide" *Am. J. Psychiatry* **121**:610–611 (1964).

61   Leavitt, op. cit., p. 317.

62   Ibid., p. 314.

63   G. Greaves, "Sexual Disturbances among Chronic Amphetamine Users," *J. Nerv. Ment. Dis.* **155**:363–365 (1972).

64   Leavitt, op. cit., p. 89.

65   G. G. Nahas, *Marihuana—Deceptive Weed,* rev. ed. Raven, New York, 1975.

66   M. E. Corcoran, Z. Amit, C. W. Malbury, and S. Daykin, "Reduction in Copulatory Behavior of Male Rats following Hashish Injections," *Res. Commun. Chem. Pathol. Pharmacol.* **7**:779–782 (1974).

67   A. Merari, A. Barak, and M. Plaves, "Effects of 1(2)-Tetrahydrocannabinol on the Male Rat," *Psychopharmalogia* **28**:243–246 (1973).

68   R. C. Kolodny, W. H. Masters, R. M. Kolodner, and G. Toro, "Depressed Plasma Testosterone Levels after Chronic Intensive Marijuana Use," *N. Engl. J. Med.* **290**(16):872–874 (1974).

69   J. Harmon and M. A. Aliapoulios, "Gynecomastia in Marihuana Users," *N. Engl. J. Med.* **287**:936 (1972).

70   G. M. Everett, "Amyl Nitrite ("Poppers") as an Aphrodisiac," in M. Sandler and G. L. Gessa (eds.), *Sexual Behavior: Pharmacology and Biochemistry,* Raven, New York, 1975b, pp. 97–98.

71   A. H. Walton, *Aphrodisiacs: From Legend to Prescription,* Associated Booksellers, Westport, Ct., 1958.

72   Leavitt, op. cit., p. 311.

73   F. Sicuteri, E. DelBene, and B. Anselmi, "Aphrodisiac Effects of Testosterone in Parachlorophenylalanine-Treated Sexually Deficient Men," in M. Sandler and G. L. Gessa (eds.), *Sexual Behavior: Pharmacology and Biochemistry,* New York, 1975, pp. 335–340.

74   O. Benkert, G. Crombach, and G. Kockott, "Effect of L-Dopa on Sexually Impotent Patients," *Psychopharmacologia* **23**:91–95 (1972).

75   A. A. Bartholomew, "A Long-Acting Phenothiazine as a Possible Agent to Control Deviant Sexual Behavior," *Am. J. Psychiatry* **124**:917–923 (1968).

76   G. Tennent, J. Bancroft, and J. Cass, "The Control of Deviant Sexual Behavior by Drugs: A Double Blind Controlled Study of Benperidol, Chlorpromazine, and Placebo," *Arch. Sex Behav.* **3**:261–271 (1974).

77   L. H. Field, "Benperidol in the Treatment of Sexual Offenders," *Med. Sci. Law* **13**:195–196 (1973).

78   E. R. Pinta, "Treatment of Obsessive Homosexual Pedophilic Fantasies with Medroxyprogesterone Acetate," *Biol. Psychiatry* **13**:369–373 (1978).

79   J. Bancroft, G. Tennent, K. Loucas, and J. Cass, "The Control of Deviant Sexual Behavior by Drugs," *Br. J. Psychiatry* **125**:310–315 (1974).

80   P. Saba, F. Salvadorini, F. Glaeone, C. Pellicano, and E. Rainer, "Antiandrogen Treatment in Sexually Abnormal Subjects with Neuropsychiatric Disorders," in M. Sandler and G. L. Gessa (eds.), *Sexual Behavior: Pharmacology and Biochemistry,* Raven, New York, 1975.

81   D. P. Baron and H. R. Unger, "A Clinical Trial of Cyproterone Acetate for Sexual Deviancy," *N. Z. Med. J.* **85**:366 (1977).

82   F. Ferracuti and R. Bartilotti, "Technical and Legal Aspects of Pharmacologic

Treatment of Sex Offenders," in M. Sandler and G. L. Gessa (eds.), *Sexual Behavior: Pharmacology and Biochemistry,* Raven, New York, 1975.

83   H. R. Unger, "Cyproterone and Hypersexuality," *N. Z. Med. J.* **86**:39–40 (1977).

84   H. A. Budd, "Brompheniramine in Treatment of Retrograde Ejaculation," *Urology* **6**:131 (1975).

85   V. A. Andalaro and A. Dube, "Treatment of Retrograde Ejaculation with Bromphendramine," *Urology* **5**:520–522 (1975).

86   K. Stockamp, F. Scheiter, and J. E. Altwein, "Alpha-Adrenergic Drugs in Retrograde Ejaculation," *Fertil. Steril.* **25**:817–820 (1974).

87   D. W. Lording, "Impotence: Role of Drug and Hormonal Treatment," *Drugs* **15**:144–150 (1978).

88   J. W. Mudd, "Impotence Responsive to Glyceryl Trinitrate," *Am. J. Psychiatry* **13**:922–925 (1977).

89   B. Ambrosi, R. Bara, and G. Faglia, "Bromocriptine in Impotence," *Lancet* **2**:987 (1977a).

90   B. Ambrosi et al., "Study of the Effects of Bromocriptine on Sexual Impotence," *Clin. Endocrinol.* **7**:417–421 (1977b).

91   D. Renshaw, "Impotence—Some Causes and Cures," *Am. Fam. Physician* **17**:143–146 (1978).

92   J. Teter, "Treatment of Endocrine Impotence," *Br. Med. J.* **4**:114 (1972).

93   H. S. Kupperman, "Impotence," *Am. Fam. Physician* **18**:21, 24, 28 July, 1978.

94   L. V. Sy and V. S. Fang, "Restoration of Plasma Testosterone Level in Uremic Men with Clomiphene Citrate," *J. Clin. Endocrinol. Metab.* **43**(6):1370–1377 (1976).

95   O. Benkert, R. Jordan, H. G. Danlen, H. P. G. Schneider, and G. Gammel, "Sexual Impotence: A Double Blind Study of LHRH Nasal Spray versus Placebo," *Neuropsychobiology* **1**:203–210 (1975).

96   A. J. Cooper, A. A. Ismail, T. Harding, and D. N. Love, "Effects of Clomiphene in Impotence. A Clinical and Endocrine Study," *Br. J. Psychiatry* **120**:62–69 (1972).

97   T. F. Davies, et al., "A Double Blind Cross Over Trial of Gonadotropin Releasing Factor in Sexually Impotent Men," *Clin. Endocrinol.* **5**:601–607 (1976).

98   W. W. Miller, "Afrodex in the Treatment of Male Impotence: A Double-Blind Cross-Over Study," *Curr. Ther. Res.* **10**:354–359 (1968).

99   J. J. Sobotka, "An Evaluation of Afrodex in the Management of Male Impotency: A Double-Blind Cross-Over Study," *Curr. Ther. Res.* **11**:87–94 (1969).

100 R. Margolis, P. Prietro, L. Stein, and S. Chin, "Statistical Summary of 10,000 Male Cases Using Afrodex in Treatment of Impotence," *Curr. Ther. Res.* **13**:616–622 (1971).

101 T. Jokobovits, "The Treatment of Impotence with Methyltestosterone Thyroid (100 Patients—Double Blind Study)," *Fertil. Steril.* **21**:32–35 (1970).

102 S. L. Fellman, D. W. Hastings, H. S. Kupperman, and W. W. Miller, "Should Androgens be Used to Treat Impotence in Men Over 50?" *Med. Aspects of Hum. Sexual.* **9**:32–43 (1975).

103 S. Maneksha and T. V. Harry, "Lorazepam in Sexual Disorders," *Br. J. Clin. Pract.* **29**:175–176 (1975).

Chapter 14

Sexually Transmitted Disease

Diseases and conditions which are spread by sexual contact have become nearly endemic in the American population. The goals of this chapter are to increase the nurse's knowledge of the effects of these diseases on sexual health and to provide guidelines for nursing intervention with infected clients. Education of the client is emphasized as well as prevention of disease.

The term *venereal disease* is not used in this chapter. Instead, all infections and conditions which are transmitted primarily by sexual intercourse are included. (Elsewhere, syphilis and gonorrhea are called major venereal diseases; lymphogranuloma venereum, granuloma inguinale, and chancroid are called minor venereal diseases.) The chapter concentrates on the psychosexual implications of diseases which usually require sexual contact for transfer from one person to another. These diseases include, in addition to major and minor venereal diseases, monilia, trichomonas, cancer of the cervix, genital herpes, *Hemophilus vaginalis*, genital or venereal warts (condyloma acuminatum), pubic lice, and scabies.

Some STDs (sexually transmitted diseases) can be transmitted through close physical contact other than sexual intercourse. Generally, however, sexual contact is the mode of transmission. Herein lies the basic problem of STD diagnosis, treatment, and follow-up: the infected person is confronted with verifiable evidence that he or she has had close physical contact with another infected individual. Sexually transmitted diseases are present in epidemic proportion not because they are difficult to diagnose or treat, but because of the social, moral, and sexual implications of these diseases.

Social influences have convinced many people that those who have a sexually transmitted disease are unclean or promiscuous or both. Cleanliness and numbers of sexual partners do influence the likelihood of contracting an STD, but many perfectly clean people with only one sexual partner still have these diseases. The myths about catching gonorrhea from doorknobs or toilet seats reflect attempts to deny the sexual nature of the infection.

PERSONAL RELATIONSHIPS

Relationships between people are altered by the introduction of an STD. Nurses may provide needed counseling to individuals, partners, couples, and families in regard to an STD as it affects their relationships.

Clients may pose difficult questions. "How can I ever tell my wife I have syphilis?" "If I got gonorrhea from my husband, I'll divorce him." "How can I have trich? I never sleep with anyone but Fred and I know he isn't having sex with anybody else." "Couldn't you just treat me and not say anything to my husband?" "Couldn't you treat my girlfriend without telling her what the medicine is for?"

Conflict between honesty and sympathy results. The client must know the correct diagnosis and must receive the safest and most effective treatment. Giving information about the disease is an essential nursing intervention, and is the basis for counseling a client about STD. Common myths and fallacies about STD may be worrisome to the client unless the nurse is able to dispel these with accurate, nonjudgmental facts (see Table 14-1).

Finding out that a sexual partner has an STD can be devastating to a sexual relationship or it can be simply a condition requiring treatment. If the partnership is based on mutual trust and fidelity, then the basis of the relationship may be jeopardized. If the relationship assumes open sexual contacts with others, the STD might not threaten the partners. In taking the sexual history, the nurse can determine the nature of the client's sexual relationships, and can adjust information, permission, and specific suggestions to fit each unique situation.

Strategies which can help clients deal with their own feelings and with the reactions of their partners include:

1   Role playing or cognitive rehearsal. The nurse plays the client and the client plays the partner. This arrangement allows the nurse to make nondirective suggestions and to be a role model for the client. The client might be told to fantasize the worst reaction the partner might possibly have as well as the reaction he or she wishes the partner might have.

2   The client might be helped to write a note or letter to the partner. This tactic allows the partner to react alone, then (when the initial shock is past) to react with the client.

3   The nurse and client could tell the partner together. The nurse then is

Table 14-1   Myths and Facts about Sexually Transmitted Disease

Myth	Fact
Yeast infections only affect females.	Both men and women can have yeast. The disease can be transmitted from one partner to the other, "ping-pong" fashion.
You can get GC by taking a bath after someone who has it.	*Neisseria* die very quickly when separated from human host conditions.
Men do not get trichomonas.	Men can transmit trichomonas and should be treated when partners are treated.
Syphilis cannot be treated after the chancre goes away.	Syphilis is always sensitive to penicillin. However, damage done by tertiary syphilis cannot be reversed by treatment.
There is nothing you can do to cure genital warts.	Podophyllin treatments are effective for genital warts. However, warts may reoccur after treatment.
Taking a bath after sex can prevent GC.	The bacteria invade cervical, urethral, rectal, and other mucous membranes. They are not easily reached by soap and water, although bathing may be helpful.
You are very likely to catch an STD from a prostitute.	Prostitutes usually are careful to avoid STDs, have frequent checkups, and receive treatment promptly.
Only homosexuals get rectal GC.	Anyone having anal intercourse could get rectal GC.
You can get STD from animal contacts.	No. STDs are human diseases only.
Virgins cannot get an STD.	Manual contact or oral contact can spread an STD. Yeast and trichomonas sometimes can be transmitted through nonsexual contact.
You get gonorrhea from a dirty person.	Gonorrhea can be present regardless of personal cleanliness.
Men always know it when they have gonorrhea because they have a drip from the penis and have painful urination.	Ten to forty percent of males can have active GC and have no symptoms at all.

immediately available to answer questions, circumvent erroneous ideas, and interpret the disease in terms of overall health.

4 Some clients may choose to have public health agencies contact their partners for treatment. This arrangement can be facilitated by a referral to a public health nurse.

DISCOMFORT AND TREATMENT

Many sexually transmitted diseases cause physical discomfort which in turn affects sexual pleasure. Monilial, bacterial, and trichomonas vaginitis can cause painful vaginal and labial irritation, swelling, and itching. Gonococcal urethritis in some men is extremely painful. Genital herpes in men and women can make simple walking or sitting impossible, let alone sexual intercourse. Often the pain is what causes the client to seek health care and is, therefore, beneficial. If sexual intercourse is painful, and if this is a new or different pain (some women assume intercourse is always painful), relief will be sought.

Treatment usually brings pain relief within a few days. Intramuscular (IM) penicillin (for gonorrhea) works even more quickly, causing cure in 24 hours in most situations. Other conditions, especially herpes simplex virus, type 2, and genital warts, take much longer to heal, perhaps several weeks.

Treatment of STD varies from penicillin injections to vaginal suppositories and from shampoo to sitz baths (see Table 14-2). Most STD control depends on treatment of the individual and all sexual contacts. As a result of shame or embarrassment, some people are reluctant to name their contacts, or name only one, or insist that there was no contact.

Questions about contacts must be sensitive, gentle, and nonjudgmental. The client must be told why the contact information is necessary and what will be done with the information. Confidentiality is assured. The section at the end of this chapter shows how the sexual history can be combined with an interview for contact of a person infected with gonorrhea or syphilis. A similar form of questioning could be adapted for other clients with STD.

Abstinence from intercourse for the duration of treatment is a common requirement. For some this is easy: it hurts to have intercourse and the vaginal medication may be messy. For others, particularly those who are asymptomatic, abstinence is difficult. In such cases intercourse protected by condom use might be more advisable. For GC and syphilis, abstinence is recommended until there is proof of cure (negative culture or nonreactive VDRL). For monilia and trichomonas, intercourse may be resumed (using a condom) when the woman finds it comfortable. People infected with herpes simplex virus, type 2, or genital warts may resume intercourse after treatment if there is no pain.

People frequently misinterpret health education or selectively hear only parts of what is told. As a result, some clients will not use all the medication, will fail to secure treatment for contacts, will resume intercourse without treatment, and will otherwise become reinfected. Nurses and others find this apparent disregard for health frustrating and even anger provoking. However, the situation may be caused more by social and relationship pressures than by ignorance or deliberate noncompliance. It is a rare person who can say, "I'd like to take you out tonight but we can't have sex because I'm getting treated for gonorrhea."

Occasionally there is a person who resists treatment altogether. Sometimes this is someone named as a contact of a positive case and who is totally asymptomatic. Many clinics treat gonorrhea and syphilis contacts even before the presence of the disease is verified, simply because the chances of having the disease are high with any exposure. In the case of a person unwilling to receive treatment, verification of existing disease usually convinces the client of the need for treatment. The question remains, does the fully informed, rational client have the right to refuse treatment for a communicable disease that is sexually transmitted?

Table 14-2 Summary of Sexually Transmitted Diseases

Condition	Site of infection	Etiology	Diagnosis	Incubation	Symptoms	Complications	Treatment
Gonorrhea (GC, clap, drip, dose). Resistant strains (penicillinase-producing Neisseria	Urethra, cervix, eyes, rectal area, throat	Neisseria gonorrhoeae	Gram-positive diplococci (smear is good for males only) Positive culture (for both males and females); males, urethral; females, cervical os	Approx. 1 week	Female: 40–80% are asymptomatic; may have greenish vaginal discharge Male: Discharge, dysuria (10% of males may be asymptomatic)	Ascending infection may lead to pelvic inflammatory disease in females with possible sterility Males may also be sterile as a result of ascending infection; systemic involvement includes joints, septicemia	1 g probenicid orally 4.8 million units procaine penicillin IM or 3.5 g ampicillin orally stat For allergic patients, use 2 g spectinomycin IM, (Trobicin) or 9.5 g tetracycline (total, over 4 days) Repeat cultures twice after treatment (at weekly intervals)
Syphilis (syph, bad blood)	Site of entry; later becomes systemic	Treponema pallidum	VDRL and FTA (blood screening tests); darkfield smear to look for spirochetes	9–90 days	Primary: Lesion is rounded, clean, indurated; usually is painless; may be anyplace on skin; heals in 4–12 weeks Secondary: Rash, especially on palms and soles, may itch; looks like many other conditions; rash is contagious Tertiary: Systemic, involves heart, nervous system	Brain, cardiac involvement Congenital syphilis in babies	Always sensitive to penicillin or tetracycline—never too late to treat 2.4 million units benzathine penicillin IM

Table 14-2 Summary of Sexually Transmitted Diseases (continued)

Condition	Site of infection	Etiology	Diagnosis	Incubation	Symptoms	Complications	Treatment
Candida (yeast infection, monilia)	Vagina, urethra	*Candida albicans*	Gram-stained smear; culture	Unknown	Vaginal discharge, vulval irritation; discharge is thick, white, cheesy; frequently itches May also be asymptomatic Males may notice itching, soreness of penis (treated with local application of nystatin cream)	Underlying conditions may include diabetes, pregnancy; oral contraceptives may increase incidence	Nystatin (Mycostatin, Monistat) per vaginal cream or suppository (through next menstrual period, if possible) Triple sulfa AVC Vinegar douche (1–2 tbsp white vinegar in 1 qt warm water)
Nonspecific vaginitis	Vagina	Probably *Hemophilus vaginalis* or *Mycoplasma*	"Clue cells" (vaginal epithelial cells covered by small gram-negative rods)		Vaginal discharge vulval irritation		Metronidazole (Flagyl) recently shown to be more effective than sulfa cream or oral ampicillin[1]
Trichomoniasis	Vagina, urethra	*Trichomonas vaginalis* (a parasite)	Identification of flagellated organism on wet prep. slide	4–28 days	Vaginal discharge; may be greenish-yellow, frothy, itchy; dysuria, dyspareunia Males may be asymptomatic carriers	Urethritis, cystitis	Metronidazole (Flagyl) 2 g orally over 1–5-day period; all partners should be treated; warn clients of Antabuse effect of Flagyl
Condylomata acuminatum (genital warts)	Labia, vagina, cervix, urethra, rectum, penis	Virus	By appearance (firm, polyplike growth)	Unknown	Painful; look like small mushrooms or cauliflower	Easily spread by autoinoculation; transmitted to sexual partners Spread extensively during pregnancy	Soap and water Topical application of 10 or 15% solution of podophyllin in alcohol

Disease	Site	Organism	Diagnosis	Incubation	Symptoms	Complications	Treatment
Herpes genitalis	Labia, vagina, cervix, penis, scrotum	Herpes simplex virus, type 2	By observation of lesion and by history	Unknown	Itching, discomfort; lesion may be a lump or a blister; lesion at first blistered, then is eroded leaving multiple superficial erosions	Acute pain; Danger to newborn if mother has genital herpes	Sitz bath or warm moist soaks; Pain medication
Pediculosis pubis (crabs)	Pubic hair	Phthinius pubis (crab louse)	By observation of lice and/or nits		Intense itching in pubic region	Excoriation from itching	Kwell shampoo or A-200 lotion in two applications
Scabies	Skin	Sarcoptes scabiei (mite)	By observation		Lesions are usually papular; burrows are grayish or black irregular lines on the skin; itching is usually worse at night or when patient is warm	Excoriation	Kwell shampoo or A-200 lotion after bath; repeat in 1 week
Cervical cancer	Cervix	Unknown	Pap smear; colposcopy; cervical biopsy	Unknown	May be none or perhaps vaginal discharge or dyspareunia or intramenstrual bleeding	Spread to other genital organs	Cervical conization

Source: Adapted from a table developed by M. Swenson for "Sexuality, Education, and the Family," in D. Hymovich and M. Barnard (eds.) *Family Health Care,* Vol. 1, McGraw-Hill, New York, 1979, Table 23-1, pp. 344–346.

CONTRACEPTIVES AND STD

Contraceptive use is a factor in the care of clients with STD. For many years the spread of GC and syphilis was controlled largely by the use of condoms. As recently as 15 years ago, the condom was the most popular birth control method in the United States. With the rise in usage of the oral contraceptive and the IUD came a rise in the incidence of gonorrhea and other STD. The condom is the only contraceptive device known to prevent the spread of STD effectively.

Reluctance to use condoms may be blamed at least partially on the attitudes which prevail among adolescents and young adults. Sex educators have fostered these negative feelings by presenting condoms as "necessary," "responsible," "prophylactic devices." Rarely are condoms presented as erotic or stimulating articles. Rarely do sex educators talk about condoms as part of sexual foreplay. Men who have never tried a condom may refuse to experiment with one because friends have said, "Rubbers aren't masculine" or "Rubbers are like swimming in your raincoat."

Women as well as men must be taught about the use of condoms. Women can buy and carry condoms for their own protection. Condoms are attractive to women for several reasons not commonly thought about: newer condoms are ribbed and textured to provide stimulation to the vagina and clitoris, condoms may decrease "messiness" in the minds of some women by preventing the deposit of semen in the vagina, and condoms can be erotic when the woman puts them on the penis herself.

Another barrier method of contraception, the diaphragm, also provides some protection from STD. Protection is not only the mechanical effect of the diaphragm itself, but also is provided by the contraceptive cream. Spermicidal preparations such as jelly, cream, and foam exert an antibacterial effect in the vagina, and thus may protect the user from some vaginal infections.

The Food and Drug Administration requires that packages of contraceptive pills contain the statement that the pills do not protect men or women from any venereal diseases.

In fact recent evidence indicates that the oral contraceptive pill may cause an increase in susceptibility to STD, especially gonorrhea. Possibly the vaginal pH is altered, allowing for easier growth of the bacteria. Possibly women who are taking the birth control pill may tend to have an increased number of different partners, thus increasing their risk of exposure .Research in this area is greatly needed so that risks of the birth control pill can be accurately assessed by health care professionals and by users of the pill.

The greatest threat to IUD users is any infection which can easily spread via the device to the uterine corpus, tubes, ovaries, and pelvic cavity. Gonorrhea frequently is implicated in pelvic inflammatory disease, although other pathogens can also be involved. The woman with an IUD needs to be especially aware of any vaginal infection so that she can seek treatment before the cervix and subsequently other reproductive organs are infected. In laboratory settings it has been shown that copper inhibits the growth of the gonococcus, although copper

IUDs seem not to have an effect on reducing gonorrhea in users.[2] Women with IUDs are three to five times more likely than nonusers to develop pelvic inflammatory disease (with risk of sterility).[3]

STD IN CHILDREN

Congenital syphilis and neonatal gonococcal infections in children have been pediatric concerns for years. It is possible for a fetus, a newborn, a child, or a young adolescent to develop diseases which are usually sexually transmitted. The method of transmission for children may be congenital, by vaginal delivery, by genital contact, and by nongenital means.

Congenital syphilis can be prevented by prompt treatment of the pregnant mother. If the baby develops signs of infection, various regimens of treatment with penicillin can be used. Similarly, mothers with gonorrhea can be treated to prevent transmission to the infant via the birth canal. Herpes infection in the mother probably dictates nonvaginal delivery to avoid infection of the neonate. Most cases of herpes simplex virus, type 2, in newborns are fatal.

Gonorrhea in children is becoming more common, perhaps because pediatricians are more alert to the possibility of this disease. Children should be cultured and diagnosed just as adults are and treated with reduced doses of penicillin or erythromycin. According to Folland, "the occurrence of gonorrhea in a prepubertal child identifies a group of persons who are at high risk of having gonorrhea, including the mother, father, siblings, and close personal contacts. These people should be cultured, for 20 to 50 percent will have gonorrhea."[4] The possibility of sexual abuse must always be considered in these cases, although an accurate history may be very difficult to obtain.

For adolescents, venereal diseases in all states may be diagnosed and treated without parental consent.

CONTACT INTERVIEW FOR STD

When the presence of an STD has been verified by culture or by microscopic examination, the treatment and follow-up must be done with sensitivity and seriousness. The infected person may be embarrassed, angry, and confused. The nurse in the office or the public health nurse is responsible for the identification of contacts, so that they also can be treated. The following guidelines may be helpful to the nurse conducting the contact interview.

1   Begin with an introduction of yourself, including your job title. Sometimes using only your first name puts the client at greater ease. ("My name is Marilyn, and I'm a nurse in the clinic. May I call you Diane?")

2   Explain the reason for the contact interview, including a "universality statement." ("Diane, you have a disease called gonorrhea that is usually transmitted through close physical or sexual contact. Many people have heard information about sexually transmitted diseases and sometimes there are ques-

tions about these diseases. Have you any questions now? Many people, especially women, are not at all aware that they had the disease. Did you know you had gonorrhea?'') Client may then say she was informed by a contact, or that she had symptoms. If she is totally surprised, this is a good time to help her discuss possible feelings of anger, jealousy, worry, or disbelief.

3 It there are symptoms, ask how long symptoms have been present. Did she take any action to relieve the symptoms? This group of questions will help to indicate the duration of the infection and may also give you a clue to the client's ability to use the health care system.

4 ''Gonorrhea is a serious disease that is easily cured. However, I need to know who you might have gotten the disease from through close sexual contact and who you might have given it to. These people will need treatment also.''

Other important points are:
a Contacts may be asymptomatic
b Consequences of untreated gonorrhea, including possible systemic infection, sterility, and joint involvement
c Ease and rapidity of spread

5 Assure confidentiality. People named as contacts will not know who named them. If the client prefers, she may inform her contacts herself.

6 Ask if the client is married.

7 What is the client's occupation?

8 What form of contraception does the client use, if any?

9 Never assume the client is either exclusively homosexual or exclusively heterosexual. Start with the most recent contact and go backward. For women with gonorrhea, go back 2 months. For men with gonorrhea, go back 2 weeks at least. (''Diane, who was the person you last had sexual relations or close sexual contact with?'' ''And who just before that?'' ''And before that?'') Remember, any sexual contact counts, including oral, rectal, and manual.

10 Try to get names and addresses of contacts. If this is not possible (the client does not know who the contacts are), then try to get a description, place of employment, place of contact (bar, motel, pick up, mutual friends, etc.). Any information that will assist an investigator to find the contact is helpful.

11 Recognize that STD can affect interpersonal relationships with partners. Here is the place for nursing intervention to help the client deal with contacts.

12 Explain the treatment and double check for possible drug allergies.

13 Explain the need to avoid sexual contact until cure is documented by reculture. If sexual intercourse cannot be deferred, the client must be protected by a condom.

14 Ask again for questions. This is a good time for other primary health care teaching regarding the Pap smear, self-breast examination, pregnancy and contraception, and sexual health.

Vignette

Problem List

1 Contraceptive needs
2 Sexuality education
3 Possible STD (gonorrhea)

Subjective Data

"I went to a party about a week ago and had oral sex with a couple of guys there. Now one of them calls me up and says he has the clap. Maybe I have it in my mouth? I'm really worried because I've kissed guys and people in my family and my baby sister and everything."

Objective Data

Vaginal examination reveals normal cervix. Throat shows no inflammation. Has not had soreness or swelling of nodes.

Assessment

Possibly exposed to GC via oral contact. Unlikely that simple kissing could spread disease to family members.

Intervention

Cervical culture, rectal culture, pharyngeal culture. Told we will call her with results.

Plan

1. Treat if any cultures are positive
2. Interview for names of contacts if necessary
3. Education about GC, especially about transmission
4. Take sexual history
5. Give opportunities to ask questions about sexuality

PREVENTION

Most public health programs strive to educate men and women about the symptoms, diagnosis, and treatment of STD. The primary health care approach, however, aims at the *prevention* of disease. Many cases of STD could be prevented if the public were educated with this goal in mind. Unfortunately, public health measures are restricted to screening, education, and follow-up. Actual prevention is an individual matter and an individual (or couple) responsibility.

Edward Brecher has suggested the following ways to prevent STD.[5] Although he focuses mainly on the prevention of gonorrhea and syphilis, the same methods also could help reduce the transmission of monilia, trichomonas, and possibly genital herpes.

Use of the Condom

This method alone could prevent the epidemic spread of gonorrhea (and herpes simplex virus, type 2). For young people it is an ideal method for contraception, since condoms are inexpensive, available without a prescription, available to men and women, and are effective birth control devices. Unfortunately, the condom has lost popularity as a contraceptive method and as a prophylactic measure for diseases which are sexually transmitted. The contraceptive pills and IUD have caused men to shun the "hassle" of the condom. Also, since gonorrhea and syphilis are easily cured with penicillin in most cases, there is less motivation to prevent infection.

The condom must be used throughout the sexual intercourse encounter to be effective in preventing infection. Perhaps the newer colored, ribbed, and decorated condoms might be more attractive to both men and women since they not only help prevent pregnancy and disease but also are sexually stimulating and fun.

Precoital Inspection of the Partner

Men and women can be encouraged to "sneak a peek" at the end of the penis to check for possible urethral discharge. Lesions, which could be a chancre, herpes, crab lice, excoriation, or monilial irritation might be observed and contact then avoided.

Soap and Water

Before intercourse, a shower together can be a sexually stimulating activity. External cleansing might also be a deterrent to the transmission of STD, particularly yeast and trichomonas. Douching probably does not reduce the possibility of infection by gonorrhea, syphilis, or genital herpes. It is even possible that douching after intercourse could increase the severity of a gonococcal infection.

Vaginal Contraceptives

Cream, jelly, foam, and the diaphragm provide both spermicidal and bactericidal benefits. Hence, the use of these preparations may reduce the incidence of some genital infections.

Postcoital Urination

This flushes the urethra in males and females. Since the urethra is a frequent site of infection in women and is almost always the site in men, cleansing it with urine after intercourse is a mechanical means of reducing infection. Urine usually is a clean, even sterile, liquid and effectively rinses out foreign bacteria. However, gonorrhea seems to survive well in urine, so probably this tactic would not reduce this infection.

OTHER POSSIBLE METHODS OF PREVENTION

1   Topical medications, such as sulfa preparations, which can be placed in the male urethra following exposure to gonorrhea. No product of this type is currently available for the prevention of gonorrhea.

2   Systemic preparations, such as small doses of mercury, will decrease the incidence of syphilis. However, the risk probably outweighs the potential benefits.

3   Prophylactic pills or injections: antibiotics probably are effective whether taken before or after intercourse with a partner who has gonorrhea or syphilis. To prevent the development of resistant strains, a therapeutic dose would have to be used (penicillin or tetracycline). The possibility of side effects or allergic reactions needs to be considered as a risk to prophylactic use of antibiotics.

4   Local antibiotic prophylaxis, including a foaming antibiotic tablet which is inserted into the vagina following exposure to gonorrhea, has been tested in other countries, but is not available in the United States.

5 Vaccination is a possibility for diseases such as syphilis, gonorrhea, and herpes. Research, however, is a long way from producing any generally available vaccines.

LEARNING ACTIVITIES

1 Role play a gonorrhea contact interview. The "patient" could be homosexual, heterosexual, a prostitute, married or single, or an adolescent. Practice phrasing questions with sensitivity to the feelings of the infected person and try problem-solving how best to notify contacts.

2 Find out about the incidence of STD in your community by checking with local health departments and venereal disease investigators. Is screening done routinely in clinics and doctors' offices? Are free clinics available?

3 Suggested research papers:
    a Gonorrhea and the birth control pill
    b Effect of STD on the marriage relationship
    c Situations which require abstinence from intercourse
    d Congenital syphilis or congenital herpes simplex virus, type 2

REFERENCES

1 T. A. Pheifer, P. S. Forsyth, M. A. Durfee, H. M. Pollack, and K. K. Holmes, "Nonspecific Vaginitis: Role of *Hemophilus vaginalis* and Treatment with Metronidazole," *N. Engl. J. Med.* **298**(26):1429–1433 (1978).

2 Elizabeth Barrett-Connor, "Personal Prophylaxis for Venereal Disease," *Med. Aspects Hum. Sexual.* **12**(5):150–159 (1978).

3 H. W. Ory, "A Review of the Association Between Intrauterine Contraceptive Devices and Acute Pelvic Inflammatory Disease," *J. Reprod. Med.* **20**(4):200–204 (1978).

4 D. S. Folland, "Treatment and Epidemiologic Procedures for Children with VD," *Med. Aspects Hum. Sexual.* **12**(5):51–52 (1978).

5 Edward M. Brecher, "Prevention of the Sexually Transmitted Diseases," *J. Sex Res.* **11**:318–328 (1975).

BIBLIOGRAPHY

Boston Women's Health Book Collective: "Venereal Disease," in *Our Bodies, Ourselves,* Simon and Schuster, New York, 1976.

Catterall, R. D.: *A Short Textbook of Venereology,* Lippincott, Philadelphia, 1974.

Delora, J. S., and C. A. B. Warren: "Venereal Disease," in *Understanding Sexual Interaction,* Houghton Mifflin, Boston, 1977.

Goldstein, B.: "Common Infections of the Genital Tract," in *Human Sexuality,* McGraw-Hill, New York, 1976.

Horos, C. V.: *Vaginal Health,* Tobey, New Canaan, Conn., 1975.

Chapter 15

Postcoronary

Several studies have documented a rather drastic decrease of sexual activity postmyocardial infarction.[1,2] Tuttle et al.[1] report that 10 percent of the postcoronary population studied were impotent, two-thirds had a marked and lasting reduction in frequency of intercourse, with only one-third returning to their prior level of activity.[3] One-hundred subjects were questioned (88 male and 12 female) on their sexual practices before and after an infarction. The study showed that the monthly mean frequency of sexual intercourse before the infarct was 5.2 compared with 2.7 after the infarct, while other activities for this population did not change appreciably. The reasons most often cited by these subjects for decreased sexual activity were anxiety, depression, lack of desire, fear of another attack or of sudden death, fatigue, pain, and decision of spouse.[4]

It appears that many of the alterations in sexual behavior are due to psychological reasons and inadequate information. Fears revolve around the belief that a repeat of a coronary will occur during coitus. Fear of death during coitus is frequently associated with sexual difficulty.[5-7] According to Puksta, using information from a study by Ueno of Japan:

A common but often unspoken fear of patients and their partners is the possibility of sudden death during intercourse. This is not a common occurrence and should be discussed. One pathologist reported that out of 5559 cases of endogenous sudden death only 0.6 percent (34 deaths) were due to sexual activity. Eighty percent of the 34 deaths, however, occurred during or after extramarital relations.[8]

Lack of accurate information and cultural biases reinforces fears and taboos and makes sexuality a needless stress factor for patients and partners. Controlling all types of physical exercise is one of the greatest concerns of cardiac patients and partners.

Friedman explains the measurement of oxygen consumption and quotes some of the findings of previous studies regarding exercise:

> The energy expenditure of a person at rest requires an oxygen consumption of approximately 3.5 ml. per kg. body weight per minute. This activity level is equal to one metabolic equivalent or 1 MET. Exercise above this level can then be described in multiples of METs. According to Douglas and Wilkes, the mean energy cost in METs of some common activities are: sleeping, 0.8; walking uphill at a 5% grade at three miles per hour, 4.0; sexual foreplay, 3.5; raking leaves, 4.0 to 5.0; and orgasm, 4.7 to 5.5. Heart rate has been found to correlate well with the number of METs and is also a very practical measure of oxygen consumption, and thus physical work (Green, 1975). The average man who has recovered from an uncomplicated myocardial infarction has a maximum capacity of 8–9 METs (Eliot and Miles, 1973). Thus, sexual activity is well below this upper limit.[9]

A study conducted at Downstate Medical Center, New York, in the exercise rehabilitation program of postcoronary patients indicates that oxygen requirements of coitus can be reduced with exercise training.[10] Hellerstein and Friedman[11] concluded from their study that participation in an active physical conditioning program produced significant improvement in physical fitness, blood pressure, mood, frequency, and quality of sex activity.[12]

Many medical centers assess exercise tolerance before patients leave the hospital, requiring them to walk 2500 ft and climb two flights of stairs without abnormal changes in pulse, blood pressure, and ECG (electrocardiogram).[13] For most people sexual activity would be tolerated with no appreciable change when the above activities have been mastered.

In the past, health professionals have been successful in completely ignoring sexual needs in postcoronary patients. According to Friedman:

> Physicians have usually been exposed to the same cultural norms as their patients. Sex, an uncomfortable topic, is often ignored by both physician and patient alike. However, it remains the responsibility of the physician to take the initiative and begin sexual counseling when needed. This requires time, openness, empathy, sexual knowledge, and an acceptance of the importance of sex. Those physicians with limited sexual knowledge and/or limited time can make certain that their patients receive adequate counseling from other health professionals such as nurses, social workers, or psychologists.[14]

According to Scheingold and Wagner:

Table 15-1   Cardiovascular Disruptions

Disorder	Possible effect on sexual functioning	Presumed mechanism	Accompanying common problems
Myocardial infarction	May decrease libido Impair erection Withdrawal from sexual activities (Difficulties not necessarily related to age, severity of infarct, and capacity for non-sexual activities)	Exercises increase oxygen demands and cardiac work. The excitement stage of coitus increases heart rate to as high as 170 beats per minute (average of 148.5 beats per minute). Blood pressure rises to as high as 220/110 with an average of 170/100. Respiratory rate may increase from 16 to 60 Adrenergic stimulation leads to increased heart rate, cardiac contractility, and systemic resistance Adaptation to exercise alters renal salt and water excretion, contributing to increased blood pressure and may increase serum cholesterols Alkalosis from hyperventilation may aggravate ischemia by decreasing amount and rate of oxygen release from hemoglobin	Normal slowing down process of aging and general debility Angina Depression Fear of recurrent infarct Fear of death Loss of self-esteem Reversal of sex role Change in life-style patterns and self-image Marital conflict Partner's fear of recurrent heart attack
Hypertensive vascular disease	Alterations in libido Erection difficulties Ejaculatory difficulties	Increased heart rate. Blood pressure may rise as high as 260/150 during coitus MmHg vascular reactivity to norepinephrine increases in response to the intense sexual excitement and exercise. With persisting hypertension, ventricular work increases, eventually producing left-ventricular function and reducing cardiac output. Sustained exertion and rapid heart rate eventually produce acute pulmonary edema because of decreased cardiac output and rapidly rising backward pressure	Cerebrovascular accident Diabetes Atherosclerosis Emotional difficulties

Source: Refs. 16 to 19. See Chap. 13 regarding effects of antihypertensive, diuretic drugs.

One of the most significant changes that has occurred in the treatment of heart patients has been the growing involvement of nurses in every aspect of the care of patients.[15]

Perhaps the nurse has the potential of being as therapeutic in sexual concerns as in any other aspect of health care. Seldom is the nurse considered as omnipotent as the physician by the cardiac patient, which can definitely be a plus in sexual counseling where there are very few definitive answers. However, nurses will need to earn the right to counsel the cardiac patient and partner by being aware of common problems that can accompany cardiovascular disruptions (Table 15-1) and by developing positive accepting sexual attitudes, assessment techniques, and intervention skills.

ASSESSMENT

A consultation with the physician regarding sexual activity for a particular patient is advisable. A brief history of premorbid sexual activities and preference should reveal

1 Usual type of sexual activity;
2 Preferred type of sexual activity;
3 Usual time of sexual activity;
4 Preferred time of sexual activity;
5 Amount of variety in sexual activity;
6 Previous episodes of impotence, decreased libido, and ejaculatory disorders;
7 Any chest pain, fatigue, or sleeplessness following sexual activity; and
8 Alcohol and food consumption in relation to sexual patterns.

The physical examination will reveal exercise tolerance (pulse, blood pressure, and ECG before and after exercise) and the psychological assessment will determine the existing sexual attitudes, knowledge, values, and goals of the patient and partner.

The assessment process will supply the guidelines for the need and type of permission appropriate for both patient and partner. A nurse can begin giving permission by taking a sexual history and determining the fears, concerns, anxiety, expectations, and goals of the patient and partner. An effective method to give permission to talk about sexuality is to begin with the statement, "Many people who have had cardiac symptoms have received confusing reports on the safety of sexual practices. What are some of the things you have heard?" "How do you feel about discussing sexual matters?"

PERMISSION

In the recent past, health professionals have given themselves permission to ignore sexuality, through both verbal and nonverbal communication, by claiming that sexuality is a private matter. Some clients may also use this alibi rather than risk being uncomfortable or stressed in the initial phase of sexual counseling. Consequently, permission giving may be needed and given in a slow but deliberate manner.

It is rare but occasionally patients will give themselves permission to completely ignore the illness and to go beyond their capabilities. On the other hand, there are couples who are looking for an excuse to terminate sexual intercourse and will welcome this opportunity to express their sexuality in less active ways. Permission for this group of patients should not be given without a thorough study and explanation of the underlying dynamics of needs and desires of both people involved in the relationship.

INFORMATION FOR CLIENTS

Exercise rehabilitation is often undertaken within 48 hours of a heart attack if patient is pain free and the resting pulse is between 50 and 90. The patient should be cognizant that exercise helps the heart in the following ways.

1 The heart works more efficiently.
2 The lungs are able to take in more air needed for exercise.
3 The heart muscle becomes stronger.
4 Heart rate slows—a slower heart rate means that the heart does not have to work as hard to do its job. The lower the heart rate is at rest, the lower will be the rise during activity.
5 Blood vessels become more flexible and blood pressure will not rise as high.[20]

Other information needed by postcoronary patients may be given in printed form, then followed by a discussion. This information usually includes precautions on when to avoid sexual relations and warning signs of heart strain. This form may be used in the initial phase of counseling to establish rapport. Below is an example of some of the information that can be included in printed form (developed by L. Besch):

Sexual activities.

The pattern of sexual relations you had prior to your heart attack is usually possible after recovery. It is believed by some that the same amount of energy is required for sexual intercourse as is for taking a short, brisk walk, climbing a flight of stairs, or performing simple jobs at work.

There are certain guidelines which can be followed when sexual activity is resumed:

1 Hazards lie in extremes of temperature, especially if it is hot and humid.
2 It is best to wait approximately 2 to 3 hours after eating a meal or after ingesting alcohol.
3 If you are already fatigued, it is not a good time for sexual activity. It is better to wait until you are well rested like after a nap or in the morning or on the weekend. You should rest afterward also.
4 An atmosphere of gentle relaxation is optimal. Tension and fear place added demands on your heart.
5 The position you use should be one which creates the least energy demand for the cardiac partner.
6 It is important to be comfortable about having sex. Most research indicates the relationship of the partner to the patient is an important variable.

If any one of the following symptoms occur in association with sexual activity you should consult your physician:

1 Chest pain occurring during or after sexual activity
2 Heart palpitations that continue a quarter of an hour or more after the activity has stopped

   3 Breathlessness that continues a quarter of an hour or more afterward
   4 Sleeplessness that has apparently been caused by the exertion of sex
   5 Marked fatigue the day following sexual activity[21]

Some patients and partners could benefit from and will appreciate information about the bodily reactions of the different stages of sexual responses: excitement, plateau, orgasm, and resolution in the female and male. Since most postcoronary patients are 50 years old or over, the effects of age on sex should be stressed. Some clients may remember sex as it was 15 years ago or as they wish it were. Information on the effects of age on sexuality keeps hopes and expectations somewhat in the realm of possibilities or in a realistic framework.

Clinicians disagree as to whether a patient should be told that a particular medication has the potential to affect sexual responses. The clinicians who prefer not to inform the patient of possible change claim that this psychological priming is responsible for sexual failure. They prefer to risk the chances that the patient will report the failure—if it occurs. These same clinicians may choose to give general information (''Some drugs can alter sex responses and if this occurs to you, take note of symptoms and call me or be sure to let me know about them at our next session''). The approaches to client and partner should respond to the psychosocial and physiological composite of current needs. Patients who occasionally suffer mild angina pectoris during intercourse may take nitroglycerin 10 minutes before sexual activity begins. In order for the nurse to feel assured about the accurateness of the information that is given, it is essential to keep abreast of current developments.

Suggestions

Suggestions should always be given in relation to needs and desires of the client and partner. Recommending specific positions for intercourse is somewhat controversial. Some clinicians believe that the cardiac patient should avoid the dominant ''on-top'' position due to the isometric exercises of supporting the weight of the body on the arms. Other specialists do not agree and believe that the stress of assuming a less-desired position would be more damaging for the cardiac patient. The on-top position may be modified by supporting more of the weight with the knees and legs. Other patients may need encouragement to slow down activity and experiment with touching, cuddling, body massage, and self-stimulation to decrease performance anxiety. If a patient is having difficulty or needs to be reassured about the advisability of resuming sexual activity, an ECG tape recording of the sexual act in the patient's home may be valuable. According to Friedman:

> One of the most important determinants of how well a cardiac patient will function sexually is how well his spouse is functioning, for fear and anxiety from either partner may have a dampening effect on sexual activity.[22]

Sexual Counseling

Many patients and partners may prefer individual counseling from nurses they value and trust. When a specialist is asked to counsel, the patient may feel that sexuality is different from other expected activities since it is treated differently. However, it is very important for the nurse to feel comfortable about discussing sexuality with no language barriers or topic taboos. Some cardiac groups have been formed to discuss mutual concerns. Some clients in the group may wish to be participant observers by learning from topics being discussed by others but choosing not to risk discussing their own sexuality. Self-esteem, ego needs, and body image may be bolstered by some of the members providing positive role models.

Nursing research is just beginning in this area and it will be interesting to see the outcomes of different approaches and options for client populations with cardiac difficulties.

Vignette

Problem List

The client is a 48-year-old married man 5 weeks postcoronary.

1 Postcoronary male (5 weeks)
2 Fear of death
3 Ambivalence about resuming sexual activity
4 Lack of sexual knowledge

Subjective Data

"I guess sex isn't for the man with a bad heart. My "big" days are over. No, I cannot afford to take any chances with sex. Well it is good that my wife doesn't care about it much anymore. She is also afraid that I will have another attack in bed. Well, we only had sex around two or three times each week before the heart attack so I guess it won't be missed very much—it isn't as if we were young and had to have sex."

Objective Data

Postcoronary of 5 weeks

Passed master two-step exercise test and can briskly climb two or three flights of stairs of 10 steps each

Depressive symptoms—withdrawal, marked decrease in sexual activity, sleeplessness

Assessment

Patient is at risk for discontinuing sexual activity.

Depression and compensation most likely arise out of feared or imagined loss. Needs information on sexual response cycle, energy requirements, and effects of aging. Also needs information on risks of another attack during sexual activity.

Intervention

Explain the male and female sexual response cycle and the effects of aging in both sexes.

Explain the amount of energy required for sexual intercourse.

Explain methods of determining the readiness of beginning sexual activity. Discuss fears or imagined loss.

Suggest masturbation or nondemanding stimulation from partner to reassure himself regarding sexual capabilities.

Suggest a meeting with partner to discuss communication difficulties and to determine her concerns.

Plan

Encourage patient to move back into sexual activity to help combat fears and feelings of loss. Increase knowledge of sexual responses and cardiac stress. Improve communication and help spouse with sexual concerns. Discuss when to avoid and the warning signs during sexual activity.

LEARNING ACTIVITIES

Discuss the many psychological implications of cardiac disruption on sexuality. Compare and contrast the possible effect of different types of cardiovascular disruption on sexual functioning.

Make an outline of the Table of Contents for a booklet on sex that could be used by the hospital staff to help prepare the postcoronary patient and partner for discharge. Compare your outline with that of other students.

SUGGESTED READING

Bloch, A., J. Maeder, and J. Haissly: "Sexual Problems of Myocardial Infarction," *Am. Heart J.* **90**(4):536–537 (1975).

Friedman, J. M.: "Sexual Adjustment of the Postcoronary Male," in J. LoPiccolo and L. LoPiccolo (eds.), *Handbook of Sex Therapy,* Plenum, New York, 1978, pp. 373–386.

Hellerstein, H., and E. J. Friedman: "Sexual Activity and the Postcoronary Patient," *Arch. Intern. Med.* **125**:987 (1970).

REFERENCES

1   W. B. Tuttle, W. L. Cook, and E. Fitch, "Sexual Behavior in Post Myocardial Infarction Patients," *Am. J. Cardiol.* **13**:140 (abstract) (1964).

2   A. Bloch, J. Maeder, and J. Haissly, "Sexual Problems after Myocardial Infarction," *Am. Heart J.* **90**(4):536–537 (1975).

3   Tuttle et al., op. cit.

4   Bloch et al., op. cit.

5   Ibid.

6   E. Dangrove, "Sexual Responses to Disease Processes," *J. Sex Res.* **4**:4–257 (1968).

7   D. Labby, "Sexual Concomitants of Disease and Illness," *Postgrad. Med.* **58**:105 (1975).

8   N. S. Puksta, "All about Sex: After a Coronary," *Am. J. Nurs.* **77**(4):603 (1977).

9   J. M. Friedman, "Sexual Adjustment of the Postcoronary Male," in J. LoPiccolo and L. LoPiccolo (eds.), *Handbook of Sex Therapy,* Plenum, New York, 1978, p. 378.

10 Puksta, op. cit., pp. 602–605.

11 H. Hellerstein and E. J. Friedman, "Sexual Activity and the Postcoronary Patient," *Arch. Intern. Med.* **125**:987 (1970).

12 Friedman, op. cit., p. 380.

13 L. Besch, "Human Sexuality Project: A Plan for Providing Information and Counseling to Cardiac Patients and their Partners," unpublished paper, University of Wisconsin, Madison, 1978, pp. 1–15.

14 Friedman, op. cit., p. 376.

15 L. Scheingold and N. Wagner, *Sound Sex and the Aging Heart,* Human Science, New York, 1974, p. 117.

16 G. C. Griffith, "Sexuality and the Cardiac Patient," *Heart Lung* **2**:70–73 (1973).

17 Hellerstein, op. cit.

18 A. W. Green, "Sexual Activity and the Postmyocardial Infarction Patient," *Am. Heart J.* **89**(2):246 (1975).

19 W. Oaks and John Moyer, "Sex and Hypertension, *Med. Aspects Hum. Sexual.* **6**(11):128 (1972).

20 Friedman, op. cit., p. 379.

21 L. Besch, op. cit., pp. 3–5.

22 Friedman, op. cit., p. 381.

BIBLIOGRAPHY

Abbott, M. A., and D. P. McWhirter: "Resuming Sexual Activity after Myocardial Infarction," *Med. Aspects Hum. Sexual.* **12**(6):18–29 (1978).

Abramov, L. A.: "Sexual Life and Sexual Frigidity among Women Developing Acute Myocardial Infarctions," *Psychosom. Med.* **38**(6):418–425 (1976).

Besch, L.: "Human Sexuality Project: A Plan for Providing Information and Counseling to Cardiac Patients and their Partners," unpublished paper, University of Wisconsin, Madison, 1978.

Beyer, J. C., and W. F. Enos: "Obscure Causes of Death during Sexual Activity," *Med. Aspects Hum. Sexual.* **11**(9):81 (1977).

Bloch, A., J. Maeder, and J. Haissly: "Sexual Problems after Myocardial Infarction," *Am. Heart J.* **90**(4):536–537 (1975).

Bruh, H., S. Wolf, and B. Phillips: "Depression and Death in Myocardial Infarction: A Psychosocial Study of Screening Male Coronary Patients over Nine Years," *Psychosom. Res.* **15**:305 (1971).

Cohen, B. P., B. S. Wallston, and K. A. Wallston: "Sex Counseling in Cardiac Rehabilitation," *Arch. Phys. Med. Rehabil.* **57**:473 (1976).

Dangrove, E.: "Sexual Responses to Disease Processes," *J. Sex Res.* **4**:257 (1968).

Dominian, J., and M. Skelton: "Psychological Stress in Wives of Patients with Myocardial Infarction, *Br. Med. J.* **2**:101 (1973).

Douglas, J. E., and T. D. Wilkes: "Reconditioning Cardiac Patients," *Am. Fam. Physician* **11**(1):123–129 (1975).

Eliot, R. S., and R. Miles: "Advising the Cardiac Patient about Sexual Intercourse," *Med. Aspects Hum. Sexual.* **9**:50 (1975).

Friedman, J. M.: "Sexual Adjustment of the Postcoronary Male," in J. LoPiccolo and L. LoPiccolo (eds.), *Handbook of Sex Therapy,* Plenum, New York, 1978, pp. 373–386.

Germain, C. P.: "Exercise Makes the Heart Grow Stronger," *Am. J. Nurs.* **72**:2170 (1972).

Green, A. W.: "Sexual Activity and the Postmyocardial Infarction Patient," *Am. Heart J.* **89**(2):246–252 (1975).

Griffith, G. C.: "Sexuality and the Cardiac Patient," *Heart Lung* **2**:70–73 (1973).

Hackett, R., and C. Bildeau: "Issues Raised in Group Setting by Patients Recovering from Myocardial Infarction," *Am. J. Psychiatry* **128**:105 (1971).

Hellerstein, H., and A. Ford: "Rehabilitation of the Cardiac Patient," *JAMA* **164**:225 (1957).

Hellerstein, H., and E. J. Friedman: "Sexual Activity and the Postcoronary Patient," *Arch. Intern. Med.* **125**:987–999 (1970).

Kaplan, H. S.: *The New Sex Therapy,* Brunner-Mazel, 1974, pp. 98–99.

Kent, S.: "When to Resume Sexual Activity after Myocardial Infarction," *Geriatrics* **30**:150 (1975).

Koller, R., J. W. Kennedy, J. C. Bulter, and N. Wagner: "Counseling the Coronary Patient on Sexual Activity," *Postgrad. Med.* **51**:133 (1972).

Labby, D.: "Sexual Concomitants of Disease and Illness," *Postgrad. Med.* **58**:105 (1975).

Maddox, J. W.: "Sexual Health and Health Care," *Postgrad. Med.* **58**:52–57 (1975).

Nemec, E., L. Mansfield, and J. W. Kennedy: "Heart Rate and Blood Pressure Response during Sexual Activity in Normal Males," *Am. Heart J.* **92**(3):274–277 (1976).

Niles, A. A.: "Adverse Reaction and Interaction Limiting the Use of Antihypertensive Drugs," *Am. J. Med.* **58**:493 (1975).

Oaks, Wilbur, and John Moyer: "Sex and Hypertension," *Med. Aspects Hum. Sexual.* **6**(11):128 (1972).

Puksta, N. S.: "All about Sex: After a Coronary," *Am. J. Nurs.* **77**(4):602–605 (1977).

Scalzi, C. C.: "Nursing Management of Behavioral Response following an Acute Myocardial Infarction," *Heart Lung* **2**:62–69 (1973).

Scheingold, L., and N. Wagner: *Sound Sex and the Aging Heart,* Human Science, New York, 1974.

Semmler, C., and M. Semmler: "Counseling the Coronary Patient," *Am. J. Occup. Ther.* **28**(10):609 (1974).

Skelton, M.: "Psychological Stress in Wives of Patients with Myocardial Infarction," *Br. Med. J.* **2**(101):55–58 (1973).

Stein, R. A.: "The Effect of Exercise Training on Heart Rate during Coitus in the Post Myocardial Patient," *Circulation* **51** (1975).

Tuttle, W. B., W. L. Cook, and E. Fitch: "Sexual Behavior in Post Myocardial Infarction Patients," *Am. J. Cardiol.* **13**:40 (1964).

Ueno, M.: "The So-called Coition Death," *Jap. Leg. Med.* **17**(9):330–340 (1963).

Woods, J. S.: "Drug Effects on Human Sexual Behavior," in N. Woods (ed.), *Human Sexuality in Health and Illness,* Mosby, St. Louis, 1975, p. 178.

Chapter 16

Diabetes Mellitus

This chapter provides information regarding diabetes mellitus and its effects on sexuality. The intent of the chapter is to alert the nurse to potential physiological and psychological problems for the diabetic and partner.

The number of diabetics in this country is estimated as being near 6 million. Despite advances in the treatment of diabetes mellitus, disturbances in sexual functioning, expecially secondary impotence, are common among diabetic males.[1] There has been an awareness of the problem since 1903, when the impotence was thought to be of an endocrine basis. At this time, there is an almost complete agreement that it is more likely a part of diabetic neuropathy. Clinicians report that from 37 to 50 percent of diabetic men are impotent and a small percentage (13 percent) show impotence as an initial symptom of diabetes. The specific lesion which causes impotence has not been determined; however, there is known involvement of the parasympathetic plexus.[2] According to Ellenberg:

> The finding of normal plasma testosterone values and the completely negative response to the use of testosterone in full measure are strong arguments against the significance of endocrine factors in pathogeneses of diabetic impotence.[3]

The diabetic might note a gradual decrease (over a few years) in the ability to initiate and sustain an erection. The patient will often have a persistence of libido. Organic impotence is not thought to correlate with the severity, duration of disease, stability of control, or whether oral agents or injections of insulin are used.[4] A man with diabetes, like other men, may suffer from psychogenic impotence. Organic and psychogenic impotence present a different clinical picture. They may be differentiated by the man, with psychogenic impotence, having the ability to masturbate, or the occurrence of nocturnal emission, or by nocturnal penile tumescences that can be measured by a plethysmograph monitor.[5]

Until very recently, the sexual functioning of females with diabetes was considered a reproductive function, ignored, or was believed to be normal. At this time, there is a great deal of speculation on the marked differences of sexual dysfunction that is reported in the male and female diabetic. In at least one study, there was some evidence of orgasmic difficulties in female diabetics.[6] However, in a later publication, Ellenberg reports the study of 100 females to determine the effects of diabetes on sexual functioning. The study population included about equal numbers of female diabetics with and without neuropathy. His findings indicate that these women reported normal libido and orgasmic reaction that compared favorably with the statistics for women in the nondiabetic population. Many of these subjects suffered from severe complications including retinopathy, neuropathy, enteropathy, diarrhea, cataracts, marked bladder involvement, neuropathic ulcers, and Charcot's joints. There is no scientific explanation as to the remarkable differences in the effect of diabetes on sexual function between men and women.[7] The earlier studies of females concentrated on aspects of fertility including pregnancy, birth, infant congenital defects, and infant mortality. In the reproductive aspect, the female diabetic has had difficulty; however, approximately 80 percent of the pregnancies of diabetic women terminate successfully.[8] The obstetrical aspects will not be covered in this book.

ASSESSMENT

The assessment of sexual problems of those having diabetes remains a difficult task (Table 16-1). Impotence is a frequent complication; however, the pathogenesis is not totally understood. There may be total impotence, borderline impotence, or ejaculatory difficulties. There is a danger of mistaking psychogenic impotence as being organic in nature. Another problem of assessing diabetic impotence is that many clinicians do not believe that it is related to the severity of the disease. Impotence may be one of the first symptoms of diabetes. Nurses or other health professionals have not routinely taken a sexual history. Consequently, the middle-aged man has no experience in giving this type of information and may be somewhat reluctant to admit a slowing down of his sexual powers or may not wish to risk talking about his masturbatory practices. The morning erection is a reliable indicator and may be more easily assessed than some of the other symptoms.

Changes in the routine or the capacity for sexual performance may be subtly hinted by the man or the partner. These clues should be assessed very carefully and judged by verbal and nonverbal messages to determine if the assessment

Table 16-1   Sexual Implications of Diabetes Mellitus

Possible effect on sexual functioning	Presumed mechanism	Common accompanying problems
Male		
Organic impotence (unable to maintain an erection sufficient to effect coital penetration)	Autonomic neuropathy Parasympathetic involvement	Neurogenic bladder Nephropathy Peripheral neuropathy Diabetic retinopathy Obesity
Borderline impotence (the beginning of difficulties in some diabetics)		Depression Susceptibility to infection
Retrograde ejaculation (usually occurs in long-standing insulin dependence)	Results from disturbance of the sympathetic nerve supply to the internal sphincter during orgasm. There is propulsion of seminal fluid from the posterior urethra into the bladder (see Fig. 3-17)	Sterility Microvascular changes Amputations Marital conflict Anger Anxiety
Libido unchanged		Denial
Female		
Questionable Secondary orgasmic dysfunction	Unknown, but a variety of etiologic factors are reported including neuropathy, susceptibility to infection, microvascular changes	Neuropathy Diabetic retinopathy Nephropathy Neurogenic bladder Enteropathy Neuropathic ulcers Hypertension Obesity Depression
Dyspareunia	Monilial infection (yeast multiply more rapidly in glucose environment)	Amputations Susceptibility to infection Insulin lipodystrophy
Adolescent amenorrhea	Endocrine Slowing of all growth and maturation	Obstetrical problems (toxemia of pregnancy, heavy birth weight, intrapartum death, congenital anomalies;) risk of child developing diabetes approximately 60% if both parents are diabetics, less than 25% if father is a carrier, and not significant if father has no family history of diabetes

Source: Refs. 9 to 16.

should be slowed in pace or if it proves to be too painful to talk about in long sessions. Information concerning the change should include duration, symptoms, fears, and partner reactions. Secondary impotence may be characterized by marital conflict, anger, anxiety, and denial. Some men may be very secretive about their symptoms, neglect health care, and deny concern. In some instances, the wives recognize the hostile nature of the husband's self-neglect but feel guilty for being angry with sick men. Other women focus concern about diabetes on possible complications and difficulties for themselves. Some women may feel responsible for the sexual difficulty, accuse the partner of having interest in other women, or feel depressed and regard themselves as failures or as being unimportant in the partner's life. Other women let the sexual impotence be generalized to impotence in work, social life, and in child rearing, which is detrimental to the man's ego and the relationship. How the homosexual partner reacts to impotence in the diabetic male has not been emphasized in the literature on diabetics.

Assessing unplanned pregnancies may lead to the beginning fears of decreasing sexual performance by either one or both partners. Fathering a child may bolster the ego or ward off having to accept borderline difficulties. Pregnancy may occasionally occur even when there is no erection but ejaculation of viable sperm.

If there is any possibility that the impotency could be psychogenic in nature, the nocturnal penile tumescences may be measured by a plethysmograph monitor device that can be used in the home by the client.

The problems of etiology or prognosis of sexual functioning of diabetic women have not been studied adequately to supply answers for this population. Nurses should begin a systematic approach of evaluation to determine if and what type of sexual problems are associated with diabetes in the female.

Occasionally amenorrhea occurs in young diabetics and may cause additional stress in maintaining a positive self-image. Changes in the level of blood glucose and in quantities of sugar excreted in the urine occur during the menstrual cycle. These changes can be confusing for the young female diabetic. The peer culture of the adolescent period may be responsible for additional stress and sex may be used by diabetics to prove their normalcy and acceptance by others. Specific skin lesions of diabetics are common in adolescent females and increase negative feelings of self-image. Insulin lipodystrophy may occur as tissue atrophy or hypertrophy. Atrophy is more common in children and adult females. It causes a dimpling and pitting at the injection site which is troublesome for physical attractiveness. Hypertrophy may become quite large and disfiguring.[17]

Depression is a common characteristic of all diabetics. Depressive reactions impair sexual functioning and may be seen as secondary orgasmic dysfunction in females.

The nurse may be the first health professional to be aware of some of the above indications of sexual difficulties. As mentioned before, the sexual assessment of diabetics is difficult and some physicians believe that there is a real danger of misdiagnosing organic impotence. Consequently, an early referral may be prudent.

INFORMATION AND SUGGESTIONS

After the problem or problems have been identified and if the patient has all the indications of organic impotency, the facts and the relationships of diabetes to the problem should be discussed with the client. The physician may give the initial diagnosis but the nurse should be cognizant of the follow-up that is indicated in the form of information and suggestions.

The nurse may assist clients and partners to look at the dynamics of the relationship and situations, to explore the options and choices open to them, and to evaluate what the consequences of their current choices or what the consequences of alternative choices would be.

Methods of obtaining sexual gratification other than genital-genital sex which are described in Chap. 3 should be discussed with the couple. Melman discusses two prostheses that are available:

> One is a solid silastic rod(s) which fills both corpora cavernosa and gives a sustained erection. This device can be inserted via a penile or perineal incision at low cost, with minimal risk and few complications. The erection appears normal and is of sufficient rigidity to bring both the patient and sexual partner to orgasm if they are physiologically capable. Most patients initially rebel at the thought of a sustained erection. However, after the placement of nearly 40 such prostheses no recipient has requested that the prosthetic device be removed because of that condition. By resorting to such simple devices as broad-banded athletic supporters, jockey shorts, or a light, tight-fitting corset, the erection will remain undetected when the patient is fully clothed.
>
> The second type is an inflatable device. This prosthesis is composed of inflatable silastic rods which are placed in each corpora, along with a reservoir placed underneath the erectus muscle. By pumping a valve in the scrotum, an erection can be initiated at the time of sexual arousal and detumescence achieved when another valve is squeezed after intercourse. The more natural appearance of the penis is the major advantage of this device. Disadvantages are its higher cost, longer time required for surgery, and a reported complication rate of 25 to 33 percent.[18]

Another problem that seems to cause difficulty for both male and female diabetics is the fear or wish to have children. Those that fear having diabetic children may repress sexual feelings and have had very little sexual experience. Those that wish to prove their sexual adequacy by the number of children may concentrate on procreation rather than sexual satisfaction for self or partner.

The partner of the impotent man may feel guilty, unworthy, angry, and rejected. These couples will need to understand the basis of the impotency and begin to communicate feelings and disappointments rather than act out in a destructive reciprocal manner. Some of these couples get caught in the "revolving-door" syndrome. The need to blame, or feeling guilty, becomes intensified and is a major obstacle in everyday interactions. A sadomasochistic trend may develop between partners which should be understood as the chosen method of handling feelings of unworthiness, shame, anger, triumph, and punishment. These people would probably benefit from couple or marital counseling.

The female adolescent diabetic may need support and suggestions to achieve and maintain a positive self-image. If menses are late and she feels sexually unattractive, different, or unacceptable, positive methods of compensation may be helpful. For example, developing skills to obtain a special spot in a group, such as playing a musical instrument, may pay big dividends. If the teenager feels a need to engage in alcohol or other drugs for acceptance, the danger of creating additional difficulties in recognizing an oncoming diabetic reaction should be reviewed with an information orientation rather than using an authoritarian approach that will likely create more rebellion. The female diabetic should be aware of the prevalence of yeast (monilial) infections in the vagina which is due to the fact that yeasts grow rapidly in glucose. These infections cause itching and discomfort but usually respond to Mycostatin vaginal suppositories and improved diabetic control. Oral contraceptives may require an increase in insulin but there are no known negative effects that are not noted in the nondiabetic population.

The diabetic male and female are plagued with many complications—hypertension, renal disease, retinopathy, fat dystrophy, fat atrophy (not harmful but cosmetically objectionable), skin lesions, obesity, and depression—all of which increase the incidence of sexual difficulties.

Diabetic women have a higher incidence of toxemia, stillbirth, and congenitally defective children, and should have this information early in life to prevent this from becoming an additional shock during adolescence or young adulthood. Premarital counseling should review this type of information along with genetic information about the disease. Most nondiabetic partners will have had less opportunity to have been exposed to this type of information. An open discussion with other couples with a diabetic member may be helpful. Diabetic teen clubs and diabetic camps will have done much of this preparation for adult relationships.

Patient education programs are needed to keep the knowledge and technology up to date. In some areas, after discharge from the hospital, patients and their families are invited to attend a monthly lecture series. The series may be followed by a monthly couples group session that encourages them to share experiences about coping with diabetes on a daily basis.[19]

These are only a few of the many types of information guides and suggestions that may prove helpful to diabetics and their partners. It seems apparent that nurses may find themselves sharing the leadership of the health team with patients and partners. Most of these problems will require long-term goals, planning, and follow-up to be implemented in primary and secondary health care settings. Since much of this material is in the beginning stages of development, it will behoove the nurse to keep abreast of current research and clinical findings.

ABOUT THE VIGNETTE

The month's educational program for diabetics was titled Sexuality and Diabetes. There was an increased number of females and families of diabetics attending in comparison to other monthly programs. The program was aimed at an introduction—permission giving—level to allow clients to have sexual concerns and to talk about them in a latter rap session.

The program was aimed at the basic knowledge level with a simple presentation of the male and female sexual response cycle. Following this presentation, a panel of two diabetics and two partners discussed the types of problems that they had experienced. One male was impotent and the female with diabetes had experienced fears about pregnancy and genetic possibilities. Each patient and partner openly discussed one of the following: fears, anger, guilt, goals, and the methods they used to help resolve their difficulties. This session was not meant to give answers but to create an environment in which members of the audience would feel free to talk about some of their difficulties and to suggest resources if a person wished to talk with someone in a private session.

Vignette

Problem

Mary B. chose the latter resource and set up an appointment to talk with the nurse about her concerns. Mary, a 28-year-old woman, was married to a 35-year-old man with diabetes. She had some uncomfortable feelings about what was happening to her marital and sexual relationship with her husband. Her sexual needs seemed to be increasing and her husband was having erectile problems. She felt angry and usually acted out her anger in destructive ways—leaving the house and going to a bar. She was unhappy and felt guilty after an evening on the town. She and her husband had never been able to talk about their difficulties; instead they each walked out and "let things cool off." When she heard about the sexual program, she had hoped she and Joe could attend together but he was not interested. He was angry that she had attended and could not tell him of this private counseling session.

Subjective Data

1   Change in sexual relationship.
2   Mary acts out anger in destructive ways.
3   Joe uses denial and will not seek help or talk about erectile difficulties.
4   Mary believes that not having sex is not the best method of handling their problem.

Objective Data

1   Married 5 years.
2   Joe has had diabetes for 20 years, checks his urine, takes daily insulin, and visits his physician monthly. His diabetes seems to be in good control.
3   Mary has no apparent physical problems.
4   Joe refuses to attend educational counseling sessions.

Assessment

Angry and guilty about sexual relationship.
Needs information on the relationship of diabetes to sexual dysfunction.
Needs support and direction solving problems based on marital conflict.

Intervention

Given permission to express feelings about unmet sexual needs.

Plan

1 Supply information about diabetes and sexuality to Mary in printed form that can be taken to the home.

2 Discuss with Mary alternate noncoital methods of meeting sexual needs: cuddling, massaging, oral-genital sex, etc.

3 Have Mary encourage Joe to come to counseling sessions and talk to his physician about his erectile problems.

4 Have Mary note the absence or presence of morning erections. If possible, determine if Joe has organic or psychogenic impotence.

Evaluation

Has Mary been able to understand that her destructive behavior has not been satisfying to her and has produced more difficulties for the relationship?

Has Mary been able to convince Joe to attend counseling or see his physician about his erectile problems?

Has the impotence been diagnosed as organic or psychogenic?

Has the couple increased their ability to talk about concerns instead of walking out?

Has Mary increased her knowledge about diabetes and sexuality?

LEARNING ACTIVITIES.

After 12 months of counseling Mary and Joe have resolved most of their marital conflicts concerning sexual practices. They have experimented with oral-genital sex and masturbatory activities, and Joe is enjoying a solid silastic rod penile prosthesis. Now, they have a new problem: they want a baby.

Mary insists on having the baby
Mary is against adoption
Joe is against artificial insemination

How will you help them solve this new problem?

REFERENCES

1 I. W. Campbell and B. Clarke, "Sexual Dysfunction in Diabetic Men," *Med. Aspects Hum. Sexual.* **9**(3):157 (1975).

2 A. Melman, "The Diagnosis and Therapy of Impotence Associated with Diabetes," *Sexual. Disabil.* **1**(1):52–56 (1978).

3 M. Ellenberg, "Impotence in Diabetes: The Neurologic Factor," in Joseph LoPiccolo and Leslie LoPiccolo (eds.), *Handbook of Sex Therapy,* Plenum, New York, 1978, pp. 401–431.

4 Daniel Labby, "Sexual Concomitant of Disease and Illness," *Postgrad. Med.* **58**(1):107 (1975).

5 Ellenberg, op. cit., p. 428.

6 R. Kolodny, "Sexual Dysfunction in Diabetic Females," *Diabetes* **20**(8):557–559 (1971).

7 M. Ellenberg, "Sex and the Female Diabetic," *Med. Aspects Hum. Sexual.* **11**(12):30–38 (1977).

8   Ibid.
9   Ellenberg, op. cit., p. 428.
10 M. Brooks, "Effect of Diabetes on Female Sexual Response," *Med. Aspects Hum. Sexual.* **11**(2):63 (1977).
11 M. Ellenberg, "Impotence in Diabetics: A Neurological Rather Than an Endocrinologic Problem," *Med. Aspects Hum. Sexual.* **7**:12–20 (1973).
12 J. Jaerman et al., "Impotence and Diabetes," *Diabetes* **21**(1):23–30 (1972).
13 L. Konez and M. Balodimos, "Impotence in Diabetes Mellitus," *Med. Times* **98**(8):159–169 (1970).
14 D. Renshaw, "Diabetic Impotence: A Need for Further Evaluation," *Med. Aspects Hum. Sexual.* **12**(4):19–25 (1978).
15 D. Renshaw, "Impotence in Diabetics," in J. LoPiccolo and L. LoPiccolo (eds.), *Handbook of Sex Therapy,* Plenum, New York, 1978, pp. 433–440.
16 N. Woods, *Human Sexuality in Health and Illness,* Mosby, St. Louis, 1975, pp. 124–139.
17 A. M. Fonville, "Teaching Patients to Rotate Injection Sites," *Am. J. Nurs.* **78**(5):880–882 (1978).
18 Melman, op. cit., pp. 52–56.
19 D. Small, "A Patient Education Program," *Am. J. Nurs.* **78**(5):889–891 (1978).

BIBLIOGRAPHY

Brooks, M.: "Effect of Diabetes on Female Sexual Response," *Med. Aspects Hum. Sexual.* **11**(2):63 (1977).
Campbell, I. W., and B. Clarke: "Sexual Dysfunction in Diabetic Men," *Med. Aspects Hum. Sexual.* **9**(3):157 (1975).
Ellenberg, M.: "Impotence in Diabetics: A Neurological Rather Than an Endocrinologic Problem," *Med. Aspects Hum. Sexual.* **7**:12–20 (1973).
Ellenberg, M.: "Sex and the Female Diabetic," *Med. Aspects Hum. Sexual.* **11**(12):30–38 (1977).
Ellenberg, M.: "Impotence in Diabetes: The Neurologic Factor, in J. LoPiccolo and L. LoPiccolo (eds.), *Handbood of Sex Therapy,* Plenum, New York, 1978, pp. 401–431.
Fonville, A. M.: "Teaching Patients to Rotate Injection Sites," *Am. J. Nurs.* **78**(5):880–882 (1978).
Jaerman, J., O. Vilar, A. Rivarola, J. M. Rosner, M. N. Jadzinsky, D. Fox, A. P. Lloret, L. Berstein-Hahn, and M. D. Saraceni: "Impotence and Diabetes," *Diabetes* **21**(1):23–30 (1972).
Kolodny, R.: "Sexual Dysfunction in Diabetic Females," *Diabetes* **20**(8):557–559 (1971).
Konez, L., and M. Balodimos: "Impotence in Diabetes Mellitus," *Med. Times* **98**(8):159–169 (1970).
Labby, Daniel: "Sexual Concomitant of Disease and Illness," *Postgrad. Med.* **58**(1):107 (1975).
Melman, A.: "The Diagnosis and Therapy of Impotence Associated with Diabetes," *Sexual. Disabil.* **1**(1):52–56 (1978).
Renshaw, D.: "Diabetic Impotence: A Need for Further Evaluation," *Med. Aspects Hum. Sexual.* **12**(4):19–25 (1978).
Renshaw, D.: "Impotence in Diabetics," in J. LoPiccolo and L. LoPiccolo (eds.), *Handbook of Sex Therapy,* Plenum, New York, 1978, pp. 433–440.
Small, D.: "A Patient Education Program," *Am. J. Nurs.* **78**(5):889–891 (1978).
Woods, N.: *Human Sexuality in Health and Illness,* Mosby, St. Louis, 1975, pp. 124–139.

Chapter 17

Spinal Cord Injury

SPINAL CORD INJURY

It is not known exactly how many spinal cord–injured persons live in the United States but in 1971, the number was estimated as being between 60,000 and 100,000. The number has grown in recent years due to the improved medical technology that has increased the life span of this population. During peacetime, the most prevalent cause of injury is automobile accidents, followed by motorcycle accidents, water accidents, gunshot wounds, and falls. Many of the spinal cord–injured persons are in the young or middle-aged group who had healthy bodies that became nonfunctional in a matter of minutes.[1] This chapter covers specific information for assessing and educating a spinal cord–injured person and partner. Most of the literature on sexual functioning of spinal cord injury has concentrated on the physiological aspects of sexual response. Controlled studies with a large sample size and standardized data collection procedures for investigating the psychosocial aspects of spinal-injured sexuality are few in number. According to Higgins:

> Professionals as well as cord-injured people are still to a large extent guided by the prejudices and biases of the past. The nature of sexual behavior is such that

continuing change can be expected. Future surveys of well-informed spinal-cord injured individuals will undoubtedly reveal different patterns of sexual behavior from those that are found in the sometimes naive and often misinformed cord-injured of the present.[2]

Table 17-1 presents some of the consequences of spinal cord injuries on sexuality. (See also Figs. 17-1 and 17-2 for review of the nervous system control of sexual function.)

ASSESSMENT

1   A complete neurological examination should be done by a neurologist to determine the level of lesion and the degree of completeness.

2   Physical and laboratory examinations will help determine the degree of muscular strength, muscular contractures, spasticity, urinary infection, and any other suspected health condition.

3   Psychosocial assessment will help determine mental health status, stage of mourning and loss behaviors, status of self-image, body image, performance anxieties, type and quality of interpersonal relationships, type and quality of social interactions and relationships, available supporting resources, and future goals and expectations.

4   Sexual history will reveal past and present sexual responses and options. The history should be thorough enough to determine present sexual knowledge and attitudes and establish guidelines for sex education and counseling. Some clinicians administer an attitude and knowledge inventory to determine educational needs.

5   Clarification of short- and long-term goals for client and partner (if available).

INTERVENTION

Permission

The disabled individual is sexual, which needs to be acknowledged and legitimatized. Permission to experiment with sexuality to find what is pleasurable, comforting, and acceptable helps clients feel that they have some important choices that will give them control over their lives. Some individuals feel that it is absolutely necessary to participate in the sex act to maintain self-esteem. However, there are others who will consider themselves sexual with other types of interpersonal interactions, such as a wink of an eye, a special smile, verbal compliments, help with grooming, or gentle touching. Some clients are able to concentrate on giving their partners pleasure which supplements their own pleasure. Oral-genital sex provides an excellent method of giving pleasure to a partner in some relationships.

The decision and responsibility to engage, or not engage, in specific sexual acts is the right of each individual. To maintain one's sexuality may be more difficult, but also may be more rewarding and greatly appreciated by those having a spinal cord injury. It requires a great deal of energy to repress sexual urges, quell anxieties, and overcome feelings of inadequacy. This energy can be more profitably used toward the goal of enhancing sexuality. Concentrating on abilities holds much more hope and choices than dwelling on the "terrible" disabilities. Although mourning behaviors are healthy and expected, the nurse can be instrumental in setting limits on the depth and longevity of self-destructive behaviors. Those who usually express anger through physical means such as pacing, throwing something, or walking out will need to develop verbal skills to release tension. The availability of a socially acceptable partner gives a boost to most individual's sexuality through mutual respect, caring, and pleasuring. If there is no available partner, permission and legitimatizing the need for one may be helpful.

If a client has had many negative experiences that have deflated the ego, the nurse's support and gentle push will help legitimatize the importance of continuing psychosexual development. The client must be assured that he or she has the right to be sexual and to choose his or her own methods of expression, whether it is autosexuality, homosexuality, or heterosexuality.

The nurse may find it difficult but challenging to provide help for a young, athletic person whose identity is shattered along with the spinal cord. Also, a young person who is not in an ongoing relationship and who has never experienced one may need special help with problem solving around loss, fantasies, and possible options. Some couples will be faced with very difficult decisions in regard to whether to continue their relationship and, if so, how they will secure enough support and assistance to do so.

Information

Only since 1940 have victims of spinal cord injury lived long enough to require special help with sexuality. Research findings are sparse for this population. Much of the writings come from clinical experience. In the past, approximately 80 percent of all literature dealt with mechanical and biological aspects of sexual functioning, concentrating on sex drive and the sex act of the male. This will probably change as women move into different social and work activities with environments that include more risk for accidents. Most of the current information about female sexuality deals with menstruation, fertility, and birthing, calling them all normal. Consequently, the woman's sexuality is defined as the ability to conceive and deliver normal healthy infants.[4] The information in Table 17-1 is incomplete but may prove useful to spinal cord–injured clients and their partners.

According to Cole:

> Loss of somatic sensation is frequent in paraplegia, but in the vast majority of patients, psycho-sexual content remains substantially normal in spite of loss of sensation over primary erogenous zones such as the genitals . . . Visceral stimulation is usually from an unknown origin and causes "spontaneous" erections. Such unknown stimuli may originate in the pelvic viscera, bladder, or rectum of individuals with either intact or damaged spinal cords.[5]

Table 17-1 Paraplegia and Quadriplegia

Lesions	Possible effects on sexual functioning	Presumed pathogenic mechanism	Accompanying common problems
Lesions are divided into Upper motor neuron complete Upper motor neuron incomplete Lower motor neuron complete Lower motor neuron incomplete	Erection (reflexogenic). Occurs as a result of external stimulation applied below the level of spinal cord lesion (generally to some area in pelvis or pelvic organs). Reflexogenic erection occurs more often in those people with complete upper-motor-neuron lesion at any level, with maximal evidence at the cervical level. Erection (psychogenic). Erection achieved through the use of either erotic thought or direct bodily and/or genital manipulation. Psychogenic erection may occur with incomplete lesion. Ejaculatory difficulties (reported ejaculation occurs in 7–27%. Higher incidence of ejaculation in lower lesion)	In absence of sacral cord function, reflexogenic erection is believed to originate from thoracic lumbar segments of cord. Psychogenic erection only experienced when lesion is below 12th thoracic vertebra (T12). When lesion is below T5 to T6 (and complete), erection is absent and probably due to vascular insufficiency of cord Absence of sacral cord function, pudendal nerve, and sacral plexus needed for ejaculation	Low levels of muscular strength spasticity Muscular contracture Incontinence Chronically infected testes Retrograde ejaculation Social isolation Depression (lower androgen supply) Loss of self-esteem Altered body image Performance anxieties Injury above T4 may cause hyperreflexia headaches from rise in blood pressure during sexual activity

Infertility (males)

Reflex emission may be dribbling in nature and lack projected power for impregnation

Inability of body to control temperature in scrotum to produce sperm (electroejaculation sometimes used to obtain semen for artificial insemination if sperm are normal)

Fertility (females unchanged)

Orgasmic response is usually changed

Orgasm achieved if there is some residual pelvic innervation or if patient has reassigned sensation from a neurologically intact portion of the body to the genitalia and experience orgasm in a fantasy. Many report this type of orgasm is satisfying and leads to resolution of sexual tension

Source: Anderson and Cole, Ref. 3.

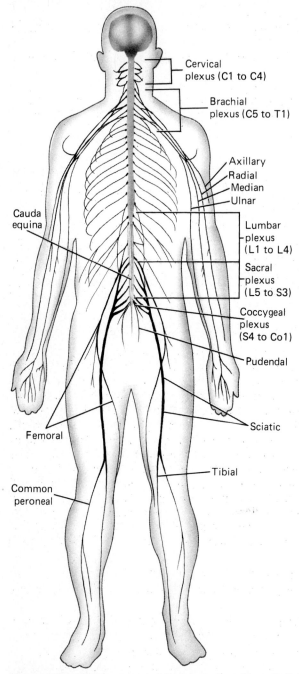

Figure 17-1 Spinal nerves and their branches. (*From E. P. Solomon and P. W. Davis, Understanding Human Anatomy and Physiology, McGraw-Hill, New York, 1978, p. 264.*)

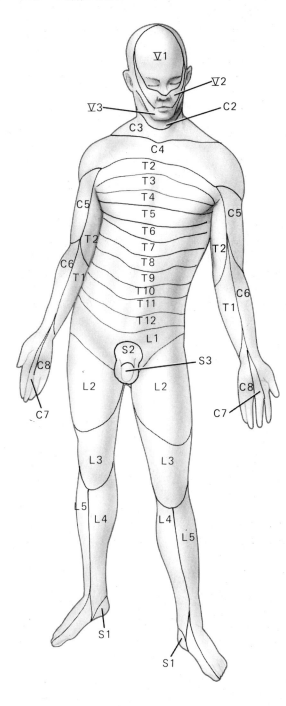

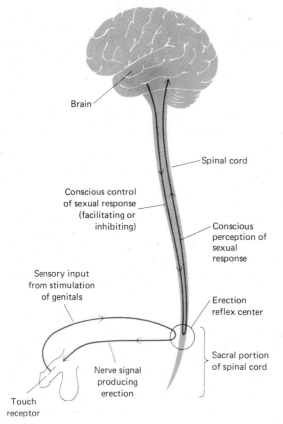

Brain

Spinal cord

Conscious control
of sexual response
(facilitating or
inhibiting)

Conscious
perception of
sexual
response

Sensory input
from stimulation
of genitals

Erection
reflex center

Sacral portion
of spinal cord

Nerve signal
producing
erection

Touch
receptor

Figure 17-2 Nervous system control of erection. Note both the reflex center in the spinal cord and the control by the brain. (*From J. Hyde, Understanding Human Sexuality, McGraw-Hill, New York, 1979, p. 174.*)

Some spinal injured males and females report orgasm in spite of complete denervation of all pelvic structures. Although this may be difficult for the able-bodied person to understand, it is reported to be entirely satisfying and leads to a comfortable resolution stage of sexual excitement. Indeed, some spinal injured adults state that they are able to concentrate on sensation from a neurologically intact portion of their bodies and reassign that sensation to their genitals, thus experiencing it in their fantasy as orgasm. Using that technique some spinal injured males report multiple orgasms.[6]

Suggestions

It seems fairly important to develop methods of emphasizing all existing physical, psychological, and social positive attitudes. If there is a special physical attractiveness, such as hair, eyes, skin, or upper torso, attention can be drawn to those areas by meticulous grooming, dress, and accessories. Many past interests and hobbies can be maintained, enlarged, and shared in various forms of social and recreational activities. Some spinal cord–injured individuals recommend being assertive and outgoing to prevent the public and associates from denying the disability and future opportunities. Successful sexual relationships appear to be an outcome and reflection of other aspects of life. Some people will find the psychological aspects of a relationship meeting sexual needs. Others will not feel they are a sexual person unless they are having a physical and psychological experience. Experimentation to find the most sensitive areas and what is pleasing leads to heightened enjoyment. If sexual intimacy is desired, below are some suggestions that others have found helpful.

Preparation
1   Overall environment, privacy, and romantic props, such as soft music, candlelight, incense, and wine help to excite and enhance sensations for some couples.

2   Good hygiene is mandatory; cleanse body, paying special attention to the genitals.

3   The bladder should be emptied as much as is possible (using Credes method). For many, there is a residual wetting problem.

4   Care should be given to appliances—remove catheter or bend and fold along shaft of the penis where it is out of the way. For females, the catheter can be pushed aside and positioned out of the way, being careful not to pull it out or block urine. If desired, a drainage tube from the bag to a large drainage bottle at the bedside may help prevent accidents. If an accident occurs, it can be cleaned up with little embarrassment if towels and other cleaning materials are handy.

5   Some couples find a water bed helpful in producing stimulation and body movement. Others enjoy reading erotic materials or engaging in body massage. Lubricating jellys and oils such as coconut oil and Kama Sutra love oils are appreciated by some couples.[7]

Sexual Activity
1   All sexual positions are possible. Some thought and experimentation with the utilization of areas of strength need to be given (e.g., the spine-injured male who has great strength in his arms may wish to create body movement with his arms and therefore would prefer the dominant or man-on-top position).

2   If there are no or very little sensations in the vagina, the partner can help determine when lubrication is necessary to prevent chafing from friction.

3   The man who has a very low injury may not have a reflex erection. "Stuffing" the penis in the vagina when there is not an erection is satisfying to some couples. The Kegel exercises* can be helpful for stuffing purposes and can heighten sensations with a flaccid penis.[8]

4   Experimentation to find the right position, pattern of pressure, and type of rhythm is necessary. Some spinal cord–injured persons find that stimulation

---

*Kegel exercises are designed to strengthen the pubococcygeus muscle and surrounding musculature. This muscle and its adjuncts help to control the urinary outlet. However, they also appear to be associated with the capacity for receiving sensory pleasure in the vaginal and clitoral areas.

around the pelvic organs or anus will produce an erection, even with a complete spinal injury.

5 If a female paraplegic or quadriplegic is wearing a catheter and desires intercourse during the menstrual period, there is a slight risk of bladder infection. A douche with cold water may stop the flow of blood and help prevent bladder infections.

6 Females should consult a contraception specialist to determine the best type of birth control for her. There are some special risks with the pill due to the chance of blood clots in the veins of legs and pelvis. The coil or intrauterine devices are also somewhat of a risk for paralyzed women. The lost sensations may prevent feelings associated with movement or penetration of the uterus wall. The manipulation of the diaphragm may be difficult but help from the partner may be available. The able-bodied partner, if there is one, may be comfortable in taking the major responsibility of birth control.

7 Spinal cord–injured males may like the option of using a penis stiffener or dildo. A stiffener is usually of hard rubber and fits over the penis which makes it stiff enough for penetration. Another method of obtaining stiffness is by silicone prosthesis, which is surgically implanted into the penis. The continuous stiffness bothers some clients. A dildo is an artificial penis, usually made of hard rubber, which can be strapped below or above the penis or can be held in the hand or mouth to supply the sensation of penile penetration if there is no penile erection.

8 Electric or battery-powered vibrators for massage and stimulation are used successfully by some couples.[9]

COUNSELING

Therapy and Educational Programs

For many, the above nursing interventions will provide adequate guidelines for successful outcomes. Those who are healthy and willing to share their experiences provide tremendous resource material for other paraplegics, quadriplegics, and partners. They serve as role models and can assist in program development.

An educational program for paraplegic, quadriplegic, and able-bodied partners was conducted in an intensive 2-day program at the University of Minnesota Medical School under the direction of Cole, Chilgren, and Rosenberg.

> The first ten hours of the workshop were spent in desensitizing the participants to explicit sexual materials so that they could deal with their own sexual feelings more easily during the remainder of the programme. Slides, speakers, panels, and films were sequenced in a deliberate manner to stimulate and facilitate the participant to deal first with nudity, then with progressively more explicit and anxiety evoking sexual material. The presentations and films explained or graphically displayed conventional aspects of human sexuality. The formal content included summaries of some of the pertinent literature recast for ready understanding by people with no medical background. Also included were movies of selected aspects of human sexuality including fantasy, male and female masturbation, male and female homosexuality, heterosexuality, sexual therapy and sexuality of the spinal cord injured person. Pornography as a desensitizing medium was utilized in saturation doses

midway through the programme. Essential to the process were small group discussions with 12 to 14 persons per group. These were led by an experienced group leader whose task was to facilitate conversation about feelings in the group.[10]

This type of program has been modified and conducted in other parts of the country. These programs combat myths, taboos, and negative attitudes and provide legitimization, information, and suggestions in a very short period of time. Further research is needed to determine the effectiveness of groups in counseling this population.

Rohme believes the public health nurse can be effective in sexual counseling for spinal cord–injured men. She presents the following example.

One twenty-four year old man with a lower motor neuron injury sustained in a car accident five years previously had flaccid paraplegia. Prior to injury he had enjoyed a very macho style of sex which stressed a variety of partners and put the emphasis on performance. His sense of manhood depended on frequent, long lasting erections. After injury he felt that without erections he "would not be of use to women." At the urging of friends he tried oral-genital sex. His religious upbringing made this a difficult decision. Initially, he reported being disgusted by the act but at the same time he was very pleased with the pleasure that he could give a partner. Consequently he set out to gain an expertise in this area. One of the most meaningful experiences he reported was a compliment one of his partners paid him when she said she felt more satisfied with him than with her usual, able-bodied lover. He was surprised to find that the women he was seeing wanted more than a stiff penis or an orgasm. They look for tenderness and someone with whom they could talk. He found that there were many other aspects of his personality that women valued.[11]

LEARNING ACTIVITY

Form small groups (10 to 12) to discuss feelings and attitudes after having viewed one or more of the following films: *Touching* (17 minutes, 16-mm film); *Don't Tell the Cripple About Sex* (30 minutes, 16-mm film); *Just What Can You Do* (20 minutes, 16-mm film); and *If Ever Two Were One* (15 minutes, 16-mm film). All the above films may be obtained or rented from Multi Media Resource Center, Inc., 540 Powell St., San Francisco, Ca. 94108.

Most of these films have been used successfully with groups of patients in educational programs.

REFERENCES

1 Glenn N. Higgins, "Aspects of Sexual Response in Adults with Spinal Cord Injury: A Review of the Literature," in J. LoPiccolo and L. LoPiccolo (eds.), *Handbook of Sex Therapy,* Plenum, New York, 1978.
2 Ibid., p. 407.
3 T. H. Anderson and T. Cole, "Sexual Counseling of the Physically Disabled," *Postgrad. Med.* **58**:117–127 (1975).
4 E. R. Griffith and R. Trieschmann, "Sexual Functioning in Women with Spinal Cord Injury," *Arch. Phys. Med. Rehabil.* **56**:18–21 (1975).

5   T. M. Cole, R. Chilgren, and P. Rosenberg, "A New Programme of Sex Education and Counseling for Spinal Cord Injured Adults and Health Care Professionals," *Paraplegia* **11**:111–124 (1973).
6   T. M. Cole, "Sexuality and the Physically Handicapped," in R. Green (ed.), *Human Sexuality: A Health Practitioner's Text,* Williams & Wilkins, Baltimore, 1975, p. 161.
7   T. O. Mooney, T. Cole, and R. Chilgren, *Sexual Options for Paraplegics and Quadriplegics,* Little, Brown, Boston, 1975.
8   Ibid., p. 102.
9   Ibid., pp. 88–92.
10 Cole, op. cit., p. 115.
11 M. W. Rohme, "The Public Health Nurse as Sexual Counselor for Spinal Cord Injured Men," *Sexual Disabil.* **2**(1):12–13 (1979).

BIBLIOGRAPHY

Anderson, T. H., and T. Cole: "Sexual Counseling of the Physically Disabled," *Postgrad. Med.* **58**:117–127 (1975).
Bidgood, F.: "Sexuality and the Handicapped," *Siecus Rep.* **11**(3):3 (1974).
Bors, E., and A. E. Comarr: "Neurological Disturbances of Sexual Function, with Special Reference to 529 Patients with Spinal Cord Injury," *Urol. Survey* **10**:191–222 (1960).
Bors, E., E. T. Engle, R. C. Rosenquist, and V. H. Hulliger: "Fertility in Paraplegic Males: A Preliminary Report of Endocrine Studies," *J. Clin. Endocrinol.* **10**:381–398 (1950).
Bregman, M. S., and R. G. Hadley: "Sexual Adjustment and Feminine Attractiveness Among Spinal Cord Injured Women," *Arch. Phys. Med. Rehabil.* **57**:448–450 (1976).
Bregman, S.: "Sexual Adjustment of Spinal Cord Injured Women," *Sexual. Disabil.* **1**(2):85–92 (1978).
Brockway, J., J. Steger, R. Berni, V. Ost, T. Williamson-Kirkland, and C. Peck: "Effectiveness of Sex Education and Counseling Program for Spinal Cord Injured Patients," *Sexual. Disabil.* **1**(2):127–136 (1978).
Cole, T.: "Reaction of the Rehabilitation Team to Patients with Sexual Problems," *Arch. Phys. Med. Rehabil.* **56**:10–11 (1975).
Cole, T. M.: "Sexuality and the Physically Handicapped," in R. Green (ed.), *Human Sexuality: A Health Practitioner's Text,* Williams & Wilkins, Baltimore, 1975, pp. 142–173.
Cole, T. M., R. Chilgren, and P. Rosenberg: "A New Programme of Sex Education and Counseling for Spinal Cord Injured Adults and Health Care Professionals," *Paraplegia* **11**:111–124 (1973).
Cole, T., and S. Cole: "The Handicapped and Sexual Health," *Siecus Rep.* **IV**(5):1–11 (1976).
Comarr, A. E.: "Observations on Menstruation and Pregnancy among Female Spinal Cord Injury Patients," *Paraplegia* **3**(4):263–272 (1966).
Comarr, A. E.: "Sex Classification and Expectations among Quadriplegic and Paraplegics," *Sexual. Disabil.* **1**(4):252–260 (1978).
Comarr, A. E., and B. Gunderson: "Sexual Function in Traumatic Paraplegia and Quadriplegia," *Amer. J. Nurs.* **75**(2):250–255 (1975).
Diamond, M.: "Sexuality and the Handicapped," *Rehabil. Lit.* **35**:34–40 (1974).

Eisenberg, M. C., and L. Rustad: "Sex Education and Counseling Program on Spinal Cord Injury Service," *Arch. Phys. Med. Rehabil.* **57**:135–140 (1976).

Griffith, E. R., M. A. Tomko, and R. Timms: "Sexual Function in Spinal Cord Injured Patients: Review," *Arch. Phys. Med. Rehabil.* **54**:539–543 (1973).

Griffith, E. R., and R. Trieschmann: "Sexual Functioning in Women with Spinal Cord Injury," *Arch. Phys. Med. Rehabil.* **56**:18–21 (1975).

Guttman, L.: "Married Life of Paraplegics and Letraplegics," *Paraplegia* **2**:182–188 (1964).

Held, J., T. Cole, C. Held, R. Anderson, and R. Chilgren: "Sexual Attitude Reassessment Workshops: Effect on Spinal Cord Injured Adults, Their Partners and Rehabilitation Professionals," *Arch. Phys. Med. Rehabil.* **56**:14–18 (1975).

Higgins, G.: "Aspects of Sexual Response in Adults with Spinal Cord Injury: A Review of the Literature," in *Handbook of Sex Therapy,* J. LoPiccolo and L. LoPiccolo (eds.), Plenum, New York, 1978.

Hohmann, W.: "Considerations in Management of Psychosexual Readjustment in Cord Injured Males," *Rehabil. Psychol.* **19**:50–58 (1972).

Jackson, F. E.: "Pregnancy Complicated by Quadriplegia: Report of Case," *Obstet. Gynecol.* **23**:620–621 (1964).

Jackson, R. W.: "Sexual Rehabilitation after Cord Injury," *Paraplegia* **10**(1):50–55 (1972).

Jochheim, K. A., and N. Wahlen: "A Study of Sexual Function in 56 Male Patients with Complete Irreversible Lesions of the Spinal Cord and Cauda Equina," *Paraplegia* **8**(3):166–172 (1970).

Mayers, K.: "Sexual and Social Concerns of the Disabled: A Group Counseling Approach," *Sexual. Disabil.* **1**(2):100–111 (1978).

Money, J.: "Phantom Orgasm in Dreams of Paraplegic Men and Women," *Arch. Gen. Psychiatry* **3**:373–382 (1960).

Mooney, T. O., T. Cole, and R. Chilgren: *Sexual Options for Paraplegics and Quadriplegics,* Little, Brown, Boston, 1975.

Neumann, R.: "Sexuality and the Spinal Cord Injured: High Drama or Improvisational Theater?" *Sexual. Disabil.* **1**(2):93–99 (1978).

Romano, M. L., and R. Lassiter: "Sexual Counseling with Spinal Cord Injured," *Arch. Phys. Med. Rehabil.* **53**:568–572 (1972).

Rossier, A. B., M. Ruffieux, and W. H. Ziegler: "Pregnancy and Labour in High Traumatic Spinal Cord Lesion," *Paraplegia* **7**:210–216 (1969).

Rowan, R. L., T. F. Howley, and H. R. Nova: "Electroejaculation," *J. Urol.* **87**:726–729 (1962).

Sadlick, M., and F. B. Penta: "Changing Nurse Attitudes toward Quadriplegics through Using Television," *Rehabil. Lit.* **36**:274–278 (1975).

Sandowski, C. L.: "Sexuality and the Paraplegic," *Rehabil. Lit.* **37**:322–327 (1976).

Talbot, H. S.: "A Report on Sexual Function in Paraplegics," *J. Urol.* **61**:265–270 (1949).

Talbot, H. S.: "Sexual Function in Paraplegics," *J. Urol.* **73**:91–100 (1955).

Talbot, H. S.: "Psycho-social Aspects of Sexuality in Spinal Cord Injury Patients," *Paraplegia* **9**:37–39 (1971).

Wachs, H., and M. Zaks: "Studies of Body Images in Men with Spinal Cord Injury," *J. Nerv. Ment. Dis.* **131**:121–127 (1960).

Weber, D. K., and H. C. Weissman: "A Review of Sexual Function following Spinal Cord Trauma," *Phys. Ther.* **51**:290–294 (1971).

Chapter 18

Surgical Interventions

The broad area of surgical interventions that result from long- or short-term serious health disorders can create or aggravate existing sexual problems and concerns. Many of the surgeries will have followed a recent devastating diagnosis of cancer. Often the client will lack sufficient time to work through shock, anger, depression, and restitution of the loss of health status before another type of health disruption or loss is created by surgical intervention. Many of these problems will be associated with loss of a body part, loss of an internal organ , loss of body function, relocation of a body orifice, unsuccessful or complications of surgery, and facing the possibility of death.

One of the major differences between a health disruption arising as a result of a chronic illness and those occurring from surgical trauma is the lack of time for psychological preparation. Surgery is responsible for sudden major body change and the client may not have had the opportunity to internalize or deal with reality regarding what the impending body function and body image would be like. Preoperative teaching and learning often concentrates on the anxiety regarding the expected surgical procedure. Some people cannot deal with the feelings of mutilation and rejection until the surgery has actually created those feelings. Some clients have a denial system that maintains unrealistic hope and fantasy ''that it will not happen to me.'' Most people have not had experiences that are quite as devastating or potentially harmful to body image and sexuality as pelvic exenteration, colostomy, penectomy, or total prostatectomy. Some surgical procedures performed on the gynecological and urogenital systems do not interfere with nerves, blood supply, or hormonal supply but are quite often responsible for psychological reactions that interfere with sexual functioning.

Some problems arise primarily from an organic basis, others from a psychological basis and some from a combination of the two. How anger, shame, and guilt reactions are related to the loss are influenced by sexual values, past sexual experiences, and life-styles. There do not seem to be many clear predictions as to how a particular individual will function sexually following surgery. Most of the studies have been conducted postoperatively and claim that the greatest attribute for "successful" postsurgical sexuality is the quality of the preoperative sexual relationship. Helping people with feelings of being punished, gaining self-esteem, improving sexual relationships, and widening the concept of sexuality will continue to present unresolved interrelated physiological and psychological complications. This chapter will present a few of the most common types of surgical procedures that present the potential of postsurgical difficulty with sexuality. The chapter is organized around loss associated with sexuality due to (1) loss of external body part; (2) loss of internal body part; (3) loss of body function; and (4) relocation of a body orifice.

LOSS OF EXTERNAL BODY PART

Mastectomy: Loss of Breast

The exact number of mastectomies that have been performed on women presently living in the United States is not known. The estimates are increasing and are in the hundreds of thousands range.[1] It is estimated that 1 of every 13 women in America will develop breast cancer.[2] Radical mastectomy is one of the most likely treatments for cancer of the breast. A radical mastectomy involves amputation of the entire breast along with pectoral muscles and lymphatic tissue which extend into the inner aspect of the affected arm.

The breast is an important aspect of female identification for many women. Size and shape of breasts are often used to reflect sexual desirability. Much emphasis has been placed on breast measurement to determine the attractiveness and desirability of the female body for certain occupations, societal functions, and sexual partners. The assigned value of the breast by a woman is based on characteristics and attributes that formulate self-concept. If positive aspects are perceived as being mainly generated from the "female" physical appearance, then the breast will most likely be an important part of self-concept. If the positive aspects of self-concept originate from intellectual capabilities or physical activities, then the breast may not be considered of any more importance than other body parts in maintaining a sense of wholeness. Breast stimulation and specific breast manipulation is experienced as pleasurable for many couples. Many men and women place a high value on the female breasts and use them as a major source of arousal during sexual activity. Consequently, the loss of a breast and body mutilation may be a significant loss to many women and may be experienced as a loss by some sexual partners. The significance of the loss and change in body image require careful assessment to determine specific meanings and needs of each individual rather than placing the dominant societal value on all women having a mastectomy.

General preoperative information will include a careful description of the operation and the expected difficulties immediately following the operation. One of the first concerns of many women after surgery is to learn the extent of the disease and the success of the operation in relation to "getting it all." After these concerns have been satisfied, a postoperative regime usually includes early mobilization of the involved side, the wearing of a temporary prosthesis, and postoperative exercises with the goal of full range of motion.

The woman may need repeated reassurance and help to identify her needs in maintaining capabilities of womanhood and sexuality. For many women, there will be the same choices and problems that were experienced by her before the mastectomy. Both the client and partner may need to talk about their fears and anxieties in resuming sexual activity. Other couples may need to hear that there is little or no hazard of resuming sexual activity and that there is no expected change in the woman's ability to give and to accept pleasure. Financial strain may prove to be a burden for some sexual relationships.

Some women may need to allow time to mourn the loss and be comfortable with their new body image before they can feel comfortable in a sexual relationship. Undressing in front of a mirror and then in the presence of the sexual partner may be helpful for women with emotional concerns of body image. For most women, a rapid return to everyday activities, as a housewife, businesswoman, teacher, or whatever her roles include, helps promote the woman's feelings of control which in return reestablishes physical and psychic well-being.

Another factor that seems to influence sexual adaptation following a mastectomy is the age of the woman. Since women outlive their spouses by several years, a breast removal may be viewed as a handicap in developing new sexual relationships. Age and its consequences have not been studied in depth to develop more than speculative statements.

Woods and Earp make some interesting points in their discussion regarding social supports:

> Women who had high numbers of physical complications with which to cope did not seem significantly influenced by the availability of social supports. Thus, one could infer, social supports have a buffering effect on depression until a threshold of physical disability is reached. From that point, the social milieu becomes less important as a determinant of mental outlook. On the other hand, when physical complications fell below this threshold, the lack of available social supports appeared to be significantly associated with depression.[3]

Penectomy: Total and Partial

Total penectomy with permanent perineal urethrostomy in the treatment of extensive carcinoma results in impotence and sterility. A penectomy is often a profound blow to the male's sense of wholeness and integrity. This surgical intervention will usually produce feelings of bodily mutilation and helplessness. With extensive carcinoma, there is the potential of physical pain, change in body image, changes in the social and family structure from financial strain, and much concern about shortened life expectancy. The above stress areas may take precedence over sex activity. Nevertheless, it remains important to understand the special symbolic meaning of a highly prized possession of a penis and how the loss of this organ affects self-esteem and the energy needed for everyday living.

Following partial penectomy, clients retain the ability to have normal erection and ejaculation. However, the length of the penis has great significance to many men and any penile loss by surgical intervention is extremely traumatic to self-esteem as it will also affect sensory perceptions. The length of the remaining penis will determine the sensory loss. These clients may be candidates for consideration of penile prosthesis. However, it is extremely important that careful assessment and counseling be done before a penile prosthesis is implanted. "The surgical procedure may result in a penis capable of being inserted into a vagina, but the client's distress about relationship problems or his concern with personal adequacy may remain unchanged."[4]

LOSS OF INTERNAL ORGANS

Prostatectomy

Most male urologic clients are in midlife, past age 50, and certain physiological changes such as a slowing of erection, decreased seminal fluid volume, and diminished ejaculatory demand are normally occurring. The above changes do not prevent the man from performing sexually in a satisfactory manner. Although there is a lack of systematic epidemiologic investigations of cancer of the prostate, it is considered one of the most common types of cancer affecting the male. Study of the age-adjusted mortality rates per 100,000 population for prostatic cancer for 24 countries shows that the rates for the United States' nonwhite population between 1950 and 1965 exceeded those for all other countries.[5] With the overall population increasing in age it is most likely that cancer of the prostate will continue to be a health problem.

According to Blandy,[6] the object of any prostatectomy is to relieve a man's urinary symptoms. There are four classic surgical approaches to the prostate gland. The first type of modern-day surgery came in the late nineteenth century with the perineal approach first used by Young and Goodfellow. Another approach used was the suprapubic or transvesicular approach developed by Fuller and Foyer. In 1943 Miller introduced the retropubic approach. One of the most commonly used surgical techniques is the transurethral approach.[7] The operative method depends on the size of the prostate, degree of renal damage, age, and health status of the patient as well as the skill of the surgeon. Another important factor is whether the gland is cancerous and, if so, the extent of the cancer.

Removal of the prostate does not cause a reduction in sexual ability. However, the radical surgical procedure, the perineal approach to the prostate, usually results in impotency.

> Radical surgical procedures may involve a widespread area richly supplied with nerve fibers that join the sympathetic hypogastric plexus to form the nerves of erection (nervi erigentis). Surgery here may interrupt the fine filaments spread out over the lateral walls of the rectum and extending anteriorly to reach the prostate, bladder, and seminal vesicles from divisions of the spinal nerves S2, S3, and S4 all of which contribute to the pudic nerve. It is also significant that the pudic artery in Alcock's canal traverses this area and supplies the corpus cavernosum penis, penile skin, and glans penis.
>
> Surgery involving this nervi plexus thus may cause permanent sexual dysfunction; it does not, however, cause loss of libido. The sex glands and endocrine system are usually not disturbed, and hormonal titers remain normal.[8]

If the surgery is for benign hyperplasia, the client should understand that his sexual abilities will most likely be about the same as before surgery if the perineal approach or radical prostatectomy is not used. There will be retrograde ejaculation, through the incompetent bladder neck. Therefore, these men and their partners should be warned not to expect an external ejaculate. Following retrograde ejaculation, the urine will be cloudy due to the semen. Significant positive feelings and self-esteem should be sponsored by significant others to help prevent a self-fulfilling prophesy that sexual activity will terminate with surgical intervention.

Some clinicians believe that the sexual status of some patients may be enhanced by prostatectomy.[9] Finkle believes that there can be psychogenic gain from prostatectomy:

> In infrequent instances an impotent aging man may "regain" his potency following prostatectomy. Again, it is probably a psychological influence which leads to renewed potency following prostatectomy. Surgical ablation of the prostate by "removing a sick gland" does not, by itself, restore potency just as removal of the gland is uncommonly a cause of impotence.[10]

Gynecological Surgery

Gynecological surgical intervention may be the treatment of choice for pelvic inflammatory disease, cysts, and pelvic cancer. Huffman reports that patients who had reconstructive operations on genitalia (repair of cystourethrocele, rectocele, enterocele, or tightening of the uterine supports without hysterectomy) rarely inquired about postoperative sexual reactions. In 317 patients seen over a period of 1 year, only 10 reported a decrease of their sexual reactions, 40 stated that their sex life was better, and 267 found their sex life unchanged.[11] (See Table 18-1 for some common surgical interventions.)

A common misinterpretation of the woman and her male partner is that vaginal intercourse will be painful and impede recovery after any type of vaginal

Table 18-1   Common Gynecological Surgeries

Surgery	Procedure
Hysterectomy	Total removal of the uterus and cervix
Salpingo-oophorectomy	Removal of the fallopian tube and ovary
Vulvectomy	
Radical	Removal of the vulva, including the labia majora, labia minora, urinary meatus, clitoris, lower one-third of the vagina, and occasionally the rectum
With lymphadenectomy	Removal of pelvic, groin, and femoral lymph nodes
Simple	Wide excision, including the labia, clitoris, meatus, and around the lesion without going into the groin or around the rectum
Exenteration	
Total	Total abdominal hysterectomy, bilateral salpingo-oophorectomy, partial or total vaginectomy, cystectomy with formation of an ileal conduit, and removal of the rectum with formation of a colostomy
Anterior	All of the above with the exception of the removal of the rectum with formation of a colostomy
Posterior	All of the above except the cystectomy and formation of an ileal conduit

Source: Saunders, Ref. 12.

surgical intervention. In some instances all sexual contacts with partners have voluntarily ceased because the issue of sexuality has never been discussed. In a simple hysterectomy with the removal of the uterus and cervix, there is no physical reason why sexual relations should be altered after the healing of the operative site. The client should be told that menses will cease and pregnancy is not possible. Early lesions have an excellent prognosis with minimum risk of recurrence.

According to Donahue:

Only patients receiving experimental protocol chemotherapy with massive bone marrow suppression and hence open to infections should avoid vaginal coitus. . . . A major problem following radical gynecologic surgery is the shortened vagina. The trifone of the bladder as well as the sigmoid colon are densely adherent to the new vaginal apex. Penile thrusting may be painful. Describing coital positions alternative to the astride posture can be most helpful. The angle of penile thrust can be further altered with pillows beneath the buttocks. The sensation of more extensive penile compression can be obtained by moistening the inner aspects of thighs with a water soluble lubricant, and then keeping the thighs well abducted. A deeper vaginal barrel can be mimicked by encircling the penile shaft with one or both palms. In addition some women find the vaginal penetration from behind, between closely abducted lubricated thighs, increases their partner's pleasure. It is important to emphasize that the foreshortened vagina cannot be forcibly dilated and that dildos are hazardous.[13]

A radical vulvectomy usually removes many of the sensory perceptors that are located in the labia majora, labia minora, clitoris, and the lower part of the vagina. Other areas such as lips, breasts, thighs, and buttocks will need to become the main source of erogenous stimulation. In pelvic exenteration, with one or two excretory conduits, many of the problems and concerns will involve an altered body image, which will be discussed in the enterostomy section. If the woman has the interest and a willing partner, developing satisfactory options will come by experimenting and evaluating the source and degree of pleasure and comfort for each person involved in the relationship.

RELOCATION OF A BODY ORIFICE

Enterostomy

Body image appears to be a major concern and adjustment for those who have had a colostomy or an ileostomy. There is a major body loss of the anus and a boundary disturbance. The boundary must include the stoma which is physically compromising and psychologically threatening. In 1952, Sutherland et al. studied Rorschach interpretations of 57 patients who had survived for 1 or more years after resection for cancer of the rectum. In this population, the presence of depression, associated with the existence of the colostomy, was frequently reported as well as an altered perception and concept of the body image, hypochondriasis, and fear of social rejection.[14] Another study conducted by Orbach and Tallent of 48 people having colostomies indicated a body image disturbance. All the subjects who participated in this investigation expressed the opinion that their bodily form had been altered in a way destructive to their physical appearance. Patients believed that their bodily intactness and integrity had been violated, and as stated by the authors, "They also facilitated an implicit attempt to deny the reality of what had been constructed in front of the body."[15] Depression and anxiety about the conceptions of bodily damage and mutilation appear to be a central theme in the literature reporting reactions of those having had ostomy surgery.[16–18]

Although there is much written regarding the care of patients with ostomies, very little research has included sexuality. Lenneberg and Rowbotham in a study of 1425 persons who were interviewed claimed that they reluctantly abandoned the idea of including questions on sexual adaptation so as not to jeopardize answers to other questions. However, these investigators did include questions of a gynecological nature. The answers to those questions supported the clinical impression that pregnancy and birthing can be safely undertaken by women with an ileostomy.[19]

A few other studies have been conducted by physicians who most often asked questions about the frequency of erection and ejaculation or frequency of sexual intercourse. One of the first and most often quoted studies was conducted by Sutherland et al.[14] on the preoperative and postoperative sexual activity of 57 patients who had colostomies for cancer. Of the 29 males, 14 were totally impotent, 5 had decreased erectile strength, and only 7 had no change postoperatively. These authors found that both the youngest (33 years) and the oldest (77 years) experienced no change in sexual patterns. They report that women subjects were resistant to any discussion of sexual matters; consequently the results were obtained from only 14 subjects and reported in general terms:

> . . . it can be stated that whenever frigidity existed prior to operation, the women have used the colostomy as a justification for cessation of intercourse. It also appears that the colostomy is a deterrent to remarriage or new sexual contacts.[20]

Dlin et al.[21] conducted a questionnaire survey among 500 members of various ostomy associations. They found that the "typical" client with an ostomy maintains an interest in sex with no change in established sex practices or in capacity to enjoy sexual intercourse. The man suffers a slight decrease in ability to maintain an erection and the woman is less able to achieve multiple orgasm. They do not believe that colostomy and ileostomy change sexual practices as much as estimates have indicated.

Dyk and Sutherland[22] investigated the adaptation of the spouse and other family members to the colostomy patient. Lowered esteem for husband was expressed by wives in several ways. Complaints included reduction in income; inconveniences by irrigation time and bathroom routines, which were a source of embarrassment in social situations; feelings of shame and frustration. The authors concluded that the spouse is frequently the key to the patient's eventual success or failure to adjust to a satisfactory life.

Most of the literature about sex after ileostomy and colostomy has been about men. The physical damage to the parasympathetic and pudendal nerves is thought to be responsible for irreversible sexual damage. Erection is impaired if the nervi erigentes are severed or their essential branches totally destroyed. According to Lyons:

> In men, reduced sexual potency and impotence are common after removal of the rectum for cancer, particularly in the elderly, but impotence is rare at any age after rectal removal for colitis.[23]

In a study comparing ileostomy and permanent colostomy, Druss et al.[24] found that there was more organic impotence and genital anesthesia in the colostomy-carcinoma group than in the ileostomy-colitis group.

In women, the statistical relationship between orgasm and removal of the rectum is unknown.[25] Weinstein claims:

> In women, since sexual enjoyment depends locally in great part upon the intact pudendal nerve and its afferent sensory nerve fibers, an active sexual life with orgasm may be resumed after an abdominoperineal operation. Fortunately, in women, the pudendal nerve is well protected even if the entire rectum is removed. This nerve still conveys sexual stimuli to the brain where they are integrated into the sexual centers.[26]

It appears that radical surgery for cancer has disastrous consequences for feelings of body image, feelings of acceptance, and sexual performance and leaves the person with a loss of health status with a continuous threat of reoccurrence of cancer. Some clients will be treated postoperatively with radiation therapy or chemotherapy, which creates additional health problems and thus additional sexual problems.

NURSING INTERVENTIONS

The decision to have an operative procedure will result in varied reactions and responses and its significance depends on a variety of factors. The impact of a surgical procedure that is experienced by the client is greatly influenced by:

1 Diagnosis or the reason for surgery
2 Significance of the loss of childbearing or fertility
3 Knowledge of anatomy and physiology
4 Meaning, assumptions, and values of sexual identity
5 Type and rationale of premorbid sex activity

Each of the above will be discussed briefly with emphasis on nursing assessment and interventions.

Diagnosis or the Reason for Surgery

Responses to surgery are influenced by the amount of choice that is perceived by the client in undergoing or not undergoing a recommended surgical intervention. Was the decision based on choice or was it forced on the client due to a disease process? Genital cancer, a dreaded disease, may also be a threat to independence, physical comfort, and survival. The surgical intervention may provide some hope for the relief of pain or bleeding urinary symptoms and still create feelings of anger, despair, and guilt. "What did I do to deserve this?" is a common concern.

> The possible link between genital herpes infections and cancer, as well as the association between prenatal stilbestrol exposure and malignancy are issues frequently brought to the clinician.[27]

However, if the client makes a decision after prolonged pelvic pain or excessive bleeding, there may be feelings of relief and hopes of improving health after the surgical procedure. Those with cancer of the colon or rectum may feel that they had no viable alternatives.

Understanding that the amount of choice, the time for preoperative or anticipatory planning, and how expectancies and past sexual experiences influence the acceptance of the surgical interventions is crucial for therapeutic nurse assessment and intervention.

Awareness of the Significance of the Loss of Childbearing or Fertility

Some women and men will need to mourn the loss of the childbearing function. The significance of the loss will often depend on the wishes and expectations of the woman and partner for future pregnancy. However, some women view themselves "desexed" without the capability of conceiving even though there is no plan or wish for future pregnancies. Other women will enjoy the freedom from concern of an unwanted pregnancy and the annoyance of routine menses. The significance of the loss cannot be judged from the values and expectations of the health personnel. For example, it is not uncommon to hear a nurse say, "I cannot understand why Mrs. S. is so upset about a hysterectomy since she has four children that she does not take care of." The nurse who bases the significance of the loss of the childbearing function on the number of children without assessing what the hysterectomy means to the client and partner will have difficulty in being therapeutic. Suppose Mr. and Mrs. S. believe or presume that the capability of conceiving is necessary in order to be an adequate sex partner or to enjoy sex relations. In this instance, the number of children would not prove to be a valid measure for the significance of the loss.

In other situations the client may feel ambivalent and behaviors will not be consistent regarding the loss of childbearing. The nurse can be helpful in explaining and clarifying feelings and expectations of the loss. Mourning the loss of childbearing and fertility should be anticipated since this function is significant for many clients for a great variety of reasons. Again, the key to successful nursing intervention is awareness of one's own feelings and values and an accurate assessment of client's knowledge, attitudes, and perception of the loss.

Knowledge of Anatomy and Physiology

The understanding of the function of the organs that will be removed or damaged and what relevant complications might be expected is very important to most clients. Simple drawings or illustrations can be helpful in reviewing the structure of internal and external genital organs, their location in the body, and their function. Misconceptions and myths can be bothersome. Repeated sessions, alone and with partner, may be needed to increase understanding of the surgical intervention.

Meaning, Assumptions, and Values of Sexual Identity

Four dimensions which include biological gender, sexual orientation, sex role, and femininity-masculinity characteristics are usually considered in sexual identity. These dimensions are interrelated and difficult to isolate for individuals or for groups of men and women in different societal subgroups. The value placed on sex organs by self, partner, and society are not static and seem to change as needs of the society change. For example, in an agricultural society with needs of a population increase, the uterus or childbearing function may have different values than when this same society moves into an industrial status with decreasing resources and a need to limit the population. Sex role, aspects of femininity-masculinity, and perhaps sexual orientation are certainly personalized but influenced by society's needs, interpersonal relations, and past sexual experiences.

Type and Rationale of Premorbid Sex Activity

Not all sex premorbid activity is alike, nor does it always occur in a "healthy" heterosexual marital relationship that is blissful and satisfying. Premorbid sex activity may include extramarital, nonmarital, autosexual, and homosexual activities. How a vaginal surgical intervention will affect a woman with no interest in vaginal intercourse is very different from the woman who believes her partner will abandon her if vaginal intercourse is not possible, even for a short period during recovery. An older woman with no partner will have less fear of abandonment but may have fears of mutilation that would interfere with auto-eroticism or seeking new partners. Removal of the rectum may prove a very difficult decision for the male homosexual because of preferred anal sexual activity. There will be some clients who will be happy for a legitimate excuse not to have sexual relations. Partners may feel this is the time for extramarital relations. Determining what the client defines as sexual preference and problem solving to help maintain or find alternate methods requires that the nurse not be bound by a definite set of "appropriate or right ways" for sexual satisfaction.

LEARNING ACTIVITIES

Imagine yourself with a colostomy. Write in order of importance those factors that you believe will be most bothersome. Describe how the colostomy will affect your sexuality.

If you were "doomed" to develop cancer of the sexual-reproductive system, what would be your major concerns? Give your rationale for choosing each specific concern.

Compare and contrast the sexual difficulties of clients who have had the following surgical interventions: mastectomy, hysterectomy, colostomy, ileostomy, and prostatectomy.

REFERENCES

1 N. F. Woods and J. Earp, "Women with Cured Breast Cancer: A Study of Mastectomy Patients in North Carolina," *Nurs. Res.* **27**(5):284 (1978).
2 H. Seidman, "Cancer Statistics, 1978: Probabilities of Eventually Developing and Dying of Cancer," *Cancer* **28**:17–44 (1978).
3 Woods and Earp, op. cit., p. 284.
4 D. Bullard, J. Mann, H. Caplan, and J. Stoklosa, "Sex Counseling and the Penile Prosthesis," *Sexual. Disabil.* **1**(3):184 (1978).
5 R. Steele, "Sexual Factors in Prostatic Cancer," *Med. Aspects Hum. Sexual.* **6**(8):70 (1972).
6 J. P. Blandy, *Transurethral Resection,* Pitman, New York, 1971, p. 127.
7 J. Comins, "Sexual Dysfunction after Prostatectomy," unpublished paper, University of Wisconsin, Madison, 1975.

8 D. Labby, "Sexual Concomitants of Disease and Illness," *Postgrad. Med.* **58**(1):110 (1975).

9 P. H. Flocks and B. J. Begley, "Urologic Problems of the Elderly," *Geriatrics* **16**(6):261–271 (1961).

10 A. L. Finkle, "The Relationship of Sexual Habits to Benign Prostate Hypertrophy," *Med. Aspects Hum. Sexual.* **1**(10):24–25 (1967).

11 J. W. Huffman, "Sexual Reactions after Gynecological Surgery," *Med. Aspects Hum. Sexual.* **3**:48 (1969).

12 S. Saunders, "Irreversible Gynecological Health Problems in Relation to Sexual Activity," unpublished paper, School of Nursing of the University of Wisconsin, Madison, 1975.

13 V. Donahue, "Sexual Rehabilitation of Gynecologic Cancer Patients," *Med. Aspects Hum. Sexual.* **12**(2):52 (1978).

14 A. Sutherland, C. Orbach, R. Dyk, R. Bard, and M. Bard, "The Psychological Impact of Cancer and Cancer Surgery," *Cancer* **5**:857–872 (1952).

15 C. E. Orbach and N. Tallent, "Body Concepts after Colostomy," *Arch. Gen. Psychiatry* **12**:126–135 (1965).

16 B. M. Dlin, A. Perlman, and E. Ringold, "Psychosexual Response to Ileostomy and Colostomy," *AORN J.* **34**:77–84 (1969).

17 R. B. Druss, J. F. O'Connor, and L. O. Stern, "Psychologic Response to Colectomy, Part II: Adjustment to a Permanent Colostomy," *Arch. Gen. Psychiatry* **20**:419–427 (1969).

18 M. Wirsching, H. J. Druner, and G. Hermann, "Results of Psychosocial Adjustment to Long-Term Colostomy," *Psychoter. Psychosom.* **26**:245–256 (1975).

19 E. Lenneberg and J. L. Rowbotham, *The Ileostomy Patient,* Charles C Thomas, Springfield, Ill., 1970.

20 A. Sutherland, op. cit., pp. 857–872.

21 B. M. Dlin, A. Perlman, and E. Ringold, "Sex after Ileostomy and Colostomy," *Med. Aspects Hum. Sexual.* **6**(7):32–43 (1972).

22 R. Dyk and A. Sutherland, "Adaptation of the Spouse and Other Family Members to the Colostomy Patient," *Cancer* **9**(1):123–138 (1956).

23 A. Lyons, "Sex after Ileostomy and Colostomy," *Med. Aspects Hum. Sexual.* **9**(1):107 (1975).

24 Druss, op. cit., pp. 419–427.

25 Lyons, op. cit., p. 107.

26 M. Weinstein, "Sexual Function after Surgery in Rectal Cancer," *Med. Aspects Hum. Sexual.* **12**(9):54 (1978).

27 Donahue, op. cit., p. 51.

BIBLIOGRAPHY

Abitbol, M. M., and J. H. Davenport: "Sexual Dysfunction after Therapy for Cervical Carcinoma," *Am. J. Obstet. Gynecol.* **119**:181–189 (1974).

Alexander, N. B.: "Towards Independence with an Ostomy," *Queen's Nurs. J.* **16**:250 (1974).

Alvin, John F.: *Sexual Hygiene and Pathology,* Lippincott, Philadelphia, 1965.

Amelar, Richard D.: *Infertility in Men,* Davis, Philadelphia, 1966.

Baumrucker, George O.: *TUR Transurethral Prostatectomy,* Williams & Wilkins, Baltimore, 1968.

Beneventi, Francis A.: *Retropubic Prostatectomy,* Charles C Thomas, Springfield, Ill., 1954.

Binder, D. P.: *Sex, Courtship and the Single Ostomate,* United Ostomy Association, Los Angeles, 1973.

Blandy, John P.: *Transurethral Resection,* Pitman, New York, 1971.

Brenton, M.: "Sex and the Physically Handicapped," *Medicine,* 29–32 (1974).

Brown, R. S., V. Haddox, A. Posada, and A. Rubio: "Social and Psychological Adjustment following Pelvic Exenteration," *Am. J. Obstet. Gynecol.* **114**:162–171 (1972).

Cherkofsy, N., et al.: "Dx: Ulcerative colitis," *Nurs. Care* **8**:10–14 (1975).

Chezem, J.: "Urinary Diversion—Select Aspects of Nursing Management," *Nurs. Clin. North Am.* **11**:445–456 (1976).

Cohen, S.: "Sex and the Ostomate: The Management of Postoperative Impotence," *Ostomy Q.* **13**(4):25–27 (1976).

Cressy, M. K.: "Psychiatric Nursing Intervention with a Colostomy Patient," *Perspect. Psychiatr. Care* **10**(2):69–71 (1972).

Cutts, S. M.: "Nursing Care Study: Prostatectomy," *Nurs. Mirror* **135**:26–27 (1972).

Dahlen, C. P., and W. E. Goodwin: "Sexual Potency after Perineal Biopsy," *J. Urol.* **77**:660 (1957).

Davis, F., et al.: "Coping with a Colostomy—The Importance of the Nurse," *Nurs. Times* **70**:580–582 (1974).

Dericks, V. C.: "Nursing Practices That Affect the Dynamics of Rehabilitation for Patients with an Ostomy, Part 4," *ANA Clinical Session,* 1974, pp. 248–253.

Dericks, V. C.: "Nursing Care of the Patient with an Ostomy," in *Nursing Care of Patients with Ostomies and Pelvic Exenterations,* American Cancer Society Professional Education Publication, 1974.

Dlin, B. M., A. Perlman, and E. Ringold: "Sex after Ileostomy or Colostomy," *Med. Aspects Hum. Sexual.* **6**(7):32–43 (1972).

Druss, R. G., J. F. O'Connor, J. F. Prudden, and L. O. Stern: "Psychologic Response to Colectomy," *Arch. Gen. Psychiatry* **18**:53–59 (1968).

Druss, R. G., J. F. O'Connor, and L. O. Stern: "Psychologic Response to Colectomy: Part II, Adjustment to a Permanent Colostomy," *Arch. Gen. Psychiatry* **20**:419–427 (1969).

Dyk, R. B., and A. Sutherland: "Adaptation of the Spouse and Other Family Members to the Colostomy Patient," *Cancer* **9**:123–138 (1956).

Fazio, V.: *Sexual Dysfunction Following Rectal Surgery,* Squibb, 1977.

Finkle, Alex F.: "Sex after Prostatectomy," *Med. Aspects Hum. Sexual.* **1,2**:40–41 (1968).

Finkle, A. L., and T. G. Moyers: "Sexual Potency in Aging Males: IV, Status of Private Patients before and after Prostatectomy," *J. Urol.* **84**:152 (1960).

Finkle, A. L., and D. V. Prian: "Sexual Potency in Elderly Men before and after Prostatectomy," *JAMA* **196**:139–143 (1966).

Finkle, A. L., T. G. Moyers, M. I. Tobenkin, and S. J. Karg: "Sexual Potency in Aging Males. Frequency of Coitus among Clinic Patients," *JAMA* **170**:1391 (1959).

Gabe, J.: "Prostatectomy: Part 1," *Nurs. Times* **60**:1012 (1964).

Gabe, J.: "Prostatectomy: Part 2," *Nurs. Times* **60**:1049 (1964).

Gallagher, K.: "Body Image Changes in the Patient with a Colostomy," *Nurs. Clin. North Am.* **7**:669–676 (1972).

Glenn, James F., and William H. Boyer (eds.): *Urologic Surgery,* Hoeber-Harper, New York, 1969.

Gold, F. M., et al.: "Sexual Potency following Simple Prostatectomy," *N.Y. State J. Med.* **69**:2987–2989 (1969).

Golub, S.: "When Your Patient's Problem Involves Sex," *RN Magazine,* March 1975, pp. 27–33.

Gorman, W.: *Body Image and the Image of the Brain,* Green, St. Louis, 1969.

Grifer, A. P.: "Loss of Sexual Function in the Male," in B. Schoenberg, A. Carr, D. Perltz, and A. Kutscher (eds.), *Loss and Grief: Psychological Management, Medical Practice,* Columbia, New York, 1970.

Gruendemann, B. J.: "The Impact of Surgery on Body Image," *Nurs. Clin. North Am.* **10**:635–643 (1975).

Harrell, H. C.: "To Lose a Breast," *Am. J. Nurs.* **72**:676–677 (1972).

Jackson, B. S.: "Colostomate's Reactions to Hospitalization and Colostomy Surgery," *Nurs. Clin. North Am.* **11**:417–425 (1976).

Kasselman, M. J.: "Nursing Care of the Patient with Benign Prostatic Hypertrophy," *Am. J. Nurs.* **66**:1026 (1966).

Katona, E.: "Patient-Centered, Living-Oriented Approach to the Patient with an Artificial Anus or Bladder," *Nurs. Clin. North Am.* **2**:623–634 (1967).

Kaufman, Joseph J.: "Urologic Factors in Impotence and Premature Ejaculation," *Med. Aspects Hum. Sexual.* **1,2**:43–48 (1967–1968).

Kolb, L. C.: "Disturbances of the Body-Image," in Silvano Arieti (ed.), *American Handbook of Psychiatry,* Basic Books, New York, 1975.

Kothari, D. R., et al.: "An Implantable Fluid Transfer System for Treatment of Impotence," *J. Biomech.* **5**(6):567–570 (1972).

Krizinofski, M. T.: "Symposium on the Patient with Long-Term Illness, Human Sexuality and Nursing Practice," *Nurs. Clin. North Am.* **8**:673–681 (1973).

Lenneberg, E., and J. L. Rowbotham: *The Ileostomy Patient,* Charles C Thomas, Springfield, Ill., 1970.

Lynn, Jack M., and Reed M. Nesbit: "The Influence upon the Incidence of Epididymitis following Transurethral Resection," *J. Urol.* **59**:72 (1948).

McCloskey, J.: "How to Make the Most of Body Image Theory in Nursing Practice," *Nursing '76,* May 1976, pp. 68–72.

MacRae, I., and G. Henderson: "Sexuality and Irreversible Health Limitations," *Nurs. Clin. North Am.* **10**(3):587–597 (1975).

Melody, G.: "Depression Reactions following Hysterectomy," *Am. J. Obst. Gynecol.* **83**:410–413 (1962).

Meyer, B. C., and A. S. Lyons: "Rectal Resection: Psychiatric and Medical Management of Sequelae: Report of a Case," *Psychosom. Med.* **19**:152–157 (1957).

"Middle Aged Male Crisis," *Med. Aspects Hum. Sexual.* **1,2**:6–13 (1968).

Mossholder, Irene B.: "When the Patient Has a Radical Retropubic Prostatectomy," *Am. J. Nurs.* **62**:101–104 (1962).

Mullens, J. E.: "Sexuality in Ostomates," *ET J.* **2**(3):1 (1975–1976).

Norris, C. M.: "The Professional Nurse and Body Image," in Carolyn Carlson (ed.), *Behavioral Concepts and Nursing Interventions,* Lippincott, Philadelphia, 1970.

Norris, C., and E. Gambrell: *Sex, Pregnancy and the Female Ostomate,* United Ostomy Association, Los Angeles, 1972.

Orbach, C. E., and N. Tallent: "Body Concepts after Colostomy," *Arch. Gen. Psychiatry* **12**:126–135 (1962).

Pearman, R. D.: "Insertion of a Silastic Penile Prothesis for the Treatment of Organic Sexual Impotence," *J. Urol.* **107**:802 (1972).

Prudden, J. F.: "Psychological Problems following Ileostomy and Colostomy," *Cancer* **28**:236–238 (1971).

Purdy, Angus: "Prostatic Tumors: Part II, Nursing Care," *Am. J. Nurs.* **56**:986–987 (1956).

Roen, Phillip R.: *Roen Atlas of Urologic Surgery*, Meredith, New York, 1967.

Rowbotham, J. L.: "Advances in Rehabilitation of Stoma Patients," *Cancer* **36**:702–704 (1975).

Roy, P. H., W. G. Sauer, O. H. Beahrs, and G. M. Farrow: "Experience with Ileostomies: Evaluation of Long-Term Rehabilitation in 497 Patients," *Am. J. Surg.* **119**:77–86 (1970).

Rush, A. M.: "Cancer and the Ostomy Patient," *Nurs. Clin. North Am.* **11**:405–415 (1976).

Sanders, Virginia E., and John G. Keuhnelian: *Urologic Nursing*, Macmillan, New York, 1970.

Schilder, P.: *The Image and Appearance of the Human Body*, Kegan Paul, Trench, Trubner, London, 1935.

Schmidt, Stanwood S., and Frank Hinman: "The Effect of Vasectomy upon the Incidence of Epididymitis after Prostatectomy: An Analysis of 810 Operations," *J. Urol.* **63**:872 (1950).

Small, S. M.: "Validation of Libido Theory," *Psychiatr. Q.* **27**:38–51 (1953).

Stahlgren, L. H., and L. K. Ferguson: "Influence on Sexual Function of Abdominoperineal Resection for Ulcerative Colitis," *N. Engl. J. Med.* **259**:873–875 (1958).

Sutherland, A. M., C. E. Orbach, R. B. Dyk, and M. Bard: "The Psychological Impact of Cancer and Cancer Surgery: Adaptation to the Dry Colostomy: Preliminary Report and Summary of Findings," *Cancer* **5**:857–872 (1952).

Turner, Roderick, and E. Belt: "A Study of 299 Consecutive Cases of Total Perineal Prostatectomy for Cancer of the Prostate," *J. Urol.* **77**:62 (1957).

Vukovich, V., and R. D. Grubb: *Care of the Ostomy Patient*, Mosby, St. Louis, 1973.

Wirsching, M., H. U. Druner, and G. Herrmann: "Results of Psychosocial Adjustment to Long-Term Colostomy," *Psychother. Psychosom.* **26**:245–256 (1975).

Woods, N. F.: "Alteration of Body Image and Sexual Adaptation: Enterostomy, Mastectomy, and Hysterectomy," in *Human Sexuality in Health and Illness*, Mosby, St. Louis, 1975.

Woods, N. F., and J. L. Earp: "Woman with Cured Breast Cancer: A Study of Mastectomy Patients in North Carolina," *Nurs. Res.* **27**(5):279–285 (1978).

Young, Hugh: "Conservative Perineal Prostatectomy," in *Classical Articles in Urology*, compiled and edited by Mark A. Inmergood, with comment by Hugh J. Jewitt, Charles C Thomas, Springfield, Ill., 1967, pp. 179–193.

Chapter 19

Sexuality and Dying

This brief chapter proposes the idea that sexuality is an important component in the lives of the terminally ill. The effect of the illness on the partner also is presented, along with guidelines for therapeutic intervention by nurses.

Sex and death may seem at first, at least, to be unrelated or even opposite events. Parents neglect death education much as they neglect sex education, and society avoids honest discussion about sexuality and dying. Certainly, sex is healthy for the living, but can it possibly also be healthy for the dying?

Individuals who are very old or who are terminally ill need loving concern and physical affection as much or more than do healthy people. Whether this kind of loving includes genital sex is entirely an individual matter. Lovemaking styles vary, but sexual needs remain even when the person is facing death. Some people merely want to be embraced and caressed. Other individuals may desire more sexual contacts than before their illness. Sex may be used as a means to decrease anxiety, increase self-esteem, or even to deny the fact that they are dying. Positive sexuality is a revitalizing and reassuring experience for healthy and ill people alike.

Factors which interfere with sexual expression of the terminally ill include the following:[1]

1 The previous experience of the patient and the partner with sex and death

2 The attitudes of family and care givers toward sexual expression in general

3 The presence or absence of physical pain or decreased range of motion

4 The attitude of family and care givers. Is the individual seen as "one of the living" or seen as "the dying patient"?

5 The perception of hope for the future

6 The official and nonofficial policies of institutions in regard to sexual expression, privacy, and the maintenance of personal dignity

Some individuals who are dying may withdraw from sexual experiences. Keleman[2] proposes a psychodynamic reason for avoiding sexuality:

> The orgastic state that produces feelings of ecstasy is a surrendering to the involuntary and to the unknown. Orgasm requires giving ourselves over to what is occurring in us. . . . The orgastic state also produces feelings of dying, raises fears of dying, because the social awareness may be threatened by the involuntary.

Even if the total involvement of orgasm does not occur, the withdrawal may occur for other reasons. The giving and receiving of pleasure may simply seem incongruous or inappropriate to the couple. Or the couple may need all their energy just to cope with the crisis of dying.

The healthy partner often experiences conflict centered around sexuality and sexual intercourse. Emotional separation as a means of anticipatory grieving causes a concomitant sexual separation. Some partners fear that they might "catch" the illness or even that death itself is contagious. Others, like the author of the following excerpt, are confused by conflicting feelings of love and hate, attachment and separation, selflessness and selfishness. The author is beginning the "letting go" process, and is experiencing anticipatory grief.

> We made love for the last time that summer. Ever since Martin had come back from Florida, lovemaking had had a particular sweetness. We knew there wasn't much more. And often, when it was over and we were lying together peacefully, I would suddenly experience such a turmoil of emotions that I didn't know how to handle them. I felt love, and the delicious sense of physical fatigue; I felt hate that the man who could make me feel this way was leaving me; I felt anxiety that it might be too much for him, fear that we might never do it again. And shame, shame for feeling this way. After all, I was healthy. Martin was dying. I knew he didn't want to die. How could I always be thinking of myself?[3]

Guilt about having sexual interest despite illness can affect either the partner or the patient. Both can also become depressed because of decreased opportunity for sexual expression. Hospitals and nursing homes, by their very nature, inhibit intimacy between sexual partners, thus compounding their guilt and frustration. The institution reflects the opinion of the culture: " . . . the terminally ill individual will neither be interested nor able to function effectively in sex.''[4] The ill person may respond to this attitude as a self-fulfilling prophecy, and become as disinterested and ineffective as is expected. If impending death has been concealed from the patient by well-meaning family and care givers, the ill individual will be further confused and angered by the behavior of those around him or her. If the patient is unaware that he or she is dying, the patient will be unable to explain the changes in levels of intimacy that are experienced. The emotional and physical estrangement may cause fantasies or rationalizations which are entirely unfounded in reality. The worst of these might be that the well partner no longer loves the ill person. Despair and hopelessness could result.

Guilt feelings in the healthy partner can also arise if sex is physically painful to the ill partner. Pain with intercourse may be caused by the disease process itself, by surgical intervention, or by drug effects. If range of motion is impaired, the partners may have to alter their usual coital positions and even their customary roles as active or passive sexual partners. Genital surgery or conditions may preclude intercourse entirely, and for some couples it will take time to learn new modes of expression.

NURSING INTERVENTION

The following suggestions for health care providers are adapted from Jaffe.[5]

1 Promote the idea that sex is good. (If nurses do not believe that sex is good, it will be difficult for them to convince others.)

2 Promote honest, complete, and loving communication about sex and about death. This communication begins in childhood with the death of pets or friends or family members and with the earliest interactions about sexuality. In order to accomplish this openness, parents may need help from the nurse in the form of reading resources, constructive conversation, and role modeling of behavior.

3 Educate other care givers, including physicians, volunteers, and nursing assistants, about sexuality and the terminally ill. Emphasize that the approach to each patient be individualized, but that most patients and families do want to talk about sexuality and terminality.

4 Emphasize to care givers and to family members that death is not contagious, and cannot be caught by intimate contact with the ill person.

5 Change the hospital environment to promote tenderness and intimacy, not abandonment. If possible, perhaps hospice or home care is preferable to the hospital. These systems promote loving care within the family and death with dignity.[6]

6 Provide a comfortable place for the well partner of the hospitalized patient. A reclining chair or an adjacent bed are best. If privacy is desired by the couple, a ''Do not disturb'' sign should be provided and must be honored by nurses and doctors alike.

7 Take a sexual history for the ill patient. Give information, permission, and specific suggestions when appropriate.

    a Information might include anticipatory guidance about sexual interest, sexual performance, the effects of drugs or treatments on sexuality, the effects of fatigue.

b   Specific suggestions might include self-pleasuring for the patient and partner, use of manual stimulation or a vibrator, or change in coital position.

8 Promote recreation and play activities if possible. Remember the relationship between appearance and morale.

9 Promote a team approach to the care of each patient. The care givers at night should be particularly sensitive to the feelings of loneliness and separation experienced by the terminally ill.

10 Encourage the well partner to give care, to touch, and to be intimate. Avoid becoming a "surrogate spouse" for the dying person. However, if the partner is unable or unwilling to give physical care, help to prevent the guilt which may be caused by the abdication of this role.

LEARNING ACTIVITIES

1 How did you learn about death? How could your education about dying have been improved?

2 Discuss your intervention in the following case: Mr. and Mrs. W. have been married for 36 years. In taking a sexual history, Mr. W. says they have not had intercourse for 6 years, "ever since she had that surgery for cancer."

3 Compare and contrast your feelings about sexual intimacy in the hospital for the following people:

a   A 16-year-old victim of Hodgkins' disease and his 15-year-old girlfriend

b   A 45-year-old patient with cancer of the vulva, scheduled for pelvic exenteration, and her husband

c   An 85-year-old man with pneumonia and his wife

d   A 35-year-old married man with leukemia and his girlfriend

4 Think about the experience of a family member who was hospitalized or who died in a hospital. How could nurses have promoted family intimacy?

REFERENCES

1   L. Jaffe, "Sex and the Terminally Ill," in H. L. Gochros (ed.), *The Sexually Oppressed,* Associated Press, New York, 1977.
2   S. Keleman, *Living Your Dying,* Random House, New York, 1974, p. 119.
3   Lynn Caine, *Widow,* Morrow, New York, 1974, p. 41.
4   Jaffe, op. cit.
5   Ibid.
6   B. J. Ward, "Hospice Home Care Program," *Nurs. Outlook* **26**:646–649 (1978).

Part Five

Advanced Intervention
and Research

Chapter 20

Education Programs

SEXUALITY IN NURSING

All previous chapters have heavily emphasized teaching and learning. Most chapters, directly or indirectly, imply that sex education has many components and requires a process that is influenced by the individual, family, school, community, and society.

Effective education in sexual health requires experiences and preparation in the *cognitive, affective,* and *transmittal* components. These three components are interrelated and somewhat dependent on each other. The cognitive component centers on information, research data, and a basic understanding of biological and psychological sexual development and functions. The affective component deals with the sexual feelings, concerns, and anxieties of self and others. The transmittal component is concerned with examining and learning various communication techniques useful in sex-related situations and applying them appropriately.[1]

How can these learning needs be met?

The *cognitive component* includes sexual anatomy, physiology, psychosexual development, psychosocial behavior, sexual variations, and the effects of drugs, disease, stress, and physical handicaps on sexual behavior. The cognitive content is usually obtained by lecture and discussion, audiovisual materials, readings, and from interactions in everyday living experiences.

The *affective component* is highly dependent on exposure and on opportunity to interact with others regarding feelings and attitudes about explicit sexual behaviors, issues, and controversial subjects. Explicit sexual films are often used to desensitize feelings and value judgments concerning sexual functions, processes, images, ideas, and practices. After viewing films that are explicit or controversial, small groups of students share their feelings, values, and conflicts regarding these topics. Increasing tolerance and understanding of attitudes and values different from one's own is a sensitization process. Writing an anonymous, introspective paper describing one's self as a sexual person helps to deal with the affective component. Some of the suggested factors to be considered by the student when writing the paper are:

1 How and when I first learned about sex
2 My feelings about being reared as a female (or male)
3 How my religious and moral beliefs affect my sexuality
4 My feelings about my current sexual activities
5 What I like most about my sexual self
6 What I like least about my sexual self
7 What I expect from my sexual self in the future

The affective component may be enhanced if these papers can be shared in a group. If the environment is too risky, then the student files them away in a drawer and examines the same topics at a later date. Exercises suggested at the end of several of the chapters and the problem-oriented vignettes deal with the affective and transmittal components.

The *transmittal component* relies heavily on the assessment, intervention, evaluation, and communication skills. The level of competence depends on former communication skills and the integration of the cognitive and affective components of sexuality. Role playing is an effective teaching strategy; each student participates as both the interviewer and as the client in investigating simulated sexual difficulties.

The Mims-Swenson Sexual Health Model provides a framework for an orderly sequence and a systematic approach to the education process for both self and clients and for program development. After having covered the content and engaged in the affective exercises in this book, it is expected that the student, with the help of peers and instructors, will be able to assess cognitive, affective, and transmittal skill levels of self. It is expected that some students will require additional study and experiences before they can attempt the nursing process beyond the basic level of the model. Some students may find that they are able to integrate some content successfully at the intermediate or advanced level of the nursing process. It is hoped that all students will have learned a great deal about self; they can acknowledge and communicate to others about any area to which it has been difficult or impossible to apply the nursing process higher than at the life experience level.

Other students will find that they can be comfortable with specific topics and know the material, but still have not mastered the transmittal skills of helping clients problem-solve around sexuality content. Or the student may find that the transmittal problem lies with "who" is having the problem (e.g., a young student, knowledgeable and comfortable with most topics of sexuality, may find it next to impossible to talk with a grandmother figure about sexual concerns). For this type of student, giving oneself permission to have additional time and experiences will probably be most prudent and beneficial for professional development.

Looking at self through autobiographies or by using attitude scales and knowledge tests at the beginning of a course of instruction provides both the student and instructor with guidelines for program development. These same tools can also provide pre- and post-self and course evaluations. Peer evaluations of transmittal skills in role playing sessions can usually provide each student with a fairly accurate assessment of functioning level in each content area.

After accurate assessment of the level of functioning, the student can transfer these skills to client populations. As noted in previous chapters of this book, educational opportunities for nurse-client interaction abound at the basic and intermediate levels of the model. Sexual health care of clients with specific health disruptions has been discussed. These same approaches can be modified to meet the needs of clients with other health disruptions, such as arthritis, renal failure, and alcoholism. Helping clients with any type of health problem that alters sexuality requires basic knowledge, comfort with the subject, respect for the client, effective communication skills, and problem-solving ability.

Since the previous chapters have concentrated on teaching and learning at the basic and intermediate levels of the model, the remainder of this chapter will highlight some of the opportunities and difficulties at the advanced level. A summary of three different kinds of programs is used to demonstrate education programs for selected populations.

PROGRAMS FOR SELECTED POPULATIONS

Children with Chronic Illness and the Developmentally Disadvantaged

Children with chronic illness and the developmentally disadvantaged require that people who plan and engage in sex education programs have many competencies. These professionals must be comfortable with the disability, be comfortable with their own sexuality, have knowledge and skill in health care of the specific disability, and have adequate preparation in specific communication skills (e.g., for blindness or deafness). These children may be victims of overprotectiveness or of avoidance regarding all aspects of their sexuality. Parents may need special help to recognize that overprotection or denial of the child's sexuality will produce an individual unprepared for interdependent adult relationships. "Society" has been prone to label the developmentally disabled as "not interested in sex" or as oversexed and dangerous. With this stigma and labeling, society has negated the need for sex education for this important group of people. Some parents and professionals are beginning to recognize that the physically and mentally disabled are sexual beings with the same desires, curiosities, hopes, and expectations as any other group of people.[2] Groups of children and parent groups with a sex education focus have proven successful in promoting awareness of the interaction of perceptions, attitudes, and cognitions around many sexual topics. The curriculum should be developed around each group's needs and goals while integrating the strengths of each group member.

Suggested curricula concepts for the developmentally disadvantaged were made by SIECUS in 1971 and are described by Spurr as:

1   Awareness of self—becoming a boy; becoming a girl; content emphasizes the role of the individual in relation to his or her environment. Identifying and recognizing parts of the body receives repetitive emphasis.
2   Physical changes and understanding of self—becoming a man; becoming a woman; bodily changes which occur during puberty and early adolescence are stressed. Students are introduced to the meaning of menstruation, intercourse, masturbation.
3   Peer relationships—boyfriends and girlfriends, with emphasis on responsibility in relationship. Important topics are dating, masculine roles, feminine roles, and family relations.
4   Responsibilities to society as men and women—contrast different lifestyles (single, married, etc.) and responsibilities of each option.

The content is presented in order of difficulty and represents the developmental needs of the different age groups.[3]

Many parents perceive that they lack knowledge and skill in how to teach their child about his or her potential for sexual functioning. In small groups parents can learn from each other. The group leader can provide and make suggestions for applying needed information. Some parents find written materials specific to the age and health condition of their child more beneficial than a group experience. A large quantity of material is being developed and produced; however, the quality of much of this material has not been tested and may not be specific enough to help many clients. Nurses with the interest and skills in developing sex education materials for this very variable population will find a fertile field for a long time to come. In some areas nursing students involved in school programs for the developmentally disadvantaged have observed that this population receives a more comprehensive approach to sex education than the remainder of the student population. They would recommend that these programs be expanded to the entire student population.

The Elderly

Another group of people who have been somewhat neglected in sex education is the elderly. As people age, the goals for sex education remain about the same as for younger adults, but it becomes increasingly difficult to acknowledge the need. "Everybody expects the elderly to know it all or know nothing and act asexual." In the past, many elderly people have resigned themselves to the prevalent taboos and stereotypes. Some elderly citizens are beginning to demand their rights. They insist that taboos and labels are no longer productive and interfere with intimate and empathic relationships.

Programs for the older citizen can assist in changing negative attitudes, removing negative sexual self-labels, and enhancing relationships. The change in attitude from sex is for the young and the "crazy or dirty old man" to sex is fun, enjoyable, and another way of expressing affection can be managed with groups or several older couples. This permission giving and change in attitudes toward sex has the potential to boost the mental health of this group of citizens.

Small group sessions of elderly couples can explore:

1 Current feelings about sex life
2 Dynamics of various types of relationships
3 Degree of change desired
4 Stereotypes and taboos versus accurate knowledge
5 Current concerns

Some aging people find it challenging to compare, and help find suitable solutions for, couples who are using or withholding sex as a punishment or as a power struggle within a marital relationship. Other couples enjoy sharing fantasies or like to report on an X-rated movie. Couples may be expected to design homework exercises that are the exact opposite of their routine behaviors. For example, the couple who has had sex relations at 10 P.M. on Saturday night, in the same bed, using the same position for the past 15 years, may be expected to share the experience of lovemaking on the living room floor, in front of the fireplace, to help replicate the playfulness and intrigue of earlier years in their lives.

Programs designed and restricted to the elderly give permission, supply information, and offer suggestions that are unique to this population. The outcomes of such programs can be evaluated in terms of liberating the elderly to engage in open communication, to change problem behaviors, and to enjoy their sexuality.

The above are only a few examples of the many groups of clients who could benefit from sex education programs. As was noted in Chap. 2, several studies have indicated that nursing schools, until the last few years, have not offered education programs that provide knowledge and clinical skills in human sexuality. A study of a continuing education program of 93 multidisciplinary health professionals, including 52 nurses, indicated that only 35 percent had experienced any type of sex education and only 6 percent had sex education past the high school level.[4] The need for workshops and inservice education programs for nurses and other health professionals is apparent if health care providers plan to include sexual health as part of total health care. Below is a summary of an example of a continuing education program conducted by the authors for nursing personnel at the University Hospitals, Wisconsin-Madison.

Nursing Personnel: Continuing Education

The population of most sexuality workshops in continuing education programs is a group of nurses who have not been exposed to education opportunities at the basic level and consequently are functioning at the life experience level. The primary objective of these programs is to explore attitudes, myths, and fallacies about sexuality. The other objectives revolve around improving self-comfort, awareness, cognitions, and the ability to communicate about common sex-related problems or issues in health care settings. The Mims-Swenson Sexual Health Model provides a theoretical framework from which to plan and implement the program. With a review of sex education history, it is easy for participants to acknowledge that they are operating at the life experience level and that some of their behaviors are more than likely destructive in health care delivery. The Sexual Health Model sets up the expectation of a realistic change from the life experience level to the basic level and places the focus on awareness, which is composed of an interaction of perceptions, attitudes, and cognitions.

Knowledge, attitudes, and perceptions can be clarified through various exercises. A discussion may be facilitated by passing out cards on which myths, value statements, and/or questions have been printed. The following are examples:

1 Love is essential to satisfying sex.
2 Sexual offense occurs because the offender is oversexed.
3 What makes a man/woman sexy?

Each group member is handed a card and is expected to share his or her values and attitudes about the statement or question. By this process the participant has an opportunity to increase self-awareness and to receive feedback from others with different values and attitudes. The participants must experience a safe environment so that they will take the opportunity to expose their attitudes and be willing to increase their tolerance and understanding of the attitudes of others.

Audiovisual material also serves to increase knowledge to desensitize, and to facilitate further discussion on values and attitudes. The Concept Media slide series on *Human Sexuality and Nursing Practice* provides common behavioral reactions of health personnel toward sex-related issues and gives fairly up-to-date information regarding sexuality in a variety of health conditions. This series gives nurses permission to try out new behaviors in their own health settings.

A word exercise similar to the "vocabulary brainstorming" technique described by Morrison and Price can be worthwhile in some professional groups. The objectives stated by Morrison and Price are (1) to provide a structure for sharing feelings about explicit vocabulary; (2) to lower inhibitions, energize members, and increase group cohesiveness; and (3) to legitimize the use of explicit sexual vocabulary.[5] The participants are asked to form groups of four or five and make a list of synonyms for penis, vagina, foreplay, sexual intercourse, and breasts. These lists are written on the blackboard and added to by other group members. Questions such as which words are most offensive and why, how do the words make you feel, and how would you react if a client used these words are raised. The importance of learning and desensitizing self to the language of sexuality in order to effectively communicate with clients with different backgrounds and needs can be emphasized.

Role playing, behavioral rehearsal, or role reversal can provide the opportunity to practice specific clinical situations. The goal of these exercises is to shape appropriate responses and to decrease maladaptive anxiety. The group will often supply relevant role-playing situations from their own clinical experiences. The seductive patient is often presented as a problem and the leader can demonstrate an appropriate way of handling the situation, or one of the members can demonstrate the way it is most often handled in the clinical setting, to facilitate further discussion.

Handouts and printed materials can be used to provide updated information on special topics of interest. Generally an evaluation form is used as one method of determining the effectiveness of the workshop. Pre- and post-attitude and knowledge scales can also be used. Nehls summarized her student experience as a leader of a continuing education program as:

> The need to be fast, flexible, a bit entertaining, and very knowledgeable of the subject area of sexuality and of group process are essential to a leader's presentation of an excellent workshop. The process of planning, implementing, and evaluating this workshop was a valuable learning experience for me. It was risk-taking, frustrating, frightening and challenging.[6]

The final chapter explores other educational opportunities in the context of therapy and research. These three advanced skills are interrelated and are often difficult to separate. Sometimes education programs look like therapy and sometimes therapy looks like an education program. Research and evaluation are important components of both education and therapy.

LEARNING ACTIVITIES

1   Discuss the qualifications that would be needed to write objectives and develop an education program for a group of sex offenders, menopausal women, preschool children, and nursing home residents.

2   What skills do you have that will be an asset in providing leadership in the sexuality education programs? What are your liabilities?

3 Evaluate or critique this book regarding strengths and weaknesses and send your response to: Professor Fern H. Mims and Melinda Swenson, 600 Highland Avenue, University of Wisconsin-Madison, Madison, Wisconsin 53792.

4 Write the objectives and develop a program for your next learning experience in sexuality.

REFERENCES

1 F. Mims, "Sexuality in the Nursing Curriculum," *Nurse Educator,* March/April 1977, pp. 20–23.

2 D. Fitzgerald and M. Fitzgerald, "Deaf People Are Sexual Too," *SIECUS Rep.* **VI**(2):13 (1977).

3 G. A. Spurr, "Sex Education and the Handicapped," *J. Sex Educ. Ther.* **2**(2):23–26 (1976).

4 F. Mims, "Human Sexuality Workshop: A Continuing Education Program," *J. Contin. Educ. Nurs.* **9**(6):29–37 (1978).

5 E. S. Morrison and M. V. Price, *Values in Sexuality—A New Approach to Sex Education,* Hart, New York, 1974.

6 N. Nehls, "Human Sexuality Workshop for Nurses' Aides—A Project Report,"unpublished paper, University of Wisconsin-Madison, 1978, p. 24.

BIBLIOGRAPHY

Brower, H. T., and L. A. Tanner: "A Study of Older Adults Attending a Program on Human Sexuality: A Pilot Study," *Nurs. Res.* **28**(1):36–40 (1979).

Downey, G. W.: "Sexuality in a Health Care Setting," *Mod. Health Care* **5**(5):20–27 (1976).

Eisenberg, M. G., and J. Falconer: "Current Trends in Sex Education Programming for the Physically Disabled: Some Guidelines for Implementation and Evaluation," *Sexual. Disabil.* **1**(1):6–15 (1978).

Held, J. P., and P. P Rosenberg: "The Care and Feeding of Small-Group Leaders of Sex Discussion Groups," *J. Sex Marital Ther.* **4**(4):292–297 (1978).

Kempton, W.: "Sex Education for the Mentally Handicapped," *Sexual. Disabil.* **1**(2):137–145 (1978).

Lief, H. I., and T. Payne: "Sexuality—Knowledge and Attitudes," *Am. J. Nurs.* **75**(11):2026–2029 (1975).

Megenity, J.: "A Plea for Sex Education in Nursing Curriculums," *Am. J. Nurs.* **75**(7):1171 (1975).

Mims, F. H.: "Human Sexuality Workshop: A Continuing Education Program," *J. Contin. Educ. Nurs.* **9**(6):29–37 (1978).

Mims, F. H.: "Sexuality in the Nursing Curriculum," *Nursing Education* March-April 1977, pp. 20–23.

Mims, F. H., L. Brown, and R. Lubow: "Human Sexuality Course Evaluation," *Nurs. Res.* **25**(3):187–192 (1976).

Mims, F. H., and M. Swenson: "A Model to Promote Sexual Health Care," *Nurs. Outlook* **26**(2):121–125 (1978).

Mims, F. H., R. Yeaworth, and S. Hornstein: "Effectiveness of an Interdisciplinary Course in Human Sexuality," *Nurs. Res.* **23**(3):248–253 (1974).

Money, J., and H. Alexander: "Films for Sex Education," *J. Sex Educ. Ther.* **2**:30–35 (1975).

Morrison, E. S., and M. V. Price: *Values in Sexuality—A New Approach to Sex Education,* Hart, New York, 1974.

Passo, S.: "Parents' Perceptions, Attitudes, and Needs Regarding Sex Education for the Child with Myelomeningocele," *Res. Nurs. Health* **1**(2):53–60 (1978).

Withersty, D. J.: "Sexual Attitudes of Hospital Personnel: A Model for Continuing Education," *Am. J. Psychiatry* **133**:572–575 (1976).

Woods, N. V., and A. Mandetta: "Changes in Students' Knowledge and Attitudes following a Course in Human Sexuality," *Nurs. Res.* **24**(1):10–15 (1975).

Chapter 21

Sexual Therapy and Research

Many nurses are interested in developing competencies in client counseling and teaching at the basic and intermediate levels of the Sexual Health Model, which were discussed in the previous chapter. However, some nurses find sexual therapy and/or research challenging and are specializing in the area of sexuality. These specialized nurses may be involved in individual, group, and couples therapy or in research projects. The objectives of this chapter are:

    1 To present some of the activities of the nurse specializing in sexual therapy for informational and referral purposes
    2 To present some of the difficulties and opportunities in research of sexual issues

THERAPIES

Therapies vary in specific clinical settings and for various populations. However, most current literature and programs presented at sexuality conferences look and sound more alike than different. Some of the specific approaches used by nurses, and discussed briefly in this chapter, include cotherapy, group therapy, masturbation therapy, and assertive therapy. A few techniques that can be used as needed in the different therapies will also be included.

Cotherapy

Many of the sex therapy programs arise from social learning and behavioral theories and are based on the principle that the dysfunction was learned and can therefore be unlearned. Often the programs have been patterned after the Masters and Johnson sex therapy program. The well-known Masters and Johnson program is a 2-week intensive therapy and always uses a male-female therapy team that focuses on the relationship. The two therapists, one male and one female, serve as a "friend in court" for the same sex partner in the relationship. Having two therapists helps to eliminate biased information, minimizes the possibility of transference, and helps to reassure the same-gender client that his or her problem, feelings, and concerns will be understood by the therapy team. The cotherapists' approach increases the opportunity to observe client reactions and increases the reliability of the interpretation and problem-solving session. The cotherapists have an opportunity to model a positive relationship and effective communication between a male and female about sexuality. The focus of the program is to educate and to improve communication. The couple observes a physical examination of each other and obtains detailed instruction in anatomy and physiology. The sensate focus that emphasizes touching and being touched is perhaps the most important technique. Sensate focus exercises help people learn to focus on sensuous pleasuring and help to eliminate being a spectator or other distractions.[1]

The Masters and Johnson program is expensive, requiring 2 weeks away from home, which may be difficult for some clients to afford. Other health cotherapy teams have developed a format of one or two sessions per week for 10 or 12 weeks. Nurses are often successful cotherapists in those therapy teams, with the other therapist being a physician or psychologist. Besides the gender dimensions, these teams offer an interdisciplinary approach. The programs often use a multitheoretical approach with behavior and social learning theories dominating, but they also apply psychodynamics, rational emotive, client-centered, and Gestalt techniques.

Individual Therapy (Psychodynamic Approach)

Some clinics use individual therapists of either gender for couples therapy. Some of the most significant differences of these therapists revolve around the conceptualization of the therapeutic process. A well-known sex therapist using a psychodynamic-oriented conceptual framework is Helen Singer Kaplan at Cornell University. According to Kaplan, "Each spouse's intrapsychic resistance and unconscious motivation, as well as the pathological dynamics of the couple's relationship, are among the factors which are considered and dealt with within the therapeutic process."[2] The nurse with a master's degree in psychiatric nursing is the most likely candidate to use the psychodynamic-oriented approach.

Group Therapy

Most nurse therapists have had a great deal of education and experience in utilizing group dynamics as a therapeutic input for change. Women's sexual therapy groups are numerous and have been very successful in giving permission to:

1 Be aware and own one's feeling
2 Take responsibility for one's own sexuality
3 Examine one's own body
4 Explore the sensuous feelings during self-stimulation
5 Have an orgasm during self-stimulation
6 Explore fantasy and pornographic materials that serve as erotica
7 Be assertive regarding sexual needs and preferences
8 Discuss sexual feelings, values, and attitudes with people who are alike and different from each other
9 Enjoy sexuality
10 Improve communication about sexuality

Reluctance and beginning anxiety of group members can be lowered by the leader suggesting formalized group tasks and exercises. An example of a beginning task is to have each member of the group draw himself or herself as a sexual being and then share this drawing with the total group. The group members give each person feedback about the drawing that can be compared with their own perceptions. This type of exercise helps to provide group trust and promotes communication and responsibility. In later group sessions, tasks that require consensus of the group concerning sexual issues (e.g., homosexuality) can be stimulating and can present a broad range of attitudes and values in what appears to be a somewhat heterogenous group.

To help individuals with specific goals, the group members and nurse leader can make suggestions for home assignments. If the member accepts the suggestion, a report of progress and problems is expected at the next meeting. Members use each other's strengths and support to improve many aspects of their sexual lives.

The nurse leader of this type of group can support a great deal of permission giving and provide accurate information concerning anatomy, physiology, sexual response cycle, and current research findings including psychosocial and psychosexual components. Suggestions for specific problems can come from the leader. However, they may be more highly valued if they are generated from the members. Nurses have found this type of group helpful with nonorgasmic women, menopausal women, divorced women, and sexually abused women. A group with a slightly different approach can be helpful to teens with unwanted pregnancies, parents of teens with unwanted pregnancies, or clients with specific health disruptions (e.g., alcoholism). Each group will identify its own goals and the success will be influenced by the motivation of the group members and the comfort and skill of the leader.

Other Approaches

Masturbation Program   Another treatment approach used by nurses in therapy of sexual dysfunction is a step-by-step masturbation program. This program is useful for:

1   Relieving performance anxiety with a partner
2   Enabling the client to determine what types of stimulation are most sensuous
3   Helping the client locate the sensitive areas and the amount of pressure that is uncomfortable
4   Becoming orgasmic
5   Practicing the squeeze technique to control premature ejaculation
6   Satisfying own sexual needs for those without partners

These masturbatory treatment approaches have been developed using a detailed step-by-step approach with visual and tactile explanation of the body. The plan locates sensitive areas and concentrates on developing comfort and feelings of pleasure. For some clients an electric vibrator provides a quicker method for success than relying on manual stimulation. After masturbation therapy, some clients have the ultimate goal of becoming orgasmic with vaginal intercourse. These clients need additional exercises with concentration of physical sensations and masturbatory activities approximating intercourse.

Dilators (Used for Vaginismus, Psychogenic Dyspareunia, and Coital Phobia)   Psychodynamic approaches concentrate on relieving some of the stress of the deeper underlying etiologic factors. Along with this psychogenic approach, various sexual tasks are employed. Lubricated vaginal dilators may be inserted into the vagina to help convince the woman that the vagina will expand, the pain will not be unbearable, and there will be little or no bleeding. The partner may become involved in the treatment by using his fingers first and then dilators of graduated size in a systematic desensitization treatment plan.

Using Fantasy and Pornography   Fantasy and pornography are sometimes used to enhance sexual arousal. These types of materials can help the client become less involved in obsessions over performance. Explanation and specific suggestions can be beneficial to clients in identifying therapeutic techniques to overcome cognitive control in psychogenic problems. The client is expected to replace the irrational control with rational thoughts about sexuality.[3]

Assertive Training   In the past few years nurses have become active in helping women to overcome inhibitions about personal needs, making social contacts, and maintaining equal power in relationships. This skill can be used to overcome inhibitions about communicating identified sexual needs and preferences. Assertive training may also be useful to boost self-esteem when a client is feeling unworthy of the affection from the partner.

"Squeeze" Technique In 1956 James Semans introduced the Semans' procedure to help the male with ejaculatory control. The principle of the Semans' technique is to increase the intensity and duration of stimulation. The penis is stimulated until ejaculation is nearly imminent and at this point the stimulation is stopped. After the sensation of ejaculation has subsided, the stimulation begins again. This pause, or stop-and-go method, increases the duration of penile stimulation and the control of ejaculation.[4]

This procedure was modified by Masters and Johnson and called the "squeeze technique." The woman stimulates the man's genitals and then uses a firm squeeze on the frenulum for 3 to 4 seconds, when a pause is needed to control ejaculation (Fig. 21-1). The urge to ejaculate, and sometimes the erection, is lost, and further stimulation can begin in 15 to 30 seconds. This procedure is continued several times. Gradually the man gains control over ejaculation.[5]

Kegel Exercises Exercises designed by Kegel in 1952 to strengthen the pubococcygeal muscle are now being used to increase sexual pleasure or orgasmic potential for the woman with weak musculature. Increasing the tone of the pubococcygeal muscle also increases the pleasure of her partner. The client can find the pubococcygeal by determining the contraction that controls the stop of urine. Once the woman begins contractions (10 or more), the exercises should be done 6 or 7 times each day until muscle tone increases.

Other Therapies Other therapies used in the treatment of sexual dysfunction are hypnosis, drug therapy, and mechanotherapy (artificial penis, penile ring). These methods are not discussed in this chapter since nurses are not as likely to be involved in their use. Also, the results of these therapies are inconclusive or have not been very impressive in their effectiveness.

Vignette

Problem
Married 21-year-old white female with presenting complaint of "fear of having sexual intercourse." Feels guilty denying spouse sexual gratification and would like to have a family in a few years. (Highlights of each office visit are summarized below.)

First Visit (Ann)
Assessment
Sexual history reveals:

1 No sexual encounter by an adult in childhood.
2 Masturbatory activity began at age 14.
3 Orgasmic with self-stimulation since age 15 or 16.
4 Client describes childhood as happy until father died when she was 11 years old. She was extremely close to her father and felt "no just God would take away someone that was loved so dearly." (She cried when speaking about father, who had died 10 years ago.)

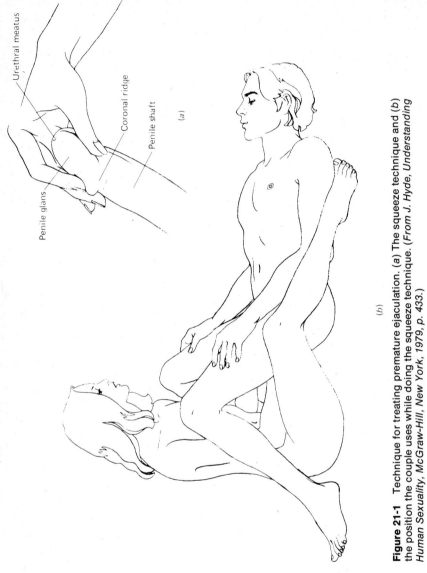

Urethral meatus

Coronal ridge

Penile shaft

Penile glans

(a)

(b)

Figure 21-1 Technique for treating premature ejaculation. (a) The squeeze technique and (b) the position the couple uses while doing the squeeze technique. (*From J. Hyde, Understanding Human Sexuality, McGraw-Hill, New York, 1979, p. 433.*)

5   Mother was affectionate with client and they discussed sex rather easily, including masturbation, menstruation, and sexual intercourse.

6   Married 2 years ago the first man she dated. Spouse is a virgin.

7   Lovemaking consists of kissing, breast fondling, and mutual masturbation.

8   Client describes her fear of intercourse with an association of excruciating pain and torrential bleeding.

Physical examination revealed no abnormalities.

Second Visit (Spouse John)
Assessment
Presenting complaint:

1   "Help me have intercourse with my wife."

2   Beginning to feel incompetent and having erection problems.

3   Describes the relationship as healthy and happy except in sexual activity.

4   Believes some of their problems relate to the unresolved death of Ann's father.

Physical examination revealed no abnormalities.

Third Visit (Couple)
Assessment

1   Ann revealed she was afraid "to love too much because she might lose John like she did her father." (Cried when talking about father.)

2   Ann would like John to change his personal hygiene routines and bathe more often.

3   Neither partner wanted to be responsible for initiating sexual activity.

4   Both partners revealed performance concerns.

5   Both partners had adequate knowledge of male and female sexual anatomy and physiology.

6   Contract of 12 weeks of treatment (client goal—vaginal intercourse).

Fourth Visit (Couple)
Intervention
Roundtable discussion of:

1   Unresolved loss (Ann)

2   Performance concerns

3   Identification of irrational beliefs and fears:
    a   Lose spouse if become too involved
    b   Vagina too small for penis
    c   Intercourse is extremely painful
    d   Both partners feared fundamental assertiveness of sexual intercourse

4   Began assignment of sensate focus exercises (explanation of each other's bodies by touch, smell, taste, and seeing)

Fifth, Sixth, and Seventh Visits (Ann)
Intervention (Plan—Psychodynamic Approach and Deconditioning Exercises)

1   Therapist dealt with unresolved death of father

2   Continuation of sensate exercises at home (body massage, practicing "I" statements, improving verbal and nonverbal communication)

Eighth Visit (Couple)
Intervention (Plan—Deconditioning and Cognitive Input)

  1 Deconditioning technique—an office demonstration of the use of graduated vaginal dilators by nurse therapist. Spouse participated. The couple was to practice using the dilators at home with no attempt at sexual intercourse. The purpose of the dilators was to:
    a Decrease sensitivity of vagina
    b Convince the client that vagina was not too small for penis
    c Help increase assertiveness of spouse

Ninth Visit (Couple)
Intervention (Plan—Working toward Assertive Behavior and Social Learning)

  1 Discussion and role playing of assertive behaviors in expressing feelings and taking responsibility for own sexuality
  2 Discussion of distaste of partner's and own ineffectiveness and talk about self-assertive approaches and responses
  3 Suggestions for modifying negative self-perceptions of each partner

Tenth Visit (Couple)
Intervention (Plan—Social Learning Approach with Information and Suggestions on Sexual Activity)

  1 Viewed film on coital techniques for information and suggestions.
  2 Discussion of the film with therapist.
  3 Therapist modeled self-assertive behaviors and beliefs in the discussion.

Eleventh Visit (Couple)

  1 Couple reported having had vaginal intercourse several times during the week (the goals of the couple were achieved).
  2 John reported satisfaction. Ann was nonorgasmic with vaginal intercourse but was happy with her progress.
  3 The couple wished to terminate therapy and work toward more sexual gratification on their own.
  4 They evaluated the treatment as a success and will contact the therapist if and when they desire professional help in the future.

Summary

Nurses are already involved in individual, cotherapy, and group therapies and all these skills can be utilized in sexual therapy. Some of the dysfunctions that are treatable by these therapies include premature ejaculation, orgasmic dysfunction, psychogenic dyspareunia, psychogenic impotence, vaginismus, and coital phobias. In most instances the client should have a thorough physical examination before attempting treatment of sexual dysfunctions. These same treatment formats can be used with clients in anticipatory guidance or for those with problems centered around other aspects of sexuality. Most nurses use a multitheoretical approach with emphasis on social learning, behavior, and psychoanalytic theories with conceptualizations from psychodynamic, client-centered, systems, and behavior approaches. Below is a vignette demonstrating an eclectic approach used by a cotherapy team composed of a psychiatric nurse and a psychiatrist.

RESEARCH

Sex research, although increasing, is still plagued with many problems. Nursing is just beginning to conduct clinical studies with a major focus of sexuality. Sampling of a population becomes a specific problem when many individuals are too sensitive, or believe sexual issues are too private, to volunteer as participants in sex research. The problem of nonparticipation would not be so detrimental to a study if those who refused to be subjects were identical to those who volunteered. This is very unlikely and consequently the study probably begins with a biased sample. For example, Farkas et al. report:

> Personality, sexuality and demographic differences were examined in volunteers and nonvolunteers for a laboratory study of male sexual arousal. Subjects were 108 participants in a questionnaire study entitled "Personality and Sexuality," who were then asked to volunteer for a second study which necessitated watching sexually explicit films, being partially undressed in an experimental chamber, and having penile diameter measured via a strain gauge device. Volunteers for the second study were found to be less guilty, less sexually fearful, more sexually experienced, and older than nonvolunteers. Volunteers also reported a higher incidence of post erectile difficulties and tended to be white or of mixed racial heritage, as opposed to being Oriental. Other personality variables did not discriminate between the two groups. The results indicate that future research in human sexuality using the laboratory analytic method must impose strict limits on generalization from the research data.[6]

Methodological Problems

Not much sex research has occurred in a controlled laboratory setting and often relies on respondents' self-reports. The reliability of self-reports of sexual behavior is questionable. Distortions may occur as overexaggerations. Or the respondents may deny or minimize sexual activity. Self-reports are probably influenced by what is accepted as the norm of the group to which the subject identifies. For example, a teenager may have problems acknowledging virginity when the verbal and nonverbal messages are received that being sexually active is not only accepted but expected.

Some studies rely on recall of sexual activity of many previous years. The reliability of what people choose to remember about sexual activity brings forth another great possibility of distortion. Some people remember the painful aspects while others choose to remember the "good ole days."

The use of questionnaires or interviews has both advantages and disadvantages. Questionnaires are less costly. The subject may feel that there is a greater probability of anonymity and respond more honestly than in a face-to-face interview. The subject will usually have more time to recall or think through the answers, which may cause less pressure and more comfort in answering. On the other hand, use of the personal interview may be more flexible and convince the subject of the importance of the research. Consequently, more thoughtful and sincere answers may be forthcoming. Subjects may feel some pressure to answer all questions that would be left blank in the questionnaire. The interview may provide more flexibility, which could be a strength in some studies. A disadvantage of the interview is noted by extraneous factors, such as skill of the interviewer in eliminating verbal and nonverbal cues in accepting responses. A researcher may not get honest answers but rather ones that the subject believes are acceptable to the interviewer.

Researchers in sexuality are also handicapped by extraordinary safeguards—a need based on the feeling that sex is somehow more sacred than other forms of human behavior. Some professionals believe that questioning people about their sexual behavior is stressful and might be harmful to mental health. Nurses need to find appropriate methods of testing this hypothesis. Informed consent usually includes:

1   Purpose of the study
2   Exactly what will be expected of the subject
3   That all persons consulted about being a subject must feel that there is a free choice not to participate
4   A person's health care will not be affected if the choice is made not to participate
5   Subjects must feel free to withdraw from the study at any time

Some of the research projects which have had nurses as the principal investigators include the following populations:

1   Rape victims
2   Incest victims
3   Teenage fertility control
4   Teenage unwanted pregnancy
5   Second trimester abortion seekers
6   Menopausal women
7   Clients with an ostomy
8   Medical and nursing student sex education
9   Parents of teenagers with unwanted pregnancies
10   Parents of children with myelomeningocele
11   Women with mastectomies
12   Residents of nursing homes

Much of the literature on the subject of human sexuality is based on clinical studies. There is a lack of descriptive and controlled research in this area. As nurses become more knowledgeable about and comfortable with sexuality, they may be surprised to find opportunities to study etiology, preventive measures, and treatment approaches in sexual health care with many different populations.

PROFESSIONAL ISSUES

There has been a heated dialogue for several years between professionals regarding *who* is qualified to conduct sex therapy, counseling, and formalized sex education programs. Some professionals believe that the purpose of sex therapy is to modify ineffective behaviors. They rely heavily on a reeducational approach, which is seen as a behavioral approach. Other professionals view this approach as overly simplistic and naive and believe that the psychodynamics of a sexual relationship requires explanation by a qualified practitioner. The two approaches require very different credentials and qualifications for the therapist or counselor. The established mental health professionals tend to argue that sex therapists should be qualified psychotherapists. They believe that sexual dysfunction is often related to the couple's emotional relationship, poor communication, hostility, guilt, and sex role problems and should be treated only by those who can put the dysfunction in the context of couples or family systems problems. The sex therapists who are not psychotherapists claim that educational and behavioral approaches have more evidence of success than do the psychotherapies. Educators and the writers of self-help programs claim success without any direct contact with a therapist. It seems most likely, at this stage of development, that different approaches are needed to treat different types of sexual dysfunctions. Because none of the approaches can boast about success through documented empirical research, the need for this data is apparent.

It is more than likely that the need for the more simplistic treatment approaches will change as the citizenry is exposed to a cultural acceptance of sexuality and more information is available to all age groups of the society. The nurse in both primary and secondary settings can be expected to have a fair amount of input into the positive change and growth processes.

Another concern of health professionals is that there is no control over who claims to be a "sex therapist." Those in the mental health profession may not have had any formalized course work in sexuality or any supervised practical experience under a master practitioner. The continuing education workshops for these mental health practitioners are not qualified to train sex therapists in a 1- or 2-day workshop. However, there are some continuing education programs that require 6 months of formal course work and intense supervision and do meet the demands of professional expertise.

According to J. LoPiccolo:

> The total lack of control over who can be a sex therapist is indeed the current state of affairs. There are absolutely no legal restraints to prevent anyone from hanging up a shingle proclaiming his status as a sex therapist. Anyone familiar with the national scene in sex therapy can cite any number of "sex therapists" who, before they became sex therapists, were not involved in any sort of therapy or human health services activity. While state licensing laws and professional societies prevent quacks from representing themselves as physicians, psychologists, and psychiatrists

and, in some states, marriage counselors, the field legally is wide open for anyone who wants to open the "Jones County Center for Sex Therapy."[7]

The American Association of Sex Educators, Counselors, and Therapists, Washington, D.C., has made some attempts to screen and certify qualified sex educators and sex therapists. This organization receives applause from some professionals and an equal amount of criticism from others.

The nurse interested in becoming a sex therapist, sex counselor, or sex educator needs to explore all the pros and cons of different approaches of those already established in the field. The nurse who is interested in finding qualified persons for referral purposes needs to be reminded that the qualifications of those claiming to be sex educators, counselors, and therapists range from persons having attended a 1-day workshop to those who have psychotherapy skills with many years of successful treatment of sexual dysfunction. The field is growing and becoming more respectable, and the client population is asking for more qualified professionals.

LEARNING ACTIVITIES

1 If you were a nurse sex therapist, what group of clients would you prefer to treat? Outline your theoretical approach.

2 Make a list of five research studies that you believe would be the most helpful in the promotion of sexual health care. Be prepared to give your rationale for your priorities.

SUGGESTED READING

Hogan, D.: "The Effectiveness of Sex Therapy: A Review of the Literature," in J. LoPiccolo and L. LoPiccolo (eds.), *Handbook of Sex Therapy*, Plenum, New York, 1978, pp. 57–81.

Kaplan, Helen: *The New Sex Therapy*, Brunner-Mazel, New York, 1974, pp. 187–247.

Masters, William H., and V. Johnson: *Human Sexual Inadequacy*, Little, Brown, Boston, 1970, pp. 24–91.

REFERENCES

1 William H. Masters and Virginia Johnson, *Human Sexual Inadequacy*, Boston, Little, Brown, 1970, pp. 24–91.

2 Helen S. Kaplan, *The New Sex Therapy*, Brunner-Mazel, New York, 1974, p. 198.

3 D. Hogan, "The Effectiveness of Sex Therapy: A Review of the Literature," in J. LoPiccolo and L. LoPiccolo (eds.), *Handbook of Sex Therapy*, Plenum, New York, 1978, pp. 57–81.

4 J. Semans, "Premature Ejaculation: A New Approach," *A. Med. J.* **49**:353–358 (1956).

5 William H. Masters, op. cit., pp. 102–106.

6 Gary M. Farkas, Larry F. Sine, and Ian M. Evans, "Personality, Sexuality and

Demographic Differences between Volunteers and Nonvolunteers for a Laboratory Study of Male Sexual Behavior," *Arch. Sex. Behav.* **7**(6):513 (1978).

7 J. LoPiccolo and L. LoPiccolo, *Handbook of Sex Therapy,* Plenum, New York, 1978, p. 516.

BIBLIOGRAPHY

Therapy

Annon, Jack S.: *The Behavior Treatment of Sexual Problems,* vol. 1, Mercantile, Honolulu, 1974.

Annon, Jack S.: *The Behavior Treatment of Sexual Disorders,* vol. 2, Mercantile, Honolulu, 1975.

Barbach, L. C.: "Group Treatment of Preorgasmic Women," *J. Sex Marital Ther.* **1**:139–145 (1974).

Barbach, L. C.: *For Yourself: The Fulfillment of Female Sexuality,* Signet, New York, 1975.

Clifford, R.: "Development of Masturbation in College Women," *Arch. Sex. Behav.* **7**(6):559–575 (1978).

Coen, S. J.: "Sexual Interviewing, Evaluation, and Therapy: Psychoanalytic Emphasis on the Use of Sexual Fantasy," *Arch. Sex. Behav.* **7**(3):229–241 (1978).

Dengrove, E.: "Behavioral Therapy of Impotence," *J. Sex Res.* **7**:177–183 (1971).

Ellis, A., and R. R. Grieger: "The Rational-Emotive Approach to Sex Therapy," in *Rational Emotive Therapy,* Springer, New York, 1977, chap. 12, pp. 198–216.

Foster, A. L.: "Changes in Marital Sexual Relationships following Treatment for Sexual Dysfunctioning," *J. Sex Marital Ther.* **4**(3):186–198 (1978).

Golden, J.: "Group vs. Couple Treatment of Sexual Dysfunction," *Arch. Sex. Behav.* **7**(6):593–603 (1978).

Hartman, W., and M. Fithian: *Treatment of Sexual Dysfunction,* Center for Marital and Sexual Studies, Long Beach, Calif, 1972.

Hoon, E. F., and P. Hoon: "Types of Sexual Expression in Women: Clinical Implications of Multivariate Analysis," *Arch. Sex. Behav.* **7**(2):105–117 (1978).

Kaplan, H. S.: *The New Sex Therapy,* Brunner-Mazel, New York, 1974.

Kilman, P. R.: "The Treatment of Primary and Secondary Orgasmic Dysfunction: A Methodological Review of the Literature since 1970," *J. Sex Marital Ther.* **4**(3):155–177 (1978).

Kilman, P. R., and R. Auerbach: "Treatment of Premature Ejaculation and Psychogenic Impotence: A Critical Review of the Literature," *Arch. Sex. Behav.* vol. 8, no. 1, 1979, pp. 81–100.

LoPiccolo, J., and W. C. Lobitz: "The Role of Masturbation in the Treatment of Orgasmic Dysfunction," *Arch. Sex. Behav.* **2**(2):163–172 (1972).

LoPiccolo, J., and E. P. LoPiccolo: *Handbook of Sex Therapy,* Plenum, New York, 1978.

Masters, W. H., and V. E. Johnson: *Human Sexual Inadequacy,* Little, Brown, Boston, 1970.

McGuire, L. S.: "Sexual Dysfunction in Women Who Were Molested as Children: One Response Pattern and Suggestions for Treatment," *J. Sex Marital Ther.* **4**(1):11–16 (1978).

McWhirter, D. P., and A. M. Mattison: "The Treatment of Sexual Dysfunction in Gay Male Couples," *J. Sex Marital Ther.* **4**(3):213–218 (1978).

Munjack, D. J., and L. J. Oziel: "Resistance in the Behavioral Treatment of Sexual Dysfunctions," *J. Sex Marital Ther.* **4**(2):122–139 (1978).

O'Leary, K. D., and G. T. Wilson: *Behavior Therapy,* Prentice-Hall, Englewood Cliffs, N.J., 1975, chap. 11, pp. 289–329.

Rowland, K. F., and S. N. Haynes: "A Sexual Enhancement Program for Elderly Couples," *J. Sex Marital Ther.* **4**(2):91–114 (1978).

Segraves, R. T.: "Conditioning Masturbatory Fantasies in Sex Therapy," *J. Educ. Ther.* **2**(2):53–54 (1976).

Sotile, W. M., and P. Kilmann: "Effects of Group Systematic Desensitization of Female Orgasmic Dysfunction," *Arch. Sex. Behav.* **7**(5):477–493 (1978).

Tsai, M., and N. N. Wagner: "Therapy Groups for Women Sexually Molested as Children," *Arch. Sex. Behav.* **7**(5):417–429 (1978).

Research

Bell, A., and M. Weinberg: *Homosexualities—A Study of Diversity among Men and Women,* Simon and Schuster, New York, 1978.

Bureau, J.: "Sexual Identity and Eroticism," in R. Gemme and C. C. Wheeler (eds.), *Progress in Sexology,* Plenum, New York, 1977, pp. 43–62.

Burgess, A. W., and L. L. Holmstrom: "Crisis and Counseling Requests of Rape Victims, *Nurs. Res.* **23**(3):196–203 (1974).

Goodwin, T.: "Sexual Concerns and Questions Which Patients Present to Registered Nurses in Selected Areas of Nursing Practice," unpublished thesis, University of Cincinnati—College of Nursing and Health, 1975.

Green, R., and J. Money (eds.): *Transsexualism and Sex Reassignment,* Johns Hopkins, Baltimore, 1969.

Groth, A. N., and A. J. Birnbaum: "Adult Sexual Orientation and Attraction to Underage Persons," *Arch. Sex. Behav.* **7**(3):175–183 (1978).

Hite, S.: *The Hite Report,* Macmillan, New York, 1976.

Keller, M. L., S. Ward, and J. Johnson: "The Relationship between Menopausal Symptoms and Sex Role Attributes," unpublished thesis, School of Nursing, University of Wisconsin-Madison, 1978.

Kinsey, A. C., W. B. Pomeroy, and C. Martin: *Sexual Behavior in the Human Male,* Saunders, Philadelphia, 1948.

Kinsey, A. C., W. B. Pomeroy, and C. Martin: *Sexual Behavior in the Human Female,* Saunders, Philadelphia, 1953.

Lamont, J. A.: "Vaginismus," in R. Gemme and C. C. Wheeler (eds.), *Progress in Sexology,* Plenum, New York, 1976, pp. 185–204.

Masters, W. H., and V. E. Johnson: *Human Sexual Response,* Little, Brown, Boston, 1966.

Masters, W. H., and V. E. Johnson: *Human Sexual Inadequacy,* Little, Brown, Boston, 1970.

Money, J. (ed.): *Sex Research,* Johns Hopkins, Baltimore, 1965.

Money, J.: "Role of Fantasy in Pair-Bonding and Erotic Performance," in R. Gemme and C. Wheeler (eds.), *Progress in Sexology,* Plenum, New York, 1977, pp. 259–266.

Money, J., and A. Ehrhart: *Man and Woman Boy and Girl,* Johns Hopkins, Baltimore, 1972.

Perlman, D., W. Josephson, W. Hwang, H. Begum, and T. Thomas: "Cross Cultural Analysis of Students' Sexual Standards," *Arch. Sex. Behav.* **7**(6):521–545 (1978).

Saghir, M., and E. Robins: *Male and Female Homosexuality,* Williams & Wilkins, Baltimore, 1973.

Seidl, A.: "Nurses' Attitudes toward Homosexuality," unpublished thesis, School of Nursing, University of Wisconsin-Madison, 1976.

Spence, J. T., and R. L. Helmreich: *Masculinity and Femininity,* University of Texas Press, Austin, 1978.

Woods, N. F., and J. A. Earp: "Women with Cured Breast Cancer," *Nurs. Res.* **27**(5):279–285 (1978).

Index

Index